THE STRUGGLE FOR MASTERY IN IRELAND, 1442–1540

Irish Historical Monograph Series

ISSN 1740-1097

Series editors

Marie Therese Flanagan, Queen's University, Belfast
Eunan O'Halpin, Trinity College, Dublin
David Hayton, Queen's University, Belfast
Fearghal McGarry, Queen's University, Belfast

Previous titles in the series are listed at the back of the volume.

THE STRUGGLE FOR MASTERY IN IRELAND, 1442–1540

Culture, Politics and
Kildare-Ormond Rivalry

Alan Kelly

THE BOYDELL PRESS

© Alan Kelly 2024

All Rights Reserved. Except as permitted under current legislation no part of this work may be photocopied, stored in a retrieval system, published, performed in public, adapted, broadcast, transmitted, recorded or reproduced in any form or by any means, without the prior permission of the copyright owner

The right of Alan Kelly to be identified as the author of this work has been asserted in accordance with sections 77 and 78 of the Copyright, Designs and Patents Act 1988

First published 2024
The Boydell Press, Woodbridge

ISBN 978-1-83765-052-1

The Boydell Press is an imprint of Boydell & Brewer Ltd
PO Box 9, Woodbridge, Suffolk IP12 3DF, UK
and of Boydell & Brewer Inc.
668 Mt Hope Avenue, Rochester, NY 14620–2731, USA
website: www.boydellandbrewer.com

A CIP catalogue record for this title is available from the British Library

The publisher has no responsibility for the continued existence or accuracy of URLs for external or third-party internet websites referred to in this book, and does not guarantee that any content on such websites is, or will remain, accurate or appropriate

This publication is printed on acid-free paper

Contents

List of abbreviations vi
Preface viii
Conventions xi

Introduction 1

1. White Earl to the Great Earl, 1442-96 16
2. Late Yorkist, early Tudor 'Butler Expugnatio' 43
3. Kildare Renaissance, 1496-1522 60
4. *Salus Populi*, Geraldine 'decay', c. 1512-19 76
5. Geraldine 'decay', 1522-34 99
6. Aristocratic entente, Kildare c. 1524-34 120
7. Rebellion, State Paper Dark Age, 1534-40 137

Conclusion 154

Bibliography 157
Index 183

List of abbreviations

AFM	*Annála Ríoghachta Éireann: Annals of the kingdom of Ireland by the Four Masters from the earliest period to the year 1616*, ed. J. O'Donovan (7 vols, Dublin, 1851)
ALC	*The Annals of Loch Cé: a chronicle of Irish affairs, 1014-1690*, ed. W. M. Hennessy (2 vols, London, 1871)
AU	*Annála Uladh, Annals of Ulster*, ed. W. M. Hennessy and B. MacCarthy (4 vols, Dublin, 1887-1901)
BL	British Library
Bodl.	Bodleian Library, Oxford
Cal. Carew	*Calendar of the Carew manuscripts preserved in the archiepiscopal library at Lambeth, 1515- 1574*, ed. W. Bullen and J. S. Brewer (6 vols, London, 1867-73)
Cal. S. P. Ire.	*Calendar of State Papers Ireland, Tudor period, 1509-1547*, ed. Steven G. Ellis and James Murray (Dublin, 2017)
CHI	*Cambridge History of Ireland*, eds Brendan Smith, i, Jane Ohlmeyer, ii (4 vols, Cambridge, 2018)
CIRCLE	CIRCLE, A Calendar of Irish Chancery Letters, c. 1244-1509, online at chancery.tcd.ie
CPR	*Calendar of entries in the Papal registers relating to Great Britain and Ireland*, eds J. A. Twemlow, iii-xvii, Michael J. Haren, xviii (23 vols, London, 1897-2008)
DIB	*Dictionary of Irish Biography*, ed. James McGuire and James Quinn (9 vols, Cambridge, 2009)
Ger. med. Ire.	Peter Crooks and Sean Duffy (eds), *The Geraldines and medieval Ireland: the making of a myth* (Dublin, 2016)
HI	*History Ireland*
HJ	*Historical Journal*
IHS	*Irish Historical Studies*
JKAH	*Journal of the Kerry Archaeological and Historical Society*
JKA	*Journal of the County Kildare Archaeological Society*
JRHA	*Journal of the Royal Historical and Archaeological Association of Ireland*
JRSA	*Journal of the Royal Society of Antiquaries of Ireland*

LIST OF ABBREVIATIONS

LP	*Letters and papers, foreign and domestic, Henry VIII*, eds J. S. Brewer, R. H. Brodie and J. Gairdner (21 vols, London, 1862-1932)
LPL	Lambeth Palace Library
NHI	Art Cosgrove (ed.), *A New History of Ireland* (9 vols, Oxford, 1987), ii
NLI	National Library of Ireland
ODNB	*Oxford Dictionary of National Biography*, ed. H. D. G. Matthew and B. Harrison (60 vols, Oxford, 2004)
Ormond deeds	*Calendar of Ormond deeds*, ed. E. Curtis (6 vols, Dublin, 1932-43)
PHCC	*Proceedings of the Harvard Celtic Colloquium*
PRIA	*Proceedings of the Royal Irish Academy*
RIA	Royal Irish Academy
SP	The National Archives, Kew, State Papers
S.P. Hen. VIII	*State Papers, Henry VIII* (11 vols, London, 1830-52)

Preface

The Kildare rebellion of 1534 has long been recognised by historians as a central event in early modern Ireland and indeed modern Irish history in general. Signalling the collapse of aristocratic rule and the onset of the conquest of Ireland by the Tudor state, this watershed in Irish history has largely been understood through the State Papers. Acknowledged to overemphasise the critics of Kildare, the near exclusivity of this archive has left an imbalanced, teleological impression. More insidiously, having obscured the circumstances surrounding the rebellion, the heightened significance of state correspondence has been to the detriment of other materials and methodologies. Indeed, with the emergence of the State Papers and the elevated magnitude of the rebellion, there was a strong sense that a critical epoch both began and ended at this juncture. Furthermore, this imbalance has been compounded by their highly selective arrangement and publication in the 1830s as the *State Papers King Henry the Eighth*. This canon of documents remains central to the existing historiography but as invaluable as they are, the State Papers are at once limited in their ability to explain events and also deeply misleading concerning the events they describe.

This study seeks to break free from the prison house of the State Paper hegemony. Recent studies have left an opening for a greater consideration of alternative approaches and often overlooked, fragmentary material. By uncovering alternative evidence in literary culture, material culture and oral culture (that is literary texts, poems, paintings, architecture), which have been neglected in conventional scholarship, it not only brings to light a whole set of dimensions obscured by the intensely political focus of the State Papers, it also offers a radically original way of reading the material therein. Out of this there has emerged a new understanding of the struggle for mastery in early sixteenth-century Ireland. This intense rivalry and push for supremacy between the leading old colonial nobility took place within a far broader and far more contested milieu than has hitherto been appreciated.

Older uncritical accounts, assuming that 1534 was part of some grand process of state formation under the so-called 'new monarchs' have long since been discounted. But more recent studies, based on deep research and richly informed by the results of comparative analysis, have fundamentally challenged that conclusion.[1] The Kildare rebellion was neither willed nor sought for. In fact, there was

---

[1] Brendan Bradshaw, *The Irish constitutional revolution of the sixteenth century* (Cambridge, 1979); Steven G. Ellis, *Reform and revival: English government in Ireland 1470–1534* (Woodbridge, 1986); S. G. Ellis, *Tudor Ireland: crown, community and the conflict of cultures, 1470–1603* (London, 1985),

PREFACE

not a single individual who desired the rebellion to take place. And yet it did – with consequences the majority of historians have regarded as momentous. The inadequacy of explanations regarding this event is due, this study argues, to the fact that historians have been looking in the wrong place. All of the interpretations, however they disagree among themselves, have been based on the same set of administrative sources, thereby perpetuating the primacy of such material.

Underlying this was a contest concerning the character of Irish politics and society as a whole. In contrast to the traditional view of the island as a land of conquest to be fully colonised by the Cambro-Normans, the Geraldines over time elaborated a more far-reaching concept of island-wide integration. This involved the recognition and co-option of leading figures within Gaelic Ireland.[2] It is in the context of the broadening of the concept of Ireland, that a range of artistic, literary and cultural pursuits acquires a very distinct significance. Within the timeframe of what follows, this more ambitious understanding of Ireland as an integrated polity was sometimes shared by the Kildares' greatest feudal rivals, the Butlers of Ormond when they themselves were the dominant lord. Most notably, the White Earl of Ormond assumed a broad approach when commanding considerable power in the early fifteenth century. But the gradual diminution of their influence and the rise of the Kildare Geraldines necessitated a revival of, for both political and ideological reasons, traditional Cambro-Norman concepts of conquest. There occurred through the late fifteenth and early sixteenth centuries, a culture war that utilised a variety of cultural expressions which were in essence part of the political war between the two Houses competing for hegemony across the island of Ireland. Exploring the contours of this cultural war at once shows how high the stakes were and how intense this competition was. It is a study which neither subscribes to the older notions of the rise of the Tudor state, nor the more recent ones of accident and contingency; but one which shows that the Kildare programme for ascendancy was more ambitious, more sophisticated

---

rev. 1998: Ellis, *Ireland in the age of the Tudors*; Ciaran Brady, *The chief governors: the rise and fall of reform government in Tudor Ireland, 1536–1588* (Cambridge, 1994); S. G. Ellis, *Tudor frontiers and noble power: the making of the British state* (Oxford, 1995). Recent scholarship has offered significant advances: David Heffernan, *Debating Tudor policy in sixteenth-century Ireland: 'reform' treatises and political discourse* (Manchester, 2018); Christopher Maginn and S. G. Ellis, *The Tudor discovery of Ireland* (Dublin, 2015).

[2] A ruling border magnate faced many strategic and cultural challenges. See esp. Ellis for the relationship between the English lowland core and the peripheral marches. The heart of this central region was the Tudor court, which in turn viewed the realm as a whole unit: Ellis, *Tudor frontiers*, pp 10, 140–1. For a specific perspective from the court of Henry VIII, see for instance, Kevin Sharpe, *Selling the Tudor monarchy: authority and image in sixteenth-century England* (New Haven, CT, 2009), pp 152–62. In relation to 'collaboration' between the old colonial nobility and the ascendant Kildare Geraldines, see Gerald Power, *A European frontier elite: the nobility of the English Pale in Tudor Ireland, 1496–1566* (Hannover, 2012), pp 47–75.

PREFACE

and more subtle than has been understood. But it also was, precisely for this, more vulnerable to the unanticipated crisis of the Tudor political intervention in Ireland and the challenge of the Tudor Reformation.

❧

I have many to thank from the time it has taken this study to take shape. Firstly, in the Department of History, Trinity College Dublin: Dr Peter Crooks for his counsel and expertise, Professor Micheál Ó Siochrú, Dr Robert Armstrong and Ms Joanne Lynch. My thanks to St Patrick's College, Maynooth for permission to use the portrait of the ninth earl of Kildare for the cover illustration (with the assistance of Rev. Prof. Michael Mullaney and Rev. Dr John-Paul Sheridan). From Maynooth, I also wish to note several mentors: Dr Kieran McGroarty, Dr Maeve O'Brien, Professor William Tobin, Professor Vincent Comerford, Professor Raymond Gillespie, the late Mr John Bradley, Professor Colm Lennon and in particular Dr Jacinta Prunty. My thanks to the following experts: Dr David Heffernan, Dr Caoimhe Whelan, Dr Lynn Kilgannon, Dr Liam O'Rourke, Dr Sean Cunningham, Professor Marian Lyons, Dr Katharine Simms, Professor Christopher Maginn, Professor Eoin Mac Cárthaigh, Sho Makino and John Shearer (Verger, Temple Church). Also, Feargal Lennon and Shane Pettit, scholars who have assisted with reading and research material.

A special note of appreciation must be given to Professor Steven Ellis. He has generously given his time to repeatedly read my work in great detail and I am grateful for his expertise and kind advice. Similarly, a hearty thanks to Dr James Murray, who has devoted much time to assist with this study. I have greatly benefited from Jim's insights and affable guidance. My sincere thanks to Boydell and Brewer; Professor David Hayton and especially my editor, Peter Sowden. A personal note of gratitude for my loving parents, Tom Joe and Bríd. But most of all, for my beloved wife Helène, who has suffered with this project from the outset. Ineffably, and for all else, this book is dedicated to her.

Finally, I acknowledge two teachers. Having first kindled a scholarly enthusiasm many years ago, the late Dr Joe Ducke remains in my thoughts. My chief debt of gratitude is to Professor Ciaran Brady, who I am grateful to count as a mentor and a friend. On many occasions, with my head full of thoughts from our conversations I have happily paced the distinctive grey corridors of Trinity's Arts Building and pounded a well-worn track from Ciaran's office to the Berkeley or National Library. With energy and wit, he has steered this study for years since having first prompted me to consider why Chaucerian conceit may appear in a 'state paper'. I remain captivated to this day. Without his guidance (and perpetual 'after-sales service') this book would not have materialised.

Trinity College Dublin
Michaelmas Term, 2022

Conventions

The eighth and ninth earls of Kildare are referred to as Gearóid (Gerald) Mór and Gearóid Óg Fitzgerald; however this can misleadingly suggest that they were entirely Gaelicised. I have retained them for the sake of recognisability although I am aware of the incongruities that arise as a result.

For the most part, contractions and abbreviations have been silently extended. When citing manuscript sources, some mid-sentence capitals have been changed to lower case. In terms of coinage, pounds, both Irish and sterling, circulated in Ireland after 1460. An Irish pound was worth roughly two-thirds of a pound sterling (13s 4d), but reference is made only to the English value. Following the custom in the Tudor realm, the year has been taken to begin on 1 January instead of 25 March.

Introduction

On 11 June 1534, the feast of St Barnabas, Thomas Fitzgerald, Lord Offaly, withdrew his allegiance to the crown, setting in motion a string of unintended and destructive consequences. This revolt has since been seen as the dramatic climax of Kildare conflict with both the crown and their old colonial rivals, in which the Geraldines overreached to their ruin. While the tenures of the eighth and ninth earls of Kildare are known to mark the zenith of the Leinster Geraldines' ascendancy, their rise under the seventh earl, Thomas Fitzgerald, has been understudied. Furthermore, insufficient prior contextualisation has been given to the rise and fall of the Butlers of Ormond, roughly under the Lancastrian crown. Within a few generations, James Butler the White Earl (fourth) of Ormond (1393–1452) and later Gearóid Mór Fitzgerald the Great Earl (eighth) of Kildare (c. 1456–1513) governed as dominant ruling magnates while adopting a broad pan-cultural approach to the maintenance of power. This study begins with an examination of the expressions of power in late medieval and early Tudor Ireland while comparing the ascendancy of the White Earl and the Great Earl as governors. The timeframe of this study commences with the final lord lieutenancy of the White Earl of Ormond, at which point the relations between the Butlers and the Kildare Geraldines were cordial. In developing the argument that non-state paper sources are best interpreted through alternative conceptual tools, this opening chapter examines the fourth earl of Ormond whose supremacy was based on alliances with a considerable network of Gaelic lords. His ascendancy was augmented through extensive cultural patronage that was often non-textual. It was not until the decline of the Butlers alongside the rise of the Kildare Geraldines that these positions and strategies were reversed.

The foremost houses of the old colonial community, active both in the colony and among the Irishry, sustained an equilibrium where stability was largely preserved. This involved the use of Irish extortions, or coign and livery, to deploy a lord's *manraed* or armed forces.[1] Military support from England was not provided in any meaningful sense and little effort was made to reverse a colony which was in decline until the 1470s. War in France and dynastic strife drained English treasure and political will, adding to the neglect of its Irish lordship. The apathy of

---

[1] The term is associated with England's northern marches but is accurate in this context: S. G. Ellis, 'A crisis of lordship: Robert Ogle, fifth lord Ogle, and the rule of early Tudor Northumberland' in *Northern History*, 55 (2018), pp 61–75.

Lionel of Antwerp (1366), the failure of Richard II (1399) and the ineffectiveness of Henry VI, followed by the hardening Yorkist-Lancastrian divides between Geraldines and Butlers, further weakened the colony. A measure of stability came with the victory of Edward IV and the danger of conflict between a Yorkist leaning Lordship of Ireland and a Lancastrian king was averted. In 1462, a Lancastrian invasion led by Sir John Butler exposed the shortcomings of the Dublin administration and it required the intervention of the Desmond Fitzgeralds to defeat the insurgent Polestown Butlers at Piltown. Thomas Fitzgerald earl of Desmond was executed in 1468, marking the end of a short-lived Desmond ascendancy and the estrangement of the Munster Geraldines from the crown. Desmond would later reappear in the interventionist rhetoric written in the 1510s, guilty of original sin as allegedly the first to impose coign and livery on the king's subjects. According to early Tudor proponents for conquest, this had accelerated the decay of the colony. Sir John Tiptoft, a humanist literatus and a proponent of brutality a century before Spenser, led one of few interventions which achieved little but exposed the limits of direct crown authority.[2] The Kildare Geraldines prospered through the prudent administration and expansion of their assets, *manraed* and efficient, often ruthless exploitation of favourable circumstances in Ireland and at Court. In the 1450s, their income was modest. Following the abeyance of the seventh earl of Kildare, the earldom was at first worth just over £250 a year.[3] Through the consolidation of their core estates from Maynooth to the upper Barrow valley, Kildare had secured the western defences of the Pale and was ideally placed to further expand into south Leinster, dominating both Gaelic and marcher lords in key locations. From their strategic stronghold, this Kildare nexus extended through the marches, Limerick and east Ulster as an island-wide network of followers. Gearóid Mór Fitzgerald strengthened the Geraldine position despite the appointment of Henry Lord Grey in 1479. Kildare's Yorkist pedigree led to rebellion in 1487 and conflict in the 1490s, culminating in a royal summons and imprisonment in the Tower in 1495. Outbreaks of violence had shaken the Pale as Geraldine-Butler feuding erupted on Kildare's removal from office. Nonetheless, cleared of charges of treason and surviving a hostile atmosphere at Court, he re-emerged with favour in 1496.

---

[2] Tiptoft's reputation as a book collector has long been acknowledged: R. J. Mitchell, *John Tiptoft (1427-1470)* (London, 1938), pp 17, 56, 74, 151-2, 170-1; Art Cosgrove, 'The execution of the earl of Desmond, 1468' in *JKAH*, 8 (1975), pp 11-27. For Spenser, see Ciaran Brady, 'Spenser, plantation and government policy' in Richard McCabe (ed.), *The Oxford handbook of Edmund Spenser* (Oxford, 2010), pp 86-105; David Edwards, 'Spenser's *View* and martial law in Ireland' in Hiram Morgan (ed.), *Political ideology in Ireland, 1541-1641* (Dublin, 1999), pp 127-57.
[3] Ellis, *Tudor frontiers*, pp 107-18.

INTRODUCTION

The deputyship of Sir Edward Poynings, quite surprisingly, was to endure for centuries in constitutional terms, with the enactment of legislation curbing the powers of the governor and Irish parliament.[4] 1496 signalled the stabilisation of relations between Henry Tudor and his leading Irish magnate. Kildare was married to the king's cousin Elizabeth St John and steps were taken to pacify Geraldine-Butler animosity. For much of his career, Gearóid Mór Fitzgerald maintained amicable dealings with Thomas Butler, seventh earl of Ormond, who resided at Court. Kildare led a series of successful campaigns across the island, including a celebrated victory in a pitched battle at Knockdoe (1504) for which he was honoured as a knight of the Garter. Upon his death in 1513 he was interred in his chantry chapel in Christ Church Cathedral and his obituaries, written by both Gael and Gall, trumpeted his virtues and achievements.

From the 1460s, in response to the ascendant Geraldines, complaints of a decaying colony increased. Over time, pleas for crown intervention became distinctly regional in scope. The rhetoric produced by those in opposition projected this stance through a traditional, insular understanding of the twelfth-century account of the original conquest, the *Expugnatio Hibernica*. Although these positions unfolded in terms of factional conflict between Kildare and Ormond, along with other anti-Geraldine proponents of 'conquest', they were alternating positions that were fundamentally more determined by their standpoint in terms of political power than by factional rivalry.

In chapter two and in subsequent chapters, an insular yet aggressive push for 'conquest' will be examined with attention to a number of Hiberno-English editions of the *Expugnatio* which appeared in the late fifteenth century. These highly significant literary sources provide an added dimension beyond the standard written material. As a projection of their broad view on noble governance in Ireland, the major cultural endeavours of the ascendant Kildare Geraldines are discussed in chapter three, including their extensive humanist patronage and relations with the Gherardini of Florence. The broad humanist patronage of the ascendant house of Kildare in some ways represented a far-reaching view that the twelfth-century conquest of Ireland was complete. Although artistic, scholarly and ecclesiastical patronage was pursued by the entire aristocracy, through the luxury of holding power the strategies of a dominant magnate allowed for broad cultural projects to become a greater priority.[5]

---

[4] David B. Quinn, 'Early interpretation of Poynings' Law, 1494-1534' in *IHS*, 2 (1940-1), pp 241-54; D. B. Quinn, 'Hegemony of the earls of Kildare, 1494-1520' in *NHI*, pp 638-61; R. D. Edwards and T. W. Moody, 'The history of Poynings' Law: Part I, 1494-1615' in *IHS*, 2 (1940-1), pp 415-24; James Kelly, *Poynings' law and the making of law in Ireland, 1660-1800* (Dublin, 2007).

[5] The most notorious exaction was known as coign and livery. These oppressive Gaelic customs were considered to be a major factor in the decline of English common law in the late

Chapters four and five return to the State Papers and quasi-state paper material which projected an opposing perspective.[6] With particular attention to the 'State' (c. 1515) this outlook was bolstered through prophetic discourse and by stressing the incomplete nature of the conquest which had caused the colony to decay. Underlying this was an insular, archaic understanding of the history of the conquest, which through Giraldus was prophetic history.[7] This standpoint came to be voiced through the literature of decay, wherein the 'evils' of a dominant magnate could only be remedied through military conquest. Anti-Geraldine sentiment was further embittered by the reality that Kildare adequately defended the Yorkist Pale while also extending the southern limits of the maghery (or 'plain', as the Pale was often referred to).[8] In opposing Kildare, the proponents of 'conquest' attacked what they presented as the Geraldine-induced 'decay' of the Englishry.

A number of key figures stood independently from these leading rival magnates. It was not the case that the entire old colonial community has been polarised toward either camp. Yet an interchange of ideas evidently took place between like-minded interest groups and there was some political unity among anti-Geraldines. Alliances were complex and fluid, yet many figures were compelled to have dealings with Kildare or Ormond.[9] Within the Pale and in government circles, a lobby to garrison Leinster existed in opposition to Kildare. Led by Ormond

---

medieval Lordship of Ireland: C. A. Empey and Katharine Simms, 'Ordinances of the White Earl and the problem of coign in the later middle ages' in *PRIA*, 75C (1975), pp 161-87. For related military extortions, see S. G. Ellis, 'Taxation and defence in late medieval Ireland: the survival of scutage' in *JRSA*, 107 (1977), pp 5-28.

[6] Recent scholarship in this area has significantly aided this study. See esp., Heffernan, *Tudor policy*; Maginn and Ellis, *Tudor discov. Ire.*; Michael Bennett, 'The Libelle of English policy: the matter of Ireland' in Linda Clark (ed.), *The fifteenth century XV: writing, records and rhetoric* (Woodbridge, 2017), pp 1-20; Chad Marshall, 'The reform treatises and discourse of early Tudor Ireland, c. 1515-1541' (Ph.D., University of Tasmania, 2018).

[7] Barbara L. McCauley, 'Giraldus "Silvester" of Wales and his *Prophetic history of Ireland*: Merlin's role in the *Expugnatio Hibernica*' in *Quondam et Futurus*, 3 (1993), pp 41-62; Caoimhe Whelan, 'Translating the *Expugnatio Hibernica*: A vernacular English history in late medieval Ireland' in C. Griffin and E. Purcell (eds), *Text, transmission and transformation in the European middle ages, 1000-1500* (Turnhout, 2018), pp 165-92; Peter Crooks, 'The structure of politics in theory and practice, 1210- 1541' in *CHI*, i, 447, 463.

[8] There has been a shift in how Gearóid Mór Fitzgerald appears in the historiography and his role in advancing the Pale: S. G. Ellis, *Ireland's English Pale* (Woodbridge, 2021); S. G. Ellis, 'Great earl of Kildare (1456-1513) and the creation of the English Pale' in *Ger. med. Ire.*, pp 325-40. Accounts written during the early decades of the Irish Free State by Donough Bryan and Edmund Curtis portrayed a quasi-independent earl of Kildare: Donough Bryan, *The great earl of Kildare* (Dublin, 1933), p. 263.

[9] For example, Sir William Darcy of Platten was an ally of Kildare up to 1515 at which point he issued his vehemently anti-Geraldine treatise the 'Decay of Ireland': S. G. Ellis, 'An English gentleman and his community: Sir William Darcy of Platten' in Vincent Carey and

INTRODUCTION

(or Ossory) this 'Butler conquest' lobby was aggressively sought by the Cowleys, Robert and Walter.[10] Of fundamental importance was the strategic Barrow valley. Given the potential threats from the north, along with Scottish incursions in east Ulster, it is curious that there was such weight behind the drive to intervene in south Leinster. Related here were the geopolitical interests of the city of Waterford and its influential civic oligarchy. Indeed, the city held Ormondist sympathies and for much time shared a Lancastrian allegiance. The mayors of Waterford represented interests that stood to gain from securing the Barrow valley which, as Finglas stated, was 'key and hyeway' for the region.[11]

Chapter six turns to Gearóid Óg Fitzgerald and an aristocratic *rapprochement* between Kildare and leading peers at Court. Gearóid Óg was raised at Court, married to a high-ranking noblewoman and as demonstrated by his *Rental*, the ninth earl received a strong inheritance.[12] Acknowledged as the 'gretest improver' of his estate, his tenure as earl and deputy oversaw the continuation of earlier Geraldine political, martial and cultural projects.[13] Kildare's critics were vocal on both sides of the Irish Sea but he acquired allies among the leading peers of the realm. A sense of Geraldine exceptionalism and indispensability was intensified as the legitimacy of Geraldine rule was augmented through material culture, Renaissance humanism and ecclesiastical patronage. By the time of Fitzgerald's alliance with Norfolk in the 1520s and also Wiltshire and Dorset in the 1530s, the Kildare position was projected through cultural expressions of an increasingly refined nature. This chapter also focuses on the patterns of competition within how court culture operates as the manner in which court culture was conducted was not simply societal or customary but was simultaneously tied to politics, patronage and competition. In connecting with preceding chapters, it is here argued that as rivalries were played out in this arena under the civil guise of life at

---

Ute Lotz-Heumann (eds), *Taking sides? colonial and confessional mentalities in early modern Ireland* (Dublin, 2003), pp 19–41.

[10] Heffernan, *Tudor policy*, pp 33–45, 56–62; David Edwards, *The Ormond lordship in County Kilkenny, 1515–1642: the rise and fall of Butler feudal power* (Dublin, 2003), pp 40–2.

[11] SP 60/2/7, f. 21v. A long literary tradition tells of the city's call to arms since the conquest: St John Seymour, *Anglo-Irish literature, 1200–1582* (Dublin, 1929), p. 88. Waterford privileges and Desmond-Ormond feuding reverberate in the sixteenth century. Thomas Butler, tenth earl of Ormond wrote to Sussex concerning the 'grete charges (for) bulded defense of the haven (after Desmond) spoyled and burned vyllyges within my contrey': BL, Titus B.XII, f. 76r.

[12] See conventions. It is remarkable how terminology can consolidate what is essentially an interpretative position. It seems that the ninth earl was first referred to as Gearóid Óg in the Gaelic annals. He was styled as such by nationalist historians since the eighteenth century and this was reinforced by influential scholars from early in the twentieth century: AFM, 1514; ALC, 1519; Edmund Curtis, *A history of medieval Ireland* (Dublin, 1938); Edmund Curtis, *A history of Ireland* (New York, 1939).

[13] *Crown surveys of lands, 1540–1, with the Kildare Rental begun in 1518*, ed. Gearóid MacNiocaill (Dublin, 1992); SP 60/3, f. 2v.

the Tudor Court, the Kildares held the upper hand. On the eve of the revolt, the house of Kildare enjoyed unprecedented military and strategic supremacy along with a sizeable income.[14] Long-standing cultural endeavours were continually expanding being unveiled as late as 1533. For instance, the cataloguing of the earl's library was perhaps an indication of expanding the collection while the ornate 'Rent Table' was an expensive and long-term project that was merely completed in 1533. Yet beyond 1534, Kildare's renaissance humanist diplomacy, and even the elaborate political treatises of earlier decades were abruptly out of fashion in favour of the concise state memorandum. Geraldine aristocratic overtures were destroyed by double blow of the Reformation and failure of the 1534 revolt.

In the final chapters, Cromwellian reform and the 'conquest' lobbyists are explored along with the Kildare rebellion of 1534. Here, the mysteries surrounding the motives of Thomas Fitzgerald, Lord Offaly, in rebelling, the murder of Archbishop John Alen and the appeal to Rome were not resolved, but deepened. It was perhaps considered to be less a gamble than the Yorkist coup d'état of 1487, intended initially as a resurgence or temporary withdrawal of allegiance. The decision to revolt was also born of a misplaced sense of Geraldine exceptionalism that ran deeper than historians have hitherto realised. On 11 June, the 'dice' were cast, as early modern antiquarians have attested, but the killing of Alen in late July changed the entire complexion of the revolt.[15] Thomas became the tenth earl of Kildare after the death of his father in September. Even after Kildare's eventual surrender and imprisonment in the Tower, dire circumstances did not prevent the possibility of a pardon from being entertained. Up to a point, with this in mind the final chapter considers the fate of the push for regional 'conquest', most vocally presented by Robert and Walter Cowley, which was sealed with the fall of Cromwell in 1540. The executions, post-rebellion devastation, crisis of policy and reconstruction in the late 1530s have diverted attention from the specific nature of the struggle that had taken place. What had been at stake between the house of Kildare and the house of Ormond was not fundamentally strategies to govern Ireland, but rather competition over the governance of Ireland, which was pursued in alternate ways relative to their wider political authority. With this in mind, as the concluding sections shall argue, each vision was overshadowed by the dramatic upheaval at Court and even further afield, with lasting implications. Yet among the wide range of momentous consequences, the unprecedented rift with Rome dealt a blow to Kildare ecclesiastical patronage and the Geraldine

---

[14] Ellis, *Tudor frontiers*, pp 113–42.
[15] James Ware, *The antiquities and history of Ireland* (5 vols, Dublin, 1705), ii, 89.

modus operandi, but ironically, the proponents of 'conquest' were also undone by the religious Reformation.[16]

❧

Underpinning this narrative are significant archival influences. The voluminous collection of extant documents categorised as the State Papers, in contrast to exiguous unconventional sources, have traditionally and understandably been seen as the foundation stone for the study of sixteenth-century Ireland.[17] The circumstances surrounding their arrangement are remarkable.[18] They form an in-depth collection which was the first of numerous major antiquarian projects of this nature in the nineteenth century.[19] In 1831 a royal commission under William IV set out the foundation records of the state.[20] A prevailing view of this historiographical climate was the inevitable overthrow of late medieval lords with the rising power of the king.[21] These documents were collected in the aftermath of 1534 and as such, they represent an attempt to make sense of the rebellion

---

[16] Grey, St Leger and Walsh distanced themselves from the 'traitor Garret' but the nature and substance of their policy was broad and inclusive like that of Kildare prior to 1534.

[17] The printed State Papers are reliable transcripts. The only textual liberties I have found are rare instances of exclamation marks inserted to give a sense of romantic apostrophe. For example, the 'State' (c. 1515); 'what pytte is to heere, what rueth is to reportte, there is no tounge that canne tell, ne penne that canne wryte!': *S.P. Hen. VIII*, ii, 14. However, they were products of a particular historiographical climate. For example, the respected Victorian editor of the chancery rolls, James Morrin, dismissed Henry VII's Ireland as 'a scene of tumult and violence': *Calendar of the patent and close rolls of the chancery of Ireland in the reigns of Henry VIII, Edward VI, Mary and Elizabeth*, ed. J. Morrin (2 vols, Dublin, 1861), i, p. xiii.

[18] Housed in The National Archives at Kew, volumes SP 60/1 to SP 60/11 predate 1540. *S.P. Hen. VIII* comprises mostly of documents from these volumes but some entries are selected from Lambeth Palace Library and the British Library. A notable state paper manuscript printed elsewhere is the 'Breviat' of Patrick Finglas: SP 60/2, ff 17r-26v. See also David Heffernan, 'Patrick Finglas' A Breviat of the conquest of Ireland and the decay of the same, c. 1535 and the Tudor Conquest of Ireland' in *Sixteenth Century Journal*, 49 (2017), pp 369-88. A well-known different version printed in Harris, *Hibernica* was based on TCD, MS 842, ff 22r-33r. See *Hibernica: or some ancient pieces relating to Ireland*, ed. Walter Harris (Dublin, 1770), pp 79-103. A version can also be found in Maginn and Ellis, *Tudor discov. Ire.*, pp 69-79.

[19] *S.P. Hen. VIII*, ii, iii; *Cal. S. P. Ire.*, ed. Ellis and Murray. See also, the earlier calendar edited by Bullen and Brewer, and to a lesser extent the itemisations edited by Hamilton: *Cal. Carew*; *Cal. State Papers relating to Ireland of the reigns of Henry VIII, Edward VI, Mary and Elizabeth*, ed. Hans Hamilton (11 vols, London, 1860).

[20] They were subsequently published as the 'State papers...under the authority of his majesty's commission [for] king Henry the Eighth.' As part of an Imperial state building enterprise, they were deemed as the core sources for the understanding of the early sixteenth century. They were to be printed while preserving their antiquated 'manner and form' as they were 'presented to the Board of Commissioners.': *S.P. Hen. VIII*, ii, p. ix.

[21] The commissioners herald the sources for the reign of Henry VIII by noting the centrality of the monarch 'as soon as the barbarous ages had passed away and the intercourse of nations began to be carried on by other instruments than the sword': *S.P. Hen. VIII*, i, p. ix.

by necessarily over representing the critics of the Geraldines. This narrative was all the more pronounced as it was recounted through selective textual correspondence with Court. The image of squabbling chieftains in the Irish annals and state paper pessimism was grimly accepted into the age of modern scholarship. While sensitive to its polemic nature, historians have nonetheless moved beyond traditional interpretations to more nuanced understandings.[22]

Archival peculiarities include the remarkable opening document chosen for *State Papers Henry VIII*, which was essentially a renaissance text (see chapter four).[23] Although they are largely a collection of administrative letters, they are neither a definitive corpus of such interactions nor are they exclusively comprised of conventional correspondences.[24] Two main points spring from this archival critique. By focusing on what appeared to be mainly documentary correspondence and deeming these sources as 'the State Papers', alternative material has been marginalised leading to a misleading impression that other sources were marginal prior to the rebellion. Indeed, the emblematic destruction of the monasteries and what was a cultural and not merely an ecclesiastical break with Rome overshadowed how political argument was expressed in early Tudor Ireland. From a long-established tradition, these sources have become rather inflexibly deemed

---

[22] Christopher Maginn, 'Continuity and change: 1470-1550' in *CHI*, i, 300-28; Heffernan, *Tudor policy*, pp xx, 2-3, 12-27; Herbert Woods, *A Guide to the records deposited in the Public Record Office of Ireland* (Dublin, 1919). Ellis has cautioned against their *ex parte* statements: S. G. Ellis, 'The English Pale: a 'failed entity'?' in *HI*, 19 (2011), pp 14-17; Ellis, *Reform and revival*, p. 2; Ellis, *Ire. Tudors*, pp 191-2. See also, MacNeill's 'painful perusal' of the archive in 1919: Eoin MacNeill, *Phases of Irish history* (Dublin, 1919), p. 347. A century later, as John McCafferty calls for a cultural history of the State Papers, he observes that from the moment the archive came into existence it became politicised: John McCafferty, 'State papers, state formation: anxiety and the SP 60-63 archive', Tudor and Stuart Ireland Conference, TCD (16 Aug. 2019). For the 'castle-centric' view afforded by the state papers, see Sarah Covington, Valerie McGowan-Doyle and Vincent Carey (eds), *Early modern Ireland: new sources, methods and perspectives* (London, 2018), intro., pp 1-26; Constantia Maxwell, *Irish history from contemporary sources 1509-1610* (London, 1923), p. 20. For the exaggerated dearth of 1922, see Ciarán Brady and Raymond Gillespie (eds), *Natives and newcomers: essays on the making of Irish colonial society, 1534-1641* (Dublin, 1986), p. 21. The explosion in the Public Record Office of Ireland in 1922 destroyed entire classes of records, which further elevated the value of the State Papers. However, many documents can be reconstructed from alternative sources: Peter Crooks and Ciarán Wallace, 'The records of a country are its noblest inheritance (Beyond 2022: Ireland's Virtual Record Treasury Research Project)' in *HI*, 28 (2020), pp 48-51.

[23] Furthermore, a long verse ballad, part of a correspondence dating to 1536 (but originally written in 1487-8) has only been published in editions by Croker (1866) and Carpenter (2003). But neither collection note the manuscript at its present location: SP 60/2, ff 52r-55v. See *Popular songs of Ireland*, ed. Crofton Croker (Dublin, 1866), p. 294; *Verse in English from Tudor and Stuart Ireland*, ed. Andrew Carpenter (Cork, 2003); *Cal. S. P. Ire.*, ed. Ellis and Murray, p. 44.

[24] Unusual documents include Thomas Cromwell's *Ordinances for the governance of Ireland* and the 'curse' proclaimed against Thomas Fitzgerald, Lord Offaly. These were, however, generally produced during a specific period toward the mid-sixteenth century.

INTRODUCTION

the exclusive and definitive source for historians. Reinforced by the commission of 1831, the arrangement of these sources shaped a teleological approach to the 1534 Kildare rebellion and offer a misleadingly linear thrust to what has become known as the Tudor conquest. Secondly, perceptions of the colony in Ireland were deeply influenced by a relationship to power which generally dictated two alternating perspectives. The State Papers provide a deceptive, though appealing illusion that government in Ireland inevitably lay with those opposed to Kildare, but this was not simply a manifestation of Geraldine-Butler conflict. The State Paper paradigm obscured the rich patterns of cultural projections that were an expression of perspective in terms of power. An ascendant ruling magnate, either Butler or Geraldine, was compelled to operate in island-wide terms and as a result conveyed their outlook through broad patronage of a culturally diverse nature.

The late medieval Lordship of Ireland has received greater attention since the turn of the century, augmenting the well-established body of work which revitalised the subject in the late twentieth century.[25] However there has always been a sense of allure to the epic saga of the Geraldine-Butler feud as a coda to medieval Ireland. Indeed, within a generation of the calamity of 1534, the story of the rise and fall of the Kildare Geraldines had become legendary. Elizabethans saw these great feudal adversaries as clashing blindly 'with tooth and naile to overthrow one the other by hook and by crooke to be in authoritie superious', and were ultimately demonised by Spenser with their 'cries Scythian like as Crom abo and Butler abo'.[26] The course of scholarship has moved from the antiquarians of the Enlightenment, the grand state archival enterprises of the nineteenth century to nationalist and revisionist history.[27] Although as recently

---

[25] The State Papers are central to the historiography: Bradshaw, *Const. rev.*; Ellis, *Reform and revival*; Ellis, *Tudor frontiers*; Ellis, *Ire. Tudors*; Brady, *Chief gov.*; Colm Lennon, *Sixteenth-century Ireland: the incomplete conquest* (Dublin, 1994); Heffernan, *Tudor policy*.

[26] C. W. Fitzgerald, *The earls of Kildare and their ancestors from 1057 to 1773* (Dublin, 1858); Raphael Holinshed, *Chronicles of England, Scotlande and Irelande* (6 vols., London, 1807–8), i, 82; *Ireland under Elizabeth and James the First described by Edmund Spenser, by Sir John Davies and by Fynes Moryson*, ed. Henry Morley (London, 1890), p. 92; Ciaran Brady, *A Viceroy's vindication?: Sir Henry Sidney's memoir of service in Ireland 1556–1578* (Cork, 2002); Patricia Palmer, *Language and conquest in early modern Ireland: English renaissance literature and Elizabethan imperial expansion* (Cambridge, 2001), pp 16, 104–5; Brendan Bradshaw, Andrew Hadfield, Willy Maley (eds), *Representing Ireland: literature and the origins of conflict, 1534–1660* (Cambridge, 1993); J. P. Montaño, *The roots of English colonialism in Ireland* (Cambridge, 2011); Willy Maley, *Salvaging Spenser: colonialism, culture and identity* (Manchester, 1997); D. B. Quinn, *The Elizabethans and the Irish* (Washington, DC, 1966), pp 53, 83; Vincent Carey, 'John Derricke's Image of Ireland, Sir Henry Sidney, and the massacre at Mullaghmast, 1578', in *IHS*, 31 (1998–9), pp 305–27.

[27] Ciaran Brady, '"Constructive and instrumental": The dilemma of Ireland's first "new historians"' in C. Brady (ed.), *Interpreting Irish History: the debate on historical revisionism* (Dublin, 1994), pp 3–31. For the slow shift from a nationalist agenda, see S. G. Ellis, 'Nationalist historiography

as the 1920s, G. H. Orpen remarked that as medieval Ireland passed into early modernity, the old colonial aristocracy had been in 'spurious imitation' of the wild Irish, a point echoed in Constantia Maxwell on the stygian 'gloom' of the State Papers.[28] The issues of acculturation, crown policy and the state of the colony were revisited by historians over the course of the twentieth century.[29] A nuanced picture of the colony, its neighbouring territories and the wider world continues to emerge.[30] Once chiefly concerned with narrow concepts of factional conflict, many historians of late medieval Ireland appreciate that feuding amongst the old colonial community also unfolded through diplomacy and arbitration that were largely regulated through English institutions. The court culture of the Gaelic and marcher lords, most notably the junior branches of the leading old colonial houses, shared many of these mediatory functions. Geraldine-Butler rivalry was consistently fierce, at times violent, but evidence also points to a richer more complex narrative.[31]

---

and the English and Gaelic worlds in the late middle ages' in *IHS*, 25 (1986-7), pp 1-18. In the early twentieth century, separatist leanings in the late medieval colony were put forward by Edmund Curtis and Donough Bryan. Also in this nationalist tradition, see James Lydon, *The Lordship of Ireland in the middle ages* (Toronto, 1972); James Lydon, *Ireland in the later middle ages* (Dublin, 1973). The question of conquest and resistance in constitutional terms are considered from a nationalist perspective in Bradshaw, *Const. rev.*

[28] G. H. Orpen, *Ireland under the Normans, 1216-1333* (4 vols, Oxford, 1920), iv, 249; Maxwell, *Irish hist.*, pp 5, 19-25.

[29] Quinn, White and Bradshaw drew heavily from a number of key reform treatises. From the 1970s, the study of the late medieval Gaelic world was reinvigorated. See esp., K. W. Nicholls, *Gaelic and gaelicised Ireland in the middle ages* (Dublin, 1972); Art Cosgrove, 'Ireland beyond the Pale 1399-1460' in *NHI*, pp 569-90; Katharine Simms, *From Kings to warlords: the changing political structure of Gaelic Ireland in the later middle ages* (Woodbridge, 1987). For an informative historiographical overview see Heffernan, *Tudor policy*, pp xvii-xxv, 21-3. Bradshaw's ideological and constitutional analysis of early Tudor treatises and state records represented a milestone in considering the centralisation of crown policy. The State Papers tend to underline Bradshaw's 'revolution' both in government and in terms of early Tudor reformers: Bradshaw, *Const. rev.*, pp 36-7.

[30] For instance, see Maginn, 'Continuity and change', pp 300-28; Maginn and Ellis, *Tudor discov. Ire.*; Sparky Booker, *Cultural exchange and identity in late medieval Ireland: the English and Irish of the four obedient shires* (Cambridge, 2018); Power, *Eur. frontier elite*; Thomas Herron and Michael Potterton (eds), *Ireland in the Renaissance, c. 1540-1660* (Dublin, 2007).

[31] Historians have advised that the longstanding narrative of internecine feuding which preceded an Elizabethan military conquest has subverted perceptions of late medieval and Tudor Ireland: Ellis, *Reform and revival*; Ellis, *Tudor frontiers*; Ellis, *Ire. Tudors*, p. 11; Brady, *Chief gov.*, pp 169-73. Crooks responds to the traditional concept of Ireland as a scene of late medieval desolation. Cautioning against an emphasis on disorder, the regulatory nature of English institutions, arbitration, compensation and marriages formed a sophisticated colonial identity that prospered within flexible structures: Peter Crooks, 'Factions, feuds and noble power in the lordship of Ireland, c. 1356-1496' in *IHS*, 35 (2006-7), pp 425-54.

INTRODUCTION

The ground-breaking scholarship of Ellis significantly revised traditional interpretations, observing a modest yet tangible revival of English institutions from the late fifteenth century. By comparing conditions in the Lordship of Ireland with those of the northern marches, Ellis has re-evaluated the relationship between lowland England and the crown's peripheral territories.[32] The *realpolitik* underlying Tudor reform has been examined to lasting influence with Brady's *Chief Governors*. In recent years, the late medieval roots of sixteenth-century policy have been traced in a dual approach of discovery and reform by Maginn and Ellis. Heffernan has explored the large corpus of extant policy papers and the long-term impact of early Henrician treatises. In his study of the policy debate, Heffernan invites historians to further explore the themes that can be found running through the large body of reform literature.[33]

Prompted by a dearth of records or a tradition of neglect, studies of Tudor Ireland have tended to overlook the fifteenth century and its warring lordships. The power of the great lordships has been seen as a decentralisation from Court or Dublin. Recent work has focused on viewing Yorkist and early Tudor Ireland in continuum, reconsidering the traditional impression of feuds as merely internecine conflict.[34] Simms has formed a detailed picture of lordship, society and

---

[32] Ellis, *Reform and revival*; Ellis, *Tudor frontiers*. Ellis has also challenged the image of the eighth earl of Kildare as a semi-independent magnate and has reassessed the role of the Leinster Geraldines in advancing the southern Pale maghery. Recent publications include, Ellis, *Ireland's English Pale* and a paper on the career and legacy of Gearóid Mór Fitzgerald in *Ger. Med. Ire*. Donough Bryan in the 1930s and James Lydon in the 1970s assessed Gearóid Mór as a mostly benign source of stability: Bryan, *Great earl*; Lydon, *Ire. middle ages*; Ellis, *Reform and revival*, pp 10-20, 67-86. See also, Marian Lyons, *Gearóid Óg Fitzgerald, ninth earl of Kildare* (Dundalk, 1998), Marian Lyons, *Church and society in County Kildare* (Dublin, 2000), pp 44-52.

[33] Lennon, *Sixteenth-cen. Ire.*; Ciaran Brady, 'From policy to power: the evolution of Tudor reform strategies in sixteenth-century Ireland' in Brian MacCuarta (ed.), *Reshaping Ireland, 1550-1700: colonisation and its consequences, essays presented to Nicholas Canny* (Dublin, 2011), pp 21-42, at pp 21-6. Reform treatises were subject to a variety of interpretations: Brady, *Chief gov.*, pp 2-4; Heffernan, *Tudor policy*, pp 217-19; Maginn and Ellis, *Tudor discov. Ire.*, pp 22-3, 113-34. The standpoint of native and marcher lords has recently been explored. In contrast to an English perspective from the maghery, those in the Irishry viewed the frontier as being culturally fluid: Christopher Maginn, 'Gaelic Ireland's English frontiers in the late middle ages' in *PRIA*, 110C (2010), pp 181-3. For wider affinities amongst the Gaelic Irish, see Simon Egan, 'A playground of the Scots? Gaelic Ireland and the Stewart monarchy in the late fourteenth and fifteenth centuries' in Linda Clark (ed.), *The fifteenth century XVI* (Woodbridge, 2018), pp 105-21; Simon Egan, 'An Irish context to a Scottish disaster: James IV, the O'Donnells of Tyrconnell and the road to Flodden' in Katharine Simms and Joseph Mannion (eds), *Politics, kinship and culture in Gaelic Ireland, c. 1100-c. 1690: essays for the Irish chiefs' and clans' prize in history* (2 vols, Dublin, 2018), ii, 10-16. For acculturation in the Pale, see Booker, *Cult. exch. med. Ire.*, pp 24-44, 97-142. There were limits to the symbiotic relations between cultures: Ellis, *Ireland's English Pale*, pp 9-12, 46-7.

[34] Ellis, *Reform and revival*, pp 1-11, 206-7; Crooks, 'Structure of politics', pp 441-68. For an exploration of historical consciousness among the colonists: Robin Frame, 'Contexts, divisions

culture in late medieval Ulster which has proven essential for understanding wider Irish politics throughout this period and into the reign of Henry VIII.[35] Ecclesiastical patronage has been studied as a conduit for the projection of cultural and political perspectives.[36] In contrast to early Tudor polemic, neither the Church *inter Hibernicos* nor *inter Anglicos* were in complete decay. In this broad, often polemic context, the late medieval church (and in particular the Knights Hospitaller) was of fundamental importance. Historians generally concur that religion was not a major factor in causing the 1534 rebellion. However, this may be tentatively qualified given the scope of ecclesiastical patronage and the use of the church for diplomatic overtures.[37] Alongside studies of aristocratic delegation

---

and unities: perspectives from the later middle ages' in *CHI*, i, 523-50. Studies have regarded Ireland's sixteenth century, moreover, modern Ireland to have begun in 1534: T. W. Moody and F. X. Martin (eds), *The course of Irish history* (Cork, 1967); Art Cosgrove (ed.), *NHI*; D. B. Quinn, 'Henry VIII and Ireland, 1509-1534' in *IHS*, 12 (1960-1), pp 318-44; D. B. Quinn, 'Aristocratic autonomy, 1460-1494' in *NHI*, pp 591-618; D. B. Quinn, 'The re-emergence of English policy as a major factor in Irish affairs, 1520-34' in *NHI*, pp 662-87; Christopher Maginn, *'Civilizing' Gaelic Leinster: the extension of Tudor rule in the O'Byrne and O'Toole Lordships* (Dublin, 2005), ch. 1; Maginn, 'Continuity and change'; Crooks, 'Factions, feuds', pp 425-54; A. J. Otway-Ruthven, *A history of medieval Ireland* (London, 1968), pp 373-408; C. A. Empey, 'The Butler lordship in Ireland' (Ph.D., Trinity College Dublin, 1970); Empey and Simms, 'Ordinances of the White Earl', pp 161-87; Lydon, *Ire. middle ages*, p. 143.

[35] In addition, see Simms's rendering of Gaelic literary sources for political analysis: Katharine Simms, 'Bardic poetry as a historical source' in Tom Dunne (ed.), *The writer as witness: literature as historical evidence. Historical Studies XVI* (Cork, 1987), pp 58-75. Simms's most recent work returns to the political relations between Gaelic Ulster and the English and Scottish realms. The cultural dynamism of Gaelic Ulster transcended political divides: Katharine Simms, *Gaelic Ulster in the middle ages: history, culture and society* (Dublin, 2020). Also breaking with the traditional chronology of 1534 are studies of ecclesiastical domains. Murray, Lyons and Scott have respectively treated of Dublin and the dioceses of Kildare and Meath. John McCafferty's recent edition of ecclesiastical records offers a unique insight on Uriel during this understudied period: *The act book of the diocese of Armagh 1518-1522*, ed. John MacCafferty (Dublin, 2020); Lyons, *Church and soc.*; James Murray, *Enforcing the English reformation in Ireland, clerical resistance and political conflict in the diocese of Dublin* (Cambridge, 2009); James Murray, 'Archbishop Alen, Tudor reform and the Kildare rebellion' in *PRIA*, 89C (1989), pp 1-15; Brendan Scott, *Religion and reformation in the Tudor diocese of Meath* (Dublin, 2007), pp 36-7. See also, Colm Lennon, *The lords of Dublin in the age of reformation* (Dublin, 1989), pp 19-33.

[36] For instance, see Murray, *Enf. Eng. ref. Ire*. From a different standpoint, recent work includes Raymond Gillespie's interpretation of the Book of Fenagh as an artefact of political import: Raymond Gillespie, 'Saints and Manuscripts in sixteenth-century Breifne' in *Breifne*, 11 (2008), pp 533-56; Raymond Gillespie, Salvador Ryan and Brendan Scott (eds), *Making the Book of Fenagh: context and text* (Cavan, 2016). Studies have also shown in certain cases the Irish church was reasonably prosperous, with new church buildings and the creation of new parishes: Lyons, *Church and soc.*, pp 53-8; Henry A. Jefferies, *Priests and prelates of Armagh in the age of reformations, 1518-1558* (Dublin, 1997).

[37] Exceptions to this general consensus notably include Robert Dudley Edwards and more recently Henry Jefferies: Robert Dudley Edwards, *Church and state in Tudor Ireland* (Dublin,

INTRODUCTION

and the politics of the Kildare ascendancy, the current established historiography offers a greater understanding of Henrician reform and the debate for policy. The failure of reform and lack of a coherent crown strategy has been examined in detail and with attention to treatises and state records. However, greater attention may be devoted to the aforementioned push for 'conquest' in Leinster, before and after 1534.[38]

In the light of the interpretative problems arising from the analysis of purely textual materials, the insights derived from recent literary and cultural theory acquire a greater relevance. In recent decades, historians of late medieval and early modern Europe and England have succeeded in deepening our understandings of the culture of the period. The political mechanisms as to how court culture works has been studied in histories of late medieval and Tudor England.[39] In broad conceptual terms, this study also draws from the many literary scholars whose specialist fields range from intellectual thought to anthropology.[40] There

---

1935); Henry Jefferies, *The Irish Church and the Tudor reformations* (Dublin, 2010). For a different view, see Bradshaw, *Const. rev.*, pp 60-80. For the disruption of ecclesiastical patronage in the 1530s, see Brendan Bradshaw, 'Sword and strategy in the reformation in Ireland' in *HJ*, 21 (1978), p. 497.

[38] Bradshaw, *Const. rev.*, pp 85-163; Ellis, *Reform and revival*; Ellis, *Tudor frontiers*, pp 96, 152-3; Ellis, *Ire. Tudors*, chs 5-6, Lennon, *Sixteenth-cen. Ire.*, chs 3-4; Brady, *Chief gov.*, pp 1-25; Heffernan, *Tudor policy*, pp 119, 150, 223. The centrality of certain key early Henrician treatises for crown policy was widely discussed in the mid- to late twentieth century: Dean White, 'The Tudor plantations in Ireland before 1571' (Ph.D., Trinity College Dublin, 1968); Bradshaw, *Const. rev.* Maginn and Heffernan have examined calls for the 'reduction of Leinster': Maginn, 'Civ.' Gaelic Leinster; Heffernan, 'Finglas' breviate', pp 369-88; David Heffernan, 'Complaint and reform in late Elizabethan Dublin, 1579-94' in Kathleen Miller and Crawford Gribben (eds), *Dublin: Renaissance city of literature* (Manchester, 2017), p. 79.

[39] See esp., Sharpe, *Tudor mon.* This bibliography has expanded since the 1980s. Notable works from this period include David Starkey (ed.), *The English court from the wars of the Roses to the civil war* (London, 1987); Alistair Fox, *Politics and literature in the reigns of Henry VII and Henry VIII* (Oxford, 1989). Fox is informative whereby politics and court culture may only be fully appreciated through the inclusion of literary sources: Alistair Fox and John Guy (eds), *Reassessing the Henrician age: humanism, politics and reform, 1500-1550* (Oxford, 1986); John Guy, *The reign of Elizabeth I: court and culture in the last decade* (Cambridge, 1995); John Guy, *The Tudor monarchy* (London, 1997); Natalie Mears, 'Courts, courtiers and culture in Tudor England' in *HJ*, 46 (2003), pp 703-22; Natalie Mears, *Queenship and political discourse in the Elizabethan realms* (Cambridge, 2005); James Simpson, *Reform and cultural revolution: the Oxford English literary history, 1350-1547* (Oxford, 2002), pp 191-255; Susan Brigden, *London and the reformation* (Oxford, 1989); Susan Brigden, *Thomas Wyatt: the heart's forest* (London, 2014); John Guy, *Henry VIII: The quest for fame* (London, 2018).

[40] For studies of a vibrant system of readership and symbolic culture, see A. B. Ferguson, *Clio unbound: perception of the social and cultural past in Renaissance England* (Durham, NC, 1979); A. B. Ferguson, *The articulate citizen and the English Renaissance* (Durham, NC, 1965); Margaret Hodgen, *Early anthropology in the sixteenth and seventeenth centuries* (London, 1964). Several older publications remain useful for earlier influences and traditions: A. Lovejoy and G. Boas,

has been something of a delay in applying such techniques to early Tudor Ireland but efforts have been made to correct this imbalance. From modest beginnings in the early 1900s, early surveys of Hiberno-English literature witnessed a lacuna from the mid-fifteenth century to the 1550s. For example, Flower stated that the *literati* of both Gael and Gall were devastated during this period, casually noting the Fitzgeralds as the 'Greeks and Florentines of Ireland'.[41] Subsequent scholars grappled with what had almost become an accepted late medieval literary void.[42] Renaissance culture, the Geraldines and the dynamism of textual, oral and non-verbal modes have also received greater attention in recent decades.[43] The

---

Primitivism and related ideas in antiquity (Baltimore, MD, 1935); George Boas, *Primitivism and related ideas in the middle ages* (Baltimore, MD, 1948). Also, see G. L. Campbell, *Strange creatures: anthropology in antiquity* (London, 2006), ch. 7; Seán Duffy, *Ireland in the middle ages* (Dublin, 1997), pp 7-27.

[41] Seymour, *Anglo-Irish literature*, pp 2-9; Robin Flower, *The Irish tradition* (Oxford, 1947), pp 145-65. As late as the twentieth century, writers have often looked disdainfully upon the possibility of an Irish milieu in early Tudor literature. Writing in the 1920s, the literary historian John Berdan's extensive studies contain a matter Victorian attitude where the works of English writers were exclusively Anglo-centric. To demonstrate, even Surrey's 'Fair Geraldine', writes Berdan, 'surely (requires) no necessity for more than a bare statement (which is that) the basis of the story is to be found in the sonnet': John Berdan, *Early Tudor poetry* (New York, 1920), p. 516.

[42] A. J. Fletcher, *Drama and the performing arts in pre-Cromwellian Ireland: a repertory of sources and documents from the earliest times until c. 1642* (Cambridge, 2001). Also, see *Verse in Eng. Tudor Stuart Ire.*, ed. Carpenter. Acculturation in the marches generated a unique and distinctly polemic Gaelic literature: Katharine Simms, 'Bards and barons: the Anglo-Irish aristocracy and the native culture' in Robert Bartlett and Angus MacKay (eds), *Medieval frontier societies* (Oxford, 1992), pp 177-97; Katharine Simms, 'The barefoot kings: literary image and reality in later medieval Ireland' in *PHCC*, 30 (2010), pp 1-21. Also, see Caoimhe Whelan, 'James Yonge and the writing of history in late medieval Dublin' in Seán Duffy (ed.), *Medieval Dublin XIII* (Dublin, 2011), pp 183-95.

[43] Colm Lennon, Aisling Byrne, Marian Lyons and Michael Potterton have produced scholarship which has influenced this study, while the recent MACMORRIS project under Patricia Palmer has broken new ground in uncovering the sixteenth-century Irish Renaissance: Colm Lennon, 'The Fitzgeralds of Kildare and the building of a dynastic image, 1500-1630' in W. Nolan and T. McGrath (eds), *Kildare: history and society* (Dublin, 2006), pp 195-211; Marian Lyons, 'The Kildare ascendancy' and Colm Lennon, 'The making of the Geraldines: the Kildare Fitzgeralds and their historians' in Patrick Cosgrove, Terence Dooley and Karol Mullaney-Dignam (eds), *Aspects of aristocratic life: essays on the Fitzgeralds and Carton House* (Dublin, 2014), pp 48-59, 71-8; Michael Potterton and Thomas Herron (eds), *Dublin and the Pale in the Renaissance c. 1540-1600* (Dublin, 2011); Thomas Herron and Michael Potterton (eds), *Ireland in the Renaissance c. 1540-1660* (Dublin, 2007); Aisling Byrne, 'The earls of Kildare and their books at the end of the middle ages' in *The Library: Transactions of the Bibliographical Society*, 14 (2013), pp 129-53; Aisling Byrne, 'The Geraldines and the culture of the wider world' in Peter Crooks and Sean Duffy (eds), *The Geraldines and medieval Ireland: the making of a myth* (Dublin, 2016), pp 278-91; Patricia Palmer (principal investigator), *Mapping actors and communities: a model of research in Renaissance Ireland in the 16th and 17th centuries* (MACMORRIS), macmorris.maynoothuniversity.ie.

INTRODUCTION

co-existence of oral and textual culture has been addressed. The use of textual modes in the Pale with legal, political and social associations differed from Gaelic customs. Oral, textual and material culture have long been understudied, but are now the focus of major scholarship. Of note is Flavin's research which sheds light on a sophisticated range of consumer goods from overseas. Flavin depicts a complex socio-political situation in the 1520s–30s when the Irish gentry maintained a taste for archaic fashions.[44] While studies of material culture continue to offer insights, fresh conceptual approaches have also been integrated in the historiography.[45] These recent endeavours are indeed welcome additions, as greater attention is presently devoted to the study of late medieval and early modern Ireland.

---

[44] Raymond Gillespie, *Reading Ireland: print, reading and social change in early modern Ireland* (Manchester, 2005), pp 26–60. Historians have acknowledged the interchangeable nature of oral and written traditions in Ireland as with further afield: Carpenter, *Verse Tudor and Stuart Ire.*, p. 10; Adam Fox, *Oral and literate culture in England, 1500–1700* (Oxford, 2000). In this context, Flavin is conscious of the traditional medieval style suit of armour on the effigy of Piers Butler: Susan Flavin, *Consumption and culture in sixteenth-century Ireland: saffron, stockings and silk* (Woodbridge, 2014), pp 95, 139–40, 245–8.

[45] For instance, Brendan Kane's exploration of honour and renaissance culture in post-reformation Ireland has been the focus of well-regarded research: Brendan Kane, *The politics and culture of honour in Britain and Ireland, c. 1541–1641* (Cambridge, 2010); Brendan Kane, 'A world of honour: aristocratic *mentalité*' in *CHI*, ii, pp 482–505; Thomas Herron and Brendan Kane, *Nobility and newcomers in Renaissance Ireland* (Washington, DC, 2013).

1

White Earl to the Great Earl, 1442-96

The first four earls of Ormond augmented their inheritance and title over the centuries, enjoying a continual rise since the founding of the comital houses in 1326. Located between both Geraldine earldoms, the Butlers of Ormond did, however, face geographical disadvantages and Kilkenny castle was some distance from the administrative centre of the Lordship.[1] By the time James Butler, the 'White Earl' of Ormond, served as deputy Lieutenant for the third time in 1442, he was the most prominent old colonial magnate in the early fifteenth century.[2] Despite acrimony with the Talbots and insidious Geraldine-Butler feuding in Munster, Ormond's career in general was marked by a broad vision that echoed his dominance.[3] This feuding was intermittent. Ormond maintained good relations with Desmond in the 1420s as commissioners of the peace were well briefed but by 1441 co-operation had ceased.[4] As governor, warlord and politician he was belligerent, successfully holding power in what was a ruthlessly competitive environment. Like his bitter rival, John Talbot, Shakespeare's 'great Alcides of the field', Ormond served in France under Henry V up to 1420.[5] Efficient

---

[1] However, it was not limited to the 'frugal amenities' of Kilkenny castle that were memorably conjured by Hilary Mantel, imagining Anne Boleyn 'on special occasions (as) she hacks on the poor dirt roads to Dublin': Hilary Mantel, *Bring up the bodies* (London, 2012). See esp., Colm Lennon, 'Pedagogy and reform: the influence of Peter White on Irish scholarship in the Renaissance' and Paul Cockerham, '"To mak a tombe for the earl of Ormon and to set it up in Iarland": Renaissance ideas in Irish funeral monuments' in Thomas Herron and Michael Potterton (eds), *Ireland in the Renaissance c. 1540–1660* (Dublin, 2007), pp 43-51, 195-230.

[2] James Lydon, *Ireland in the later middle ages* (Dublin, 1973), p. 135; Robin Frame, 'Contexts, divisions and unities: perspectives from the later middle ages' in *CHI*, i, 541-3.

[3] The outward looking nature of his tenure can be compared with the Great Earl of Kildare: C. A. Empey, 'The Butler lordship in Ireland' (Ph.D., Trinity College Dublin, 1970), p. 257; Michael Bennett, 'Late medieval Ireland in a wider world' in *CHI*, i, 341-2; David Edwards, *The Ormond lordship in County Kilkenny, 1515–1642: the rise and fall of Butler feudal power* (Dublin, 2003), pp 2-4.

[4] Peter Crooks, 'The ascent and descent of Desmond under Lancaster and York' in *Ger. Med. Ire.*, p. 229; CIRCLE, Patent Roll 8 Henry V, no. 18; A. J. Otway-Ruthven, *A history of medieval Ireland* (London, 1968), p. 376.

[5] R. A. Griffiths, *The Reign of Henry VI* (Cheltenham, 1998), p. 413; E. A. E. Matthew, 'The governing of the Lancastrian lordship of Ireland in the time of James Butler, fourth earl of Ormond c. 1420-1452' (Ph.D., Durham University, 1994), p. 212; David Beresford, 'The Butlers in England and Ireland, 1405–1515' (Ph.D., Trinity College Dublin, 1999), pp 42-9; M. C. Griffith, 'The Talbot-Ormond struggle for control of the Anglo-Irish government, 1414-47'

and aggressive, as demonstrated by the regulations of coign in his 'Ordinances', Ormond's *patria* and patronage were also broad in scope.[6] The Ormond strategy in Ulster had been to counterbalance O'Neill and O'Donnell. Even as Richard Nugent, baron of Delvin, held the viceregal office in 1448-9, peace in Uriel and south-east Ulster 'twene english and yrish (was made) by auctoritie of (the) depute and the Eirle of Ormond'.[7] In 1449, when Ormond intervened in the O'Reilly lordship, he was indispensable as Richard duke of York pursued the vestigial earldom of Ulster.[8]

Ormond-Talbot feuding erupted again in the early 1440s.[9] Archbishop of Dublin Richard Talbot and the (disputed) Geraldine prior of Kilmainham Thomas Fitzgerald had been vehemently opposed, with 'malice', to Ormond.[10] Giles Thorndon originally a royal intermediary serving as Treasurer was driven from Ireland under intimidation from the deputy Lieutenant. He was accused of having consorted 'with...Thomas Fitzmorice, a notorious traitor...broken the king's prison and gaol in which lay Brother Thomas Fitzgerot styling himself prior of the Hospital of St John of Jerusalem in Ireland'.[11] A colourful counter-accusation of treason and necromancy was filed by Thorndon and Fitzgerald once they fled to England where Ormond was condemned for misuse of the seal. The alarming drop in revenues added to the *gravitas* of the charges.[12] This intense

---

in *IHS*, 2 (1940-1), p. 394. Memories of bitter feuding with Talbot were opportunistically conjured a century later in Ormondist complaints that he had brought 'Leynster to disobedience and destruction': *Ormond deeds*, iv, 209.

[6] C. A. Empey and Katharine Simms, 'Ordinances of the White Earl and the problem of coign in the later middle ages' in *PRIA*, 75C (1975); Empey, 'Butler lordship', pp 257-79; James Lydon, *The Lordship of Ireland in the middle ages* (Toronto, 1972), pp 130-3; Bradshaw, *Const. rev.*, p. 13. The ordinances were distinctly Gaelic in character: Kenneth Nicholls, 'Anglo-French Ireland and after' in *Peritia*, 1 (1982), p. 401; K. W. Nicholls, *Gaelic and gaelicised Ireland in the middle ages* (Dublin, 1972), pp 36, 46.

[7] *Registrum Iohannis Mey. The Register of John Mey, Archbishop of Armagh, 1443-1456*, ed. W. G. H. Quigley (Belfast, 1972), p. 168. Archbishop Mey of Armagh had previously warned that the English of Uriel stood in 'drede of perell': *Reg. Mey*, p. lxxv; Katharine Simms, *Gaelic Ulster in the middle ages: history, culture and society* (Dublin, 2020), pp 172-4; Matthew, 'Lancastrian lordship', pp 360-1. Ormond's policy in Ulster was similar to that of Kildare from the 1470s, distributing influence between and seeking to avoid a concentration of power: Simms, *Gaelic Ulster*, pp 202-3. Henry VIII attempted to do likewise with Kildare and Ormond in the 1520s.

[8] Simms, *Gaelic Ulster*, pp 179-86; Simms, '"The King's friend": O'Neill, the crown and the earldom of Ulster' in Lydon (ed.), *England and Ireland in the later middle ages*, pp 214-36.

[9] Griffith, 'Talbot-Ormond struggle', pp 372-6; Otway-Ruthven, *Medieval Ire.*, p. 376.

[10] *A roll of the proceedings of the king's council in Ireland*, ed. James Graves (London, 1877), pp 303-4; Matthew, 'Lancastrian lordship', pp 346-63.

[11] *Ormond deeds*, iii, 142.

[12] Suitability to rule depended in some measure on respectability along with dignified noble stock. Eleanor duchess of Gloucester's trial for witchcraft 1441 destroyed Humphrey's political credibility, and it is curious that the White Earl's bitter enemies led by Giles Thorndon

struggle was exacerbated by Geraldine-Butler rivalry although Desmond and Ormond were in fact at peace from 1442-4. But Geraldine control of the Knights Hospitallers represented a change from previous decades. When under Butler influence, Gerald Fitzthomas, father to Prior Thomas Fitzgerald, claimed manors in Kildare which passed to Ormond in 1432 through his marriage to Elizabeth Fitzgerald, widow of John Grey, the second baron Grey of Codnor, and daughter of the fifth earl of Kildare.[13] The removal of Prior Thomas Fitzgerald in 1447 prompted a dramatic challenge for trial by combat, the knight being 'appayryde in Smethfylde...fulle clenely harnyssed, redy wythe alle hys fetys abd wyth allehys wepyns, kepynge the fylde tylle hyghe none'. A generation later the event was chronicled in print, 'the priour of Kylmain (Kilmainham) appeled the erle of Urmond of treason wich had a day assigned to them to fight in smythfeld and the listis wer made and feld drassid (field dressed)'.[14]

Discontent lingered, even with the cancellation of the commission of oyer and terminer issued to the former prior. Ormond had been acquitted of treason; yet Archbishop Talbot continued to condemn 'de abusu Regiminis Jacobi comitis Ormoniae (misrule of the earl of Ormond) dum esset locumtenens Hiberniae (as governor of Ireland)'.[15] Historians have recognised these events as the last echoes of the Ormond-Talbot feud which abated with the marriage of the earl's daughter Elizabeth Butler and Talbot's son in 1444.[16] While Ormond navigated decades of political opposition and litigation, he secured influence throughout the Irishry, orchestrating an effective approach to regional affairs. In east Munster, possibly with the aid of the Cahir Butlers, Desmond raids on the Ormond lordship shattered a peace that had been kept since 1442.[17] Partisan reports painted the Geraldine-Butler struggle in Munster as the 'greate distruction of all the contry'.[18] In 1443 the archdiocesan council of Armagh

---

attempted to charge Ormond with necromancy in the mid-1440s: *Proceedings and ordinances of the Privy Council of England*, ed. Nicolas Harris (7 vols, London, 1834-7), v, 297, 301, 304-5, 325-34; S. G. Ellis, *Ireland in the age of the Tudors* (London, 1998), pp 23-6.

[13] *Crown surveys of lands, 1540-1, with the Kildare Rental begun in 1518*, ed. Gearóid MacNiocaill (Dublin, 1992); *The Red Book of the earls of Kildare*, ed. Gearóid MacNiocall (Dublin, 1992), p. 146; Matthew, 'Lancastrian lordship', p. 346.

[14] *Roll of the Proceedings of the King's Council in Ireland*, pp l-li; *Saint Alban's Chronicle (1485)*, pp 422-3.

[15] James Ware, *The antiquities and history of Ireland* (5 vols, Dublin, 1705), ii, 323. A brass of Richard Talbot survives from St Patrick's Cathedral around the time of his death, c. 1449. Of note are a series of canons and choristers on either side of the archbishop: John Crawford and Raymond Gillespie (eds), *St Patrick's Cathedral, Dublin: a history* (Dublin, 2009), p. 51.

[16] Otway-Ruthven, *Medieval Ire.*, p. 379.

[17] Empey and Simms, 'Ordinances of the White Earl', pp 164-8. Desmond may have nursed a grudge with the reversal of a marriage agreement from 1429: Crooks, 'Desmond under Lancaster and York', p. 242.

[18] *Original letters illustrative of English history*, ed. Henry Ellis (11 vols, London, 1824-6), i, 61.

exaggerated accounts of an 'immense war' in east Ulster for the purpose of non-attendance in parliament.[19] Since the 1410s, Desmond interfered with the Butlers of Cahir, which caused unrest ('propter dissensionem') in Carrick.[20] Intense attacks from Desmond in 1444 and 1446 'preyed and burned' the town while tensions also mounted between the Polestown and Cahir cadets. Conflict among the junior Butlers was largely contained by the fourth earl of Ormond but while he was at Court his deputy Edmund MacRichard was captured by Piers FitzJames of Cahir in 1447. From England, Ormond arranged for declarations of denunciation to be issued by the commons of Tipperary and Kilkenny against Desmond, which were sent to the king's council.[21] However, more important in terms of concrete administration were the set of regulations that became known as the 'Ordinances of the White Earl'.

After 1432 much of Kildare and the Barrow valley passed to Ormond and prior to 1444, as governor he had taken Shrewsbury's rents in Wexford into crown hands.[22] Both in response to these fractious marcher conditions exacerbated by feuding magnates and in order to manage his lands, a broad series of bureaucratic measures were taken. For instance, a rental of lordships in Kilkenny and Waterford was made in 1444.[23] Better known are the regulations for the exactions of coign (provision and lodgings for militia), referred to as the 'Ordinances of the White Earl', for Kilkenny and Tipperary. Necessary for the upkeep of a ruling magnate's *manraed*, it suggested a strong degree of control imposed by Ormond.[24] The liberty of Tipperary had fallen into abeyance in the early fifteenth century and was merged with Kilkenny, which, although a royal county, was in practice within the earl's *patria*.[25] Statutes for the regulation of coign were enacted in Ormond's absence. Driven by the anxieties of the 1540s, the gentry of Tipperary later claimed that 'the white James Erle of Ormonde...comyttid to sundrye personnes...the rule and governance...in hisabsence...(causing) malicious division and rancour betwene themselves.' But Ormond's 'hope they would have governed

---

[19] Brendan Smith, *Crisis and survival in late medieval Ireland: the English of Louth and their neighbours, 1330–1450* (Oxford, 2013), p. 213.

[20] *The Red Book of Ormond*, ed. N. B. White (Dublin, 1932), p. 121; Empey and Simms, 'Ordinances of the White Earl', pp 166–7.

[21] Empey, 'Butler lordship', pp xxxiii–xxxv, p. 279; Crooks, 'Desmond under Lancaster and York', pp 243–4.

[22] Otway-Ruthven, *Medieval Ire.*, p. 347.

[23] *Ormond deeds*, iii, 104, 155. The Red Book of Ormond originates from the fourteenth century. James Butler, second earl of Ormond prohibited marchers to intervene in disputes concerning cattle raids. Established in 1361, his ordinances were copied in the seventeenth century: SP 46/130, f. 32.

[24] These regulations have been cited as evidence of Butler autonomy to the point of separatism: Bradshaw, *Const. rev.*, p. 19.

[25] Empey and Simms, 'Ordinances of the White Earl', p. 168.

the cuntry well in his absennce' was justified.[26] York's lieutenancy at first held much promise for widespread stability and when Butler was appointed Deputy Lieutenant in September 1450 he campaigned successfully with Desmond in Munster, the midlands and Ulster. Co-operation between Ormond and Desmond in 'reforming' Limerick, the midlands and south Ulster was omitted from this complaint.[27] The Yorkist party established by Richard Plantagenet in the 1450s did not polarise the Geraldines and Butlers from the outset.[28] Ormond-Desmond rivalry was ever present and their feuding was highly destructive.[29] But as with the above petition from the gentlemen of Tipperary the 1530s State Papers tended to overstate and misleadingly simplify 'tholde malice' between Desmond and Ormond for the entire reign of Henry VI.[30]

While Ormond served as the leading old colonial magnate his position was at times challenged to the point of being displaced. With Sir John Talbot's first term as lord lieutenant (1414-21), it seems that Ormond was compelled to alter his stance on the governance of the colony. Projections of this shift in perspective are to be found in the sources. By 1421, to counter Talbot's growing hold of the governorship, he had allied with Archbishop Swayne of Armagh, who dealt firmly with the Church *inter Hibernicos*, and Christopher Preston, Lord Gormanstown, before collating a petition against Talbot.[31] It was claimed that the land had fallen from order to decay and that corruption was rife in the chancery and the king's bench. The seizure of estates as crown lands 'by the lieutenant's orders' was condemned, yet Ormond did likewise by absorbing Shrewsbury's rents in Wexford prior to 1444. The history of Giraldus was referred to in describing the destructive oppression of 'coynes'.[32] By citing the *Expugnatio* in this context, the rhetorical

---

[26] In reference to the capture of Edmund MacRichard by Cahir in 1447: *Ormond deeds*, iv, 210.
[27] *Ormond deeds*, iv, 210.
[28] For a critique of Campion and what he saw as the 'imperfect' reflection of the civil war in England see: Crooks, 'Desmond under Lancaster and York', pp 223-4. Ormond and York maintained a constructive relationship at this time: Otway-Ruthven, *Medieval Ire.*, p. 384. In the 1460s, an elegy for York perhaps flatteringly celebrates his establishment of 'peacable' government, 'en Erllande mist til gouvernement, tout le pais rygla paisiblement': *Political poems and songs relating to English history*, ed. Thomas Wright (2 vols, London, 1861), ii, 157.
[29] Empey, 'Butler lordship', pp 274-5; Ellis, *Ire. Tudors*, pp 56-7; Anthony McCormack, *The earldom of Desmond, 1463-1583: the decline and crisis of a feudal lordship* (Dublin, 2005).
[30] *Ormond deeds*, iv, 210; SP 60/4, f. 10r.
[31] Archiepiscopal declarations can be highly politicised and often resound with the perspectives of a ruling magnate or an opposing power block. For example, in 1443 a statement from Armagh exaggerated the dangers of attending Parliament due to 'immense war' in the region: *The register of John Swayne, archbishop of Armagh and primate of Ireland, 1418-1439, with some entries of earlier and later archbishops*, ed. D. A. Chart (Belfast, 1935), p. 190; Smith, *Crisis and survival*, p. 213.
[32] Peter Crooks, 'Factionalism and noble power in English Ireland, c. 1361-1423' (Ph.D., Trinity College Dublin, 2007), pp 378-80; *Proc. ord. Privy Council Eng.*, ii, 43-52.

justification was revealing. The petition spoke of 'le lyvre de Cambrense' and ancient historians of England ('anxiens estories dengletere'), the five-fold rights of the English crown in Ireland alongside the submissions made to Richard II.[33] Archbishop Swayne and Preston bore the letter to England. Later in 1446, with Talbot again as governor, Ormond was reluctant to co-operate. According to Richard duke of York, Ormond maintained that 'it shall never bee chronicled, nor remaine in scripture, by the grace of God, that Ireland was lost by my negligence'.[34]

Also of relevance here is the well-known *Libelle of Englishe Polycye*, commissioned by Ormond at some stage prior to the mid-1430s. In circulation by 1436, this political poem advocated for the protection of English interests through naval power and it reflected the mercantile value of the port towns and Butler regional interests, particularly the city of Waterford. Michael Bennett has drawn attention to the 'matter of Ireland' of the fifteenth century with reference to the striking parallels between the 'Libelle' and the early Tudor tract, *Salus Populi* (see chapter four). Both were renaissance texts designed to sway policy, but the narrow focus on securing the Englishry while sidelining broad conciliar approaches to the Irishry appears to reflect the White Earl's relationship to power at a moment of anxiety. Perhaps reflecting an uncertain hold on the viceregal office or competition from Talbot, the writer states that Ormond 'speke to me fulle late whyche was a lorde of ful grete astate, that expensis of one yere don in France' would suffice to conquer Ireland. The *Libelle* can be interpreted as a move against aristocratic delegation and alliance with the native Irish lords: 'God forbede that a wylde Yrishe wyrlynge shoulde be chosen for to be there kynge'.[35] In points later echoed in both the *Salus Populi* and anti-Geraldine advocates for intervention, 'moche glorye' may be attained in Ireland, granting 'salvacioun to Englaunde and to alle Englyshe menne.' Ireland offers the prospect of a crusade to the west, to salvage a land 'so riche' and fertile, 'in all Christendome, ys no grounde ne londe to Yrelond lyche'.[36]

---

[33] Peter Crooks, 'Factions, feuds and noble power in the lordship of Ireland, c. 1356–1496' in *IHS*, 35 (2006–7), pp 51–2. For the adaptability of the *Expugnatio* to immediate circumstances, see *Proc. ord. Privy Council Eng.*, ii, 51–2. For contemporaries, the *Expugnatio* itself represented a firm symbolic statement: Frame, 'Contexts, divisions', pp 528, 535–6.

[34] Otway-Ruthven, *Medieval Ire.*, p. 382; Edmund Campion, *A historie of Ireland* (Dublin, 1809), p. 198.

[35] *Political poems*, pp 187–9; Michael Bennett, 'The Libelle of English policy: the matter of Ireland' in Linda Clark (ed.), *The fifteenth century XV: writing, records and rhetoric* (Woodbridge, 2017), pp 1–20; *The libelle of Englyshe polycye: a poem on the use of sea power, 1436*, ed. George Warner (Oxford, 1926), pp 36–8; V. J. Scattergood, 'The libelle of Englyshe polycye: the nation and its place' in Helen Cooney (ed.), *Nation, court and culture: new essays on fifteenth-century English poetry* (Dublin, 2001), pp 28–49; Alexandra Petrina, *Cultural politics in fifteenth-century England: The case of Humphrey, duke of Gloucester* (Boston, MA, 2004), p. 321.

[36] There are parallels between the *Libelle* with its regional focus and the later pleas to intervene in south Leinster in the 1530s: *Political poems*, pp 157–9, 186–7. For the historical symbolism

The White Earl's patronage had a lasting legacy and later generations of Butlers accentuated the flexible link between the *Expugnatio* and an insular, entrenched political programme. This strategic and rhetorical concept of crusade was particularly, although problematically, relevant to circumstances in late medieval Ireland. Given that there was already an established church, the suggestion of a crusade may seem tendentious. But since the twelfth-century conquest of Ireland, as Kathryn Hurlock observes, the rhetoric of the conquest remained couched in terms of a crusade thereafter.[37]

Under the fourth earl, the cultural reach of Ormond spanned from Gaelicised marcher lords to the Lancastrian Court.[38] While this patronage did reflect certain local and regional issues, an underlying theme was the broad aristocratic overlordship of the White Earl, prevailing against rivals while confidently projecting an expansive vision of the colony. There exists in the Bodleian Library a number of remarkable documents pertaining to the fourth earl of Ormond, which includes the well-known dual manuscript of the *Expugnatio Hibernica-Gouernaunce of Prynces* but also and an illustrated heraldic record.[39] James Yonge, notary, was commissioned for the manuscript. Yonge was a beneficiary of the White Earl's rule and he was imprisoned after resisting John Talbot's appointment as lord lieutenant in 1414. Employed by Ormond prior to 1420, for the rest of his career Yonge supported his patron through his written work and political activism.[40] The *Expugnatio-Gouernaunce* was commissioned in the early 1420s and in the context of Talbot-Ormond rivalry, it arguably represented the White Earl at a crossroads. Varying approaches to the governance of Ireland may be projected, from the more insular, regional approach represented by the *Expugnatio* to a broader

---

of crusade, see Kevin Sharpe, *Selling the Tudor monarchy: authority and image in sixteenth-century England* (New Haven, CT, 2009), p. 12.

[37] Kathryn Hurlock, 'Crusading rhetoric and Anglo-Irish relations, c. 1300–1600' in Edward Coleman, Paul Duffy and Tadhg O'Keeffe (eds), *Ireland and the Crusades* (Dublin, 2022), pp 164–77; E. A. E. Matthew, 'Henry V and the proposal for an Irish crusade' in Brendan Smith (ed.), *Ireland and the English world in the late middle ages* (Basingstoke, 2009), pp 161–75.

[38] Katharine Simms, 'Bards and barons: the Anglo-Irish aristocracy and the native culture' in Robert Bartlett and Angus MacKay (eds), *Medieval frontier societies* (Oxford, 1992), pp 177–97, see pp 190–7 for Talbot-Ormond variance.

[39] Bodl., MS Rawl. B 490, ff 50–90; Bodl., MS Rawl. B 496, ff 7r–16v.

[40] A number of his texts survive although he most likely produced a much larger body of work: St John Seymour, *Anglo-Irish literature, 1200–1582* (Dublin, 1929); Caoimhe Whelan, 'The notary's tale' in Sparky Booker and C. N. Peters (eds), *Tales of medieval Dublin* (Dublin, 2014), pp 113–34; Caoimhe Whelan, 'James Yonge and the writing of history in late medieval Dublin' in Seán Duffy (ed.), *Medieval Dublin XIII* (Dublin, 2011), pp 183–95; Theresa O'Byrne, 'Centre or periphery? The role of Dublin in James Yonge's *Memoriale*' (1412) in Kathleen Miller and Crawford Gribben (eds), *Dublin: Renaissance city of literature* (Manchester, 2017), pp 18–25.

alternative suggested by the *Gouernaunce*. Other relevant sources include records of legislation, peerage, chronicles and humanist literature. The preservation of Ormondist *res gestae* reveals certain calculated representations. As shall be seen in chapters two, four and five, later generations were mindful as to how these could be modified to suit changing circumstances.[41]

The *Expugnatio* will be the focus of chapter two where its providence and redactions will be analysed in more detail, but the *Gouernaunce* is here of use in considering the fourth earl's perspective. The *Gouernaunce of Prynces* or 'Secreta Secretorum' was a pseudo-Aristotelian 'mirror for princes', that during the Middle Ages was believed to be advice imparted from Aristotle to his pupil Alexander. The Alexander romance (life and legacy of Alexander III of Macedon) was popular among the aristocracy of medieval Europe but given the cross-cultural nature of practical governance in Ireland, the cult of Alexander assumed a greater meaning for an old colonial ruling magnate.[42] The *Gouernaunce* had a particular appeal in its praise of princely and scholarly attributes, along with a celebration of the concept of broad conquest. Figures from classical antiquity 'conquerid more al the worlde by connynge and study of clergeable bokys than by assautes of battaill'.[43] However, there was also contrary advice with the aggressive removal of native marcher lords, the 'roote of the nettille' such as the O'Dempsey 'of whom spronge the wedis that as myche in mi tyme have destruede of the comyte of Kyldare'.[44] As Whelan observes, the White Earl's *Gouernaunce* reflected the rivalry with Talbot and the latter is most likely in Yonge's mind when 'other governors' are denounced.[45] But

---

[41] The later fifteenth-century copy of this manuscript without the *Gouernaunce*, TCD MS 592, is of relevance as a part of an anti-Geraldine, 'conquest' perspective.

[42] As demonstrated by the contents of their library, the eighth and ninth earls of Kildare took an interest in the Alexander romance. Indeed, Kildare's 'liber Alixandre maugne' (see ch. 3) was one of two gilded books in their library: BL, Harleian MS 3756, f. 190v. A case can be made for the obituaries of both the White Earl and the Great Earl as in some way reflecting the chivalric values of the cult of Alexander: BL, Add. MS 4787, f. 251v. Flattisbury wrote that Kildare was *justiciarius* for '33 annorum'. Ellis has noted this discrepancy as Kildare was in fact deputy for just over thirty years: S. G. Ellis, 'Great earl of Kildare (1456-1513) and the creation of the English Pale' in Peter Crooks and Sean Duffy (eds), *The Geraldines and medieval Ireland: the making of a myth* (Dublin, 2016), pp 325-9; BL, Add. MS 4792, f. 6r.

[43] Bodl., MS Rawl. B 490, f. 28v.

[44] Bodl., MS Rawl. B 490, f. 28v. The text trumpets Butler achievements; 'good pees in leynstere and many othyr commendable dedis of armes he did elsware. (Alexander's virtues) by witte and connynge... gouerbaunce of a roelme is not doyne at will sauve by good renoune': Bodl., MS Rawl. B 490, ff 33; Whelan, 'Notary's tale', pp 113-34. Whelan also notes the influence of the *Gouernaunce* in the preamble to the attainder of Shane O'Neill in 1569. Also, see Ciaran Brady, 'Making good: new perspectives on the English in early modern Ireland' in Ciaran Brady and Jane Ohlmeyer (eds), *British interventions in early modern Ireland* (Cambridge, 2005), pp 1-3; Ciarán Brady, *Shane O'Neill* (Dundalk, 1996).

[45] 'methynketh hit apperyth oft tymes by diuers Englyshe captanys of Irland that haue bene

the overarching image of Ormond as governor in the *Gouernaunce* is that of a ruling magnate with considerable island-wide influence 'thys erle through the grace of god...to Pees reformed...brenys of Thomon..bourkes of connaught and monstre... leys..mcmahens, oneyle boy'.[46] Other documents obliquely reflecting Ormond's broad reach include an account of the 'Purgutario' undertaken by a Hungarian lord and an Italian to Lough Derg.[47] Given the circumstances surrounding the commissioning of the dual codex with its distinctive and diverging implications, consideration was perhaps devoted to future select emphasis. Turning briefly to Ormond's counterpart, Talbot on the other hand exploited a particular courtly connection. An indication of this can be seen in the finely illustrated 'Talbot-Shrewsbury book', dedicated to Margaret of Anjou on her betrothal to the king. The manuscript is a collection of chivalric romances and treatises and features an illustration of Talbot himself dressed in garter robes presenting the gift in the royal presence. The ceremony is decorated in detail, including a Talbot white dog in the foreground.[48]

Heraldic records most likely produced by the White Earl were propagandist in nature. Under their respective arms, listed after the 'Count mareshal', are Ormond, followed by the Geraldines of Munster and Leinster. Enumerated on the next folio leaf are 'Mauricius Purcell, Freyng, Blaunchevyle (and) Purcell.' By elevating the lesser lords of Ormond, the earl is attending to his feudal base. Contrary to the image offered elsewhere, the armed forces provided by these lords include native kern. A captaincy of kern was shared by two Purcell, an example of hereditary 'captaynes of the kerne' in County Kilkenny.[49] Early in his Lieutenancy,

---

now byth whos neclygence... haue destrued hanselfe har naciones har landis': Bodl., MS Rawl. B 490, f. 43v; Whelan, 'Notary's tale', pp 113-34; Whelan, 'James Yonge', pp 183-95.

[46] Bodl., MS Rawl. B 490, f. 55v.

[47] BL, Royal MS 10, B.IX (available on microfilm, NLI, pos. 1451). Yonge was commissioned to write this account which chronicles the experiences of a Hungarian noble Laurence Rathold and an Italian merchant Antonio Mannini. Also, see Michael Bennett, 'Late medieval Ireland in a wider world' in *CHI*, i, 338-9, 351.

[48] BL, Royal MS E.IV, f. 2v. This heraldic symbol was popularly associated with Talbot's chivalric prowess, a contemporaneous verse affectionately referring to him as 'owre good dogge' in France: *Political poems*, ii, pp 221-3. The text concludes with the statutes of the Order of the Garter which was illustrated with Talbot heraldry: BL, Royal MS E.IV, f. 439r.

[49] Bodl., MS Rawl. B 484, ff 7r-16v; Empey and Simms, 'Ordinances of the White Earl', p. 171; K. W. Nicholls, *Gaelic and gaelicised Ireland in the middle ages* (Dublin, 1972), p. 40; H. J. Hore and J. Graves (eds), *The social state of the southern and eastern counties of Ireland in the sixteenth century* (Dublin, 1870), pp 97-8. For the 'Freyng', de la Freigne as a 'knightly race' in Ormond folklore see the annals of John Clynn: *The Annals of John Clyn*, ed. Bernadette Williams (Dublin, 2007), p. 66; William Healy, *The history and antiquities of County Kilkenny* (Kilkenny, 1893), p. 274. Ormond claimed de facto heraldic jurisdiction through his agent John Kitely who was made King of Arms in Ireland: *Issues of the exchequer from Henry III to Henry VI*, ed. Frederick Devon (London, 1837), p. 459.

a *rapprochement* appeared to have emerged between Richard Plantagenet, duke of York, and Ormond who was the natural choice to assist in the management of his estates in Ireland. Evidence of this can be found in the Butler and York arms displayed on the pillar piscina of the Cathedral of St Patrick, Trim.[50] York was likely the aforementioned 'Count mareshal' in Ormond's heraldic records and among York's titles in Ireland was lord of Trim.[51] The material culture and the legacy of the White Earl are attested to in the will of Thomas Butler, seventh earl of Ormond, who solemnly recalled how his father:

> delyvred unto me a lytle whyte horne of ivory garnyssed at both thendes with golde and a corse therunto of whyte sylke barred with barres of gold thereuppon the wych was myn ancestors at fyrst tyme they were called to honour and hath sythen contynually remained in the same blode for wych cause my said lord and ffather commaunded me...to the honour of the same bloode...I woll..unto Sir Thomas Boleyn...heire apparaunt'.[52]

Ecclesiastical patronage included the church of St Thomas of Acon (a military order) in London. Through this church, a link was fostered between the cult of St Thomas Becket and the earls of Ormond.[53] Endeavours of a religious nature also included plans for a pilgrimage to Rome accompanied by his 'suite to the number of twenty-five'.[54]

The considerable extent to which Ormond operated in the Gaelic sphere necessitated an intercultural outlook.[55] A large body of politically charged bardic literature shows that the Butlers preceded the Geraldines in substantial patronage of Gaelic literature and *seanchaide*.[56] Cross cultural in its content, the themes of war and diplomacy dominate the Irish poems commissioned by the fourth

---

[50] Michael Potterton, *Medieval Trim: history and archaeology* (Dublin, 2005), pp 404-8; Elizabeth Hickey, 'Royal heraldry and some Irish arms at Trim' in *Ríocht na Midhe*, 8 (1998-9), pp 129-31; Helen Roe, *Medieval fonts of Meath* (Navan, 1968), pp 102-3; Karen Ralph, 'Medieval antiquarianism: the Butlers and artistic patronage in fifteenth-century Ireland' in *Eolas*, 7 (2014), pp 4-5.
[51] Bodl., MS Rawl. B 484, f. 7r; Edmund Curtis, 'Richard, duke of York, as viceroy of Ireland, 1447-1460; with unpublished materials for his relations with native chiefs' in *JRSA*, 2 (1932), pp 158-86.
[52] Beresford, 'Butlers in England and Ireland', p. 301. Curious parallels can be made with a medieval Irish artifact. The ancient kingship of Leinster was associated with the MacMurrough charter horn of Cualu, which was refurbished in the fifteenth century: Simms, 'Barefoot kings', pp 7-8.
[53] Beresford, 'Butlers in England and Ireland', ch. 2.
[54] *CPR*, viii, 278.
[55] Simms, 'Gaelic culture and society' in *CHI*, i, 428; Nicholls, *Gaelic and gaelicised Ire.*, pp 36-46.
[56] The Gaelic term for historical writing. Also, see Katharine Simms, 'Bardic poetry as a historical source' in Tom Dunne (ed.), *The writer as witness: literature as historical evidence. Historical Studies XVI* (Cork, 1987), pp 58-75; Katharine Simms, 'Geraldines and Gaelic

earl and the Butler cadet families which also related to Ormondist interests across the island of Ireland.[57] In 1447, when Ormond returned to Ireland and reached an accord with Talbot, the occasion was celebrated by the *filí* as the deeds of certain old colonial lords were often preserved in encomiastic bardic verse.[58] Patronage in the vernacular Gaelic Irish by the marcher English lords in general, but Ormond in particular mirrored political interests. A significant collection of poems relating to the Ormond lordship under the fourth and fifth earls reflected a broad outlook in cultural and political terms. For instance, the mediatory roles of Butler allies such as the Purcells were praised for their hopes to 'unite the nobles of Ireland, both Gael and Gall'.[59] An elegy for James Purcell, baron of Loughmoe, was strongly influenced by the Arthurian traditions which illustrated the cultural complexity of the marches. Through creating a sense of *mythos*, unifying concepts could be stressed: 'Cing Artúir dá credit cách' [Arthur to whom all gave allegiance].[60] In a likely reference to his funeral, there was much grief 'on going from Holy Cross' a Cistercian abbey which prospered through Butler patronage in the mid-fifteenth century. The cloisters and chapter house were renovated, while in the early to mid-1400s a unique example of secular art in the form of a wall painting was commissioned.[61] At this time the order of Cistercians had permitted ornamental plaster walls. Influenced by English styles, the painting illustrates the aristocratic pursuit of a stag hunt. A similar scene was evoked in the words of the mid-fifteenth-century Hiberno-English poet of the Ormondist Tipperary poems who described a deer chase in praise of Piaras Butler, lord of Cahir: 'ag fiadhach Cláir mhín Mhumhan, tír fanar cháir Cathughadh' [on the fair plain of Munster, a land worth fighting for].[62] Rivalries among the

---

culture' in *Ger. Med. Ire.*, p. 269; D. B. Quinn, *The Elizabethans and the Irish* (Washington, DC, 1966), p. 2.

[57] *Poems on the Butlers of Ormond, Cahir and Dunboyne AD 1400–1650*, ed. James Carney (Dublin, 1945); C. A. Empey, 'The Butler Lordship' in *Journal of the Butler Society*, 13 (1970–71), pp 174–80, 183–5. The author was a Hiberno-Norman poet: *Poems on marcher lords: from a sixteenth-century Tipperary manuscript*, ed. Anne O'Sullivan and Padraig Ó Riain (London, 1987), p. xxi.

[58] Simms, 'Gaelic culture', p. 428; Françoise Henry and Geneviève Marsh-Micheli, 'Manuscripts and illuminations, 1169–1603' in *NHI*, 801; Katharine Simms, *From Kings to warlords: the changing political structure of Gaelic Ireland in the later middle ages* (Woodbridge, 1987), pp 4–5; see also, Bradshaw, *Const. rev.*, p. 22.

[59] *Poems on marcher lords*, p. 23.

[60] Prominent also is the claiming of the sword by Galahad. See *Poems on marcher lords*, pp 28–31. The malleability of bardic verse suited colonial lords: Simms, 'Bards and barons', p. 182.

[61] *Poems on marcher lords*, p. 23; Roger Stalley, *The Cistercian monasteries of Ireland* (New Haven, CT, 1987), pp 112–4; Colmcille Ó Conbhuidhe, *The Cistercian abbeys of Tipperary* (Dublin, 1999), pp 87, 202; Ellis, *Ire. Tudors*, p. 39.

[62] *Poems on marcher lords*, p. 90; Harold G. Leask, *Irish churches and monastic buildings* (3 vols, Dundalk, 1960), iii, 60–8; Rachel Moss, *Art and devotion in late medieval Ireland* (Dublin, 2006),

Butler cadets and Desmond-Ormond feuding were also themes in this collection of bardic verse.[63]

The most important compendium of Irish literature associated with the fourth earl of Ormond is the 'Book of the White Earl', a large manuscript presently housed in the Bodleian Library.[64] Containing a selection of middle Irish texts, including a narrative of the crusades, its most remarkable component is the illustrated 'Book of Pottlerath' and a copy of the eleventh-century *Saltair Chaisil* (Saltair of Cashel).[65] The symbolism of the *Saltair* is emphasised by Simms as the *patria* of the White Earl included the cathedral's sacred ground. Through this association, Ormond was linked to the prestige of the archiepiscopal see.[66] A variety of religious accounts dedicated to Edmund MacRichard Butler dating to the 1450s are also of note. According to Empey, the courts of the junior branches were a world apart from the aristocratic pomp of the leading old colonial magnates.[67] However, the political rhythms of how court culture operated were comparable. In the case of the Butler cadets based in the marches, the dominance of the White Earl and his broad vision of governance was projected through patronage of vernacular literature.

❧

The absence and subsequent decline of the Butlers following the death of the White Earl, coupled with the establishment of a Yorkist Lordship of Ireland made way for a Desmond ascendancy.[68] It was in the 1460s that the Fitzgeralds of Desmond then sprang to dominance although for centuries their power had extended far beyond their provincial powerbase in Munster. Their position was

---

pp viii, 67–8; Ó Conbhuidhe, *Cistercian Tipperary*, pp 271–5; H. S. Crawford, 'Mural painting in Holycross abbey' in *JRSA*, 5 (1915), pp 149–50. For the Kildare Geraldines and the hunt, see Colm Lennon, *Sixteenth-century Ireland: the incomplete conquest* (Dublin, 1994), p. 73; Colm Lennon, 'The making of the Geraldines: the Kildare Fitzgeralds and their historians' in Patrick Cosgrove, Terence Dooley and Karol Mullaney-Dignam (eds), *Aspects of aristocratic life: essays on the Fitzgeralds and Carton House* (Dublin, 2014), pp 71–8.

[63] James Purcell's attack on Carrick, Philip Hackett's 'fame' in thwarting Desmond: *Poems on marcher lords*, pp 35, 67–8, 79–81. The latter event took place in 1462, at which point the house of Desmond was dominant: Crooks, 'Factions, feuds and noble power', p. 429. A relationship between the Abbey of Holy Cross and Maynooth later appears to have emerged in the 1470s. An indication of this survives in a (grant) 'da [unu] orte et [unu] tenete in Maynoth' to the abbot and convent: NLI, D 1790.

[64] Bodl., MS Laud Misc. 610.

[65] Bodl., MS Laud Misc. 610, ff 1r–58v, 73r–122v.

[66] Empey and Simms, 'Ordinances of the White Earl', p. 168; Simms, 'Geraldines and Gaelic culture', p. 269; Henry and Marsh-Micheli, 'Manuscripts and illuminations', pp 800–3.

[67] Empey and Simms, 'Ordinances of the White Earl', p. 165.

[68] The fifth and sixth earls of Ormond were either absent or under attainder. The liberty of Tipperary was affected by conflict between the Polestown and Cahir Butlers which had previously been curtailed by the fourth earl of Ormond: Empey, 'The Butler lordship', pp 278–9.

overturned with the sudden execution of Thomas Fitzgerald, earl of Desmond to widespread 'grete astonishment' in 1468.[69] Early in the reign of Henry VIII, anti-Geraldines recounted the 1460s as a dark turning point, but at the time, stability provided by aristocratic governance was a cause for optimism.[70] Richard, duke of York, seized the opportunity to profit from the rise of the Geraldines, and a crucial parliament at Drogheda in 1460 underlined factional divides while reinforcing the idea of aristocratic delegation in the lordship.[71]

From the 1450s the Lancastrian earls of Ormond had relocated to England and remained absent aside from the disastrous campaign that culminated with defeat at Piltown in 1462. By 1464 both Desmond and Kildare blocked Ormond's return.[72] But the years immediately preceding Piltown were arguably as significant as the battle itself. The parliament of 1460 claimed dominion over 'Irish enemies which never king of England did heretofore' while the revenues of absentees were to be used for defence.[73] The anti-Yorkist prior of Kilmainham Thomas Talbot, a rival to James Keating, was denounced along with Ormond's associate Thomas Bathe, the 'pretended (baron) Louth'.[74] Although York was killed at Wakefield, the major reversal at Towton resulted in the execution of James, fifth earl of Ormond. The following year witnessed sporadic violence in Leinster with Sir

[69] Crooks, 'Desmond under Lancaster and York', pp 233-42; BL, Add. MS 4792, f. 77r. The Munster Geraldines were a formidable force for long spells in the preceding centuries. Desmond's power in the mid-fifteenth century remains understated: McCormack, *Earl. Desmond*, pp 18-24.

[70] William Darcy's 'Decay of Ireland' stated that the seventh earl of Desmond was the 'fyrste man that ever put coyne and lyverie on the kynges subiectes.' See Maginn and Ellis, *Tudor discov. Ire.*, p. 91. Throughout the Tudor era from Patrick Finglas to Davies and Spenser, exaggerations of feuding and disorder 'between the Earles of Ormond and Desmond' crystalised into fact. SP 60/2, ff 17-19; John Davies, *A discoverie of the true causes why Ireland was never entirely subdued* (1612), p. 149; for the 'imperfect' reflection of the 'Wars of the Roses' in Ireland see, Crooks, 'Desmond under Lancaster and York'; for a more traditional overview see Art Cosgrove, 'The Gaelic Resurgence and the Geraldine Supremacy: c. 1400-1534' in T. W. Moody and F. X. Martin (eds), *The course of Irish history* (Cork, 1967), pp 159-61.

[71] Ellis, *Ire. Tudors*, pp 59-61. The Desmond landed base in Munster was bolstered from the early fifteenth century where they were also well placed to protect key port towns: Kenneth Nicholls, 'The development of lordship in County Cork' in Patrick O'Flanagan and Cornelius Buttimer (eds), in *Cork: history and society* (Cork, 1993), pp 166-7; Nicholls, *Gaelic and gaelicised Ire.*, pp 162-3. The earl secured the support of the mayor of Cork. In 1445 Desmond defended what he stressed as the 'four shires' of Munster: Crooks, 'Desmond under Lancaster and York', pp 234-5, 240, 257-8.

[72] In 1459 James Ormond was made a Knight of the Garter in reward for his loyalty to the house of Lancaster: Edwards, *Ormond lordship*, pp 81-90; Matthew, 'Lancastrian lordship', pp 157-8, 322, 432-51; Donough Bryan, *Great earl of Kildare* (Dublin, 1933), p. 3.

[73] Raphael Holinshed, *Chronicles of England, Scotlande and Irelande* (6 vols., London, 1807-8), i, 257; Otway-Ruthven, *Medieval Ire.*, p. 387.

[74] *Calendar of Close Rolls Henry VI: 1451-1461*, ed. C. T. Flower (6 vols, London, 1947), vi, 405.

John Butler capturing Waterford. Raids by Desmond on the Ormond lordship were partly successful. Bardic sources recounted the defeat of Desmond 'before Fethard' as the Ormond captain Philip Hackett 'gave way to none'.[75] The battle of Piltown was a decisive engagement, with Butler losses evoked in the annals numbering 'four hundred and ten of the slain interred besides the number who were devoured by dogs and birds of prey'.[76] The Geraldines consequently 'took Kilkenny and the other towns in the country of the Butlers' reinforcing their victory by securing treasures while, according to Davies, 'almost all the townesmen of Kilkenny were slaine'.[77] Thomas, seventh earl of Desmond, succeeded his father on 2 August 1462 whose tenure was characterised by 'high pollitique wit, reule, manhood (and) wisdom'.[78] In a parliament held in Wexford, 1463, Desmond and Kildare were exempt from an act of Resumption, a moment later lamented by William Darcy who wrote that all fell 'so fowrthe to the howse of Yorke'.[79] The cross-cultural governance of Desmond, later demonised by Darcy as having begun the 'abhomynable ordre of coyne and lyvere' on Palesmen, was in reality more balanced than the view offered in the polemic of early Tudor reformers.[80] Desmond's personal council reflected the cultural duality of his lordship, but the defence of the king's subjects remained a priority, despite the distance from Dublin.[81] Desmond benefited from the restoration of Kildare in 1454 and both Geraldine houses extended their control beyond their respective *patria* from the mid-fifteenth century.[82] His influence throughout the island was signalled by the adherence of the O'Donnell of Tír Conaill and the MacWilliam Burke among 'many others' recorded in both the annals and bardic literature.[83]

---

[75] *Poems on marcher lords*, pp 78-9, 117; Crooks, 'Factions, feuds', p. 429.

[76] AFM, 1462; McCormack, *Earl. Desmond*, pp 59-61; Ellis, *Ire. Tudors*, pp 64-5.

[77] AFM, 1462; Davies relied on 'Baron Finglas in his discourse of the decay of Ireland' who in turn took a polemicist stance; Davies, *Discoverie*, p. 149; SP 60/2, ff 18-19.

[78] CIRCLE, Patent Roll 3, Edward IV.

[79] *Statute rolls of the parliament of Ireland, first to the twelfth years of the reign of king Edward IV*, ed. H. F. Berry (Dublin, 1914), pp 42-3; Crooks, 'Desmond under Lancaster and York', p. 249; LPL, MS 635, ff 187; Christopher Maginn and S. G. Ellis, *Tudor discovery of Ireland* (Dublin, 2015), p. 92.

[80] LPL, MS 635, ff 137; Sparky Booker, 'The Geraldines and the Irish: intermarriage, ecclesiastical patronage and status' in Peter Crooks and Sean Duffy (eds), *The Geraldines and medieval Ireland: the making of a myth* (Dublin, 2016), pp 292-310.

[81] McCormack, *Earl. Desmond*, pp 41-5, 61-3. For an overview of native customs in Desmond see Nicholls, *Gaelic and gaelicised Ire.*, pp 37-8, 68-9.

[82] Booker, 'Geraldines and the Irish', p. 309.

[83] AFM, 1463, 1464; Simms, *Gaelic Ulster*, pp 197-8. For Yorkist allegiances amongst the Gaelic Irish, see Egan, 'Irish context to a Scottish disaster', pp 10-16; For the O'Donnells in later bardic literature, see Eoin Mac Cárthaigh, 'Dia libh, a uaisle Éireann (1641)' in *Ériu*, 52 (2002), pp 89-121; Eoin Mac Cárthaigh, 'The O'Donnells at war in the 1640s and early 1650s' (Pamphlet), Paul Walsh Memorial Lecture 7 (Maynooth, 2022), pp 1-21.

Hugh Roe O'Donnell served Desmond with forays into Leinster and Connaught in 1464 and 1467, while Kildare profited from the continued Yorkist loyalties among Ulster lords in the late fifteenth century.[84]

The 1460s witnessed a Desmond renaissance with the governance of Ireland under the seventh and eighth earls, yet it is notable that the Desmond-Florentine correspondence of the 1440s has received far less attention than the Kildare-Gherardini sources of the 1510s.[85] The Florentine humanist Leonardo Bruni attempted to contact the Fitzgeralds of Desmond and dispatched a letter in 1440.[86] In 1443 a petition from the sixth earl of Desmond to the king was endorsed which rendered Giovanni Betti de Gherardini, the bearer of letters to Desmond, a 'king's man' ('Johann de Geraldyns merchaunt de Florence et servitear a nostra dis cousin').[87] Thomas Fitzgerald has been regarded as a renaissance prince and bardic verse under his patronage ambitiously elevated a Geraldine conquest to the realm of *mythos*. In surveying the earliest invasions of Ireland, 'Ga med ngabhal fuair Ére [how many times has Ireland been conquered]?', the twelfth-century exploits of Maurice Fitzgerald were seen as the true conquest.[88] Desmond's outlook was, as Crooks observes, cosmopolitan in the widest sense, from the presentation of their origins to the culmination, later pursued by Kildare, of a Geraldine narrative of how the colony was to be perceived.[89]

Following the Geraldine victory at Piltown, Edmund MacRichard Butler was taken hostage and the aforementioned *Saltair* was exchanged as part of the ransom. There subsequently appeared an extraordinarily piece of evidence that testified to the centrality of symbolism to aristocratic rivalry.[90] Desmond's exaction of the artefact was marked by the following inscription:

Saltair mic Rd buitl[er] i em burgt in tsater suo nogo dtca maidm baile inspiull ar iarl uruman ar mcruesd Iaiarla dsmuman…do bained in leab[a]r s[e]o na

---

[84] Simms, *Gaelic Ireland*, pp 195, 202–3.

[85] Crooks has examined the role of James Fitzgerald, sixth earl of Desmond, through literature and material culture, in studying his dynastic propagation: Crooks, 'Desmond under Lancaster and York', pp 235–7.

[86] Crooks, 'Desmond under Lancaster and York', p. 237; Michael Potterton, 'The Fitzgeralds, Florence, St Fiachra and a few fragments' in Michael Potterton and Thomas Herron (eds), *Dublin and the Pale in the Renaissance, c. 1540–1660* (Dublin, 2007), p. 24.

[87] Crooks, 'Desmond under Lancaster and York', p. 238; Aisling Byrne, 'Geraldines and the culture of the wider world' in *Ger. Med. Ire.*, p. 279.

[88] 'Muiris Mac Gerailt as a sgath do bhi an banbu do-chi cach a comhardha.' Seamus Pender, 'O Clery Genealogies' in *Analecta Hibernica*, 18 (1951), pp 169–72; Simms, 'Geraldines and Gaelic culture', pp 270–1; Bradshaw, *Const. rev.*, p. 22; Otway-Ruthven, *Medieval Ire.*, p. 386.

[89] Lennon, 'Making of the Geraldines', pp 71–8; Crooks, 'Desmond under Lancaster and York', p. 237.

[90] Simms, 'Geraldines and Gaelic culture', p. 268; Henry and Marsh-Micheli, 'Manuscripts and illuminations', p. 803.

carrugi as fuasgd mcruisded isse in mcr sin do chur na leabra sin scrib dofe no gur bain tomas iarla desm[ond] amac iad.

[The Psalter of Edmund son of Richard Butler to whom this psalter belonged until the defeat inflicted upon him and the earl of Ormond by Thomas earl of Desmond at Piltown when this book and the book of Carrick were exacted as a ransom for MacRichard. And it was he who had these books written for himself until the earl of Desmond exacted them.][91]

Additional marginal entries show that the manuscript was passed on to successive earls of Desmond.[92] But it is the above inscription by recording a politically charged key moment that shows the importance of literature as a medium.

The ecclesiastical and humanist projects undertaken by Desmond in the early 1460s befitted those of a ruling magnate. An act for the establishment of a university at Drogheda was passed in 1463 and the following year a collegiate church was founded in Youghal where the chancel of a pre-existing edifice was rebuilt as part of the endeavour. In November 1464 Thomas, seventh earl of Kildare, (deputising for his cousin) and Joan, countess of Desmond, dedicated the Franciscan church at Adare, wherein the annals record the Geraldines as having 'erected a tomb'.[93] Remarkably, in a move to strengthen and extend regional Geraldine patronage, Kildare and Desmond also initiated a foundation charter in Dunsany Church in 1465.

Yet this Desmond hegemony was short lived. Sir John Tiptoft arrived as viceroy in 1467 with 700 archers and also, as historians have noted, with his considerable collection of humanist books.[94] The sudden and shocking execution ('decapitato') of Desmond in 1468 prompted a violent Geraldine response especially in Leinster where the O'Connor and Kavanagh were stirred into action.[95] Kildare's eventual pardon was preceded by what Crooks describes as a momentary decision to

---

[91] Bodl., MS Laud Misc. 610, f. 110v; see also, Anne O'Sullivan and William O'Sullivan, 'Three notes on Laud Misc. 610 (or the Book of Pottlerath)' in *Celtica* 9 (1971), p. 146.

[92] Simms, 'Geraldines and Gaelic culture', p. 269; Charles Plummer, 'Colophons and marginalia of Irish scribes' in *Proceedings of the British Academy*, 11 (1926), p. 39; Miles Dillon, 'Laud Misc. 610 (cont.)' in *Celtica* 6 (1963), p. 143. Prior to 1500, the earls of Kildare held a 'Saltir Casshill' in their library: BL, Harleian MS 3756, f. 97v.

[93] Leask, *Irish churches*, iii, 28, 124; AFM, 1464; Tadhg O'Keeffe, *Medieval Irish buildings* (Dublin, 2015), p. 133; Crooks, 'Desmond under Lancaster and York', p. 250.

[94] Peter Crooks, 'The structure of politics in theory and practice, 1210- 1541' in *CHI*, i, 468; Brendan O'Connell and Karen Hodder (eds), *Transmission and generation in medieval and Renaissance literature: essays in honour of John Scattergood* (Dublin, 2012).

[95] BL, Add. MS 4792, f. 77r; AFM, 1470; Crooks, 'Desmond under Lancaster and York', pp 233-42; Otway-Ruthven, *Medieval Ire.*, pp 392-3.

terminate Geraldine governance of the lordship leading to the accidental rise of Kildare.[96] It was, however, an event which Kildare exploited.

The steady decline of the Butlers throughout Yorkist Ireland occurred as Thomas, seventh earl of Kildare, conveniently served as governor. By 1470, the centre of power in the lordship had shifted to Dublin and the colony's institutions were modestly restored.[97] The rise of the Geraldines from these humble standings when the earldom was restored in 1454 served the crown's interests.[98] The Kildare estate was promptly organised as the breadth and scope of Kildare governance expanded through continued hold of the viceregal sword.[99] The influence and military prowess of the Leinster Geraldines, through the utilisation of public office and private resources, largely drove this improvement of English institutions. From subjugating O'Connor Faly in 1459, reclaiming their ancestral manor of Rathangan to securing the Barrow valley, the Kildares achieved gains of strategic importance in Leinster. Along with landed estates in Munster, Lecale and parts of east Ulster were later integrated into the Geraldine landed patrimony.[100] The importance of the O'Connor Faly was also recorded in bardic literature. As a source of armed men, 'O Conor that was king, his ketherin [kern] he gan bring'.[101] Throughout the 1470s, this influence was also demonstrated through Geraldine ecclesiastical patronage in the church *inter Anglicos* and *inter Hibernicos*.[102] In 1473 Parliament had warned that the maghery was devoid of a defence force but in 1474 Kildare established the Fraternity of Arms of St George for this purpose.[103] Revenues from poundage to fund the order was insufficient but Kildare could

---

[96] Crooks, 'Desmond under Lancaster and York', p. 228; S. G. Ellis, *Reform and revival: English government in Ireland 1470–1534* (Woodbridge, 1986), p. 28; Art Cosgrove, 'The execution of the earl of Desmond, 1468' in *JKAH*, 8 (1975), p. 16.

[97] Ellis, *Reform and revival*, p. 3; Ellis, *Ire. Tudors*, pp 51–69, 70–5; Edwards, *Ormond lordship*, pp 79–82; Beresford, 'Butlers in England and Ireland', chs 3–4.

[98] For Geraldine-Butler contention and the manor of Maynooth in the 1450s, see Raymond Gillespie, 'The Fitzgeralds and the making of the manor of Maynooth' in Patrick Cosgrove, Terence Dooley and Karol Mullaney-Dignam (eds), *Aspects of aristocratic life: essays on the Fitzgeralds and Carton House* (Dublin, 2014), pp 40–1; Ellis, *Ire. Tudors*, p. 57; *Ormond deeds*, iii, 83–5.

[99] See for example, Simms, *Gaelic Ulster*, p. 193.

[100] Ellis, 'Great earl', pp 334–8; S. G. Ellis, *Tudor frontiers and noble power: the making of the British state* (Oxford, 1995), pp 58–61; Lennon, *Sixteenth-cen. Ire.*, pp 71–2; AFM, 1459; Cormac Ó Cléirigh, 'The O'Connor Faly lordship of Offaly, 1395–1513' in *PRIA*, 96C (1996), pp 87–102.

[101] Seymour, *Anglo-Irish literature*, p. 85.

[102] Ellis, *Reform and revival*, pp 12–14, 78–9; Marian Lyons, *Church and society in County Kildare* (Dublin, 2000), pp 66–7; Marian Lyons, 'The onset of religious reform: 1460–1550' in *CHI*, i, 509–10; Bryan, *Great earl*, pp 189, 260.

[103] Bryan, *Great earl*, p. 15. Enemies of the ninth earl of Kildare later pointed to this year as a turning point in the decay of the lordship. In 1534 it had been '60 wynters' since Kildare monopolised the deputyship: SP 60/2, f. 32v.

exact extortions to remedy a shortfall.[104] The 'quasi-regal' status enjoyed by Kildare was bolstered through cross-cultural endeavours that came to fruition from the late fifteenth century and shown by Ellis, acculturation in the marches was the norm during this period. England was an exception with its focus on uniformity.[105]

※

Within two years of succeeding his father as the eighth earl of Kildare, Gearóid Mór Fitzgerald had thwarted the efforts of Lord Grey as governor.[106] In 1479 he was also made viceroy under Richard, duke of York, 'be loved boy' of Edward IV in what promised to be a *rapprochement* between the houses of York and Kildare.[107] Much scholarship has been devoted to the continued rise of Kildare in Yorkist Ireland, with particular attention to the agreements, alliances, tributes and accounts outlined in the *Kildare Rental*.[108] The island-wide nature of the Kildare network was, according to Lennon, bastard feudalism epitomised.[109] Ellis notes that Kildare's parliament in Limerick in 1483 was the first time that it took place in the city.[110] Yet the broad geographical reach of the eighth earl in particular allowed for many aims of both king and viceroy to be satisfied through the practical policy of aristocratic delegation.[111] Instructions given by Richard III in 1484 reflected a similar policy to that of his predecessor in 1479, to the benefit of the Kildare Geraldines. Pursuit of the king's 'right and enherytance of his erldom of Wolstre' had been an aim since the restoration of Edward IV and Richard proclaimed that 'no man can do more than his said cousyn [Kildare] seeing and considred that the gret onealle that had married the said erles sustre'.[112]

---

[104] S. G. Ellis, *Ireland's English Pale* (Woodbridge, 2021), pp 24-5.

[105] Lennon, *Sixteenth-cen. Ire.*, pp 75-8; Colm Lennon, 'The confraternities and cultural duality in Ireland, 1450-1550' in Christopher F. Black and Pamela Gravestock (eds), *Early modern confraternities in Europe and the Americas: international and interdisciplinary perspectives* (Aldershot, 2007), pp 36-7, 40-1. Ellis, *Tudor frontiers*, pp 46-9; Ellis, 'Great earl', p. 346; Simms, *Kings to warlords*, p. 19.

[106] Ellis, *Ire. Tudors*, pp 76-7; Bryan, *Great earl*, pp 27-38. Bryan notes that the seventh earl most likely died of plague. Had he been killed in battle it would have been recorded.

[107] An endenture seeking 'proffitte pease and tranquility of his said land... during the tyme of the pleasure of the said boy' was an indication of a close relationship between Kildare and the king: SP 46/130, f. 12v; Maginn and Ellis, *Tudor discov. Ire.*, p. 117.

[108] *Crown surveys*, pp 264-77; D. B. Quinn, 'The re-emergence of English policy as a major factor in Irish affairs, 1520-34' in *NHI*, 662-87; Ellis, *Ire. Tudors*, pp 98-118; Ellis, *Tudor frontiers*, pp 109-19.

[109] Lennon, *Sixteenth-cen. Ire.*, pp 75-6.

[110] Ellis, *Ire. Tudors*, p. 80.

[111] Ellis, *Reform and revival*, p. 61; Lennon, *Sixteenth-cen. Ire.*, pp 75-8; Marian Lyons, 'Kildare ascendancy' in Patrick Cosgrove, Terence Dooley and Karol Mullaney-Dignam (eds), *Aspects of aristocratic life: essays on the Fitzgeralds and Carton House* (Dublin, 2014), pp 48-55.

[112] BL, Harleian MS 433, f. 266v; Simms, *Gaelic Ireland*, pp 192-3.

A key marriage alliance was that of Eleanor to Con Mór O'Neill in 1480, who was denizened as an Englishman thereafter, an unusual occurrence.[113] The king also expressed a desire for O'Donnell to be his 'ligeman or true peax man that his said cousin of Kyldare shalbe contente to so recyve and entre him'.[114] The crown sought peace with Desmond along with broadly seeking the 'weele of this land of Irland (through) good rule and politique guyding'.[115] Such an outlook suggested an affirmation of Kildare. Despite indifference at Court, it is evident that Kildare was necessary in allaying the problematic regions across the island. It was prudent to use the earl to stabilise Ulster and curtail Scottish incursions. By the end of the decade, Kildare had a firm hand in Ulster politics, even to the detriment of the Scots, namely the earl of Argyll and lord of Lorne, Colin Campbell. In 1474, a parliamentary address to the king declared that there were Scots in Ulster to the alarming 'nomber of xm' [10,000], and remembered the 'grete conquest that [Edward the] bruse som tyme sen.' An immediate threat were those who 'entred and dwellen in Ullester...and dayly conspiren to subdue al thys land to the obeysaunce of the kyng of Scottes'.[116] Subsequent correspondence between Argyll and the king illustrates the Geraldine reach in north-east Ulster and the Lordship of the Isles. Argyll stressed his 'fidelity' to the king and complained against Kildare incursions in his lordship.[117]

In conjunction with a broad geographical outlook and in contrast to the allegations of critics, Gearóid Mór Fitzgerald advanced the extent of the Pale. The defence of county Kildare was essentially tied to that of the Dublin and Meath marches.[118] The eighth earl of Kildare was especially active in securing lands directly to the west and south of the maghery. A priority for Kildare was the

---

[113] Kildare was in various ways promoting the use of common law. See Booker, 'Geraldines and the Irish', pp 292–3; Sparky Booker, *Cultural exchange and identity in late medieval Ireland: the English and Irish of the four obedient shires* (Cambridge, 2018), p. 162; AFM, 1480; Ellis, *Tudor frontiers*, pp 192–3; Bryan, *Great earl*, p. 55.

[114] BL, Harleian MS 433, f. 266v.

[115] This possibly reflects a lack of interest in Ireland. At court, it was apparently not well known that Thomas seventh earl of Kildare was dead: Maginn and Ellis, *Tudor discov. Ire.*, p. 117; BL, Harleian MS 433, f. 242; *Letters and papers illustrative of the reigns of Richard III and Henry VII*, ed. James Gairdner (3 vols, London, 1861–3), ii, 91–3.

[116] Bryan, *Great earl*, pp 18–22; Otway-Ruthven, *Medieval Ire.*, p. 396.

[117] BL, Titus B.VIII, ff 161.

[118] In the 1930s, Donough Bryan claimed that the great earl did nothing to further the limits of the Pale while Bradshaw later argued that the eighth earl sought to annex the Pale. Ellis has written extensively on the uncelebrated achievements of Gearóid Mór in securing and advancing the Pale maghery though this outcome was not necessarily aspirational: Bryan, *Great earl*, p. x; Bradshaw, *Const. rev.*, p. 31; Ellis, *Reform and revival*; Ellis, 'Great earl', p. 332; Ellis, *Tudor frontiers*, p. 121. Also, see Ellis, *Ireland's English Pale*.

reclaiming of Rathangan, Lea and Morrett and also Kilcullen, all of which lay outside the maghery in the 1450s.[119] Athy prospered in the late fifteenth century and was made a borough by 1515. South of Dublin, construction work and fortifications to safeguard against the O'Toole along with the rebuilding of Powerscourt 'cost the [eighth] erle of Kildare and thinhabitauntis of the countre of dublin 4 or 5000 markis'. The bridges of Athy and Woodstock were secured.[120] Kildare was in a position to relieve the financial burden for the defence of the Englishry which was traditionally borne by the colonists in general.[121] Continuing an outward-looking policy enabled by the Geraldines, the final parliament of Richard III requested an assessment for the 'true means of recovering all the waste lands of the county of Carlow to be populated by the king's subjects'.[122] Fercullen was purged of the O'Tooles and Kildare often seized marchlands as 'swordlands' across south Leinster.[123] Kildare bought old titles, thereby removing the Irish from certain lands in south Dublin and the Barrow valley.[124] A remarkable surge in the rates of tillage around the four obedient shires testifies to a measure of stability. Maginn has observed that this unexpectedly occurred in locations where the topography was not amenable to grain-based agriculture south of Dublin.[125] Kildare efforts directly impacted the Cooley ('Coyle') peninsula where, according to Elizabeth St John the 'landes was conqueste...of the wylde irish enemyes bi grete defecutes [difficulty] and to his grete coste and charge'.[126] Most telling of all was the Act of Marches and Maghery (1488) which regulated the imposition of coign and livery in both areas. In the 1510s a copy of the act stressed how 'the actes of marches and maugeries which extended with the shyres' for instance at Kilcullen which had been outside the limits. At the same time the document condemned the 'treacon of therle...of Kyldare' in supporting Simnel.[127] The primary concern of the king's deputy in Ireland was defence of the maghery, a task which Kildare effectively achieved, although his enemies exploited the means to this end as Kildare's cross-cultural endeavours were seen as causing the decay of the Englishry.

The earl prospered in the early 1480s and his hold on strategic interests included a line of estates acquired from Carlow castle to Leighlinbridge. His *manraed* expanded and allies were granted favourable treatment in both common

---

[119] Ellis, 'Great earl', pp 325-40; Ellis, *Tudor Frontiers*, pp 111-14, 120-34.
[120] Ellis, 'Great earl', p. 335; SP 60/3, f. 171r; SP 60/2, f. 145r.
[121] Ellis, *Reform and revival*, p. 50; D. B. Quinn, 'Anglo-Irish local government 1485-1534' in *IHS*, 1 (1938-9), pp 366-81.
[122] *Statute rolls of the parliament of Ireland, Edward IV*, ed. James Morrisey (Dublin, 1939), p. 71.
[123] Lennon, *Sixteenth-cen. Ire.*, p. 72; Ellis, *Tudor frontiers*, pp 56-61, 116-18.
[124] SP 60/1, ff 31; Ellis, *Reform and revival*, p. 60.
[125] Maginn, *'Civ.' Gaelic Leinster*, p. 29.
[126] SP 60/1, f. 29r; *Cal. S. P. Ire.*, p. 2.
[127] NLI, MS 2507, f. 57v.

and marcher law.[128] Despite tremendous uncertainty following Henry Tudor's invasion and victory at Bosworth, Kildare neither anticipated his interests to be significantly altered, nor did he expect the new regime to survive. In throwing his weight behind the pretender Simnel, Kildare ensured that the courts were kept in the name of 'Edward VI' while coins were struck accordingly. These were calculated measures based on Henry Tudor's precarious claim and possibly also by Kildare's insights on the new king's limited knowledge of Ireland.[129] But the failed rebellion of 1487 did little to diminish Kildare's standing in the Lordship of Ireland. While anti-Geraldines later remembered the 'right high offences' committed by Kildare in 1487, the subsequent expedition of Sir Richard Edgecombe confirmed the earl's advantageous position.[130] The account of Edgecombe's voyage exposed the limits of the crown and the necessity for aristocratic delegation.[131] There was possibly a Butler subplot to O'Neill infighting as Henry Óg O'Neill, a distant relative of the White Earl, killed Con Mór when claiming the lordship of Tyrone.[132]

Kildare's position to hold power across the island in the name of the crown was then tested in the 1490s. The rebellion with Perkin Warbeck was problematic for Kildare, especially as Desmond and many Gaelic lords supported the pretender, with Hugh Roe O'Donnell conspiring with James IV of Scotland.[133] By way of avoiding a summons to Court, the king was notified that his presence in Ireland was required by 'my cousynes in especiall therle of dessemond and the lord bourk of Connaught... to abide for their defence and to apece such varience...betwixt the said erle and lord bourke.' Kildare also impressed upon the new king the unprecedented value of Geraldine delegation, stressing the 'laboure and peyn I have susteyned to sett your said subjects in ease...others whose ancestors was never

---

[128] For example, in what transpired to be the final parliament of Richard III, Cahir O'Connor received a grant of 40d per ploughland in County Meath as reward for military service in the name of the king: *Stat. Rolls Ed. IV*, p. 77; Bryan, *Great earl*, pp 60, 82–3.

[129] LPL, MS 632, ff 256; BL, Add. MS 4791, ff 135; NLI, D 1855; Maginn and Ellis, *Tudor discov. Ire.*, p. 116; Ellis, 'Great earl', p. 329; Randolph Jones, 'Janico Markys, Dublin and the coronation of 'Edward VI' in 1487' in Seán Duffy (ed.), *Medieval Dublin XIV: Proceedings of the friends of medieval Dublin symposium 2012* (Dublin, 2014), pp 185–209; Sean Cunningham, *Henry VII* (London, 2007), p. 55.

[130] SP 60/1, f. 133r; *SP Henry VIII*, ii, 143. Writing in 1537, Chief Justice Luttrell saw this as a watershed in Kildare-induced decay as 'within 50 yeres' from 1487 Gearóid Mór Fitzgerald first cessed County Kildare, which was then 'encreased' by his son: SP 60/5, f. 41r. Henry did not wish to see a return to the factional wars of the fifteenth century: Ellis, 'Great earl', pp 325–40; Maginn and Ellis, *Tudor discov. Ire.*, pp 119–21.

[131] Maginn and Ellis, *Tudor discov. Ire.*, p. 20.

[132] AFM, 1494. An inaugural bardic poem affirms Henry's 'best right to the land of Ireland' and proclaims that 'harshness is joined to that right (go ccuire a crúaidh leisin ccert...ní fhuighidh úain dú hoigreacht)': Simms, *Gaelic Ulster*, p. 204.

[133] A Desmond-O'Donnell Yorkist alliance from 1464 was still honoured: Simms, *Gaelic Ulster*, p. 203.

bonden to noon of your progenytours, kynges of England before this time'.[134] His role as mediator in Ulster had long been recognised but Kildare's influence in Connaught and along the western seaboard was echoed by Desmond and Piers Butler who wrote to the king noting Kildare's capacity to quell 'distencone ye dependith (to) be therin...and the lords boryke of Connaght and other lordis in yt...to be mortale warre and grete sheding of crystyn blode by the yrysh as which can in no wise ne endid ner posid without our said good lorde be presently'.[135] The Book of Howth records that due to 'variance' with Ormond 'and the rest of the Butlers,' Kildare 'married his sister called Lady Margaret to one Persse Butler for policy'.[136] It transpired to be a noteworthy match. Relations between Kildare and Ormond who was at Court, were amicable at this time and would remain so until his death in 1515. It was while under the protection of Gearóid Mór that Piers Butler killed Sir James Ormond in 1497.[137] Five years earlier, *de facto* war had broken out between Kildare and Sir James, the sixth earl's illegitimate son, who had been sent along with Thomas Garth and 200 men. The well-known episode recalled by Sir Gerald Shanesson was a display of Kildare strength. However, when he 'hanged [Garth's] son...kylled them of Dublin upon Oxmantowne Greene' it was more due to factional rivalry rather than what Shanesson saw as 'resistance' to the crown. Kildare 'by craft and policy called the citizens of Dublinye out upon Oxmantoune Green and in wars set upon them and slew many of them'.[138] Within a generation, as Ellis writes, the earl's exploits had become the stuff of legend.[139] Conflict with Sir James threatened to upset what until then had been a co-operative relationship between Kildare and Thomas Butler, absentee seventh earl of Ormond. Kildare warned that his 'bace cosyn with the kingis Irish enemyes... set his moost noble auctoritie in hurt' and the annals recorded that 'Kildare itself were burned by the son of the earl of Ormond'.[140] In themes that arose in later decades, regional interests in south Leinster relating to the Barrow valley and the city of Waterford were pressed. John Wyse, chief baron of the exchequer and special justice for counties Kilkenny and Waterford, alleged in 1493 that 'lords... and commons [were] day to day robbed and expelled from their goods [in] danger

---

[134] Bryan, *Great earl*, pp 146-7; Otway-Ruthven, *Medieval Ire.*, p. 406.
[135] SP 46/100, f. 20; AFM, 1491.
[136] *Cal. Carew*, v. 176.
[137] Edwards, *Ormond lordship*, p. 83.
[138] SP 60/2, f. 10v; Ellis, 'Great earl', pp 325-40; *Cal. Carew*, v. 176; Agnes Conway, *Henry VII's relations with Scotland and Ireland 1485-1498* (Cambridge, 1932), p. 55. See also Damien Duffy, *Aristocratic women in Ireland, 1450-1660: the Ormond family, power and politics* (Woodbridge, 2021), pp 76-8.
[139] Ellis, 'Great earl', pp 325-40. Dublin mayor Jancis Markys was seen as an opponent and was killed by the Geraldines: Jones, 'Janico Markys', p. 204; BL, Add. MS 4791, f. 135r.
[140] *Letters and papers R. III Hen. VII*, ii, 56; AFM, 1493.

and peril of the road [and to the loss of the] king's revenues'.[141] Here, allegations and counter-claims were reminiscent of the Talbot-Ormond variance and in late 1493 the king confided that the old colonial aristocracy 'have not improved my lordship there all this while since our ancestors conquered there'.[142]

Having been implicated with Warbeck, Kildare was removed as deputy and replaced with Sir Edward Poynings who was charged with securing Ireland against the second Yorkist pretender. Maintaining that he 'never lay with ne ayded, comferted ne supported hym' (Warbeck) Kildare alerted Thomas Butler that his illegitimate son 'pubblisheth and name hymself erle of Ormound [as he] provoket and styrreth Irishmen' to the detriment of Kilkenny and Tipperary. Kildare also warned that in Ormond lands, Sir James 'spareth no churches ne religious places both hath spoyled them'.[143] Yorkist rebels failed to take Waterford but Kildare's arrest and attainder on account of his 'great and manifold treasons' prompted further violence.[144] Desmond advanced in Leinster and Kildare's allies in Ulster moved against Poynings. The annals preserved a sense of foreboding when the earl was 'sent over to England' and while there was uncertainty, Poynings' defensive policy reflected an obvious need for the resources and *manraed* of a ruling magnate.[145]

Initiatives under seventh and eighth earls of Kildare were often notable for their symbolic import. The military function of the Fraternity of Arms of St George carried chivalric and courtly associations although it was eventually undone by its Geraldine-Yorkist partisan complexion.[146] While Parliament wrote to the king touching the 'recouere of the sayd land' stating that the 'furst conquest therof was obtened with...a small nombre of Englyssh men', the Fraternity of Arms of St George was to comprise of the thirteen 'most noble and worthy in the four shires'.[147] It was in the chivalric martial tradition of the Hapsburgs and the cult of St George but it was also of particular interest to both Kildare and Edward IV.[148]

---

[141] *Statute rolls of the Irish parliament: Richard III - Henry VIII*, ed. Philomena Connolly (Dublin, 2002), p. 95.
[142] Ware, *Antiq. and history of Ire.*, ii, 26.
[143] *Letters and papers R. III Hen. VII*, ii, 56; C. W. Fitzgerald, *Earls of Kildare and their ancestors from 1057 to 1773* (Dublin, 1858), p. 192.
[144] LPL, MS 632, f. 255; Conway, *Hen. VII Sco. Ire.*, pp 216-17; Bryan, *Great earl*, pp 188-91.
[145] Simms, *Gaelic Ulster*, pp 204-5; AFM, 1494; Quinn, 'English policy', p. 642. For documents relating to Poynings, see Conway, *Hen. VII Sco. Ire.*, pp 201-19.
[146] Ellis, *Reform and revival*, p. 53; Ellis, *Ire. Tudors*, pp 73-4; Linzi Simpson, 'The early Geraldine castles of Ireland: some case studies' in Peter Crooks and Sean Duffy (eds), *The Geraldines and medieval Ireland: the making of a myth* (Dublin, 2016), p. 140.
[147] Maginn and Ellis, *Tudor discov. Ire.*, pp 32-3; Bryan, *Great earl*, pp 20-1; Lennon, *Sixteenth-cen. Ire.*, p. 74; Thomas More, *History of Ireland* (4 vols, Paris, 1840), ii, 288.
[148] Lennon, *Sixteenth-cen. Ire.*, p. 84; Bryan, *Great earl*, p. 269.

Relevant items in the earl's library before 1500 include 'Saint George is passion' and the crusading themes: 'Lanncelott du lake' and the 'sege of Jerusalem'.[149] Yorkist-Burgundian patronage of both the Alexander romance and the *Receueil des Histoires de Troie* in the 1470s arguably influenced Kildare's collection.[150] Echoing Ormond's control over the office of King of Arms during the 1420s, under Gearóid Mór Fitzgerald this guild had also incorporated the charge of the Fraternity of Arms in Ireland.[151]

The legitimation of Kildare power by royal mandate (for example in 1479 and 1484) was accompanied by overt symbolism. For instance, in 1479, a groat and half-groat of Edward IV were struck in the mint of Trim which featured the Kildare arms.[152] Such endeavours projected meaning in different ways, yet a central approach was nonetheless reinforced. Gearóid Mór Fitzgerald became captain of the Fraternity of Arms of St George on succeeding his father, an appointment that was associated with an interest in chivalric literature and the cult of St George. The symbolic and temporal roles of chivalric orders retained a special significance for the seventh and eighth earls of Kildare. This applied also to ecclesiastical powers in general but the Order of St John of Jerusalem in particular. The mediatory role of the church in Yorkist Ireland is evident in a variety of sources from the diplomacy of Archbishop of Armagh Edmund Connesburgh in resolving 'certain strifes, discords and controversies between certain magnates' (1475) to the elegy for the Archbishop of Cashel John Cantwell (b. 1482) who as a 'peacemaker' kept all from going to Rome ('le cách don Róimh ní rachthai).[153]

---

[149] BL, Harleian MS 3756, ff 97; Andrea Ruddick, *English identity and political culture in the fourteenth century* (Cambridge, 2013), pp 292–3; Jonathan Good, *The cult of St George in medieval England* (Woodbridge, 2009), pp 86–7; H. B. Clarke, 'Angliores ipsis Anglis: the place of medieval Dubliners in English history' in H. B. Clarke, Jacinta Prunty and Mark Hennessy (eds), *Surveying Ireland's past: multidisciplinary essays in honour of Anngret Simms* (Dublin, 2004), p. 57. For the reign of Henry VIII, see Sharpe, *Tudor mon.*, p. 150.

[150] Margaret duchess of Burgundy by 'the commandemet of the right hye myghty and vertuouse Pryncesse' commissioned the text which was promptly translated and printed in English: Raoul Le Fèvre, *Recuyell of the Historyes of Troye* (Bruges, 1473), p. 2. Aisling Byrne, 'The earls of Kildare and their books at the end of the middle ages' in *The Library: Transactions of the Bibliographical Society*, 14 (2013), pp 129–53.

[151] F. X. Martin, 'The crowning of a king at Dublin, 24 May 1487' in *Hermathena*, 144 (1988), pp 7–34.

[152] On the obverse of each coin, the Fitzgerald saltire was placed on either side of the royal arms: Aquilla Smith, 'On the Irish coins of Edward IV' in *Transactions of the Royal Irish Academy*, 19 (1841), pp 31–3, 48–9. Enactments for the uniform acceptance of coinage were made in 1483, with specific provisions against the burgesses of Waterford, Kilkenny and Limerick should they refuse to obey the statute. Bryan notes that anti-Kildare sentiment in these towns may have prompted such a response: Bryan, *Great earl*, pp 74–5.

[153] *Cal. Patent Rolls, 1447–1485*, pp 71–9, Otway-Ruthven, *Medieval Ire.*, p. 397, *Poems on marcher lords*, pp 4–5.

The governance of both the seventh and eighth earls of Kildare were buttressed by a broad range of cultural and symbolic initiatives, the character and purpose of which will be discussed in greater detail below.

Amid the unrest between 1485 and the indenture between Kildare and Henry VII in 1496, the symbolic import of certain developments has been overlooked. The governance of Gearóid Mór Fitzgerald was such that destruction and construction often occurred simultaneously, a point memorably underlined in the biography of the Great Earl.[154] As Ellis explains, the *Rental* probably preserved agreements made in earlier decades which were always enforceable through violence. Likewise, the Kildare library inventory *c.* 1500 reflected the interests and pursuits of the preceding century.[155] The very act of compiling a library catalogue signalled continual expansion. These early sources arguably also provide glimpses of the Great Earl's manipulation of court ritual, routine and pageantry. There was a deliberate poise in the absence of Kildare on pilgrimage as Edgecombe for days 'laie stille at Duvelyn abidyng the comyng of therle' in June 1488.[156] In the context of noble etiquette, this could be interpreted as a projection of aristocratic assuredness. Tension between Kildare and Edgecombe was marked by 'right felle' words and 'angry' debate. But interactions largely unfolded within formal diplomatic structures. The earl's delaying tactics were apparently not deemed honourable, but Edgecombe's account preserves a sense of ceremony and the structured routine of hospitality. All parties concerned were alive to the rhythms of formal entertainment, 'good cher' provided by the old colonial nobility.[157] In the same year for instance, Kildare and Sir Rowland FitzEustace financed a new chantry endowment with John Estrete, the earl's agent at Court, which included daily mass and a large weekly choir celebration of the Eucharist.[158] The symbolism of Kildare ecclesiastical patronage and chivalric prowess with the Fraternity of Arms of St George were also to be found with the Knights Hospitaller and its

---

[154] Bryan, *Great earl*, p. 260. There was often a deliberate symbolic purpose behind the construction of a library: Richard Ovenden, *Burning the books: a history of the deliberate destruction of knowledge* (London, 2020), p. 8. Also, see Raymond Gillespie, 'Books, politics and society in Renaissance Dublin' in Kathleen Miller and Crawford Gribben (eds), *Dublin: Renaissance city of literature* (Manchester, 2017), pp 38–54.

[155] Ellis, 'Great earl', pp 325–40; Lennon, *Sixteenth-cen. Ire.*, pp 75–8; Caoimhe Whelan, 'TCD MS. 592: A Hiberno-English translation of Gerald of Wales' on the conquest of Ireland', plenary lecture delivered at Beyond the Book of Kells: The stories of eight other medieval manuscripts from the library of Trinity College Dublin, Trinity College Dublin (5 Dec. 2017).

[156] BL, Titus B.XI, f. 285r.

[157] BL Titus B.XI, f. 283v, 284r.

[158] Marian Lyons, 'Sidelights on the Kildare ascendancy: a survey of Geraldine involvement in the Church, *c.* 1470-*c.* 1520' in *Archiium. Hibernicum*, 48 (1994), pp 82–3; Raymond Gillespie, 'Singing and society 1540–1700', Choral music in Ireland: history and evolution, Chamber Choir Ireland (31 Jan. 2020).

Geraldine master, James Keating. In 1494 Poynings' Parliament denounced Keating as 'intrused pryor of Seint Johns...to the utter dystruccon of the same Religion [having] presumyd withoute thauctoritie of the great master of the Rodes thasssent of the king'. The 'mysgovernaunce' of Keating and Kildare prompted enactments that required priors of Kilmainham to be 'of English blood'.[159]

In 1496, a peace marked by a tripartite indenture represented a turning point in relations between Gearóid Mór and Henry Tudor. Kildare's situation appeared insecure on his departure for England but the terms of his restoration were favourable. The generous terms indicated the low priority of the lordship, which cost the crown £23,000 since 1491 and the failure of interregnum governors Gormanstown, Poynings and Delvin played into Kildare hands.[160] Petitions for Kildare's return were led by Desmond with Piers Butler who had plagued Sir James Ormond's efforts in Ireland.[161] Kildare was to curtail Desmond should he 'rebell or offende his grace' but his chief priority was the modest requirement to defend the lordship.[162] A key stipulation of the bond was the long-standing 'great and haynoux discord discencion and varience that have be betwix theis ii noble blodes of the land of Irland called botellers and Geraldynes'. Bearing in mind the eventual shortcomings of Poynings' military reach, the old colonial ruling elite were to 'gyve occasion from hensforth to be werred upon (the Irishry) thuttermost of their powers...and quarrell according to their duetie and ligeaunce'.[163] An earlier draft of the indenture perhaps overtly dwelled on 'any cause or occasion happened between them' which was crossed out in the manuscript.[164] Kildare was married to Elizabeth St John, the kings's 'nigh kynneswoman and of his noble blood', a match that brought significant landed estates.[165] By December 1496 Kildare had also inherited strategic lands in Lecale including the manors of Strangford and Ardglass with the death of Sir Rowland FitzEustace, the father of Gearóid Mór's first wife, Alison.[166] The agreeable terms given to Kildare in 'ner trouble upon

---

[159] Conway, *Hen. VII Sco. Ire.*, pp 210-11.

[160] Kildare's replacements lacked the resources and *manraed* to rule with lasting effect: S. G. Ellis, 'Henry VII and Ireland, 1491-1496' in James Lydon (ed.), *England and Ireland in the later middle ages: essays in honour of Jocelyn Otway-Ruthven* (Dublin, 1981), pp 242-3; Ellis, *Reform and revival*, pp 25-7; Ellis, 'Great earl', p. 331; Ellis, *Ire. Tudors*, p. 97; G. O. Sayles, 'The vindication of the earl of Kildare from treason, 1496' in *IHS*, 7 (1950-1), pp 46-7. Donough Bryan writes of the hopelessness of his situation on departure for England and Crooks has noted Kildare's likely gratitude on his return: AFM, 1494; Bryan, *Great earl*, p. 198; Crooks, 'Factions, feuds', p. 425.

[161] Maginn and Ellis, *Tudor discov. Ire.*, p. 123; Sayles, 'Vindication of Kildare', pp 39-47.

[162] Conway, *Hen. VII Sco. Ire.*, p. 212; Ellis, *Ire. Tudors*, p. 14, Lennon, *Sixteenth-cen. Ire.*, pp 69-70; Quinn, 'English policy', pp 646-8; Ellis, 'Henry VII and Ireland', pp 250-4.

[163] Conway, *Hen. VII Sco. Ire.*, pp 226-9.

[164] SP 46/100, f. 20r.

[165] Conway, *Hen. VII Sco. Ire.*, pp 231-2.

[166] Simms, *Gaelic Ulster*, p. 212; *Crown surveys*, pp 319-21.

kynges subgets ne cause to be trobled vexed by colore of his office or odrewise' specified (in a re-written sentence) that 'deet and tityll of land alwayes exaept'.[167] As a draft of the indenture, details in the manuscript hint at a softening of the crown's stance. The king was seen to have acted as a 'poletique prince', prudently appointing Kildare as 'primum hominis auctoritas apud Hybernos'.[168] The crown benefited from a broad return to order, as Ralph Verney wrote to Reginald Bray of 'Irishmen of the south and west partys of the land so that now thanked be God the kynge hathe peace in all the lande without strake or great charge or coste'.[169]

It was in many ways, and despite the upholding of Poynings' law, a return to aristocratic delegation.[170] After 1496 there was, as historians observe, a different tone to Kildare's administration.[171] The agreement enabled further Geraldine expansion while opponents pushed for alternative strategies, with distinctively couched rhetoric. Having surveyed the political priorities and by extension the cultural patronage of Ireland's foremost late medieval old colonial magnates, the next chapter shifts in focus to more specific influences. I have derived much profit from the recent scholarship devoted to the reception of Giraldus Cambrensis in the fifteenth and sixteenth centuries. In what follows, attention is given to strategic and political use of the *Expugnatio* which sprang from deep-rooted interests and far-reaching implications.

---

[167] Struck through was the following; 'for any cause or occasion hapened betwen them': SP 46/100, f. 20r.
[168] Edward Hall, *Vnion of the two noble and illustrate famelies of Lancastre and Yorke* (1548), p. 37.
[169] Conway, *Hen. VII Sco. Ire.*, pp 233-4.
[170] Ellis, *Tudor frontiers*, p. 50.
[171] Ellis, 'Great earl', p. 332; Crooks, 'Factions, feuds', pp 425-6.

2

Late Yorkist, early Tudor 'Butler Expugnatio'

The *Expugnatio Hibernica* of Giraldus Cambrensis, that indispensable twelfth-century work, much revered by those of English Ireland, evolved through remarkable change in the fifteenth and early sixteenth centuries. During this period a key shift occurred as various translation and redactions appeared, the political and historical significance of which remains a matter of debate. In what follows, a preliminary account of contextual circumstances along with related themes returns to the time of the White Earl. Also, in order to better understand this extraordinary development of the use of the *Expugnatio*, a discussion of the relevant Hiberno-English editions is required.

There was a late medieval surge of interest in the *Expugnatio Hibernica* which reflected contention over precisely how the text was interpreted.[1] Driven by historical argument and approaches to the government of Ireland, a cluster of Hiberno-English editions of the *Expugnatio* appeared over the fifteenth century.[2]

---

[1] In order to understand the continuing significance of this twelfth-century text it is necessary to firstly become acquainted with the original contents as it was read in the fifteenth century. Written before 1189, Giraldus generally wrote of the initial arrival of the Cambro-Norman knights, the establishment of the colony under Robert Fitzgilbert and Henry II and their triumphs while outnumbered against an uncivilised, uncultured Irishry. The *Expugnatio* was split into two books, further divided into 40 and 45 chapters respectively. A third book 'concerning prophecies' was unfinished or has not survived. The idea of focusing on a 'conquest' in south Leinster was indelibly tied to the *Expugnatio*. A key moment recounts the intervention of Henry II in Ireland on behalf of Diarmuid MacMurrough (claimant to the kingship of Leinster), the arrival of Robert Fitzstephen and the subjugation of Wexford. Also, see Seán Duffy, *Ireland in the middle ages* (Dublin, 1997), pp 59-75; James Lydon, *The Lordship of Ireland in the middle ages* (Toronto, 1972), pp 32-52; Robin Frame, *Colonial Ireland, 1169-1369* (Dublin, 1981); Michael Richter, *Giraldus Cambrensis: the growth of the Welsh nation* (Aberystwyth, 1972), pp 190-200; John Gillingham, *The English in the twelfth century: imperialism, national identity and political values* (Woodbridge, 2000). Attention is here concentrated on the uses of the *Expugnatio* toward the close of the fifteenth century, but for later use of Giraldus, for instance, see Alan Ford, 'The Irish historical renaissance and the shaping of Protestant history' in Alan Ford and John McCafferty (eds), *The origins of sectarianism in early modern Ireland* (Cambridge, 2005), pp 131-6. Elizabethans were keenly aware of the history of the conquest and were selective in points of emphasis: Hiram Morgan (ed.), *Political ideology in Ireland, 1541-1641* (Dublin, 1999) (see in particular the editor's introduction, pp 9-21).

[2] These have recently been the subject of significant scholarship. Byrne has focused on a Kildare viewpoint, stressing the local relevance of Giraldus for the Fitzgeralds. Whelan has extensively contextualised and analysed the late fifteenth-century versions of the *Expugnatio*, in particular TCD, MS 592: Aisling Byrne, 'Family, locality and nationality: vernacular

The *Expugnatio* was a Geraldine panegyric and Giraldus himself was an ancestor of the Fitzgeralds. However, there are many important elements in this history that allow it to be read as the core chronicle that represented the entire colonial community. The tradition of conquest universally cherished by the colonists applied as much to the Butlers of Ormond, the Darcys of Platten or indeed any Cambro-Norman descendant. It came to be that in the debate for policy, a narrow, militaristic understanding of the *Expugnatio* could reveal that its advocate was challenging those in a position of power. In this sense, a literal projection of the text was the testament of those in retreat. Given the island-wide, pan-cultural nature of Kildare governance in late medieval Ireland, the *Expugnatio* could be utilised to denounce a conciliar outlook towards native lords, deviation from the king's laws and most damningly of all, the use of Gaelic extortions. The Hiberno-English *Expugnatio*, and in particular the later copy of the White Earl's manuscript (TCD, MS 592), reflected a fierce debate over the nature of the colonial inheritance, begging the question as to whether the *Expugnatio* still signified the exclusion of the Irishry or if there were alternative ways of allocating power. The *Expugnatio* was a highly politicised text throughout the later middle ages, long before the Elizabethan link between Giraldus and punitive crown policy in Ireland. It seems that as the later copy of the White Earl's *Expugnatio* was commissioned (referred to from here as the 'Butler *Expugnatio*') and was subsequently discussed, the *Expugnatio* could more readily represent a firm anti-Irish policy of entrenchment to cleanse the Englishry of native evils. By arresting the alleged 'decay' of the lordship, the broad pan-cultural following of a ruling magnate may be undermined. Therefore, the challenge of understanding the various projections of opposing strategies in the pursuit of power in late medieval Ireland is to re-evaluate the *Expugnatio*. It remained a Fitzgerald panegyric, but due to its universal value to the colonists it could also be utilised as a rhetorical weapon against the native customs that bolstered their position.

Throughout the late medieval period, Giraldus was essentially seen as the authority on the conquest. A short-hand reference to his name, or simply 'Cambrensis', often sufficed to inform the reader of the source.[3] By the late

---

adaptations of the *Expugnatio Hibernica* in late medieval Ireland', *Medium Ævum*, 82 (2013), pp 101–18; Caoimhe Whelan, 'The *Expugnatio Hibernica* in medieval Ireland' in Georgia Henley and A. J. McMullen (eds), *New perspectives on Gerald of Wales* (Cardiff, 2018), pp 243–58; Caoimhe Whelan, 'Translating the *Expugnatio Hibernica*: A vernacular English history in late medieval Ireland' in C. Griffin and E. Purcell (eds), *Text, transmission and transformation in the European middle ages, 1000–1500* (Turnhout, 2018).

[3] Whelan, 'Translating *Ex.*', p. 246. Instances include 'le lyvre de Cambrense' cited by the white earl and the copy of 'Cambrensis' owned by Kildare in 1500: Peter Crooks, 'Factions, feuds and noble power in the lordship of Ireland, *c*. 1356–1496' in *IHS*, 35 (2006–7), pp 51–2; BL, Harleian MS 3756, f. 97r. For the *Expugnatio* and the reinforcement of the dichotomy between native and colonist, see Christopher Maginn and S. G. Ellis, *Tudor discovery of Ireland*

fifteenth century, an uncompromising, entrenched and culturally homogenous conception of the colony emerged as a powerful symbol anti-Geraldine policy. Its universal value to crown subjects, strategic fluidity and prophetic import allowed for polemic use which rendered the *Expugnatio* an ideal foundation text for anti-Geraldine rhetoric up to the 1530s. Certain projections of the *Expugnatio* reinforced such a perspective and these are discussed below. I will discuss the broad political and cultural Geraldine response to this in chapter three, where it can be properly seen in relation to the direct and aggressive nature of the opposing position.

Five extant Hiberno-English editions of the *Expugnatio* were produced over the fifteenth century. One of these is a fragment and of the other four, the 'Butler Expugnatio' appears to be the most recent.[4] From the Yorkist to the early Tudor period, the White Earl's Hiberno-English *Expugnatio* was also the only copy which can be attributed to a particular lord at the time of its commissioning. Darcy of Platten, Co. Meath possessed a copy at some stage after its production (BL, Add. MS 40674). This was most likely passed on to the early Tudor reformer and former Kildare ally, William Darcy.[5] The fourth surviving complete Hiberno-English edition was written by an unknown scribe Thomas Bray and now is now housed in Lambeth Palace (LPL, MS 598).[6] Palaeographical analysis indicates each edition to the fifteenth century.[7] The late fifteenth-century corpus of Hiberno-English

---

(Dublin, 2015), pp 113–14. Recent scholarship on seventeenth-century historical argument and political discourse includes Eamon Darcy, *The Irish rebellion of 1641 and the wars of the three kingdoms* (Woodbridge, 2013), pp 11–35.

[4] It is a copy of the White Earl's manuscript (Rawl. B 490). Each appears in a neat hand and their aesthetic presentation exceeds that of LPL, MS 598 and BL, Add. MS 40674. TCD, MS 592 and Bodl., MS Rawl. B 490 were extensively highlighted and include marginal annotations in a later, possibly early sixteenth-century hand.

[5] An active readership is suggested by marginal highlights and in particular the Darcy heraldry. Whelan, '*Ex. Hib.* Ire.', p. 245.

[6] LPL, MS 598 and BL, Add. MS 40674 have some crudely decorative calligraphy and annotated margins. Although some effort was made to enhance the appearance of both the manuscripts, aesthetically, they are inferior to the White Earl's edition and its copy. Block prints were used to clarify the opening lines of chapters one and two in the 'Darcy Expugnatio' and the manuscript features an illustration of the Darcy coat of arms. Numerous parts of the text are highlighted with what appear to be crosses of St Brigid. The 'Bray Expugnatio' most distinctively contains one very small grotesque illustration and another larger image of a bloodied, decapitated head. There are also a number of crosses at the margins throughout the manuscript.

[7] Byrne, Esposito, and McCauley date TCD, MS 592 to the late fifteenth century. Byrne and Esposito date Bodl., MS Rawl. B 490 to the late fifteenth century. F. J. Furnival dated TCD, MS 592 and Bodl., MS Rawl. B 490, before 1440. See Byrne, 'Vernacular *Expug.*', p. 104; Mario Esposito, 'The English conquest of Ireland' in *Notes and queries*, 75 (1917), pp 495–6; Barbara Lynne McCauley, 'A critical edition of the English conquest of Ireland, a medieval Hiberno-English manuscript from the Latin of Giraldus Cambrensis' *Expugnatio Hibernica*' (Ph.D., Florida State University, 1993). Scholars have argued that these Hiberno-English manuscripts

editions were abbreviations of the twelfth-century Latin. For example, the 'Butler Expugnatio' is bound in fifty-six standard folio pages and divided into sixty-two unnumbered sections equating to chapters. Speeches and descriptions were shortened, and most allusive classical and biblical references are omitted: yet they were faithful to the overall thrust of the original text. However, the manuscript contains a greater number of marginal highlights than the original manuscript commissioned by the White Earl.[8] The dedication to the fourth earl of Ormond is copied at the end of the manuscript which also contains a fragment of the White Earl's *Gouernaunce of Prynces*. The significance of this 'Butler Expugnatio' in its later fifteenth-century literary, historical and didactic context has also been the focus of recent studies.[9] Its distinctive marginalia reflected ongoing concerns in the late medieval colony. Largely ecclesiastical in nature, these textual peculiarities point to what Whelan describes as an ongoing moral struggle and a need to safeguard the lordship by avoiding sin. It appears to have represented a political stance that excluded native Irish lords.

There are two main aspects to consider in relation to selective points of emphasis in the manuscript. Firstly, a primary concern was the concept of 'cleansing' or purifying the colony. Narrative inserted from the *Topographia Hibernia* (extracts from which were unique to the fifteenth-century Hiberno-English versions) related to the morality of the 'conquest'. The *Expugnatio* readily represented the evils of Irish customs and a need to purify the lordship. Highlighted in red ink, a late medieval reader was also to *nota bene* the Synod of Cashel (1172) which stated that the king's claim to Ireland was 'imaden the counsaylle of Cashel' to purge the island 'of the

---

were orientated toward Ireland rather than the wider world: Caoimhe Whelan, 'Translating Cambrensis: The history of the late medieval English conquest of Ireland' (Ph.D., Trinity College Dublin, 2015). Giraldus was widely circulated in England and beyond during this period, Maginn and Ellis, *Tudor discov. Ire.*, p. 114; Whelan, '*Ex. Hib.* Ire.', p. 245.

[8] Whelan has discerned three scribal hands and that the dialect changes over time. The third hand writes from f. 12r to the end of the manuscript: Caoimhe Whelan, 'TCD MS. 592: A Hiberno-English translation of Gerald of Wales' on the conquest of Ireland', plenary lecture delivered at Beyond the Book of Kells: The stories of eight other medieval manuscripts from the library of Trinity College Dublin, Trinity College Dublin (5 Dec. 2017). Bodl., MS Rawl. B 490, begins with the *Expugnatio* which spans the first 72 folio pages and is divided into two books with 28 and 34 chapters respectively. The textual narrative is essentially identical to TCD, MS 592 and there are some similarities between their marginal illustrations. A christogram ('ihs') enclosed by a quadrangle is particular to Bodl., MS Rawl. B 490, but there are comparable illustrations in TCD, MS 592. Bodl., MS Rawl. B 490, f. 35v; TCD, MS 592, ff 18v, 26r.

[9] The translator of TCD, MS 592 is unlikely to have been James Yonge as it does not contain his distinctive signature endnote. Whelan concludes that there was a strong ecclesiastical undercurrent throughout the manuscript: Whelan, '*Ex. Hib.* Ire.', p. 245; Whelan, 'Translating Ex.', pp 165–92. McCauley has suggested that Yonge was the translator: McCauley, 'Critical ed. English conquest', p. v.

unclene lyf'.[10] Also related to the theme of entrenchment is an inscription, 'oor lady mercy helpe' with a cruciform below. It is stated that the health of the colony depended on atonement for 'haye synnes': the same folk wayes este entombuet whych synes or than that shold have power for to done hame the same wiech for haye synnes'.[11] Related to this theme are symbolic overtures that reinforce the need for purification and entrenchment. Marginalia to the side of chapter 24 highlights a 'fyre oot of the eeste' and a side note in Latin with red ink points to the king's first arrival, 'de primo...in hib[er]n[ia]'. On the opposite folio page is an extended marginal note in a later, possibly Tudor hand: the 'kynge brought 400 grete shippes unto Ireland and such to timie subdued the whole lande beinge govrend by the king all submittyd to the kynge excepte the kinge of conacht'.[12] Possibly connected to the theme of purification is an illustration that resembles the chancel steps of a church that can be found alongside the unpopular governorship of William Fitzaldelin.

Secondly, the theme of a colonial siege mentality was accentuated. Attention was drawn to accounts for 'Englysshmen...assayled within har castell', and further examples can be found in chapters 18 and 19. Here, the verso margin is illustrated with a large and distinctive sword-like image. Inscribed in a slightly later hand are the reading aids 'dermot mcmurrough dyed' and 'the aryvall of men of norway' aside the deeds of Miles de Cogan in Dublin. Highlighted passages also include the sieges of Waterford and Dublin. A textual peculiarity also reinforces this theme. The manuscript includes two extracts from Giraldus' *Topographia*. One of which can be found after an account of the siege of Dublin, with MacMurrough and its 'cytezens ouer al other hated weren of hym'.[13] Inserted here was a miracle taken from the *Topographia*, an account of an immovable cross ('rood') in Christ Church Cathedral as the city was under threat.

The manuscript is unique in providing additional information regarding Thomas Becket. A reading aid ('the archbishop of Canterbury called Tho becket 1171') is accompanied with an extended passage that also includes a marginal illustration. A prophecy of Merlin with this extended reference to Thomas Becket suggested an interventionist perspective.[14] There were also links between Ormond and Becket.

---

[10] TCD, MS 592, f. 18v.
[11] TCD, MS 592, f. 24v.
[12] TCD, MS 592, f. 12v.
[13] TCD, MS 592, ff 7r, 8r, 10r, 23v.
[14] 'myracles that yn the worldes en-dyng yn the west of the world... prynces and hey menn shal come out of the este ynto the weste and lout ham to the newe martyres fot-stappes. Al tys was openly iseyd of the holy martyr Seynt Thomas [miracles that in the world's ending in the west of the world...princes and high men shall come out of the east into the west...to the new martyr's footsteps. All this was openly said of the holy martyr Saint Thomas]': TCD, MS 592, ff 9; Caoimhe Whelan, 'The notary's tale' in Sparky Booker and C. N. Peters (eds), *Tales of medieval Dublin* (Dublin, 2014), pp 113-34; Caoimhe Whelan, 'James Yonge and the writing of history in late medieval Dublin' in Seán Duffy (ed.), *Medieval Dublin XIII* (Dublin, 2011), pp 183-95.

The White Earl claimed descent from Becket's sister and the connection between the saint was enthusiastically fostered at this time.[15] The (hospital) church of Saint Thomas of Acon in London, where orisons were 'ordeyned and establyshed' by the White Earl, was originally the birthplace of Becket who was the hospital's patron saint.[16] It is possible that this Ormondist sacred space appears in the 'Butler Expugnatio'. A coloured sketch of what vaguely appears to be a shrine or church is inserted in the margin of the manuscript. It may be an image of Canterbury or considering the provenance of the manuscript and the context of its late fifteenth-century readership, it is possibly alluding to Saint Thomas of Acon.[17] Another extended reference to the *Topographia* related to a prophecy on the morality of the conquest and divination through dialogue. It was a further passage that could symbolise crown intervention, recounting a revelation that spoke of the 'syns of the land' which may be purged if the colonists remain virtuous.[18]

By the close of the fifteenth century the Kildares held an Irish language version of Giraldus. This suggests that Giraldus, or even the conquest, was seen neither solely as an Anglophone nor (in ecclesiastical terms) a Gregorian project. Kildare's library contained numerous copies of Giraldus at turn of the sixteenth century. No text survives but it seems that along with a Latin, English and Irish copy of the *Topographia*, an Irish edition of the *Expugnatio* was stored in Maynooth castle. Furthermore, Kildare allusions to the *Expugnatio* were not conveyed through state memoranda or through exclusively English texts. In 1507 references to Geraldine *res gestae* were written for an Italian reader while corresponding with the Gherardini of Florence. No extant Hiberno-English copy of the *Expugnatio* can be definitively traced to Kildare.[19] Although the Fitzgeralds could cite the *Expugnatio* as a segment of their family history, it was merely part of a much broader English and European,

---

[15] For the link between the cult of St Thomas Becket and the earls of Ormond, see Anne Sutton, 'The Hospital of St Thomas of Acre of London: the search for patronage, liturgical improvement, and a school, under Master John Neel, 1420-63' in Clive Burgess and Martin Heale (eds), *The late medieval English college and its context* (York, 2008), pp 199, 202-5.

[16] Joan, countess of Ormond, the first wife of the white earl (d. 1430) was buried in the Mercers' chapel of the church as was Thomas, the seventh earl, in 1515: David Beresford, 'The Butlers in England and Ireland, 1405-1515' (Ph.D., Trinity College Dublin, 1999), pp 298-9.

[17] In the background of the sketch are lines that resemble the surface of water, perhaps the Thames which flowed south of St Thomas of Acon: TCD, MS 592, f. 9r.

[18] 'Yn awodde of m[ea]th of aprest... wolf that lay ther... spake to hym and bad hym that he shold nat be adredde... and seyd tha[t] for the syns of the land[es] folke' there would be a reckoning. TCD, MS 592, f. 24v. Also, see Whelan, '*Ex. Hib. Ire.*', pp 243-58. Tracts written in the early decades of Henry VIII's reign reflect the import of such discourse. In the chapters that follow, see in relation to the *Salus Populi* and revelation through the secret divine. See also, ch. 5 and the 'Discourse' (c. 1526) and Kildare's use of Irish extortions was couched in terms of wolves and lambs: BL, Lansdowne MS 159, ff 7.

[19] Aisling Byrne suggests that the Irish version held in Maynooth was a translation of the earlier Hiberno-English copy of the *Expugnatio*: Byrne, 'Vernacular *Expug.*', p. 101.

Geraldine renaissance milieu. This fits with the wide-ranging cultural inclusiveness of the Geraldine administration of Ireland which will be discussed at greater length in the following chapter. Based on extant evidence, Maynooth was where a Gaelic manuscript of the *Expugnatio* could be found at this time.[20] As the Hiberno-English texts were intended for an old colonial or English audience, Kildare perhaps had a different use for Giraldus. If the eighth or ninth earls of Kildare intended meaning with a 'Geraldine Expugnatio', it was a more complicated projection.

※

This evolving use of the *Expugnatio* suggests a consideration of related evidence. A range of contemporaneous sources both in Ireland and at Court relate to perceptions of the colony which in ways touched upon the question of conquest. According to Kildare's enemies, the Lordship of Ireland could not be purified if a ruling magnate governed through broad, pan-cultural means. If the 'Butler Expugnatio' can generally be dated to the mid-fifteenth century or the 1460s it was commissioned during a time of Ormond decline. Partly due to the earl's absence, their Lancastrian affinity and the ongoing feud with Desmond, Butler fortunes contrasted to those of Kildare.[21]

The death of the White Earl in 1452 marked a turning point.[22] An Ormond 'fragmenta historia' and obituaries for the White Earl signified a loss of leadership as the fourth earl's legacy stands out from his predecessors and immediate heirs.[23] The fifth earl of Ormond was executed after the battle of Towton while the mid- to late fifteenth century also saw infighting among the Butler Polestown and Cahir cadets, 'manu equali'.[24] As the earldom declined, Ormondist or at least anti-Geraldine opinion did not remain silent. Following the Butler defeat at Piltown complaints were voiced against native influences in the Barrow valley, with Castledermot, one of the 'keys of Leinster' allegedly under Gaelic control.[25] Meanwhile, the fortification of the region and defence of the southern Pale did

---

[20] Byrne considers that the *Expugnatio* was not always especially culturally divisive, unlike in the later sixteenth century when English officials invoked the idea of 're-conquest': Byrne, 'Vernacular *Expug.*', p. 105.

[21] S. G. Ellis, *Ireland in the age of the Tudors* (London, 1998), pp 51–69; David Edwards, *The Ormond lordship in County Kilkenny, 1515–1642: the rise and fall of Butler feudal power* (Dublin, 2003), pp 79–90; A. J. Otway-Ruthven, *A history of medieval Ireland* (London, 1968), pp 376, 385; Beresford, 'Butlers in England and Ireland', chs 3–4.

[22] Otway-Ruthven underlines the fact that an entire older generation of lords died: Otway-Ruthven, *Medieval Ire.*, pp 376–85.

[23] He was entombed in 'marie. virginius', St Mary's Abbey, Dublin: BL, Add. MS 4792, f. 77r; BL, Vespasian D.X, f. 138v.

[24] *Ormond deeds*, iii, pp 260–1.

[25] M. C. Griffith, 'The Talbot-Ormond struggle for control of the Anglo-Irish government, 1414–47' in *IHS*, 2 (1940–1), p. 396.

little to aid the Ormond lordship.[26] An anti-Geraldine grudge was nursed since the 1460s, as demonstrated by Henrician documents which preserve a certain historical sense of awareness. See for instance, Darcy's 'Artycles of the sore dekaye of the kynges subietes' as Ormond-Desmond hostility did not abate until a truce in 1486.[27] As can be seen in the state paper archive, the year 1474 was bitterly remembered for the following '60 wynters' as the moment Kildare dominated the governorship.[28] It was in this year that that the earldom of Ormond was restored in Ireland under John Butler, the sixth earl. Meanwhile, there was intense debate over crown policy in Ireland, specifically the 'nombre of Englysh men' required and the matter of the Scots 'conspiren to subdue al thys land'.[29] The continued rise of the Kildares was by no means inevitable and a stable regime under Edward IV considered closer attention to the Lordship of Ireland. In what was a forerunner to subsequent treatises, c. 1474 'Enstruccyons [for the] relief [of Ireland]' emphasised the 'pitiose decay' of the land while heightening a sense of alarm by means of prophetic discourse. In this particular instance, following a reference to crown revenues from the Bann fisheries, a 'whyte lyon' was to 'wyn this land'.[30]

With the death of Thomas, seventh earl of Kildare, in 1478 (possibly of 'la plage de pestilence' which afflicted the colony) some measures were also taken to limit the powers of the governor, specifically the ability to alienate landed rights of the crown and to grant licences in mortmain.[31] Archbishop Edmund Connesburgh took the muster of 200 archers sent by Edward IV in June 1477 to support the governor, Bishop Sherwood of Meath (whose commission as governor was later annulled and Kildare then elected justiciar), and was then ordered to arbitrate 'certain strifes, discords and controversies between certain magnates in Ireland'.[32] The mediatory role of the church can also be seen in Ormondist bardic literature from the marches when Archbishop of Cashel John Cantwell curtailed the 'growth of every evil' and ensured that 'all would not be going to Rome (le cách don Róimh

---

[26] S. G. Ellis, 'Great earl of Kildare (1456-1513) and the creation of the English Pale' in *Ger. Med. Ire.*, pp 325-40.

[27] LPL, MS 635, ff 188r-189v; Maginn and Ellis, *Tudor discov. Ire.*, p. 91.

[28] SP 60/2, f. 32v.

[29] Otway-Ruthven, *Medieval Ire.*, p. 396; Maginn and Ellis, *Tudor discov. Ire.*, pp 32-3.

[30] Ellis has flagged this as a prequel to later reform tracts: S. G. Ellis, *Ireland's English Pale* (Woodbridge, 2021), pp 24-5; Maginn and Ellis, *Tudor Discov.*, pp 32-3. It appears to have been a reference to John de Courcy and his conquest of Ulster. Giraldus referred to him as the 'white knight', but the lion also symbolised the Earl Marshal: Donough Bryan, *Great earl of Kildare* (Dublin, 1933), pp 18-22; Gerald of Wales, *Expugnatio Hibernica, the conquest of Ireland*, ed. A. B. Scott and F. X. Martin (Dublin, 1978), p. 175 (II. 17).

[31] Bryan, *Great earl*, pp 27-8; S. G. Ellis, *Reform and revival: English government in Ireland 1470-1534* (Woodbridge, 1986), p. 21.

[32] *Cal. Pat. Rolls, 1476-1485*, pp 71, 79. I am grateful here for the assistance of Professor Steven Ellis.

ní rachaí)'.[33] His death in 1482 was mourned as a loss to regional interests from an Ormond perspective. While Thomas, seventh earl of Ormond, was in favour at the late Yorkist and early Tudor Court, Piers Butler of Polestown (son of Sir James Butler) managed the Ormond lordship in Ireland.[34] In conjunction with Thomas, Gearóid Mór Fitzgerald managed part of the Ormond estate but Piers Butler also enjoyed a significant power base. In 1485 Piers was married to Kildare's daughter Margaret Fitzgerald, 'for policy, being in variance with James Butler, earl of Wormane...Sir James could not well attend to war with the earl of Kildare'.[35] Despite their weakened lordship, the Butlers of Ormond remained in a position to exert some influence and it was perhaps on rising from its lowest ebb from 1462 until the 1480s that in Gowran, Carrick or Kilkenny their views on the colony were manifested in a projection of the *Expugnatio* that emphasised entrenchment. The decision to omit the *Gouernaunce of Prynces* and replicate the White Earl's *Expugnatio* seems to reflect a narrow Butler perspective by the later fifteenth century. Devoid of the *Gouernaunce* (bar a column of text), the *Expugnatio* with its own marginalia inserted and coloured over time appears to relate to the Geraldine-induced decay of the lordship. For instance, a highlighted reading aid warning that the 'Iresshe men bene false of kynd' resonated with such concerns.[36] The vivid complaints of decay and the push for regional entrenchment that can be traced in the State Papers of Henry VIII are arguably symbolised in the marginalia of TCD, MS 592. These side notes, reading aids and illustrations were selectively inserted at some stage between the commissioning of the manuscript and arguably, the 1530s.[37]

The manuscript appears to have been written in a south Leinster or Waterford dialect.[38] Given the Butler interests in Waterford, a tentative connection with related literary polemic may be traced, unveiling of propagandist motives across a range of sources. Ongoing readership of the *Expugnatio* accentuated certain viewpoints, which in ways matched anti-Geraldine rhetoric. The dichotomy between obedient Butler adherents and the Yorkist Geraldines was underlined by Edgecombe's propagandist account and other documents that regard the city

---

[33] *Poems on marcher lords: from a sixteenth-century Tipperary manuscript*, ed. Anne O'Sullivan and Padraig Ó Riain (London, 1987), p. 5.

[34] *Original letters illustrative of English history*, ed. Henry Ellis (4 vols, London, 1827), i, 147.

[35] *Cal. Carew*, v. 176. He did not enjoy the advantages afforded to the white earl of Ormond: C. A. Empey and Katharine Simms, 'Ordinances of the White Earl and the problem of coign in the later middle ages' in *PRIA*, 75C (1975), pp 173-4.

[36] The Kildare library at this time contained a 'liber Alixandre maugne' which was plausibly the *Gouernaunce* as it was believed to be a text originally written for Alexander III of Macedon.

[37] The opening and closing folio pages are slightly damaged. Whelan notes that the manuscript was likely to have been unbound for some time. This perhaps also indicates continued use and readership. The differing scribal hands and slight changes in dialect also perhaps indicate a late medieval and early Tudor interest in the manuscript.

[38] Caoimhe Whelan, 'TCD MS. 592'.

of Waterford as a loyal bastion.[39] Henry Tudor consulted with Ormond, who was then in favour at Court and chamberlain to the queen, on how to respond to the Simnel rebellion.[40] Butler and Waterford allegiance to the Tudor cause was celebrated in the ballad royal verse, 'O ye citizens of that faire citie' which appears to have circulated widely and even appeared in the State Papers of Henry VIII. Subsequent chronicles were thus shaped by these polemic influences and a Waterford correspondent writing to Court referred to the rebellion by blanketing 'all the norte' as having 'yelded obedience' to the pretender. In fact, the Archbishop of Armagh Octavian de Palatio was among those who had resisted.[41] The 'false land full of rebellion' beyond Waterford, as the author recounted, added weight to later appeals on the city's part from More to Wolsey for 'speciall favour' and to remember the 'duty of allegiance [shown by] John Butler maior of Waterford'.[42] The ballad itself was later recited and recalled, as when a correspondent cited the opening lines 'in Englysh ryme as followeth' which was deemed sufficient to remind the reader.[43] In the 1490s John Wyse sought protection for the king's highway along the Barrow valley to Waterford. Sir James Ormond defended his attacks on the Geraldine region, drawing parallels with the threat from the Turks.[44] Perspectives of the colony and the rhetoric of crusade characterised a message from the king to Charles VIII where 'Irlandois sauvages' in need of 'policie et justice' were differentiated from the other Irish who spoke English.[45] Meanwhile, Poynings' parliament of 1494 legislated in a manner that was anti-Kildare in both explicit and subtle ways. Given Geraldine sanctioned raids on the Pale in the preceding years the image of a vulnerable maghery and marches 'wher through Irishemen doo great hurtes by their oft skulles and making prayes' could be

---

[39] Kildare 'hath always been and is [an] utter enemye to the said Citie'. Stoking fears of Scottish intrigue through Geraldine Yorkist sympathies in Ulster, Edgecombe also possibly exaggerated that news of the death of James III was the 'the common voice... in the cite of Duvelyn and all the contry' on 18 July: BL, Titus B.IX, ff 332v, 334r. He was most likely killed at the Battle of Sauchieburn, 11 June.

[40] Maginn and Ellis, *Tudor discov. Ire.*, p. 122.

[41] SP 63/214, f. 19r. See also in relation to the 'othe off the ffremen' of Waterford: *The great parchment book of Waterford: liber antiquissimus civitatis Waterfordiae*, ed. Niall J. Byrne (Dublin, 2007), p. 49.

[42] SP 60/2, f. 54r; BL, Titus XI., ii, f. 341r; SP 63/214, f. 19r.

[43] SP 63/214, f. 20r. A copy of the poem was sent from Wyse to Cromwell in 1536: SP 60/2, f. 52v.

[44] *Statute rolls of the Irish parliament: Richard III - Henry VIII*, ed. Philomena Connolly (Dublin, 2002), p. 95. C. W. Fitzgerald, *Earls of Kildare and their ancestors from 1057 to 1773* (Dublin, 1858), p. 192; AFM, 1493; *History of the Church of Ireland*, ed. Richard Mant (London, 1839), p. 104.

[45] 'Comme font ceulx de sond Royaulme et les autres Irland [— —] langue Angloise': BL, Caligula D.VI, f. 19r.

emphasised for political purposes.[46] Chapter four of the same gave voice to the plight of the 'poore trewe erthe tillers' who suffer through Irish extortions.[47]

In fact, the eighth earl of Kildare did much to increase the rate of tillage in the Englishry.[48] Partisan accounts such as the Book of Howth portrayed a dull-witted Gearóid Mór Fitzgerald. In 1495 courtiers allegedly 'did but jest at his demeanour and doings [in the royal presence, where] the king and the lords could not hold the laughter, but the earl never changed countenance but told his tale as though he were among his fellows in his country'.[49] Although it was his son the ninth earl who was reared at Court, it is implausible that Gearóid Mór would be embarrassingly out of touch with courtly decorum in this manner. As has been argued with reference to Edgecombe, he would have been alive to the rhythms of court culture as a political arena. His sense of honour appears in the annals of 1492 when 'Con O'Connor was slain by the people of the earl of Kildare for having in jest thrown a pole at the Earl'.[50] Even by the time of his death, his legacy and deeds during this period were distorted. In 1513 a 'note' on the Act of Marches and Maghery tied the 'treacon of therle of therle of Kildare' to 'coyn and lyvry which is thevery occacone of the mysery of Ireland'.[51]

Despite good relations for much of the period between the seventh earl of Ormond and his 'cosyn' Kildare, Thomas Butler's position at Court and the questionable loyalty of the Geraldines apparently required a firm anti-Irish perspective on his part within formal courtly circles. Certain anti-Yorkist literature of Henry Tudor's Court, some of which was loosely associated with Ormond, offers snapshots of a decaying Lordship of Ireland. The court poet, Andreas Ammonius, came under the patronage of Ormond during the later years of Henry VII.[52] Ammonius found favour in England and in praise of Mountjoy he referred

---

[46] AFM, 1492, 1494. Conway comments on the symbolism of the iron helmet or 'skull': Agnes Conway, *Henry VII's relations with Scotland and Ireland 1485-1498* (Cambridge, 1932), p. 215.

[47] Conway, *Hen. VII Sco. Ire.*, p. 202.

[48] S. G. Ellis, 'The English Pale: a 'failed entity'?' in *HI*, 19 (2011), pp 14-17. See also Ellis, *Ireland's English Pale*, pp 98-9, 108, 131-5.

[49] Popular sources recall colourful scenes in an exchange that strangely resembled the eighth earl's interrogation in 1495-6, Wolsey confronted an obstreperous ninth earl of Kildare as 'king' of Ireland: *Cal. Carew*, v, 180; Richard Bagwell, *Ireland under the Tudors* (3 vols, London, 1885), i, 148.

[50] AFM, 1492.

[51] NLI, MS 2507, f. 57v. See also Polydore Vergil's polemic written in the early decades of the sixteenth century on the folly of the Yorkist pretenders in Ireland: Eric Haywood, 'Humanism's priorities and empire's prerogatives: Polydore Vergil's *Description of Ireland*' in *PRIA*, 109C (2009), p. 237.

[52] Susan Brigden, *London and the reformation* (Oxford, 1989), p. 83; Aysha Pollnitz, *Princely education in early modern Britain* (Cambridge, 2015), pp 34-57; Sean Cunningham, *Henry VII* (London, 2007), pp 253-72; Thomas Penn, *Winter king: Henry VII and the dawn of Tudor England* (London, 2011), p. 356; Gilbert Tournoy, 'The unrecorded poetical production of Andreas

to Henry VIII as 'our Octavius'.[53] Either incidentally or intentionally, his verse depicts Geraldine-induced decay in Ireland. His first poem, 'to the English lord, Mountjoy', related in part to the 1487 Simnel rebellion. Ammonius treats of a land of perpetual violence ('nec agrestis Hybernia cessat') and equated Yorkist rebels with those of Roman Pannonia ('Ungrus Pannoniam, Scotus Hiberniam').[54] Ammonius was closely connected to the royal tutor, poet and historian Bernard Andreas who produced two main works, *Historia Henrici Septimi* and a celebration of his achievements based on the labours of Hercules, *Les Douze Triomphes de Henry VII*.[55] Also using classical analogies, his chronicle of the life of Henry Tudor portrayed the Geraldine-Yorkist Irish as the Germanic Teutoni ('Teutonum quam Hibernorum').[56] Accounts of Ireland at the Court of Henry VII are scarce and lacking in detail but some profit may be derived from these extracts given the aforementioned context. An appeal for conquest is not put forward, but the image of Ireland provided here could be used to justify military intervention.

While not directly linked with the *Expugnatio* or its late medieval readership, the concepts of conquest, crusade and the often-contentious nature of ecclesiastical patronage converge with the Knights Hospitaller. The Order of Knights of the Hospital of Saint John of Jerusalem, Knights Hospitaller or simply (according to John Rawson) the 'religion', was a theatre of factional strife in

---

Ammonius' in *Humanistica Lovaniensia: Journal of Neo-Latin Studies*, 37 (1988), pp 257-60; D. R. Carlson, 'Three Tudor epigrams' in *Humanistica Lovaniensia: Journal of Neo-Latin Studies*, 45 (1996), pp 189-200.

[53] Ammonius was in England by 1506, probably having travelled there with the papal nuncio Silvestro Gigli. Gigli carried the papal cap and sword to the king having been sent by Julius II in 1505. In 1509 Ammonius was secretary to William Blount, Lord Mountjoy, stepson of Ormond, and by 1511 was Latin secretary to Henry VIII. Cardinal Julius de Medici wrote to the king in 1514 relaying papal approval of Ammonius, 'cuis secretarim' as papal collector in England. He received benefices in Gloucester and Worcestershire from Richard Fox and Gigli. Around this time, Ammonius also was in possession of a 'white Irish horse', possibly a gift by means of Ormond: BL, Vitellius B.II, ff 66v, 71v, 105; SP 1/9, 92r; SP 1/10, f. 5r. Written between 1503 and 1511, a select compilation of his poems was printed in Paris in 1511.

[54] Pannonia Superior was a Roman province north of the Danube. In 193 CE it was from this province that Septimus Severus began a coup d'état and became emperor. There are obvious parallels here with Ireland in 1487-8. Irishmen were vaguely deemed uncivilised or a human subspecies ('hyblaeis apibus gens numerosior'): *Andrea Ammonii carmina omnia*, ed. Clemente Pizzi (Florence, 1958), pp 5, 12; *Dizionaris biografico delgi Italiani*, ed. Gilbert Tournoy (Rome, 1989), pp xxxvii, 236-41.

[55] In his own words, 'Ammonius regius scriba ad Bernardum Andream regium poetam': *Dizionaris biografico*, p. 264.

[56] *Memorials of Henry VII*, ed. James Gairdner (London, 1858), p. 50. The Germanic Teutoni resisted Rome in the Cimbrian War during the first-century BCE. A late medieval English courtly audience may have been aware of this event as translations of the histories of Livy were in circulation by the end of the fifteenth century. The panegyric verse of Andreas compared Yorkist Ireland to something of a Homeric cyclopean 'caverne': *Memorials*, p. 222.

pre-Reformation Ireland as various interests sought to control the Hospitallers in Ireland.[57] The Hospitallers held sway throughout the island but unlike many orders they were closely associated with the English colony and enjoyed a privileged position in late medieval Ireland.[58] Their symbolic role in matters of state ranged from political to cultural. For instance, the lord deputy was customarily a guest of honour at annual performances of religious drama in liturgical and civic ceremonies.[59] In addition they were 'beyond time and memory possessed of diverse possessions as well spiritual as temporall in this land...lawful[ly dealing]... within the Irishry'.[60] Although mostly dealing with an earlier period, Helen Nicholson and Paolo Virtuani highlight that an increasingly secularised Knights Hospitaller did bear arms, albeit rarely, within Christendom.[61] Of fundamental importance was their broad capacity to mobilise political will and raise revenue but it was also their embodiment of chivalry and crusade that was relevant to the projection of policy in Ireland. From an old colonial perspective, allusions to crusade varied depending on a lord's relationship to power. An ascendant ruling magnate may voice the precedence of serving religion against the Turks if this facilitated continued rule through aristocratic delegation. Those seeking crown intervention would prioritise the conquest of Ireland in terms that effectively implied a crusade. Expedient governance of the lordship under Kildare liberated resources for foreign affairs. Furthermore, such a policy would be a first step in the process of crusade in the Holy Land.[62] Finite resources rendered the outright pursuit of either option unlikely but those were points of emphasis in relation to political power.[63] The *Expugnatio* itself recounted a westward religious crusade and as a prophetic history was also a rhetorical advantage for the proponents of

---

[57] SP 60/1, f. 77r.

[58] Brendan Scott, 'The Knights Hospitaller in Tudor Ireland: their dissolution and attempted revival' in Martin Browne and Colman Ó Clabaigh (eds), *Soldiers of Christ: the Knights Hospitaller and the Knights Templar in medieval Ireland* (Dublin, 2016), pp 47–60.

[59] In 1528, Piers Butler was accompanied by John Rawson for a Passion drama at Hoggin Green staged by the Hospitallers, All Hallows and Holy Trinity: St John Seymour, *Anglo-Irish literature, 1200–1582* (Dublin, 1929), pp 118–23, 126–7.

[60] *Statute rolls of the parliament of Ireland, Edward IV*, ed. James Morrisey (Dublin, 1939), p. 217.

[61] Paolo Virtuani, '*Tuitio fidei?* The Irish Hospitallers at war' in Edward Coleman, Paul Duffy and Tadhg O'Keeffe (eds), *Ireland and the Crusades* (Dublin, 2022), pp 121–8; Helen Nicholson, 'The Hospitallers and Templars' involvement in warfare on the frontiers of the British Isles in the late thirteenth and early fourteenth centuries' in Jürgen Sarnowsky (ed.), *Ordines militaris colloquia Torunesia historica* (Toruń, 2012), pp 105–19.

[62] The *Salus Populi* and its state paper for instance portray the conquest of Ireland as a springboard to greater fame against the Turks.

[63] An Anglo-Imperial treaty ratified at Windsor, which included Cardinal de Medici and the Florentine Republic, was characterised by a 'crusade' against the French and the Turks: *Calendar of State Papers and manuscripts in the archives and collections of Milan, 1385–1618*, ed. A. B. Hinds (16 vols, London, 1912), i, 421–2.

conquest. The anti-Geraldine 'State' (c. 1515) prophesied a conquest of Ireland, the 'crystyn lande…[with] most soulles damned' as a necessary step in reclaiming the 'great citie of Constantinople'.[64] It was in this context that for generations the Butlers and other critics of Kildare clung to the memory of the 'cankerid malicious rebellion rotid in theym evyr sithens' the 1460s.[65] It was therefore not only preferable to control the Hospitallers in Ireland, but also desirable to more effectively project how the needs of the colony were best served. For a dominant magnate it was an eastward conquest for Christendom.

Reinforcing the fourth earl of Ormond's position, Thomas Butler, illegitimate son of the White Earl and veteran of the French wars, led the order in Ireland in the 1410s. This 'pryor of Kilmaynam', according to John Page, court poet of Henry V, was praised for his exploits at Harflete, where he was 'well arayde of warre' with 'xv hundryd fyughtyng men'.[66] By the 1430s contention over the Hospitallers had further intensified factional divides. Kildare's grandson Thomas Fitzgerald was appointed prior, to the outcries of 'contempt, rebellion, and dilapidation of the goods of the said hospital' in 1447.[67] Ormond wrote of 'certaine poyntys of treson' against the prior which prompted the dramatic spectacle of a challenge in Smithfield, with Fitzgerald 'fulle clenly harnyssyd, redy why the alle hys fetys and whythe alle hys wepyns, kepynge the fylde tylle hyghe none'.[68] A mid-fifteenth-century power shift saw a number of English-born priors serving under Lancastrian kings before the tempestuous priorate of James Keating under the Kildare Geraldines. Keating aggressively extended his landed base and political power, enabling him to supersede Lord Deputy Bishop Sherwood in 1475-7.[69] Keating also declared the Earl Marshal's estates in Wexford 'by his deed quit claimed' to the Hospitallers, a move that prompted opposition and required papal intervention to legitimise the claim.[70]

A frequent recipient of parliamentary privileges, for instance with Roland FitzEustace in 1477, by 1482 the Grand Master and Marmaduke Lomley struggled to dislodge Keating.[71] His career unfolded alongside the rise of Kildare and by

---

[64] BL, Add. MS 4792, ff 100v, 110v.
[65] For example, in 1535 Ossory wrote that Desmond's 'duetie of alegeaunce that a subgiet oght to owe his Prince [was from this moment] as a Turk is to believe in Christ': *S.P. Hen. VIII*, ii, 229-30.
[66] *Historical collections of a citizen of London in the fifteenth-century*, ed. James Gairdner (London, 1876), pp 12-13.
[67] AFM, 1438; C. L. Falkiner, 'The Hospital of St John of Jerusalem in Ireland' in *PRIA*, 26 (1906-7), p. 299.
[68] *Historical collections*, p. 187.
[69] *Stat. Rolls Ed. IV*, p. 107.
[70] *Stat. Rolls Ed. IV*, pp 609-11; *Dignitas Decani St Patrick's Cathedral Dublin*, ed. Newport White (Dublin, 1957), p. 75.
[71] Lomley complained that he was stripped of 'all manner evidences, writings, bulls and letters, which I brought with me in that behalf into Ireland': *Stat. Rolls Ed. IV*, p. 332; *Collectanea de*

association, the eighth earl himself has been viewed in a similar light. Keating was deprived of office by the Grand Master for subordination and in 1483 his replacement Marmaduke Lomley appealed to the king 'againes one frere James Keteng' who 'violently' held him captive in Kilsaran.[72] In June 1484 Archbishop de Palatio wrote to the king on behalf of Lomley against 'pretended friar [olim priorem prioratus]' Keating.[73] In 1488 Keating was 'specially noted among all chief causes' of the Yorkist rebellion.[74] Kildare personally valued the Hospitallers and their potential influence.

Two of Gearóid Mór Fitzgerald's sons were 'knights of the Rhodes' while his library held much literature relating to the crusades in general and chivalric orders in particular.[75] The library contained 'the sege of the Rodes' which may have been a copy of a text printed in the Low Countries, the *Siege of Rhodes* translated by court poet John Kay and dedicated to Edward IV in 1482.[76] Through the Hospitallers, European contacts were utilised after 1534 when Gerald, eleventh earl of Kildare, was accompanied by a host of their knights.[77]

In the 1510s and 1520s, conflict involving the Hospitallers in Ireland under Henry VIII was proximate to contention over colonial policy. An early Tudor intervention materialised with the appointment of Sir John Rawson in 1511, which obstructed Geraldine influence. Rawson was regarded by the king for his outstanding individual merit ('ipsius merito').[78] His brother Richard was prebendary of St Stephen's Chapel, Westminster in 1511 and royal chaplain by 1520. John Rawson had joined the Hospitallers by 1497 and was thereafter engaged in diplomatic missions to Rome and Venice.[79] In contrast to his predecessors in Kilmainham, Rawson was a resolute appointment from a crown perspective.[80]

---

rebus Hibernicis, ed. Walter Harris (20 vols, Dublin, 1786), xiv, 230. Note the later similarities with Archbishop John Alen in 1534; James Murray, 'Archbishop Alen, Tudor reform and the Kildare rebellion' in *PRIA*, 89C (1989), pp 1–16.

[72] *Registrum Octaviani alias Liber Niger*, ed. Mario A. Sughi (2 vols, Dublin, 1999), ii, 185.

[73] *Reg. Oct.*, ii, 264.

[74] BL, Titus B.XI, f. 334v. See also BL, Add. MS 4792, ff 56

[75] Bryan, *Great earl*, p. 92; Aisling Byrne, 'The Geraldines and the culture of the wider world' in Peter Crooks and Seán Duffy (eds), *The Geraldines and medieval Ireland: the making of a myth* (Dublin, 2016), p. 286; Gregory O'Malley, *The Knights Hospitaller of the English langue, 1460–1565* (Oxford, 2005), pp 240–55.

[76] Guillaume Caoursin, *The siege of Rhodes* (London, 1482), pp i–iii.

[77] Vincent Carey, *Surviving the Tudors: the 'wizard' earl of Kildare and English rule in Ireland, 1537–1586* (Dublin, 2002), pp 44–9; A. Valkenburg, 'A study in diplomacy, Gerald, eleventh earl of Kildare 1525–85' in *JKA*, 14 (1965), p. 297.

[78] BL, Otho C.IX, f. 32r. For Hospitaller influence beyond the Tudor marches, for instance, see the correspondence between James IV and the Grand Master at Rhodes: *Letters and papers illustrative of the reigns of Richard III and Henry VII*, ed. James Gairdner (3 vols, London, 1861–3), ii, 262.

[79] *Calendar of State Papers Venice*, ed. Rawdon Brown (11 vols, London, 1864), ii, 64.

[80] Scott, 'Knights Hospitaller', p. 48; D. B. Quinn, 'The re-emergence of English policy as a major factor in Irish affairs, 1520–34' in *NHI*, pp 655–8.

Within a year, Rawson faced problems reflecting cultural and political divides that became a matter for the king's close attention. An Irish adversary of Rawson, Brother Edmund Seix had been granted the valuable Hospitaller manor of Kilsaran in Uriel to which the crown objected.[81] Seix countered that anti-Irish impositions violated the rules of the order. Under the rules of the order, Seix argued a credible case. However, a letter from the king to Rhodes, written in the hand of Andreas Ammonius, warned of a disruption of revenues ('reditus') and denounced the Irish degeneracy of Seix ('edmundo cesse homini hibernico').[82] The crown was wary of interference in the lordship through the Hospitallers. Ammonius appealed to the Grand Master as a broad-thinking man ('contemplationis virum') and for the true religion ('uram religione') on behalf of the king.[83] In 1518 Rawson was summoned to Rhodes and the king granted licence to leave in 1519 although this was postponed. Evidence exists, albeit fragmentary and allusive, as to Rawson's disposition and interests through patronage. In 1520 an inventory recorded by a monk of the London Carthusian Priory of Mount Grace noted 'a newe mantell by the gyfte of Syr John Rawson knyght of the Rhodes' and a 'prntyd portewe by the gyft of mr Rawson'.[84] It is likely that Rawson bestowed this penitential breviary and cloak while holding office in Ireland. By the time Kildare was restored, both Rawson brothers were industriously following the king's bidding.[85] Kildare, perhaps in an effort to deflect the crown's intervention through the Hospitallers, in 1522 exerted pressure on Rawson to 'have gonne to the service of...religion at the Rodes'.[86] This prior was no friend of Gearóid Óg and Rawson accused the earl of coercing him 'ayenst my will, to graunte and lett owt certayn my fermys and tithis to the Erle of Kyldare'.[87] In contrast to the previous generation where Keating strengthened Kildare's hand, Rawson was of a different political stamp. However, the underlying dynamics and perspectives in relation to power remained comparable to those of the preceding century.

In bridging the late fifteenth and early sixteenth centuries, observations may be taken from contextualising the copy of the *Expugnatio* which came into the

---

[81] In 1484, the king and Grand Master at Rhodes were petitioned on behalf of Prior Marmaduke Lomley against James Keating 'olim priorem prioratus' for the custody of Kilsaran: *Reg. Oct.*, ii, 264, 638.
[82] BL, Otho C.XI, f. 32r; O'Malley, *Knights Hospitaller*, p. 251.
[83] BL, Otho C.XI, ff 26-32. See also *Registrum de Kilmainham: register of chapter acts of the Hospital of Saint John of Jerusalem in Ireland, 1326–1339*, ed. Charles McNeill (Dublin, 1932), p. 167.
[84] SP 1/19, ff 169.
[85] In 1523, Richard was knighted and appointed 'receiver of petitions for Gascony and other parts beyond the seas': *Athenae Cantabrigienses 1500–1585*, ed. H. C. Cooper and Thompson Cooper (London, 1858), p. 82.
[86] SP 60/1, f. 77r.
[87] *Crown surveys of lands, 1540–1, with the Kildare Rental begun in 1518*, ed. Gearóid MacNiocaill (Dublin, 1992), pp 242, 291; SP 60/1, f. 77r.

hands of the Darcies of Platten but it uncertain who originally commissioned the manuscript.[88] It is likely that either John Darcy (d. 1483) or his son acquired the manuscript.[89] John's son, Sir William Darcy, was a figure of note.[90] Initially an ally of Gearóid Mór Fitzgerald, his relationship with Kildare soured around 1513 at which time Darcy prepared his influential 'Artycles' concerning the decay of Ireland, becoming in Bradshaw's words, 'the father of the movement for political reformation' in early Tudor Ireland. The manuscript experienced an afterlife of sorts in the form of this treatise, which was in some measure shaped by the *Expugnatio* in constructing an anti-Geraldine narrative of decay. Presented to the Privy Council in 1515, Darcy evidently enjoyed political favour and his premise also carried much currency. Reflecting not merely an anti-Kildare lobby, animosity with Desmond since the 1460s is present here from the outset.[91] Although the treatise was formally brought to the attention of Henry VIII, Darcy's 'Artycles' touched upon the bitter divisions of an earlier generation with the notable denunciation of Desmond as the 'fyrste man that ever put coyne and lyverie on the kynges subiectes'. It remained unforgotten and was presented as part of a yawning Geraldine problem even as Kildare was the driving force for decay.[92]

---

[88] BL Add. MS 40674. Entitled 'de expugnatione Hiberniae' and containing 35 folio pages, at a later stage, the Darcy arms were inserted in the manuscript.

[89] The fourteenth-century governorship of their forefather John Darcy ('Justiciario Hibernie') was noted in the register. The manuscript includes later medieval or sixteenth-century marginal notes as reading aids for this particular part of the text: Bodl., MS Rawl. B 501, f. 21r. See also *Reg. Kilmainham*, p. 21. Familial or dynastic propaganda can appear in varied ways and in a range of sources. For instance, in the Book of Howth, St Laurence's ancestor, 'Sir John (de Courcy) was alter Ercules': *Cal. Carew*, v. 87; Sparky Booker, 'The Knight's Tale' in Sparky Booker and C. N. Peters (eds), *Tales of medieval Dublin* (Dublin, 2014), pp 135-48; Valerie McGowan-Doyle, *The Book of Howth: Elizabethan conquest and the old English* (Cork, 2011); Thomas Herron, 'Introduction: a fragmented Renaissance' in Thomas Herron and Michael Potterton (eds), *Ireland in the Renaissance c. 1540–1660* (Dublin, 2007), p. 21.

[90] Ellis, 'Darcy of Platten', pp 19-41.

[91] LPL, MS 635, ff 188r; Maginn and Ellis, Tudor discov. Ire., p. 91; David Heffernan, *Debating Tudor policy in sixteenth-century Ireland: 'reform' treatises and political discourse* (Manchester, 2018), pp 30-2; Brendan Bradshaw, *Irish constitutional revolution of the sixteenth century* (Cambridge, 1979), pp 37-43; Robin Frame, 'Contexts, divisions and unities: perspectives from the later middle ages' in CHI, i, pp 528-35, 541. See also below, ch. 4.

[92] Maginn and Ellis, *Tudor discov. Ire.*, p. 91; LPL, MS 635, f. 188r. Palmer offers an account of early modern Irish literature in the context of conquest, violence and cultural assimilation are considered: Patricia Palmer, *The severed head and the grafted tongue: literature, translation and violence in early modern Ireland* (Cambridge, 2019), pp 1-35. It is possible that the points of emphasis in LPL, MS 598 differ from the perspectives in Geraldine manuscripts through their respective positions of power. For humanist concepts of decay framed through nature and art, see Dorothy Koenigsberger, *Renaissance man and creative thinking: a history of concepts of harmony, 1400–1700* (Hassocks, 1979), pp xi-xiii, 266-72.

3

Kildare Renaissance, 1496–1522

For reasons other than those of the romantic narratives of the Great Earl 'reigning royally', Kildare's epithet is apt.[1] In the context of what is here discussed, the sheer scope and significance of the Kildare project may add to established scholarship. In recent decades, the range of factors behind Kildare's prominence, his capacity in terms of *manraed*, estate management, distribution of patronage along with a myriad of political, social and also cultural approaches have been studied.[2] From the mutually agreeable bond of 1496, he was in the position to comfortably fulfil the obligation to defend the Pale and the king was satisfied with the relative security and financial viability of the colony with its English institutions in reasonable order.[3] Prompted by a 'long tyme (of) great and haynoux discord discention and variance', a tripartite indenture marked a calming of Geraldine-Butler tensions.[4]

---

[1] For this antiquated tradition, see *The spirit of the nation: ballads and songs by the writers of 'The Nation' with original and ancient music* (Dublin, 1845), pp 91–5; Brian Fitzgerald, *The Geraldines: an experiment in Irish government, 1165–1601* (London, 1951), pp 93–202; C. W. Fitzgerald, *Earls of Kildare and their ancestors from 1057 to 1773* (Dublin, 1858); Donough Bryan, *Great earl of Kildare* (Dublin, 1933); Edmund Curtis, *A history of medieval Ireland* (London, 1938), pp 383–4.

[2] Ellis, *Tudor frontiers*, pp 18–45; Ellis, *Ire. Tudors*; Colm Lennon, *Sixteenth-century Ireland: the incomplete conquest* (Dublin, 1994). More recently, see Marian Lyons, 'Kildare ascendancy' in Patrick Cosgrove, Terence Dooley and Karol Mullaney-Dignam (eds), *Aspects of aristocratic life: essays on the Fitzgeralds and Carton House* (Dublin, 2014), pp 47–59; Vincent Carey, *Surviving the Tudors: the 'wizard' earl of Kildare and English rule in Ireland, 1537–1586* (Dublin, 2002), pp 16–22; Aisling Byrne, 'Geraldines and the culture of the wider world', Sparky Booker, 'The Geraldines and the Irish: intermarriage, ecclesiastical patronage and status' and S. G. Ellis, 'Great earl of Kildare (1456–1513) and the creation of the English Pale' in *Ger. Med. Ire.*, pp 278–91, 292–324, 325–340.

[3] D. B. Quinn, 'Hegemony of the earls of Kildare, 1494–1520' in *NHI*, pp 646–8; S. G. Ellis, 'Henry VII and Ireland, 1491–1496' in James Lydon (ed.), *England and Ireland in the later middle ages: essays in honour of Jocelyn Otway-Ruthven* (Dublin, 1981), pp 250–4. For the year as a turning point, see Peter Crooks, 'Factions, feuds and noble power in the lordship of Ireland, c. 1356–1496' in *IHS*, 35 (2006–7), pp 425–54; Ellis, 'Great earl', pp 325–340; Christopher Maginn, 'Continuity and change: 1470–1550' in *CHI*, i, 300; S. G. Ellis, *Reform and revival: English government in Ireland 1470–1534* (Woodbridge, 1986), pp 170–2; S. G. Ellis, *Ireland in the age of the Tudors* (London, 1998), p. 14; Lennon, *Sixteenth-cen. Ire.*, pp 66–86. The king's ignorance of the cultural unity of Gaelic Ireland has been argued: Quinn, 'Hegemony of the earls of Kildare, 1494–1520', pp 638–61.

[4] Agnes Conway, *Henry VII's relations with Scotland and Ireland 1485–1498* (Cambridge, 1932), pp 227–9.

Kildare held parliament at Castledermot in 1499, augmenting the 1488 Act of Marches and Maghery with meaures for 'thencreasinge of Englishe manners and conditions'.[5] The political nous of the Great Earl was demonstrated in his constructive relationship with Thomas Butler, even after what had transpired in the preceding years. Writing two months before Piers Butler killed Sir James of Ormond, whose enemies by then even included James Wise of Waterford, the earl required Kildare to have his 'landes there in fferme'.[6] Gearóid Mór Fitzgerald did not simply manage Ormond estates but also Piers Butler himself, and Kildare's 'good cousinage' was an advantage to Thomas Butler distanced from Ireland at Court. Ormond's debt of gratitude stemmed from the 'letting of the third parte of my landis in your partes' and Pier's 'drede' of Kildare.[7] Ormond accounts reflect concerns that in 1499, 'lawes of yrlond...noyr manne holde hyes londis by eyrre wtowtte any clayme the lorde schall neuur have recouvre'.[8] A debt of gratitude may be seen in an appeal for restitution of his prisages of wines through parliamentary grant and was exempted from absentee legislation shortly thereafter.[9]

At Court, Kildare's agent Thomas Kent procured the co-operation of Ormond while the king's 'poletique' approach was similar to the policies of the late Yorkist crown.[10] Kildare also campaigned widely, and with few exceptions, successfully. According to Verney, the immediate impact of Kildare's restoration subdued 'Irishmen of all the southe and west partys of the land' and aside from the forcing of MacMurrough-Kavanagh from Carlow castle, the 'kynge hath peace in all the lande without strake or...great charge or coste'.[11] From 1498 to 1503 Kildare campaigned in Connaught, aligned his interests with Henry O'Neill and secured his new lands in east Ulster. With O'Donnell and Maguire, Kildare took Dungannon castle with heavy cannon and dislodged Savage from Lecale. Gaelic annals later recounted the 'power of the earl of Cill-dara' having expelled Savage, who held the seneschalsy of the earldom of Ulster since the 1430s. Kildare's 1503 campaigns in Lecale were later portrayed by his enemies as the cause of an influx of Scots comparable to the Bruce invasion, a criticism that nonetheless implied a position of strength.[12] It was a coup to reach an accord with O'Donnell, who

---

[5] S. G. Ellis, *Ireland's English Pale* (Woodbridge, 2021), introduction and ch. 1; Ellis, 'Great earl', p. 332; CPR, pp 128-9.
[6] SP 46/130 f. 23r, *Ormond deeds*, iii, 336-7; Conway, *Hen. VII Sco. Ire.*, p. 239; Ellis, 'Great earl', pp 325-40.
[7] SP 46/130 f. 23r.
[8] SP 1/231, f. 306v.
[9] SP 46/130, f. 23r.
[10] Edward Hall, *Vnion of the two noble and illustrate famelies of Lancastre and Yorke* (1548), p. 10.
[11] Conway, *Hen. VII Sco. Ire.*, pp 233-4.
[12] SP 60/2, f. 35v; AFM 1498; K. W. Nicholls, *Gaelic and gaelicised Ireland in the middle ages* (Dublin, 1972), p. 195; ALC, 1519.

submitted to the earl in Dublin.[13] Marriage to Elizabeth St John, the king's 'nigh kynneswoman and of his noble blood', accompanied Honiley manor and estates while Gearóid Óg's later marriage to Elizabeth Zouche secured further lands.[14]

Kildare projected a desire and a capacity to safeguard the remotest corners of the Englishry. Victory at the battle of Knockdoe could have been presented at Court as a defence of English institutions, specifically Galway's chartered liberties. How the townsfolk perceived the situation is uncertain. Even less clear were the wider political consequences; however there was much to trumpet from a Geraldine standpoint as an obvious statement of Kildare power. Traversing the island, leading a force comprised of Ulster lords with those of the Pale and defeating Clanrickard Burke demonstrated logistical, political and military prowess.[15] If the event spurred a reaction from the king, it was a complex response. Firstly, Kildare was made a Knight of the Garter. Yet in 1506, the king considered a 'viage personal in his most noble person'. It did not materialise, but its purposed aim to reduce the 'wild Irish' signified reservations as to the imperfect, pan-cultural character of aristocratic delegation.[16] In the following years, sweeping Geraldine military expeditions were conducted and the only notable defeat was the skirmish at O'Brien's bridge.

Ten years before Philip Flattisbury wrote his obituary of Gearóid Mór Fitzgerald, he had commenced the important account of tenurial and dynastic records known as the 'Red book of Kildare'.[17] Marginal notes and reading aids in the manuscript suggest consultation throughout this period. Flattisbury's role in presenting the Kildare image survives in his obituary for the eighth earl. He was, according to Flattisbury, 'qui fuit in officijs tam deputati quam Iusticiarij domini Regis in terra sua Hiberniae [the king's deputy in Ireland] per spatium

---

[13] He fostered Kildare's son Henry in return: Katharine Simms, *Gaelic Ulster in the middle ages: history, culture and society* (Dublin, 2020), p. 208.

[14] Conway, *Hen. VII Sco. Ire.*, pp 321-2; Booker, 'Geraldines and the Irish', pp 293-5.

[15] 'Bellum de Knocktoe', as it was referred to in a contemporary chronicle; BL, Add. MS 4791, f. 95r. Also, see G. A. Hayes-McCoy, *Irish battles: a military history of Ireland* (Belfast, 1989), pp 53, 65-6; Lennon, *Sixteenth-cen. Ire.*, pp 67-9; S. G. Ellis, 'The Tudors and the origins of the modern Irish states: a standing army' in Thomas Bartlett and Keith Jeffery (eds), *A military history of Ireland* (Cambridge, 1996), p. 118; Christopher Maginn, 'Gaelic Ireland's English frontiers in the late middle ages' in *PRIA*, 110C (2010), p. 186; Katharine Simms, *Gaelic Ulster in the middle ages: history, culture and society* (Dublin, 2020), p. 209. S. J. Connolly, *Contested island: Ireland 1460-1630* (Oxford, 2007) begins with this event (pp 4-5). Simon Egan observes that Knockdoe did little to alter the balance of power on the western seaboard: Simon Egan, 'Lordship and dynasty in the late medieval Irish sea world: the Hiberno-Scottish Nexus' in *Cambrian Medieval Celtic Studies*, 78 (2019), pp 1-44.

[16] *Select cases in the council of Henry VII*, ed. Bernard Quaritch (London, 1958), p. 46. Also, see Christopher Maginn and S. G. Ellis, *Tudor discovery of Ireland* (Dublin, 2015), pp 132-3; Conway, *Hen. VII Sco. Ire.*, p. 86.

[17] NLI, MS 5769 (photostat), p. 4.

33 annorum [for 33 years]', greatly advancing the king's Lordship of Ireland and defeating his enemies.[18] In succeeding his father, Gearóid Óg Fitzgerald ensured continuity in most respects, from estate management and political alliances to the completion of cultural projects.[19] Another significant book of Geraldine records was the *Kildare Rental* which was begun in 1518. Mainly concerned with Kildare's landed interests and his varied agreements with a broad array of lords, the book also lists the earl's private collections. Cromwell would later be informed that among his 'evidences and bookes' a 'booke of the landes, lately thErle of Kildares' was held by his widow, a possible reference to this account.[20] The *Rental* indicated the expansion of the Kildare *patria* as the ninth earl succeeded his father. An island-wide reach contributed to his reputation as the greatest 'improver' of his estates.[21] Military and economic gains were intertwined. Prosperity was indicated by an increase in tenants for example in the manor of Maynooth.[22] Campaigning as far north as Carrickfergus and south to the MacCarthy of Carbery, Kildare interests were protected with 'great generalship' up to the death of Gearóid Mór, and his heir continued to protect the lordship. Gunpowder delivered to 'the erle of Kyldare' was categorised along with dispatches to Berwick for defence of the north.[23] Despite a lurking Scottish presence, Ireland remained generally more secure since the pax of 1496. In 1513 the king was updated on the Scots' 'continual intelligence with the ffrenchemen...their shippes that they send into Fraunce pass on the bak syde of Irlaunde'.[24] Kildare's ability to control O'Neill and O'Donnell, to achieve, in the words of Brendan Bradshaw, diplomatic checkmate, was an effective asset to the crown. Hugh Dubh O'Donnell had submitted to Kildare (1503), thus improving relations with the English administration. What was later referred to as his 'good serwice' was, amid much ceremony, rewarded with a knighthood at Court.[25] After a brief summons to Court in 1515,

---

[18] I have been kindly assisted by Professor Steven Ellis with this transcription. This period of service as the king's deputy was just over thirty years: BL, Add. MS 4787, f. 252v; BL, Add. MS 4791, f. 135v; Ellis, 'Great earl', p. 325; Lennon, *Sixteenth-cen. Ire.*, p. 71. The annals say, 'a knight in valour and princely and religious in his words and judgement': AFM, 1514; S. G. Ellis, 'Fitzgerald, Gerald, eighth earl of Kildare (1456?-1513)', *ODNB*.

[19] Marian Lyons, *Gearóid Óg Fitzgerald, ninth earl of Kildare* (Dundalk, 1998), pp 4-5; Lennon, *Sixteenth-cen. Ire.*, p. 79.

[20] SP 60/2, ff 156r-157r.

[21] SP 60/3, f. 2r; Ellis, 'Great earl', pp 325-40.

[22] S. G. Ellis, *Tudor frontiers and noble power: the making of the British state* (Oxford, 1995), pp 125-30; Booker, 'Geraldines and the Irish', p. 309; *Crown surveys of lands, 1540-1, with the Kildare Rental begun in 1518*, ed. Gearóid MacNiocaill (Dublin, 1992), pp 232-57.

[23] SP 1/5, f. 15v; Katharine Simms, *Gaelic Ulster in the middle ages: history, culture and society* (Dublin, 2020), p. 212; AFM, 1516; ALC, 1516.

[24] BL, Galba B.III, f. 148v.

[25] SP 60/5, f. 12r; Hall, *Vnion Lancastre and Yorke*, p. 10; Brendan Bradshaw, *Irish constitutional revolution of the sixteenth century* (Cambridge, 1979).

Kildare was restored in a stronger position; the words of Polydore Vergil on the eighth earl's restoration in 1496 as 'primum hominis auctoritas apud Hybernos' are appropriate here.[26]

Meanwhile, a carefully fostered Geraldine image was projected at Court and further afield. The Book of Howth portrayed an undignified Gearóid Mór Fitzgerald devoid of the wit to appreciate courtly decorum. The opposite was more likely to be true, as he was made a Knight of the Garter within a decade. If there is an element of truth in the description, it may be that of his unchanging countenance, the effortless air of nobility and what Castiglione later termed *sprezzatura*.[27] Contemporary descriptions of his king 'suaviter ac saeviter in modo' [a calm demeanour masking a savage intensity] were equally applicable to Ireland's leading old colonial magnate.[28] His chivalric identity and heritage as a conqueror, one augmented through the Fraternity of Arms of St George and later as Knight of the Garter, continued to be projected in various ways. Far from being mere flummery, they were part of a substantive personal project that spanned generations. The extent to which he fully embraced renaissance courtiership can be seen in the more private humanist activities of collecting a library.

At some stage prior to 1531, the eighth or ninth earl acquired 'the ordre of the garter' for their library.[29] The previous governor to be made a Knight of the Garter was John Talbot, first earl of Shrewsbury and Waterford. His 'Talbot-Shrewsbury Book' presented to Margaret of Anjou in 1445 contained extracts from the order's statutes and was decorated with Talbot heraldry.[30] Similarly, Gearóid Mór propagated his *res gestae* while expanding a library that he probably inherited from his father. Late medieval readership was a dynamic, interactive process with delicate implications in terms of status and patronage. The existence of the earl's library was a symbol in itself but its extensive content and the moves to catalogue its items indicated intentions to further expand. It served an aesthetic function and in certain cases was personalised to suit liturgical or ceremonial purposes. The manuscript itemised as 'Scala Cronica in Kyldare' survives with the faintly visible inscription of what appears to be Gearóid Mór's name and family motto, '[Si dieu]

---

[26] Eric Haywood, 'Humanism's priorities and empire's prerogatives: Polydore Vergil's *Description of Ireland*' in PRIA, 109C (2009), pp 195–236; Lennon, *Sixteenth-cen. Ire.*, p. 79. See also Susan Brigden, *New worlds, lost worlds: the rule of the Tudors, 1485–1603* (London, 2001), pp 155–6.

[27] 'The king and the lords could not hold the laughter, but the earl never changed countenance, but told this tale as though he were among his fellows in his country': *Cal. Carew*, v. 180; Bradshaw, *Const. rev.*, p. 73.

[28] Thomas Penn, *Winter king: Henry VII and the dawn of Tudor England* (London, 2011), p. 78.

[29] BL, Harleian MS 3756, f. 97v.

[30] BL, Royal MS 15 E.VI, ff 439r–40v.

plet A moy cest [livre partient] G. vste kyldare'.[31] Items on Juvenal and Virgil were 'cum glosa' but more importantly, two gilded books include a 'psalterium' and a 'Liber Alexandri deauratus'.[32] The psalter survives as a finely illuminated Book of Hours inscribed with obituaries including those of the seventh and eighth earls of Kildare, along with the birth of two sons of Gearóid Óg Fitzgerald.[33] Orisons were inscribed below certain fine illustrations for example, f. 4r, and 'dylyvery' from 'paynes of purgatrey'.[34] If the ornate appearance of the manuscript mirrors its importance, the 'Liber Alexandri' is a revealing item which suggests the value placed on the chivalric medieval cult of Alexander.[35] This highly adaptable trope remains underexplored in the specific context of the late medieval old colonial community. Those particular circumstances confronted by marcher lords were later imperfectly reflected in Stanihurst's demonstrative observation that Ireland was 'in sundry ages seized of diuers good and couragious Alexanders'.[36] Kildare's

---

[31] Corpus Christi College, Cambridge MS 133, f. 3v; BL, Harleian MS 3756, f. 97r; Aisling Byrne, 'Earls of Kildare and their books at the end of the middle ages' in *The Library: Transactions of the Bibliographical Society*, 14 (2013), pp 131, 146. For the king's library, see Kevin Sharpe, *Selling the Tudor monarchy: authority and image in sixteenth-century England* (New Haven, CT, 2009), pp 86-90.

[32] Catalogued as 'Liber Alixandre maugne', c. 1500: BL, Harleian MS 3756, ff 96v, 190v.

[33] The manuscript is stored at Pierpont Morgan Library, New York, MS M.105: Byrne, 'Earls of Kildare', p. 132.

[34] The manuscript was originally illustrated in Rouen, c. 1420-25. It is attributed to the Fastolf Master, who has been associated with the Talbot Master (illustrator of the Talbot Shrewsbury Book): Hugo van der Velden, 'A prayer roll of Henry Beauchamp, earl of Warwick' in J. F. Hamburger and A. S. Korteweg (eds), *Tributes in honor of James H. Marrow: studies in painting and manuscript illumination of the late middle ages and northern renaissance* (London, 2006), p. 540.

[35] Byrne has tentatively identified a (late fifteenth century?) *Liber Alexandri magni de preliis* as a possible title for this text: Byrne, 'Earls of Kildare', p. 145.

[36] Raphael Holinshed, *Chronicles of England, Scotlande and Irelande* (6 vols, London, 1807-8), iv, p. v. The literature on the re-invention of Alexander during the middle ages is vast: Richard Stoneman, *Alexander the Great: a life in legend* (New Haven, CT, 2008). Indirectly related pseudo-Aristotelian works (see ch. 1 and the 'Secreta Secretorum') have likewise been the focus of much scholarship. The Alexander tradition was embraced by the Irish *literati*, a subject that merits further attention: George Cary, *The medieval Alexander* (Cambridge, 1956), pp 15-17, 69; Cameron Wachowich, 'In search of worlds to conquer: echoes of Alexander the Great in medieval Ireland' in *PHCC*, 36 (2016), pp 215-30; Brent Miles, *Heroic saga and classical epic in medieval Ireland* (Woodbridge, 2011), pp 49-57, 78-97, 200-3. The life of Alexander has of course been intensely contested since the Hellenic period. Classicists continue to debate the manner in which commentators across the ages have imposed preconceived or speculative ideas on Alexander. For example, see Bodil Due, 'Alexander's inspiration and ideas' in Jesper Carlsen, Bodil Due, Otto Steen Due and Birte Poulsen (eds), *Alexander the Great: reality and myth* (Rome, 1993), pp 53-60; Kieran McGroarty, 'Did Alexander the Great read Xenophon?' in Mark Humphries and Brian McGing (eds), *Hermthena: a Trinity College Dublin Review, in honour of George Huxley* (Dublin, 2006), pp 105-24. In time, the growing allure of the myth of Alexander also became increasingly malleable.

gilded 'Alixandre maugne' represented simply one strand of a multifaceted, evolving tradition – labyrinthine in its layers of complexity. However, precisely because of this, it is likely that a late medieval Hiberno-English idea of Alexander would complement the exclusive image of the White Earl or the Great Earl as ruling magnates.[37] Indeed, reports of his 'great generalship' were attested to in the English chronicles and the Irish annals. His obituaries, but in particular Flattisbury's words, exemplify this late medieval chivalric ideal in a symbolic colonial setting.[38]

Flattisbury's role in disseminating the Kildare image rendered him a likely compiler of the library catalogue and also as the scribe for the earl's correspondence with the Florentine Gherardini.[39] Referring to the earlier communication with Desmond, Kildare imparted his dynastic standing while enquiring of his 'beloved brethren' in Florence.[40] He enquired of blood relatives in France and what family members live in the 'Roman country'. Kildare also described his position as Ireland's foremost magnate and worthy descendant of the original conquest. The Geraldine origin *mythos* predated this correspondence and while the direct implications of the Gherardini correspondence are unclear, it was keenly exploited by the eighth earl. The Geraldines had by then featured in Cristoforo Landino's commentary on Dante (1481) and in Ugolino di Verino, *De Illustration Urbis Florentiae* (c. 1500) as 'the three brothers of the ancient Geraldines...to mastery as lords of Ireland'.[41] A Geraldine 'aquisto' of Ireland was recounted in Landino's Dantean guide which was itself unveiled in 1481 (reproduced in 1520) at the

---

[37] BL, Harleian MS 3756, f. 96v.
[38] AFM, 1514; ALC, 1513; BL, Add. MS 4787, f. 242v; Ellis, 'Great earl', p. 325.
[39] Lennon, *Sixteenth-cen. Ire.*, pp 83–4. Kildare's 1507 letter to his Tuscan 'cousins' has prompted interest in recent studies: Aisling Byrne, 'Geraldines and the culture of the wider world' in Crooks and Duffy (eds), *Geraldines and medieval Ireland*, pp 278–91: Michael Potterton, 'The Fitzgeralds, Florence, St Fiachra and a few fragments' in Michael Potterton and Thomas Herron (eds), *Dublin and the Pale in the Renaissance, c. 1540–1660*, pp 19–47.
[40] The original is lost. See Abraham Fitzgibbon, 'Appendix to the unpublished Geraldine documents: the Gherardini of Tuscany' in *JRHA*, 4 (1877), pp 247–9; Byrne, 'Geraldines and the culture of the wider world', p. 279; Colm Lennon, 'The making of the Geraldines: the Kildare Fitzgeralds and their historians' in Patrick Cosgrove, Terence Dooley and Karol Mullaney-Dignam (eds), *Aspects of aristocratic life: essays on the Fitzgeralds and Carton House* (Dublin, 2014), p. 71; Fitzgerald, *Geraldines*, pp 16–17. In the context of later decades, see Colm Lennon, 'Pedagogy and reform: the influence of Peter White on Irish scholarship in the Renaissance' in Thomas Herron and Michael Potterton (eds), *Ireland in the Renaissance c. 1540–1660* (Dublin, 2007), p. 51.
[41] 'Tresque Geraldina fratres de gente vetusa...quorum divida Hibernia ductu est Illos occiduis dominos Rex fecit in oris Mauritii (Geraldini)': Ugolino di Verino, *De illustration urbis Florentiae* (Paris, 1790), p. 116. Kildare was noted in a 1505 edition of Duns Scotus' *Enchiridion Fidei* printed in Venice: Michael Bennett, 'Late medieval Ireland in a wider world' in *CHI*, i, 352. See also above, ch. 1 and the bardic accounts of a 'Desmond conquest': Seamus Pender, 'O Clery Genealogies' in *Analecta Hibernica*, 18 (1951), pp 169–72.

Palazzo Vecchio, Florence. Landino places Kildare and Desmond as the foremost lords ('maxime el counte di Childariare el counte di dicimone') on the island. Both Kildare and the Florentine Gherardini corresponded in the belief that neither differed from their progenitors: 'ne noue hauno mutato ne isegne de gli anti chi gherardini'.[42] Among later sixteenth- and seventeenth-century accounts, those of Dominicus O'Daly touched upon the Geraldine vision that had broadened in the years leading up to 1534.[43] With a tone of finality, the completeness of a Geraldine conquest of Ireland through 'great feats of arms' was stressed:

> know then, that my predecessors and ancestors passed from France into England and having remained there for some time, they, in the year 1140 (1170) arrived in this island of Ireland and by their swords obtained great possessions and achieved great feats of arms; and up to the present day have increased and multiplied into many branches and families...I, by the grace of God, possess by hereditary right the earldom, and am Earl of Kildare, holding diverse castles and manors.[44]

'Illustrious' twelfth-century deeds were celebrated but the impression of Ireland as a land of conquest mirrors the circumstances of Kildare's supremacy. As 'deputy of the whole of Ireland', the conquest, and the concept of the *Expugnatio* in prophetic terms, was fulfilled. In this sense alone, the contrast with reform discourse seeking conquest was vast. The use of historical argument denoted an intent to forge a Geraldine saga with a broad scope:

> we are most desirous to know the deeds of our ancestors so that if you have in your possession any history we request you to communicate it to us. We need to know the origin of our house and their numbers, and the names of your ancestors whether there are any of them settled in France and who of our family inhabit the Roman territory. I also wish to know the transactions of the present time, for it gives me great joy always to hear news of our house. If there is anything that we can procure for you through our own labour and industry or anything you have not got, such as hawks, falcons, horses...I beg you will inform me of it as I shall in every way possible endeavour to obey your wishes. God be with you and do you love us in return. Gerald chief in Ireland of the

---

[42] Cristoforo Landino, *Opere del divino poeta Danthe consuoi cometi* (Milan, 1520), pp 10, 249, 383; Byrne, 'Geraldines wider world', p. 279.

[43] From the 'land of Heturia grew a most flourishing vine of Troy, and from Florence...that noble and ancient Geraldine offshoot advanced beyond the Irish sea to the northern shores of Ireland': Diarmaid Ó Catháin, 'Some reflexes of Latin learning and of the Renaissance in Ireland, c. 1450-c. 1600' in Jason Harris and K. C. Sidwell (eds), *Making Ireland Roman: Irish neo-Latin writers and the republic of letters* (Cork, 2009), pp 28-9.

[44] *An account of the facsimiles of the national manuscripts of Ireland*, ed. J. T. Gilbert (Dublin, 1889), p. 473.

family of the Geraldines, Earl of Kildare. Lord Deputy of the most serene King of England in Ireland.[45]

Gifts from Kildare to the king at this time included goshawks and horses, an arrangement that is similarly suggested here.[46] Kildare humanism in general and an Italianate penchant in particular, filter through a wide range of diplomatic sources.[47]

In 1516, the first edition of Ludovico Ariosto's *Orlando Furioso* appeared, canto ten of which enumerated Kildare and Desmond as Ireland's sole representatives among the elite of Christendom:

Now turn to the Irish – they are drawn up on the plain in two squadrons.
   The earl of Kildare leads the first, and the earl of Desmond, from the rugged hills,
   the other. The first has on his standard a flaming pine; the other, argent, a bend gules.[48]

In this poetic muster for crusade, the precedence of Kildare ('la prima') and Desmond ('la seconda') reflects their standing in terms of political power. It is conceivable that it echoes Gearóid Mór's communique with Florence, where peripheral attention was drawn to 'a relation of ours called therle of Desmond'.[49] To be regarded in such a work was of significance. The high profile of the author ensured a circulation among the Italian courtly elite and further afield.[50] Nicollo Machiavelli wrote in late 1517 of reading the 'fine verses of Orlando Furioso told by Ariosto (lo vro lirico...do orlando furioso dillo ariosto)' and was displeased

---

[45] *Facsimiles National Manuscripts Ire.*, p. 473.
[46] The illegal export of 'hawkis and other commodities of the land' were questioned in court records of 1510: *Red Book of the earls of Kildare*, ed. Gearóid MacNiocall (Dublin, 1992), p. 191. Agard, reporting to Cromwell in 1536, found in Fitzgerald's possession '3 or 4 caste of hawkes; and as for privey stuffe, God knowis whatt': *S.P. Hen. VIII*, ii, 244; SP 60/2, f. 131r. Through their rapprochement with Cromwell, the Butlers sent a hawk as a gift to Austin Friars in 1532: Diarmaid MacCulloch, *Thomas Cromwell: a life* (London, 2018), pp 66-7. See also below, ch. 7.
[47] Milanese state papers described Gearóid Óg as 'an English gentleman... master of practically the whole of the country': *Calendar of State Papers and manuscripts in the archives and collections of Milan, 1385-1618*, ed. A. B. Hinds (16 vols, London, 1912), i, 956. For instance, also see *S.P. Hen. VIII*, ii, 140.
[48] *Orlando Furioso: an English prose translation*, ed. Guido Waldman (Oxford, 1974), p. 102. 'Guarda Ibernesi appresso il piano | Sono due squadre, e il Conte di Childera | Mena la prima, e il Conte di Desmonda | Da fiery monti ha tratta la seconda | Nello standardo il primo ha un pino ardent | L'altro nel bianco una vermiglia banda': Ludovico Ariosto, *Orlando Furioso* (London, 1754), p. 99. Also, see Byrne, 'Geraldines wider world', p. 280.
[49] *Facsimiles National Manuscripts Ire.*, p. 473.
[50] For Ariosto and Elizabethan Ireland, see Brigden, *New worlds, lost worlds*, pp 21, 24-32; Suan Brigden, 'Becoming Italianate in sixteenth-century England', Trinity Centre for Early Modern History Seminar Series, TCD, 25 Nov. 2019.

to be overlooked in the roll of poets ('dolgo solo...ne idaro rato pomi') where he was omitted as one would exclude a dog ('inhibbi inscritto idillo comir un canae').[51] Both Machiavelli and Ariosto received d'Este patronage, notably that of Cardinal Ippolito d'Este and Marchioness of Mantua, Isabella d'Este.[52] The family enjoyed both far-reaching political and literary interests. Within a year of Ariosto's publication, a descriptive account of Chiericati's travels in Ireland written for the marchioness referred to Kildare's prominence. Chiericati observed that in mid-Ulster 'the rule of England ceases (et ivi termina il dominio di Anglia)' but the illustrious earl of Kildare was viceroy over the entire island ('da I'll conte de Childara, vicedomino di quel isola').[53]

Like many of the foremost nobility, as demonstrated by Humphrey of Lancaster, duke of Gloucester, who accumulated a library, Kildare pursued a similar project.[54] The eighth earl, and possibly his father Thomas, cultivated a literary collection of cultural, political and symbolic value. The acquisition of texts between c. 1513 and 1531 reflected deepening links with Court and the wider world. Gearóid Óg was a childhood acquaintance of the king and his upbringing at Court inspired investment in his seat of Maynooth.[55] In a humanist, transcultural manner, its contents covered the languages of late medieval English Ireland and ranged from insular psalters to works to Florentine texts. Byrne and Lennon caution against an overemphasis on Italian links, citing a greater influence from the northern renaissance.[56] Yorkist-Burgundian links had connected the late medieval and early Tudor Court with the Low Countries.[57] It is remarkable that no extensive study of the catalogue and its context has been offered until Byrne's paper, given its significance not only for the Kildares but for Ireland's renaissance.[58] Having been a long-term initiative, halted only by the rebellion of 1534, a number of archivists

---

[51] Florence, Biblioteca Nazionale Centrale di Firenze, Palatini Machiavelli I.52, f. 3r.

[52] C. P. Brand, *Ludovico Ariosto: a preface to the Orlando Furioso* (Edinburgh, 1974), pp 9, 115.

[53] J. P. Mahaffy, 'Two early tours in Ireland' in *Hermathena*, 40 (1914), pp 10-11. See also Potterton, 'Fitzgeralds, Florence', pp 19-47; Colm Lennon, 'The Fitzgeralds of Kildare and the building of a dynastic image, 1500-1630' in W. Nolan and T. McGrath (eds), *Kildare: history and society* (Dublin, 2006), pp 195-211.

[54] Alexandra Petrina, *Cultural politics in fifteenth-century England: The case of Humphrey, duke of Gloucester* (Boston, MA, 2004).

[55] A fifteen-year-old Gearóid Óg played a role in the funeral of Henry Tudor's son, Arthur: Lennon, *Sixteenth-cen. Ire.*, p. 79; Ellis, *Ire. Tudors*, pp 18-28; Ian Campbell, 'Irish political thought and intellectual history, 1550- 1730' in *CHI*, ii, pp 507-8.

[56] Byrne, 'Geraldines wider world', p. 279; Lennon, 'Fitzgeralds of Kildare', p. 205.

[57] Malcolm Vale, *The princely court: medieval courts and culture in north-west Europe, 1270-1380* (Oxford, 2001), pp 2-5; Malcolm Vale, *War and chivalry: warfare and aristocratic culture in England, France and Burgundy at the end of the middle ages* (London, 1981).

[58] The catalogue has been printed in: Bryan, *Great earl*; *Crown surveys*. Also, see Catharine Moore, 'The library lists of the eighth and ninth earls of Kildare' (M.A., Trinity College Dublin, 1997).

and learned men were employed for the project. A number of scribes were devoted to the singular task of compiling the catalogue, which itself contained fragments of aesthetic calligraphy.[59] The Kildare library was emblematic of aristocratic martial values, 'feetis of armes of chyvalry' including the crusades, the order of the Knights Garter and the cult of Alexander ('liber Alexandri...siedge of thebes') but it also embraced wider aspects. Works of classical antiquity, devotional texts and chronicles showed a worldview where Kildare, Court and the continent were interlinked. Items of immediate relevance acquired from early in the reign of Henry VIII included the 'kynge of England his answer to Lutter' and 'Sir Thomas Moore his book agayns the new opinions that hold agayns pilgrimags'.[60] Irish manuscripts on the Passion of St George (Thomas, seventh earl of Kildare, and the Fraternity of Arms of St George) and the 'Saltir Casshill', a copy of which was seized by Desmond in 1462, possibly related to the endeavours of earlier generations. Desmond was better known for his 'senchusa Geraltach' but Kildare's interest is suggested by the presence of Torna Óg Ó Maolchonaire in the 'Curragh on Briget's Eve' around the time of the eighth earl.[61]

The opulent seat of Maynooth with its pageantry, music and social pursuits and the careful projection of a dynastic image connected a considerable range of sources, overlooked in terms of political import and wider meanings.[62] At some stage in the late medieval period, stone vaults were constructed to replace wooden floors in the donjon of Maynooth castle.[63] Among the finery and trappings listed in Kildare's inventory of 1518 were gilded 'candelstyks with my lords armys', a

---

[59] For example, see the ornate capital 'In primis': BL, Harleian MS 3756, f. 96v; Byrne, 'Earls of Kildare', p. 135.

[60] For a discussion of each text, see Byrne, 'Earls of Kildare', pp 283-90.

[61] RIA, MS 23 D.17, f. 123r; Miles Dillon, 'Laud Misc. 610 (cont.)' in *Celtica* 6 (1963), pp 138-9. Bradshaw suggests that the Irish contents of the library indicated there was ethnic harmony before the 1530s: Bradshaw, *Const. rev.*, p. 27. Raymond Gillespie posits a connection between Thomas Fitzgerald as a minor with James, seventh earl of Desmond through the large number of Irish language texts: Raymond Gillespie, 'The Fitzgeralds and the making of the manor of Maynooth' in Patrick Cosgrove, Terence Dooley and Karol Mullaney-Dignam (eds), *Aspects of aristocratic life: essays on the Fitzgeralds and Carton House* (Dublin, 2014), p. 40. Simms adds that the Kildare Geraldines were relative latecomers to bardic poetry and *seanchaide*: Simms, *Gaelic Ulster*, pp 21-3, 243-58.

[62] See also Potterton, 'Fitzgeralds, Florence', pp 19-47; Raymond Gillespie, 'Singing and society 1540-1700', Choral music in Ireland: history and evolution, Chamber Choir Ireland (31 Jan. 2020); Susan Flavin, *Consumption and culture in sixteenth-century Ireland: saffron, stockings and silk* (Woodbridge, 2014), p. 121; Lennon, *Sixteenth-cen. Ire.*, p. 72.

[63] Alan Hayden, 'Maynooth castle, co. Kildare: excavation of the donjon' (unpublished archaeological report lodged with the National Monuments Service, Ireland, 2013), pp 16-17. The 'north west side of the dungen' was pounded when 'beseaged' in 1535: *S.P. Hen. VIII*, ii, 236; SP 60/2, f. 97r.

'standing cupp with a couer and my lordis armys in the myddes'.[64] Attention to detail reflected the highly refined dynamics of courtly hospitality. Sources are limited but the 'cher' referred to by Edgecombe in Maynooth was still an example of a highly charged political encounter.[65] Details for the setting can be in part recreated from the *Rental*. Ornaments of precious metal from across the continent included a number of Spanish items.[66] Contact with the Court, where the ninth earl resided for four months as recently as 1515, and the politics of gift giving may explain the origin of certain items.[67] Given the active interest in the Italian Gherardini, a Tuscan-born Bishop Alessandro Geraldini of Santa Domingo (Spain) who served at Court up to 1519 may account for some of the exchanges. A humanist scholar and tutor to Catherine of Aragon, Bishop Geraldini also served in a diplomatic capacity, advising the king in 1517 that 'de familia Geraldina' produced many eminent prelates.[68] As 'dominican bishop apud indos', he was present at Greenwich that year 'to exhort the king against the infidels'.[69] Claiming to be a historian and having written 'much that is approved by all men of learning', the pope and the emperor placed him in the service of Catherine.[70] He dined at Greenwich while the Kildare agent Anthony Knevet attended upon the Spanish ambassador and it is feasible that Kildare and the Geraldine bishop interacted through Knevet.[71]

Indeed, the eighth earl had expressed a desire to know of other Geraldines in the 'Roman country'.[72] According to Sebastian Giustinian, Wolsey held the Geraldine bishop in little regard and in 1518 a letter appealing for the king's favour included extensive references to 'fragmenta philostrati de liberalitate ad tyrii', Flavius Philostratus' *Life of Appolonius of Tyanna*, claiming that Henry is no tyrant.[73] The Butler servant Robert Cowley may have been privy to Wolsey's disapproval when later denouncing Knevet for having 'opteyned the bisshoprik of Kildare to a simple Irish preste, a vagabounde without lernyng maners of good qualitye...not worthy to bee a hally water clerc'. Cowley concluded by warning against articles presented by Bathe 'feynyng it to bee for the reformacion of Irland' and in criticising the writer's Geraldine affinity, and added the loaded remark that he had 'noo more experience of the land, then I have in Ytally'.[74] It would

---

[64] BL, Harleian MS 3756, f. 13r.
[65] BL, Titus B.XI, f. 283v.
[66] Marian Lyons, *Church and society in County Kildare* (Dublin, 2000), p. 86.
[67] For comments on gift giving, see Flavin, *Cons. cult.*, pp 5, 64, 146.
[68] *LP*, ii, 1183.
[69] *LP*, ii, 1114-15.
[70] *LP*, ii, 1301-2.
[71] *LP*, ii, 1021.
[72] Fitzgibbon, 'Gherardini of Tuscany', pp 247-9.
[73] LPL, MS 602, f. 36r.
[74] *S.P. Hen. VIII*, ii, 141-2.

have been characteristic of Wolsey to insist on the appointments to ecclesiastical office. Wolsey opposed Fitzgerald in the see of Kildare but it is also conceivable that his anti-Geraldine stance links Bishop Geraldini.[75] Despite the fragmentary records, a considerable courtly context may be gleaned from Kildare's broad dynastic vision.

A further significant characteristic of the Kildare inventory was an item that was likely to have been of regional relevance. Similar to the Butler heirloom passed from the White Earl to the seventh earl and Thomas Boleyn, the inventory also records a 'great horne, brownd with silver and gylt'.[76] Such a vessel was associated with the kingship of Leinster which the MacMurrough charter horn symbolised.[77] Surpassing even the 'great and rich' trappings of Maynooth castle, the 'Rent Table' unveiled in 1533 was another endeavour that reflected the continuity between the eighth and ninth earls.[78] That each name is carved in relief on the table suggests the fruition of a long-term project. This elaborate material symbol of overlordship sprang from the preceding decades of formal submissions and the *Rental* itself even records a ritualised 'forme of doing homage' to the earl.[79] The ideas that underlay the commissioning of the 'Rent Table' and related projects originated with the previous generation, as with the establishment of the collegiate church.

Located in front of Maynooth castle, this quasi-academic establishment was not simply a Geraldine image of princely piety.[80] Much of the original building has now been reconstructed in St Mary's Church (of Ireland) but the crypt and tower survive, its north and west sides presently adjacent to St Patrick's College, Maynooth. Founded as the College of the Blessed Virgin Mary in the devotional fashion of mainland Europe, as Lyons observes, it was a notable endeavour at a time when monasticism was in decline and learned clergy were in short supply. A licence to endow the college was granted by Archbishop of Dublin, William Rokeby in 1518. At its inception it was to support a master and five fellows along with additional clerks. Nomination of the master and sub-master was vested in the

---

[75] It was in the diocese of Kildare that Gearóid Óg Fitzgerald encountered difficulties, at least in the 1520s. During a lengthy *sede vacante*, the earl quarrelled with Wolsey but continued to enjoy many diocesan benefits throughout the decade: Lyons, *Church and soc.*, ch. 2.
[76] BL, Harleian MS 3756, f. 99v. See also David Beresford, 'The Butlers in England and Ireland, 1405-1515' (Ph.D., Trinity College Dublin, 1999), p. 301.
[77] See above, ch. 1; also Katharine Simms, 'The barefoot kings: literary image and reality in later medieval Ireland' in *PHCC*, 30 (2010), pp 7-8.
[78] 'FILIUS GERALDI'. See also below, ch. 6. The inscription on the table includes the motto of the Kildares, which commonly appeared in the deeds of both the eighth and ninth earls. See for instance the contents of their library and an early grant made in 1474 which shows the earl's seal matrix which preserves the faintly discernible motto with the Kildare arms: NLI, D 1790.
[79] BL, Harleian MS 3756, f. 48r.
[80] Lyons, *Church and soc.*, pp 36, 87-88; Bryan, *Great earl*, p. 260.

earl while the archbishop was to oversee investiture of spiritualties.[81] A separate chantry chapel seems to have been constructed within the castle grounds in the 1510s but its precise location is uncertain.[82] Geraldine ecclesiastical patronage merits, as it has already, an entire study in itself. As a central tenet of culture and politics, it underpinned much of what is discussed here. Kildare's successful exercise of power required a careful balance between the church *inter Anglicos* and *inter Hibernicos*, complicated by marches with co-existing cultures.[83] Co-operation with the church hierarchy was vital due to their role in arbitration and even mediation in the delegation of power.[84] Influence through the Knights Hospitaller has been broached in earlier chapters, yet Kildare's island-wide church patronage was sought through a variety of means. For example, through co-ordination with Desmond, Kildare distributed benefices in the diocese of Limerick.[85]

When the eighth earl was interred in his chantry chapel in Christ Church Cathedral, it sealed a significant phase in the family's ascent. Known during his lifetime as the 'lord of Kildare's chapel', this constructive chantry was erected in 1510, placed in the main body of the quire and with an altar dedicated to the Virgin Mary.[86] Its ornate wooden screens were grandiose and Anglo-centric in design, befitting his other endowments.[87] Vestments were bestowed during his life

---

[81] John Healy, *Maynooth college 1785-1895* (Dublin, 1895), pp 131-2; Lyons, *Church and soc.*, p. 87; Marian Lyons, 'The foundation of the Geraldine College of the Blessed Virgin Mary, Maynooth, 1518' in *JKA*, 18 (1994-5), pp 134-50.

[82] Gillespie, 'Manor of Maynooth', p. 42; Lyons, *Church and soc.*, p. 85.

[83] For example, in 1523 Kildare impressed upon Wolsey the *realpolitik* of seeking spiritual rights in the Irishry: SP 60/1, f. 84r; James Murray, *Enforcing the English reformation in Ireland, clerical resistance and political conflict in the diocese of Dublin* (Cambridge, 2009), pp 27, 71, 85-6; Lyons, *Church and soc.*, pp 73-4; Brendan Scott, *Religion and reformation in the Tudor diocese of Meath* (Dublin, 2007), pp 36-7.

[84] For instance, note diplomacy through Bishop Barrett of Annaghdown and indentures between Kildare and Richard III: BL, Harleian MS 433, f. 266r.

[85] The Geraldines were conservative in dispersing positions according to the recipient's cultural background: Booker, 'Geraldines and the Irish', pp 301-9; Sparky Booker, *Cultural exchange and identity in late medieval Ireland: the English and Irish of the four obedient shires* (Cambridge, 2018), pp 97-100; Katherine Walsh, 'The clerical estate in later medieval Ireland: alien settlement and society in medieval Ireland' in John Bradley (ed.), *Settlement and society in medieval Ireland* (Kilkenny, 1988), pp 361-78.

[86] Clerical assent was required: Tadhg O'Keeffe, *Medieval Irish buildings* (Dublin, 2015), p. 170. Donough Bryan cited the campaigns and patronage during 1512 as indicative of Kildare and destroyer and creator: Bryan, *Great earl*, p. 260; Roger Stalley, 'The architecture of the cathedral and priory buildings, 1250-1530' in Kenneth Milne (ed.), *Christ Church Cathedral, Dublin: a history* (Dublin, 2000), p. 105; Edward Seymour, *Christ Church Cathedral, Dublin* (Dublin, 1869), p. 31.

[87] Stalley, 'Architecture, cathedral and priory', p. 105. Relief tiles commissioned with the Kildare coat of arms were to be found at Christ Church cathedral, St Patrick's cathedral and Bective Abbey: E. S. Eames and Thomas Fanning, *Irish medieval tiles: decorated medieval paving tiles in Ireland with an inventory of sites and designs and a visual index* (Dublin, 1988), pp 47-8.

and in his will, the obits of the Cathedral noting a 'cloak of purple and cloth of gold', possibly similar to the late fifteenth-century 'Magi Cope' of Christ Church, Waterford.[88] Detailed liturgical arrangements were made and the obits were fulsome for both Thomas, seventh earl of Kildare, and his son, Gerald the lord deputy ('dominus Geraldus comes Kyldare ac deputatus Hybernie') who offered vestments of cloth of gold ('vestimentorum de panno aureo').[89] There is here a sense of the deputyship as a birthright and the ninth earl would have anticipated a comparable undertaking for his legacy. Events in the 1530s, however, would overturn any aspirations of the ninth earl for a family mausoleum in the cathedral.

It has not been widely appreciated that the formative decades after Henry VII's restoration of Gearóid Mór heralded the expanding Kildare horizons. Both a pre-existing military base and efficient estate management drove an effective island-wide strategy, which have been well studied, but their projections in cultural terms shed light on the scope of Geraldine exceptionalism. Furthermore, their particular representations of Ireland as a land of conquest were essentially characterised in conceptual terms by their present fulfilment of the twelfth-century conquest through both martial reinforcement and diplomatic means. England's priorities in terms of conquest as such were to be in France or to the east. In this sense, the aforementioned Knights Hospitaller were unique with regards to ecclesiastical patronage and political influence. Regarding policy or perspectives on conquest, Kilmainham could be seen as a weathervane. Scrutiny of the broad Kildare position materialised in the early Tudor intervention through John Rawson. The Geraldine status quo, amplified through cultural endeavours that often placed a subtle emphasis on the eastward conquest for Christendom, thus offered a different perspective on Ireland. Naturally, the ideal of crusade for Christendom was not solely a Geraldine preserve, nor was the *Expugnatio* exclusive to proponents of the military conquest of Ireland. But it became increasingly clear that priorities in terms of where conquest was to be pursued were determined by a relationship to power. The later cultural patronage of Gearóid Óg has been identified as the apotheosis of their renaissance pursuits, but projections of a Kildare image in the broadest possible sense predated even the reign of Henry VIII. In what amounted to humanist diplomacy, their construction of a dynastic identity and attention to the political rhythms of court culture reveal how Ireland's early sixteenth-century renaissance was determined by particular circumstances and moreover, distinctive Irish conditions.

---

[88] These surviving vestments were Florentine-made: Catriona MacLeod, 'Fifteenth-century vestments in Waterford' in *JRSA*, 52 (1952), pp 85-98; Seymour, *Christ Church*, p. 31.

[89] It seems that Thomas's effigy was later moved to nearby St Werburgh's Church: *The book of obits and martyrology of the cathedral church of the Holy Trinity, commonly called Christ Church, Dublin*, ed. J. C. Crosthwaite (Dublin, 1844), pp 48, 57; Stalley, 'Architecture, cathedral and priory', p. 94.

Amidst this remarkable renaissance activity there were countervailing forces which created considerable tension within the earl of Kildare's strategic operations. From the 1510s, as their enemies became increasingly vocal, the Geraldines faced growing challenges to which the following chapter is now going to turn. The interventionist anti-Geraldine lobby, with its bitter yet sophisticated rhetoric, was on the whole a response to the vigour of the Kildare position. In a sense, it also reflected the considerable scope of Geraldine monumentalism. From its inception, it appears that this movement was itself distinguished by humanist leanings and a manner of renaissance diplomacy of its own.

4

Salus Populi, Geraldine 'decay', c. 1512–19

By the death of Henry Tudor, complaints against Kildare had evolved in terms of detail, polemic import and sophistication. This literature of decay, long a feature of political commentary on the lordship, was invigorated by protégés of Wolsey. Far more so than his predecessors, the Cardinal cultivated patronage in Ireland and apparently sought, or was at least receptive to such petitions. Most notable in this respect were prelates John Kite, Hugh Inge and William Rokeby. In contrast to the impression given by the archive, criticism of Kildare-induced decay did not originate under Henry VIII much less in the year 1515 as implied in the printed State Papers.[1] A number of Henrician treatises have traditionally been associated with this *annus mirabilis* that has been seen to mark the emergence of humanist reform rhetoric in the lordship.[2] The summer months of 1515, between Sir William Darcy's indictment of Kildare at Court and the return of Gearóid Óg with favour, seems to have signalled that conquest lobbyists were regarded, in the memorable quip of one leading historian, as the 'pratlings of Polonius'.[3] The volume and vigour of anti-Kildare reform rhetoric from the late 1520s has tended to divert the attention of historians from the preceding developments and the earliest of these documents.[4] The 'poletique' and at times watchful approach of Henry Tudor came to enable diplomatic circles cultivated by Fox but more so Wolsey which offered channels of communication for voices opposed to an ascendant ruling magnate. In 1506,

---

[1] The potentially misleading categorisations and post-1534 prism of the State Papers are exemplified through analysis of its opening document entitled the 'State of Ireland and plan for its reformation (1515)'. In the nineteenth-century edition of the State Papers this tract has been dated to 1515 on the vague grounds of 'internal evidence': *S.P. Hen. VIII*, ii, p. ii. See also Christopher Maginn, 'Continuity and change: 1470-1550' in *CHI*, i, 300-28. The concept of reform was alive throughout the late medieval period: Peter Crooks, 'Factions, feuds and noble power in the lordship of Ireland, c. 1356-1496' in *IHS*, 35 (2006-7); Peter Crooks, 'The structure of politics in theory and practice, 1210- 1541' in *CHI*, i, 441-68.

[2] Bennett, Marshall and Crooks have located the tract in its earlier context. Their long-term currency, as Heffernan shows, can be seen in Elizabethan discourse but a variety of later proposals was conceived during the Henrician period.

[3] Brendan Bradshaw, *Irish constitutional revolution of the sixteenth century* (Cambridge, 1979), p. 36.

[4] David Heffernan, *Debating Tudor policy in sixteenth-century Ireland: 'reform' treatises and political discourse* (Manchester, 2018), p. 29.

when Henry VII 'entendythe god willinge to make a viage personall in his most noble personn', consideration was likely given to the disruption of Geraldine governance and patronage of office. The 'warr...continued by Ebren [O'Brien] of the wilde irishe' apparently prompted the king's intention to campaign with a force of 6000 men but the precise motive remains unclear.[5]

As early as the 1480s, Ormond and the city of Waterford, particularly the Wise family, provided the crown with what was considered valuable information regarding circumstances in the lordship. Chief baron of the exchequer John Wyse had been charged to account for the 'maner of this lande' and he has been credited with the military 'Discruption of the power of Irishmen'.[6] Wise echoed an opinion likely passed on the king, specifically to 'distrue the coyne and lyvre that [over-mighty lords] takit ther [right] that the land may the better be remedyed by you as it dyd sumtyme by your noble auncesters'.[7] Interests of the 'loyal' city of Waterford were addressed in the 1510s, while the narrative of Ireland's decay was boded forth from late in the reign of Henry VII.[8] A late fifteenth- or early sixteenth-century 'Descriptio Hiberniae' was written in this context. Locating Ireland 'west uppon Damfayse in Scotlend' the general impression of this geographical survey was one of decay.[9] The king's honour, revenues and the merits of bringing the land 'undir due obeduince' were noted, as was the annual income 'of olde tyme' over 30,000 marks from Ulster alone. Historical context is given, specifying that this was in the 'reede erll is dayes, greet besides vousons of Churches or wards... and many oyerthinges'.[10]

The Lordship of Ireland came into greater focus at Court in the early 1510s. John Rawson's appointment as prior of Kilmainham in 1511 occurred as various regional complaints regarding the decay of the Englishry were given credence.[11] As

---

[5] *Select cases in the council of Henry VII*, ed. Bernard Quaritch (London, 1958), p. 46.
[6] *Ormond deeds*, iv, 336; Christopher Maginn and S. G. Ellis, *Tudor discovery of Ireland* (Dublin, 2015), pp 41, 80-9; Heffernan, *Tudor policy*, pp 9-10.
[7] *Ormond deeds*, iv, 336-7; Maginn and Ellis, *Tudor discov. Ire.*, p. 130.
[8] See for example the confirmation of Waterford liberties: SP 60/1, ff 99; SP 60/2, f. 1r-2v. Patricians of the Pale and towns with their royal charters had a vested interest in order and participation in government: Bradshaw, *Const. rev.*, pp 34-6.
[9] See the 'State' (c. 1515) and a proposal to settle east Ulster against the Scots.
[10] SP 60/1, f. 7r. Richard de Burgh, second earl of Ulster and third baron of Connaught, was known as the 'Red Earl' (1259-1326). He was a rival of John Fitzgerald, first earl of Kildare. The period after his death was notable for the merging of Irish lineage and laws: K. W. Nicholls, *Gaelic and gaelicised Ireland in the middle ages* (Dublin, 1972), p. 12. Negligible revenue receipts during the fifteenth century had slowly improved under the early Tudors: S. G. Ellis, *Reform and revival: English government in Ireland 1470-1534* (Woodbridge, 1986); D. B. Quinn, 'Guide to English financial records for Irish history, 1461-1558, with illustrative extracts, 1461-1509' in *AH*, 10 (1941), pp 17-27.
[11] SP 60/1, ff 147; Maginn and Ellis, *Tudor discov. Ire.*, p. 143. 'In this the king takes notic that the lord master of the Rodes... by his bull utterly dischauryge Sr Robert Everes Priores (and)

Maginn observes, from this decade there were certain benign implications to the preference for the term Irish rebels as opposed to Irish enemies.[12] With O'Donnell also knighted at Court in 1511, there was an intense period of petitioning from many quarters as the new regime settled. Similarly, it seems that the death of Gearóid Mór Fitzgerald gave occasion to a wave of timely anti-Geraldine pleas. Reform literature was produced in a dynamic environment where political intelligence was actively sought and as new information became available.[13] Kite, Rokeby and Inge, in the words of the latter, were mindful of Wolsey's 'manyfole and great urgent causes' and supplicated for his 'graciouse favours'.[14] By the mid-1510s the Cardinal was informed of the 'false confederacion' between Piers Butler and Desmond with their 'grettest Irish lordes yownyng un to him' that carried the 'fere of rebellion'. Kildare was expected to act to maintain order.[15] There are, as Heffernan points out, close parallels between concerns relayed by Kite in 1514 and the 'State' (c. 1515). The tract echoed the land's resources which, 'with out helpe of godde charite off most victoriusse kynge all shall decay'.[16] According to Kite, there was honour in prioritising the conquest of Ireland and stated that the king was

> moche bounde to reforme ys lande as to mayntayne the goode order and justice off england, more bound (than) to subdueu them than Jewes or Sarycenes, for relygyon, Chrystes faithe, obedyence to the church untu us, for lakke of the temporall swerde is scant...grett revenyes of his lost ryghtes and tytles off which revenyes now agynst the chirche and chrystes faith.[17]

---

had committed to his trusty and welbeloved conncellor Sr John Rawson': BL, Add. MS 4791, f. 200v.

[12] Maginn, 'Civ.' Gaelic Leinster, p. 74.

[13] Maginn and Ellis, Tudor discov. Ire., p. 23. Although Bradshaw argues that a traditional mould had been broken through humanism and an 'Anglo-Irish reforming milieu' there was also continuity with earlier generations in terms of the basic strategy of 'conquest'. The state paper format, as Heffernan, Maginn and Ellis have recently pointed out, was new: Bradshaw, Const. rev., pp 33, 37, 49-57; Heffernan, Tudor policy, p. 30; Maginn and Ellis, Tudor discov. Ire., p. 137; Sixteenth-cen. Ire., pp 82-3. See also A. B. Ferguson, Clio unbound: perception of the social and cultural past in Renaissance England (Durham, NC, 1979); A. B. Ferguson, The articulate citizen and the English Renaissance (Durham, NC, 1965).

[14] SP 60/1, f. 8r.

[15] SP 60/1, f. 11r.

[16] The original Salus Populi is lost but fragments of narrative from it enable some reconstruction of the original document. It contained numerous sections or 'books' the first of which recounts a 'prophetic' dialogue where St Brigid received a revelation from the 'secret divine' in the form of an angel. The oppressed underclass of the king's commons made 'feble' through coign and livery are prophesied to revive by means of military intervention. See also Heffernan, Tudor policy, p. 30; Bradshaw, Const. rev., pp 49-57.

[17] SP 60/1, f. 4r. This rings true for a voice of complaint from Armagh, but the diocese of Meath, the proposed starting point for reconquest in the 'State' (c. 1515) may be considered

Kite, Inge and Rokeby were alive to the king's ambitions within and for Christendom. These were broad concepts subject to interpretation and varying points of emphasis, one of which was Pope Leo X in his desire for unity and the ideal of crusade.[18] Anxieties existed from European rivalries and a campaign against England as an alternative to war 'sur les sarrasines' was one such option.[19] In 1513 both Thomas Spinelly and Surrey scrutinised French naval activity, colourfully remarking that their intents were to 'go in to purgatory as to the trade'.[20] Some complaints against Kildare were connected to foreign intelligence, such as Bonnivet's dispatch to Wolsey touching suspicious contact between the earl and French merchants ('conte de guildarue ine Irlande qui faet pl avere mauchaines francoise').[21] William Knight (like Inge, a Wykehamist and New College Oxford alumni) vaguely warned of succour given to Castillian envoys 'by fortune in Ireland in thir wylde partes'.[22] A notable account survives of Archduke Ferdinand (younger brother of Charles) forced to land in Kinsale due to stormy seas in June 1518. Desmond appears to have corresponded with the king as a result.[23]

It was commonly acknowledged that before Surrey's term as lord lieutenant, 'so numerous (were) complaints' against Kildare, that a diverse anti-Geraldine lobby was surprisingly unified.[24] Denunciations of Kildare appeared in documents not normally perceived to be of a political nature, such as the 1513 'note' of the earlier Act of Marches and Maghery, which fused the decay of the lordship and the 'treasons' of Kildare.[25] With the succession of the ninth earl, a claim from

---

('begynne... amonges the kinges subgettes of the countye of Meathe'): SP 60/1, f. 25r. For Gaelic influences in the Meath clergy, see Michael Haren, 'Social structures of the Irish church: a new source in Papal penitentiary dispensations for illegitimacy' in Ludwig Schmugge (ed.), *Illegitimität im Spätmittelalter* (Munich, 1994), p. 212.

[18] *LP*, iii, 247-8.

[19] In this case, Wolsey was informed in 1517 that money raised by Francis I for a crusade could be used against England; 'cest tresmimal faiet donner Indnlgeres areter princes': BL, Caligula E.I, f. 177v.

[20] SP 1/3, f. 201r; BL, Galba B.III, f. 148v.

[21] BL, Caligula E.I, f. 226v.

[22] They received 'ofwoulde much humanyte as among suche people': BL, Galba B.VI, f. 56v.

[23] Hiram Morgan with Dorothy Convery, *Ireland 1518: Archduke Ferdinand's visit to Kinsale and the Dürer connection* (Cork, 2015); Hiram Morgan, 'Archduke Ferdinand's visit to Kinsale in Ireland, an extract from Le Premier voyage de Charles-Quint en Espagne, de 1517 à 1518', online at celt.ucc.ie. A colourful account by Laurent Vital spoke of the dangers beyond the walled towns ('les manans de la ville ne oseroyent aller hors de la ville en leurs affaires'): *LP*, ii, 1327-8. In terms of anthropological perceptions, it was an enthusiastic encounter with the primitive savage: *Collection des voyages des souverains des Pays-Bas*, ed. Charles Piot Gachard (4 vols, Brussels, 1881) iii, 289.

[24] AC 1519. See also Bradshaw, *Const. rev.*, p. 33; Ciaran Brady, *Chief governors: the rise and fall of reform government in Tudor Ireland, 1536-1588* (Cambridge, 1994), p. 6; Heffernan, *Tudor policy*, pp 35-6, 45.

[25] NLI, MS 2507, f. 56v. 'Sinistre' polemic was heeded to be a cause of strife in the

within the family became an issue. Complaints against Gearóid Óg by Elizabeth St John (second wife of the eighth earl) mentioning the 'uttr distruccion' of lands were scrutinised at Court. Kildare was allegedly responsible for land 'made waste bi dali oppressions of coyne and lyvre' including parts of Uriel [Louth] and Cooley ('a parcell of...landes named Coyle'). Dubious privileges were granted to the 'kyngesirishenimy called the grete o neale a shrowde presedent that the kynges depute to grant tributt...of the kynges sbjects to the kyngesirishenimyes... said landdes bieth in the possession of the said wyldirishenimyes...to the uttr distruccon of me and my children without your grace and your noble connsaill loke upon hit'.[26] The interchangeable 'kynges' and 'wylde' Irish enemies in this instance carry subtle pejorative implications. Phonetically, the term here suggests repeated use. Furthermore, O'Neill's regional incursions were pointed out in the 'State' (c. 1515) and also frequently thereafter.[27]

With Wolsey's continued elevation in the governance of the realm, he was presented with what is now printed in the *State Papers* as the 'State of Ireland and plan for its reformation (1515)'. Essentially a push for a military policy while denouncing Kildare and the decay of the lordship, the document is in many ways a most unconventional 'state paper' correspondence. Inspired by an earlier (now lost) anonymous Latin didactic text entitled *Salus Populi*, its author is known only through the pseudonym 'Pandar'.[28] The 'State' (c. 1515) offers a detailed overview of the late medieval colony, describing the geo-politics of the island and its inherent nature as a land of continual war. As with other treatises, a historical background was given on the neglect of the lordship in previous centuries and the king's lost titles. Degenerate feudal magnates had decayed English institutions while the use of native extortions was endemic.[29] The use of Irish weaponry by those of English blood had accelerated the decline of the colony and the training of skilled archers and the provision of armour were requested. The settlement of east Ulster and the reduction of a corridor linking Dublin with the southeast

---

aforementioned endentures of 1496: Agnes Conway, *Henry VII's relations with Scotland and Ireland 1485-1498* (Cambridge, 1932), pp 227-9.

[26] SP 60/1, f. 29r.

[27] In 1535 Skeffington was instructed to 'exclude Neile Mor out of our shire of Uryell ... the untrewest man towardes Us within those partes': SP 60/2, f. 189r. For Geraldine-induced decay in Uriel, see Harold O'Sullivan, 'Dynamics of regional development' in Ciaran Brady and Jane Ohlmeyer (eds), *British interventions in early modern Ireland* (Cambridge, 2005), pp 52-3.

[28] The original *Salus Populi* derived its title from *De Legibus* of Cicero: 'salus populi suprema lex esto' [the health of the people should be the highest law], promoting the idea of imperial intervention for the welfare of citizens. Inge, Kite, Darcy among others framed their work around this concept. See Heffernan, *Tudor policy*, pp 30-1; Andrew Dyck, *A commentary on Cicero, de Legibus* (Ann Arbor, MI, 2004), p. 32.

[29] Namely the earldom of Ulster since the death of the Earl Marshal: SP 60/1, ff 18.

along the Barrow valley were also presented as necessary strategies. Additionally, it was stated that a royal progress must be preceded by the removal of Hugh Boy O'Neill (Clandeboy) from Ulster as far south as Greencastle.[30] But it is also notable for its extensive cultural references and literary allusions. Classified as a state paper, its length and content resembled a substantial reform treatise but equally so, a humanist text.

The manuscript at Kew published as the 'State' (c. 1515) is not the only version of the source. An 'Abstract' of the *Salus Populi*, BL Add. MS 4792, is a sixteenth-century copy of a document that arguably predates the SP 60 manuscript. The 'Abstract' provides greater details of the original *Salus Populi* and since it more closely resembles the original 'booke in Latin', it seems to have been a bridge between the *urtext* and the 'State' (c. 1515). Differing at various stages, the 'Abstract' appears to be a slightly less polished version of the State Paper.[31] The 'State' (c. 1515) has intrigued historians since the late sixteenth century when Richard Stanihurst enumerated the 'Pandar' among the learned men of Ireland.[32] Most historians have assigned an author based solely on reading the 'state paper' manuscript. Brendan Bradshaw proposed that the tract was written by an embittered William Darcy who was excluded from Kildare's council.[33] Dean White attributed the tract to William Rokeby, on the grounds that assuming the date of the State Paper commission is correct, he was present at Court from the summer of 1515 and would have had an opportunity to present the tract in person.[34] Fitzsimons and Heffernan attribute the document to John Kite, Archbishop of Armagh, citing strong circumstantial evidence through Kite's correspondence

---

[30] Brady, *Chief gov.*, p. 249; Heffernan, *Tudor policy*, pp 10, 27–34, 64. Heffernan draws attention to this as the earliest such proposal undertaken in later policies. See also Maginn and Ellis, *Tudor discov. Ire.*; *Cal. S. P. Ire.*, ed. Ellis and Murray, pp 2–3. Of relevance here is the remonstrance against Kildare by Elizabeth St John: SP 60/1, f. 29r.

[31] A seventeenth-century copy of the 'Abstract' is housed in Trinity College Dublin: TCD, MS 842, ff 34r–49v. A further copy of this version made in the nineteenth century is stored in the John Rylands Library, Manchester, possibly transcribed by the antiquarian, Denis H. Kelly (1799–1877): Crawford MS 54 (available on microfilm, NLI, pos. 4797). Also, see Heffernan, *Tudor policy*, p. 18.

[32] Raphael Holinshed, *Chronicles of England, Scotlande and Irelande* (6 vols., London, 1807–8). Ware stated that this 'Pandarus, or the author of the book De Salute Populi' was a fifteenth-century Irish writer treating of the 'causes and calamities' of Ireland: *The whole works of Sir James Ware concerning Ireland*, ed. Walter Harris (2 vols, Dublin, 1764), ii, 90. J. A. Froude and Frederick Furnivall were similarly enticed by the enigmatic pseudonym, yet content to accept its anonymity: J. A. Froude, *The English in Ireland* (3 vols, London, 1884), i, 32. It was not until the twentieth century that attempts were made to identify the author.

[33] Bradshaw, *Const. rev.*, p. 38.

[34] Dean White, 'The Tudor plantations in Ireland before 1571' (Ph.D., Trinity College Dublin, 1968), p. 27.

with Wolsey in 1514. This particular correspondence outlined a number of concerns and proposals identical to those of the 'State' (c. 1515).[35]

Scholars have also examined the 'Abstract', with Bennett in particular focusing on the original *Salus Populi* in the light of both the 'Abstract' and the 'state paper'.[36] Bennett argues that the *Salus Populi* was a mid-fifteenth-century work by Nicholas Lassy, who it is claimed was also the author of the *Libelle of Englyshe Polycye* (1436). His recounting of the *Salus Populi* through extant material and related earlier sources demonstrates a vibrant scholarly dimension to the political discourse of Yorkist Ireland.[37] By the 1510s there was evidently a growing appetite at Court for the augmentation of policy within what the 'Abstract' describes as 'rolles of rhetoric'. This has been overlooked in terms of early Tudor Irish political rhetoric. Bennett points out a reference to the fall of Constantinople in 1453 in the final prophecy of the Pandar, which he notes as being topical in the 1460s and 1470s.[38] Despite the avenues opened by the aforementioned studies, much of the existing historiography tends to employ the 'State' (c. 1515) as the first word on Ireland under Tudor expansion. For reasons outlined below, it is here proposed that Huge Inge (Bishop of Meath 1512-21, Archbishop of Dublin 1521-8) was the author. It is also arguable that the author of the 'State' (c. 1515) was the 'Pandar' himself, on the grounds that the writer intimately identified with the original *Salus Populi*. Perhaps having been styled as such in a suggestive nod to his mentor or having been cordially given the pseudonym by Wolsey, there are various clues in the different versions that present a case for Inge's authorship.

The 'State' (c. 1515) and the 'Abstract' were likely to have been written before 1515.[39] In each case the projected re-conquest or reformation of Ireland is also expressed through prophetic narrative.[40] Such discourse can be untangled to shed

---

[35] Fiona Fitzsimons, 'Cardinal Wolsey, the native affinities and the failure of reform in Henrician Ireland', in David Edwards (ed.), *Regions and rulers in Ireland 1100-1650* (Dublin, 2004), p. 84; Heffernan, *Tudor policy*, pp 30-7.

[36] Maginn and Ellis, *Tudor discov. Ire.*, pp 137-9; Maginn, 'Continuity and change', p. 316; Michael Bennett, 'The Libelle of English policy: the matter of Ireland' in Linda Clark (ed.), *The fifteenth century XV: writing, records and rhetoric* (Woodbridge, 2017), pp 1-20; *The libelle of Englyshe polycye: a poem on the use of sea power, 1436*, ed. George Warner (Oxford, 1926), pp 36-8. See also Heffernan, *Tudor policy*, pp 30-1; Chad Marshall, 'The reform treatises and discourse of early Tudor Ireland, c. 1515-1541' (Ph.D., University of Tasmania, 2018), ch. 3.

[37] Bennett, '*Libelle*', pp 17-20.

[38] Crooks places the *Salus Populi* and its 'Abstract' in a didactic literary context of how the crown's Irish problem was framed throughout the fifteenth century, although humanist pursuits found a tangible purchase at the court of Henry VIII: Crooks, 'Structure of politics', p. 444.

[39] The State Paper commission simply mentions ill-defined 'intrinsic evidence' in dating the tract to 1515: *S.P. Hen. VIII*, ii, p. ii.

[40] This prophetic tradition was a distinctly medieval inheritance; Michael Bennett, 'Late medieval Ireland in a wider world' in *CHI*, i, 337.

light on the origins of each document as key passages in the text aid in dating the sources. The revival of English law, the suppression of Irish vices and the promotion of the 'comen wele' are also described in terms of the 'prophesie [of] all this land'. According to the 'State' (c. 1515), this prophecy was to be fulfilled by 1517, and that the reformation of Ireland could be achieved in three years.[41] The 'Abstract' foretold of a completed prophecy by 1516, with military and political reform 'within a few years'. Based on these variations it may be possible, admittedly crudely, to date the 'Abstract' and the 'State' (c. 1515) to 1513 and 1514, respectively.[42]

It appears that the 'Abstract' (although now extant in a later Tudor copy) was a reworking of the original *Salus Populi* written before the 'State' (c. 1515). The 'Abstract' was 'conceaved' from Latin to the 'English tongue' for those '[un]acquaintyd with poesie'.[43] The 'State' (c. 1515) contains literary references which suggest an advancement from the 'Abstract':[44]

> Also the nombre of the saide chief capytaines and chyeff regions excede not muche of 60. Ther be many other pety captaynes and pety regions besyde the premysseis of the Kinges Iryshe enymyes exceding the foresaid nombre that folowyth the same ordre in every poynte as muche as in them is and kepeyth the same rule after ther power that callyth them Tyshagheis that is to saye Dukes in ther langage consydering that a duke is as muche to saye as a guyder or a leader of the folke and in that consyderation every captayne maye be callyd a duke of his armye and retynue and concludeyth that a kyng is moste to be dreddeid in trone and a duke in the fylde and every man shulde dredde muche moore to dysobey his duke and captayne of the fylde then to dredde his enymye for the duke and captayne of the fylde is more then any kyng lyke as at the syge of Troye

---

[41] 'the sayde armye be on the kinges coste and charge during the space of 3 yere, or tyll the kinges sayde subgettes be put in ordre': SP 60/1, f. 24v. The 'Pandar sayeth, that the profycye of Ireland is, that in the yere of our Lorde Jhesu Cryst mdxvii, such folke, as was most feble shalbe most strong and such folke, as was moste strong, shalbe more strong, and fewe better then they was, throughe all the lande of Ireland': SP 60/1, f. 17v. In the printed State Papers, the year appears in the numerals: '1517'. This was also noted in the margin of the original manuscript with abrasive graphite pencil: S.P. Hen. VIII, ii, 10; SP 60/1, f. 17v.

[42] BL, Add. MS 4792, f. 100v. Elsewhere in the 'Abstract', less helpfully in terms of dating the source, 'enstrucions' are provided for the reformation of the Lordship of Ireland within 'the space of v yeres': BL, Add. MS 4792, f. 96r. While suggesting the above, this study will continue to refer to the 'State' (c. 1515) as such.

[43] BL, Add. MS 4792, f. 110r.

[44] For illustrative corresponding items from the 'Abstract' and the 'State' (c. 1515), respectively, see BL, Add. MS 4792, f. 98r; SP 60/1, f. 14v. 'Also the nombre of the saide chief capytaines and chif regons excede not moche of lx but beside them to be other regions and pety captaynes of the Kynges Iryshe enymyes exceding the foresaid number which call them self in ther langage tyseghs and they in every point after ther power followe the same ordre as the saide chefe captaynes do': BL, Add. MS 4792, f. 98r.

Hector that was no king was duke and governour of many a kyng and captayne of all the oste of Troye wherin was manye a noble kyng.[45]

The 'State' (c. 1515) also omitted passages of verse and Latin extracts from the 'Abstract'.[46] Certain sections of the 'Abstract' were reproduced in a more concise manner. For example, the power of Irish captains to

> make warre and pease for him self withoute lycence of there chief captayne' is described as follows in the state paper: 'chief captains...obeyeth to no other temperall person but onely to himself that is stronge and every of the said Capytaynes makeyth warre and peace for hymself and holdeith by swerde and hathe imperiall jurysdyction within his rome and obeyeth to noo other person Englyshe ne Iryshe except only to suche persones as maye subdue hym by the swerde.[47]

The 'Abstract' was originally intended for the 'kynge and his counsell', which accounts for the way 'State' (c. 1515) was filed as a carefully curated document.[48]

Evidence for Inge's authorship and aspects of his career are worth recounting. Certain passages unique to the 'Abstract' are revealing in terms of the author and his political aims. The proposal to establish a university in Athlone 'after the manner of New College Oxford' is notable.[49] There are repeated references to Oxford in the document. Hugh Inge was not only the sole former Oxfordian of the possible authors, but also one of New College. The proposal to establish a university in Athlone would be strange from the perspective of the Archbishop of Armagh. This would count against the case for Kite and also against Rokeby up to 1512. Inge was appointed to the see of Meath later in that year. Geographically,

---

[45] SP 60/1, f. 14v. While the above example draws on Homeric epic, possibly alluding to Lydgate's *Hystorye, sege and dystruccyon of Troye*, the following example includes demonstrates an apt biblical allusion in the state paper; 'Also that no ydleman stranger nor vacabond be found in therghe all the land Englyshe or Irysh on payne of his lyfe. If this land were once furnyshed in order as is aforesaid who darest be so bold in England to rebell agaynst the kynge': BL, Add. MS 4792, f. 108v. 'Also that idell man strayer ne vacabound be founde in any place throughe all the land Iryshe or Englyshe upon payn of his lyffe Also yf the King were as wyse as Salamon the Sage he shalle never subdue the wylde Iryshe to his obeysaunce withoute dreadde of the swerde and of the myght and streyngthe of his power and of his Englyshe subgettes orderyd as aforesayd for aslong as they maye resyste and save ther lyffes they wylle never obey the Kyng': SP 60/1, f. 33r.
[46] For example the introductory quatrain and concluding 'recapitalatio premisorum': BL, Add. MS 4792, ff 107r, 110r.
[47] BL, Add. MS 4792, f. 98v; SP 60/1, f. 12r.
[48] Close reading of the State Paper manuscript shows that on f. 14r, the word 'eny' was neatly inserted in a different but contemporary hand: BL, Add. MS 4792, f. 110r; SP 60/1, f. 14r.
[49] Bennett, Maginn and Ellis have drawn attention to this point: Maginn and Ellis, *Tudor discov. Ire.*, p. 137; Bennett, 'Libelle', pp 1-21. See also Heffernan, *Tudor policy*, p. 76.

medieval Meath stretched as far west as Athlone and the late medieval shire of Meath prospered from the fifteenth century.[50] Each reworking of the text was designed for a courtly reading. In the case of the 'Abstract', it was written for, or on the advice of Wolsey as Privy councillor. By 1511, Inge returned to Oxford from Rome, where he served in the papal curia and at the English hospice, where he was made a Doctor of Divinity.[51] Since their studies in Oxford where they both were students of Divinity at the same time, the careers of Wolsey and Inge rose simultaneously. Arguably, the 'Abstract' was then part of a portfolio to justify Inge's appointment to a significant position in the Lordship of Ireland. Inge probably departed Rome after the death of Walter FitzSimons, Archbishop of Dublin in May 1511, perhaps in the knowledge of having Wolsey's support to fill the vacancy. Inge was incorporated from a 'foreign university' as a Doctor of Divinity in Oxford on 3 April 1511. William Rokeby had petitioned Pope Julius II for the position but Inge enjoyed an advantage in having served in the Pontifical Curia and as warden (*custos*) of the English Hospice in Rome. Wolsey oversaw matters in the English Hospice at Rome, where many of his protégés prospered, including John Alen (later archbishop of Dublin). Inge apparently benefited from being given a fixed-term appointment as *custos* from 1496 to 1499, during which time he regularly reported to England.[52] When Sylvestro Gigli (see chapter two) and Thomas Colman vied for the mastership, the Cardinal received petitions of a sophisticated nature, particularly from later in 1515. There were many similarities between the 'State' (*c.* 1515) and Colman's correspondence with Wolsey prior to his election as master of the hospice in 1516. Gigli had informed the Cardinal that there was no suitable Englishman for the position and Colman imparted an elaborate appeal to Wolsey, offering insights through classical literature and affirming their great historical tradition ('gretes tradient histories...galli ac parentem') and referred to conflict with the Scots.[53] Inge was exposed to a vibrant culture of humanist political rhetoric during his *custodia* in Rome which was evidently harnessed in appealing to Wolsey at this time. Inge's departure during *sede vacante* may have prompted the composition of the 'Abstract' for Wolsey's file as a demonstration of his expertise. Although Inge's arrival in England may have

---

[50] S. G. Ellis, *Ireland's English Pale* (Woodbridge, 2021), pp 14, 118.
[51] *Register of the University of Oxford*, ed. C. W. Boase (2 vols, London, 1885), i, 75.
[52] Brian Newns, 'The hospice of St Thomas and the English crown 1474–1538' in J. F. Allen (ed.), *The English hospice in Rome* (Gloucester, 2005), pp 145–92, 190–2; James Willoughby, 'The library of the English hospital in Rome before 1527' in *La Bibliofilia*, 113 (2011), pp 161–4.
[53] BL, Vitellius B.II, ff 185. Scotland was on Wolsey's radar and, as Heffernan notes, the 'State' (*c.* 1515) was one of few early treatises to engage with the Scottish problem in east Ulster: Heffernan, *Tudor policy*, p. 64.

preceded Wolsey's blessing to be elevated to the seat of Dublin, by 9 February 1512 Rokeby was Archbishop elect and Inge was later appointed Bishop of Meath.[54]

The 'State' (c. 1515) could only have been fully understood by the addressee with prior knowledge of the *Salus Populi*. Assuming Wolsey was privy to this, it also seems that the 'Pandar' was a moniker or pseudonym that also denoted closeness between the author and addressee.[55] The 'Pandar', as mediator, was a suitably intimate moniker. A possible indication of such a personal relationship can be found in an appeal to Wolsey by Inge, in whom he placed his 'hole hope'.[56] The friendship of Pandarus is based on the medieval concept of *amicitia*, male fellowship and a scholarly bond possibly formed in Oxford.[57] Allusions in the 'State' (c. 1515) probed 'questions of the secrete dyvine', suggesting a student of that discipline.[58] Inge's time at the Pontifical Curia along with his doctorate in Divinity from Oxford and Rome show him to have been a scholar. Richard Bere, a friend of Erasmus, was one of his benefactors, while Wolsey of course was a major cultural patron.[59] There is a shared intimacy in the 'State' (c. 1515) through the medium of the 'Pandar'. Deeper meanings are implied as the angel 'dyd understande' Ireland, while the empathy, 'pytty' of the Pandar, co-existed with vehemently anti-Kildare sentiment and an abhorrence of Irish extortions.[60]

Inge's subsequent career and cultural patronage in some ways ran true to the diplomatic and humanist characteristics of the 'Pandar'.[61] His effective tenure as bishop of Meath and influence on the Irish council likely made him a valuable source of intelligence for the Cardinal.[62] He would later be relied upon for

---

[54] CPR, xviii, 573.

[55] The variations of the *Salus Populi* reflect different stages of editing and interaction with Wolsey, who would have witnessed similar dynamic creativity at the court of Henry Tudor. Richard Fox was referred to by his protégé, royal tutor and historian Bernard Andreas as his 'Mycenas', while Skelton was 'Calliope' to the young prince Henry: John Skelton, *Pithy pleasaunt and profitable works of maister Skelton* (London, 1568), p. 382; Thomas Penn, *Winter king: Henry VII and the dawn of Tudor England* (London, 2011), pp 102-3; Greg Walker, *John Skelton and the politics of the 1520s* (Cambridge, 1988), pp 45-6, 54-5; William Nelson, *John Skelton: laureate* (New York, 1939), p. 46.

[56] SP 60/1, f. 8r.

[57] Alcuin Blamires, *Chaucer, ethics and gender* (Oxford, 2006), p. 33.

[58] SP 60/1, f. 17v.

[59] Roger Bowers, 'The cultivation and orbit of Thomas Wolsey' in S. J. Gunn and P. G. Lindley (eds), *Cardinal Wolsey, church, state and art* (New York, 1991), p. 181. For an impressive recent study among a large bibliography for this topic, see Glenn Richardson, *Wolsey* (Oxford, 2020), esp. pp 154-7, 162-3, 183-90.

[60] SP/60, f. 17v. BL, Add. MS 4792, f. 100v. Chaucer's Pandarus empathises with Troilus' predicament: Geoffrey Chaucer. *Troylus and Cresyde* (1483), p. 20.

[61] Inge earned a reputation for loyal and diligent service. As a 'worthy English gentleman', Polydore Vergil praised his capacity to promote 'good order' in spite of the 'wild Irish': Polydore Vergil, *The Anglica historia of Polydore Vergil, A.D. 1485-1537* (London, 1950), pp 308-9.

[62] Wolsey's Irish policy from 1514 was to strengthen the core region of the lordship but he

counsel and support before and after Surrey, while proving an important voice seeking amity between Kildare and Ossory as lord chancellor.[63] With the unrest of 1527-8 in the lordship Inge came to take a softer stance with Kildare, urging the return of the earl whose 'substanciall power' could restore order. Inge was also likely acquainted with Norfolk through Thomas Bathe, who is reputed to have written 'A Discourse of the Cause of the Evil State of Ireland and of the Remedies Thereof' (c. 1526). As outlined in this treatise, Inge also foresaw 'som good ordre for this poore land...which shall sooner succede by the firme unitie of these two Erlles'.[64] While archbishop elect in 1522 he was promptly 'restorid to all the profittes...sith the decesse of the late Archebysshoppe (Rokeby)'.[65] Inge's diligent service was reflected in a refined attention to detail and symbolism. In formal correspondence he may have used watermarked paper with a matching seal matrix. An imprint of a wax seal with the image of a liborium was used when the council wrote to Wolsey in May 1528 which appears to match a watermark on a leaf in correspondence between the same in 1521. In each case, Inge was the first signatory as bounden orator.[66] While authorship of the 'State' (c. 1515) remains uncertain, it continues to shed light on policy formation but also Ireland's early Tudor renaissance.

Although the 'State' (c. 1515) was prompted by strong opinion against Kildare, this polemic context also had a bearing on its humanist and symbolic import. It demonstrated a use of renaissance learning determined shaped by conditions particular to Ireland in which the 'Pandar' exists. As a pseudonym based on the diplomatic and counselling aptitude of Pandarus in Chaucer's *Troilus and Cressidye* (c. 1380), it was a highly adaptive symbol.[67] The 'Pandar' invoked 'charity' but

---

was mindful that only a long-term vision would curb the underlying causes of decay: Fiona Fitzsimons, 'Cardinal Wolsey, the native affinities and the failure of reform in Henrician Ireland' in David Edwards (ed.), *Regions and rulers in Ireland 1100-1650* (Dublin, 2004), pp 78-9.
[63] See for example SP 60/1, ff 51, 108r, 121r-122v. Along with Bermingham, he may have had an input into the treatise, 'A Discourse of the Cause of the Evil State of Ireland and of the Remedies Thereof, c. 1526'. See also SP 60/1, ff 121r-122v; Heffernan, *Tudor policy* and below, ch. 5.
[64] SP 60/1, f. 127v.
[65] SP 60/1, f. 82r. Upon translation to office, an elliptical Gothic stone arch was commissioned for the Palace of St Sepulchre with Inge's archiepiscopal arms built in the wall above the lintel. This was constructed at the entrance facing St Patrick's cathedral. Angels are placed at either side of the coat of arms, above which is a scroll, also partly damaged bearing the motto: 'virtus nobi[llis]'. Heraldry and its meanings were a preoccupation of Wolsey's leading dependants: Diarmaid MacCulloch, *Thomas Cromwell: a life* (London, 2018), pp 172-3.
[66] SP 60/1, f. 74r, 115v.
[67] Pandarus as a symbol allows for both intellectual banter and profound philosophical reflection: David Wallace, *Chaucerian polity* (Stanford, 1997), p. 44; D. R. Woolf, *Reading history in early modern England* (Cambridge, 2000), p. 6. The pseudonym may also have been inspired by Lydgate's *Hystorye, sege and dystruccyon of Troye* (c. 1400-1450), another popular text at the

urged conquest while seeking to 'flay' the Scots. The Pandar represented the lordship's affinity with the crown and the immediate anxieties in the face of marches controlled by old colonial magnates.[68] Likewise, the lines between the political, prophetic and cultural were blurred. Wolsey as the reader, however, would have understood the 'Pandar' on a literary and political level. The 'Pandar' fitted the obvious image of the renaissance ambassador which is somewhat novel in the context of late medieval and early Tudor Ireland.[69] Symbols and literary conceit were intrinsic to the thrust of the 'State' (c. 1515), the most perceptible of which were the medicinal connotations for the reversal of Kildare-induced decay. In this analogy, the 'herbes' represented the remedy of military intervention. The harsh rhetoric, to 'purge and expulse the same' seems to have echoed Giraldus.[70] Lapses in the maintenance of archery were a cause of the enfeeblement of the king's commons and the demise of the colony. As such, the centrality of reviving the use of English weaponry was tacitly symbolised by the bowman Pandarus. Characteristic of the *de casibus* tradition, the reversal of this 'feble' state was prophesised by the 'Pandar'.[71] Here, political argument was regarded to be more effectively made through the use of stylised prose (as with Colman and Spinelly).

Yet archaic influences also underpinned the morality of the conquest through the preservation of the Latin church. The layers of meaning pertaining to history, prophecy and courtly literature in the 'State' (c. 1515) have a general appeal, but it seems that the ecclesiastical content relates to Wolsey in particular. References to the early church patricians, scripture and the discipline of Divinity were

---

early Henrician court and in print since 1513. The Kildare library contained a copy of 'Troillus', which was probably Caxton's 1483 printed edition of *Troilus and Criseyde*: Aisling Byrne, 'Earls of Kildare and their books at the end of the middle ages' in *The Library: Transactions of the Bibliographical Society*, 14 (2013), p. 150; BL, Harleian MS 3756, f. 97v.

[68] SP 60/1, f. 20r; Margaret Hodgen, *Early anthropology in the sixteenth and seventeenth centuries* (Philadelphia, 1964), p. 273.

[69] Studies have examined Renaissance diplomacy in England and Europe. See for instance, Susan Brigden, who states that although the term ambassador was not coined until later, it was nonetheless a familiar concept. Chaucer's *Troilus* is cited as an example: Susan Brigden, *Thomas Wyatt: the heart's forest* (London, 2014); Susan Brigden, 'Reformation diplomacy: Henry VIII and his ambassadors' inaugural (Mary L. Robertson lecture, Huntington Library, 22 Sept. 2014).

[70] SP 60/1, ff 24. The 'Abstract' expands on the analogy of the 'apothecary'. There is 'no other medicine' but the 'said herbes', meaning an aggressive military approach: BL, Add. MS 4792, f. 104v. See ch. 2 above; TCD, MS 592, f. 24v. In the context of Wolseian diplomacy, see also Wingfield's memoranda from the mid-1510s. For instance, he used medicinal analogies and reinforced advice by referring to where it was 'wrytyn that Troylis' acted in folly: BL, Vitellius B.XVIII, ff 104r, 117v.

[71] SP 60/1, f. 18v; BL, Add. MS 4792, f. 110v; Paul Budra, *A mirror for magistrates and the de Casibus tradition* (London, 2000), p. 18. The preservation and optimal use of archery is a common theme in Giraldus: Gerald of Wales, *Expugnatio Hibernica, the conquest of Ireland*, ed. A. B. Scott and F. X. Martin (Dublin, 1978), p. 93 (I. 30).

woven into the premise. The righteousness and 'honour eternall' of moving against Kildare was bolstered through sacred scripture, and apocalyptic visions were conjured as a reckoning for the land's 'greate wrongful extortion'.[72] In the 'Abstract', the 'remedia premissorum' justified the conquest on moral grounds, for the 'church of Chryst' and the relief of the commons.[73] Highlighted by a manacle, the bold assertion that the king 'were more honour...to surrendre his clayme therto' without intervention and 'remedye' 'under Godd, under the See Appostolycall' touches upon the Laudibiliter, and by association the *Expugnatio*.[74] The 'State' (c. 1515) echoed core themes of Giraldus, the fulfilment of the conquest through pursuing the virtuous life pleasing to God, which resonated with a late medieval reader.[75] Pope Gregory I (the Great) joins the tract's twin literary pillars of Giraldus and Chaucer in reinforcing this point. After further condemnation of Kildare, whose mortal soul is in 'grete daunger', Gregory's 'booke De Pastoralibus' is cited to denounce the degenerate Irish church in a land of constant war.[76] The influence of medieval ethnography is most notable in the Pandar's revelations. Brigid's interaction with the divine, from the 'fyrst chaptre of his booke callyd Salus Populi', was based on the *Topographia*.[77] Certain passages unique to the 'Abstract' also resonate with the *Topographia*. These include descriptions of reserves of gold ore which 'exceed the pomp of the eeste' and it also claims

---

[72] SP 60/1, f. 18r.
[73] BL, Add. MS 4792, f. 107r. On reading the 'State' (c. 1515) Bradshaw stated that its use of commonweal as a purely philosophical concept was more akin to More's *Utopia* than Dudley's *Tree of commonwealth*. The 'Abstract' may suggest otherwise: Bradshaw, *Const. rev.*, p. 49.
[74] SP 60/1, f. 21v.
[75] Caoimhe Whelan, 'Translating the *Expugnatio Hibernica*: A vernacular English history in late medieval Ireland' in C. Griffin and E. Purcell (eds), *Text, transmission and transformation in the European middle ages, 1000–1500* (Turnhout, 2018), p. 247.
[76] SP 60/1, f. 22v. The 'Abstract' manuscript is here highlighted by a manicle: BL, Add. MS 4792, f. 103v. Peter Gwyn writes of Gregorian views of the primacy of the church as being at odds with Henry Tudor's moves against individual clergy which was most unlike Dudley's *Tree of commonwealth*: Peter Gwyn, *The king's cardinal: the rise and fall of Thomas Wolsey* (London, 1990), pp 31, 44–5.
[77] The Pandar's *Salus Populi* in a sense is a quasi-Giraldus; 'the premisseis consyderyd the Pander shewyth in the fyrst chaptre of his booke callyd Salus Populi that the holly wooman Brigitta used to inquyre of her good Anglle many questions of secrete dyvine and among all other she inquyryd of what Crystyn lande was most sowlles damned, the Angell shewyd her a lande in the weste parte of the worlde': SP 60/1, ff 17v–18r. The allegories run deeper. The opening book of *Troilus and Criseyde* includes Pandarus being likewise moved to compassion, speaking of Titan's (Prometheus) fate in hell to show the extent to which he sympathises and is prepared to assist Troilus; 'swich yvel is nat alwey botelees...put not impossible thus thy cure...to come is ofte in aventure. I graunte wel that thou endurest as sharp as doth he, Ticius, in helle': Chaucer, *Troylus and Cresyde*, p. 17. Also see Ludwig Bieler, *Ireland, harbinger of the middle ages* (Oxford, 1963), pp 25–8.

that the ancient arms of Ireland feature a king on a 'golden chair', amounting to a sense of the exotic, resource-rich orient.[78]

Traditions preserved in medieval chronicles pervade the tract. While apparently associated with Giraldus, this cannot be stated with certainty. Kane argues that for the early Tudors in particular there is little evidence to show a direct and an unequivocal readership of Giraldus. Heffernan likewise points to a lack of concrete evidence and also suggests Ranulph Higden as a possible source.[79] Indeed, Higden's *Polychronicon*, Geoffrey of Monmouth and John of Fordun were redacted and in print by the 1510s.[80] The *Topographia* appears to have been a formative source for the 'State' (*c.* 1515) as it also described the land as 'voyde of poyson'. This was one of many traditions to be found in accounts passed on from classical antiquity.[81] In *c.* 1515, Ireland as an earthly paradise was not quite an appeal for benign commonwealth reform but a motive to subjugate its wretched inhabitants.[82] The use of prophecy suggests inspiration from the prophetic works of Giraldus, itself subject to polemic use. The aforementioned late medieval Hiberno-English editions of the *Expugnatio* indicate a revival of English culture.[83] Prophetic discourse often stirred controversy or caused political debate. In 1521 Wolsey examined one Thomas Gildon before council for seditious remarks 'by provesey'.[84] The thrust of the *Expugnatio* as a prophetic history against that of a barbarous people who were Christian only in name is echoed in the 'State' (*c.* 1515) on the 'crystyn lande [where] was most sowlles damned'.[85] A political proverb (discussed below) follows immediately thereafter in the text. While reference was made to decline since the twelfth and thirteenth centuries, the tract has a footing in the European events of its day. Engaging with the king's desire for crusade, the Pandar prioritised the Lordship

---

[78] A blank heraldic shield can be found in the margin of the manuscript. BL, Add. MS 4792, f. 110r. Also, see TCD, MS 842, ff 34r-49v.

[79] Heffernan, *Tudor policy*, p. 27; Brendan Kane, 'Did the Tudors read Giraldus? Gerald of Wales and early modern polemical historiography' in Georgia Henley and A. J. McMullen (eds), *New perspectives on Gerald of Wales* (Cardiff, 2018), pp 259-60.

[80] Kildare's library catalogue listed a 1482 edition of Higden as 'ffurst' among English books: Byrne, 'Earls of Kildare', p. 149; BL, Harleian MS 3756, f. 97v.

[81] BL, Add. MS 4792, f. 110v; SP 60/1, f. 18r; George Boas, *Primitivism and related ideas in the middle ages* (Baltimore, MD, 1948), pp 170-1. An enduring tradition from the middle ages placed Ireland next to the 'oceanus Hyperborens': BL, Add. MS 4787, f. 241r.

[82] See Heffernan, *Tudor policy*, pp xvii, 26; Bradshaw, *Const. rev.*, pp 48-52; Alan Kelly, 'Classical thought and primitivism in English depictions of Ireland: a case study of John Derricke's *Image of Ireland*, 1581' (M.A., Maynooth University, 2005).

[83] The *Salus Populi* stressed the moral, 'charitable' obligation to commence a conquest. Pleas for charity and 'oor ldy mcy helpe' were highlighted in the 'Butler Expugnatio' manuscript. They were likely to have been expressions of dissatisfaction with the state of the colony: SP 60/1, f. 4r; TCD, MS 592, f. 18v.

[84] SP 1/21, f. 200r.

[85] The land is visually located, 'shewed' to be in the 'weste part of the worlde': SP 60/1, f. 18r.

of Ireland as an honourable quest in itself and a springboard to 'subdue the realme of France [and] vanquyshe the turkes'.[86]

There is a distinctly literate, almost courtly sense in how the 'museis' inspire the political counsel offered in the 'State' (c. 1515). In the manuscript a manacle draws attention to this reference which also engaged with the reversal of decay and the king's honour.[87] Describing the Irishry 'lyke as at the syge of Troye' carried underlying political implications.[88] In abstract political terms, the Trojan analogy is suggestive of a siege mentality similar to the *Expugnatio*, whereby the Englishry must be safeguarded from native corruption (see chapter two). It is unsurprising that in response to Geraldine projections, opposing policies are to be reinforced through humanistic phenomena, albeit distinctively inward looking. The inventive use of history and literature included allusions to court culture. Aside from the overt symbolism of the 'Pandar' as renaissance diplomat, the rhetoric of the 'State' (c. 1515) drew upon court poets. Before the flamboyance of Surrey (Henry Howard) and Wyatt, an older generation of court poets including Andreas Ammonius and Bernard Andreas was headed by John Skelton. The latter was arguably one of the Pandar's muses.[89] The Pandar's pejorative treatment of Kildare's 'myght and power, so great worsship and riches' resonated with the 'colors, fyctions and poyses' denounced by Skelton. The writer takes issue with those who 'currifavel' at Court, an adverse term used in literary contexts to denounce deceit. Kildare's duplicity was most memorably evoked through Arthurian allusions in the 'Discourse'.[90] The 'Abstract' claims to be influenced by 'poesies laureat'. Ironically, Skelton would later vilify Wolsey in the 1520s.[91] Embedded within the 'State' (c. 1515) was a rhyming couplet: 'who so wylle in Courte dwell, he muste lerne to courry favour well'.[92] By virtue of its presence and

---

[86] SP 60/1, f. 35r. Also, see Bennett, 'Late medieval Ireland', p. 337. If the 'Pandar' is also the author of the 'Abstract' and 'State' (c. 1515), he speaks of himself in the same self-appraising manner as Giraldus. See for example in the 'Abstract': BL, Add. MS 4792, f. 110r.

[87] SP 60/1, f. 21v.

[88] SP 60/1, f. 14v.

[89] An overmighty Kildare and the fears of those around the deputy to 'shewe hym the trewth' are sentiments expressed in the 'Bowge of courte'. Printed c. 1500, it was by the 1510s an established critique: *The complete English poems of John Skelton*, ed. John Scattergood (Liverpool, 2015), pp 38–52.

[90] B. J. Whiting and H. W. Whiting, *Proverbs, sentences, and proverbial phrases from English writings mainly before 1500* (Cambridge, MA, 1968), p. 169.

[91] BL, Add. MS 4792, ff 103v, 107r, 110v. There is an element of satire in the verse quatrain that opens the 'Abstract'. It seeks to alleviate 'confusion' by reworking the *Salus Populi* and plainly set out its argument, perhaps alluding to Skelton's gripe against obscure 'fyctions'. For Skelton's attack on Wolsey see 'Why come ye nat to courte?': *English poems of John Skelton*, ed. John Scattergood, pp 244–73, 459. Also, see Walker, *Skelton and the politics of the 1520s*, pp 9–15, 124–5; David Starkey, *Henry: virtuous prince* (London, 2008), p. 37.

[92] SP 60/1, f. 22r.

the survival of the document, such passages were neither frivolous nor of marginal relevance in the quest to secure the ear of the Cardinal.

A didactic 'proverb of old date' outlined the crown's traditional domestic and foreign concerns whereby the 'pryde of Fraunce, the treason of Inglande and the warre of Ireland shall never ende'.[93] The 'warres in Fraunce and of dyverse other landes' namely the crusades for Christendom were argued to be unattainable without the initial conquest of Ireland.[94] With France as England's 'ancient enemy' the Pandar faced an uphill task in shifting attention to Ireland. Yet as Richardson notes, a war-weary England emerging from civil strife was inclined toward peace in Europe.[95] In terms of precise methods of reading, each redaction of the *Salus Populi* was intended to be received as a humanist tract.[96] The 'Abstract' begins with the rather vocal assertation that 'the Pandar of Ireland in his book of Salus Populi saith'.[97] Wolsey was aware that the king regarded 'pleasaunte letters' to 'bee his pleasure to here the same red'.[98] While recent studies have yielded much profit, the courtly and literary aspects of the 'State' (c. 1515) and related literature of decay remain understudied.

On 23 June 1515 at Greenwich, the king's council was presented with Sir William Darcy's 'Artycles'.[99] It came to mark a key date in the state paper and quasi-state paper history of Geraldine-induced decay. Finglas' initial 'brief note' on the decay of Ireland 'preferred unto kinge Henry the Eighth about the viith yere of his raigne', the timing of which may have been co-ordinated with Darcy, writing in the wake of an already submitted 'State' (c. 1515).[100] With the original *Salus Populi* an even older work, the early 1510s were a vibrant period for this literature of decay.[101] Elizabeth St John's aforementioned complaints had been filed by 1515,

---

[93] SP 60/1, f. 18r.
[94] SP 60/1, f. 18v.
[95] Glenn Richardson, *The Field of Cloth of Gold* (London, 2013), pp 2–15.
[96] The original Latin verse, the hybrid 'Abstract' and refined state paper were possibly to be read as the *Praise of Folly* or *Book of the Courtier*. The extended literary conceits suggest a courtly audience and there is arguably an oral exposition in the opening words of the 'State' (c. 1515); 'who lyste make surmyse to the king for the reformation of his lande of Ireland': SP 60/1, f. 12r.
[97] BL, Add. MS 4792, f. 96r.
[98] S.P. Hen. VIII, ii, 138; Katharine Simms, *Gaelic Ulster in the middle ages: history, culture and society* (Dublin, 2020), p. 218.
[99] The original is lost but Maginn and Ellis have collated the earliest extant manuscripts: Hatfield House Archives, Cecil Papers MS 144, ff 9, printed in Maginn and Ellis, *Tudor discov. Ire.*, pp 91–3; LPL, MS 635, ff 188, *Cal. Carew*, i, 6–8. The council meeting was more likely to have taken place on this date rather than 24 June as in the LPL manuscript: Maginn and Ellis, *Tudor discov. Ire.*, p. 45.
[100] This document is also lost: LPL, MS 635, f. 185; Maginn and Ellis, *Tudor discov. Ire.*, p. 27; Ellis, *Reform and revival*, p. 224.
[101] See also the anti-Kildare 'note' on the 1488 Act of Marches and Maghery (written c. 1513);

thus reinforcing an opportunity for Geraldine enemies to follow suit and appeal accordingly. Like the 'Pandar', Darcy and Finglas proposed that only an aggressive military policy focused on regional entrenchment could stem the Kildare-induced decay of the colony. There was evidently an appetite for reform treatises which gained traction with a use of historical argument, warning of cultural lapses from the English norm.[102] Where the 'State' (c. 1515) proposed a conquest to begin in Meath, Darcy's 'Artycles' and the treatises by Finglas are preoccupied with south Leinster.[103] But of particular note in each case was an active use of history and lively rhetoric underlining the morality of conquest. To varying degrees, Giraldus seems to have provided inspiration.[104] Through engagement with the chronicles there was an active participation in presenting the history of the colony.[105]

Darcy's 'Artycles' plunge into a rebuke of the mid-fifteenth-century Desmond misrule, claiming that James, the sixth earl, 'was the fyrste man that ever put coyne and lyverie on the kynges subiectes'.[106] Undertaking 'the saide extorcyon of coyne and lyverye', Desmond had set this precedent for well 'above L wynters'.[107] Estranged from the crown since 1468, Desmond's heirs accelerated the continual decline of the Munster Englishry, as Darcy clarifies. It was this original sin of James Fitzgerald that 'began the same ordre of coyne and lyverie', in a sense usurping the king's rights by means of 'his conquest'. Having 'used it sythens', Desmond operated as an affront to the king.[108] Darcy explained that the Butlers of Ormond were compelled to follow suit, proclaiming Desmond's culpability for the Geraldine-Butler feud in Munster. Darcy briefly accounted for the loss of Ulster from the thirteenth to fifteenth centuries to succession problems and neglect, before recounting the 'abhomynale ordre of coyne and lyverie' in the four obedient shires of Leinster. In this case it was Thomas, 'sonne to the foresaide James...put to execution' in 1468, who was responsible for the wasting of the

---

NLI, MS 2507, f. 57v. The succession of Henry VIII heralded a fresh acquisition of knowledge: Maginn and Ellis, *Tudor discov. Ire.*, p. 134. Bradshaw for example states that the young king Henry was initially indifferent to information on Ireland: Bradshaw, *Const. rev.*, pp 33-4.

[102] SP 60/1, f. 29r. Also, see Ellis, *Ireland's English Pale*, pp 131-3.

[103] SP 60/1, f. 25r.

[104] As Bradshaw has observed, if the 'State' (c. 1515) was a prophetic statement, then Darcy and Finglas wrote histories: Bradshaw, *Const. rev.*, p. 53.

[105] The closing lines of the late medieval Hiberno-English editions of the *Expugnatio* could be seen as an invitation to this end. The 'Butler Expugnatio' for instance concludes, 'Mayster Gerard ham and har gestes leveth to other that ham wrytte': TCD, MS 592, f. 28r. The folio page with the corresponding section in the 'Darcy Expugnatio' is damaged: BL, Add. MS 40674, f. 102r.

[106] Maginn and Ellis, *Tudor discov. Ire.*, p. 91; LPL, MS 635, f. 188r.

[107] '40 wynters' in the LPL manuscript. Maginn and Ellis have collated the sources offering the most accurate transcription: Maginn and Ellis, *Tudor discov. Ire.*, p. 91. Also, see Heffernan, *Tudor policy*, pp 3, 9, 30.

[108] Maginn and Ellis, *Tudor discov. Ire.*, p. 92.

lordship's core region. 'His kynnes men', the Kildares, 'began and renued' these oppressions and within a generation Leinster was 'cleane goone and decayed'. A weakened Ormond lordship was prone to Desmond interference and plagued by rivalry amongst its cadets. As can be seen during Surrey's campaign, it was in Piers Butler's interests to block Desmond's relationship with the crown. It was Darcy's soured relationship with Kildare and co-operation with Piers that largely prompted the 'Artycles'.[109] Controlling the narrative of past events was evidently an avenue of attack for those emphasising the decline of the colony.

While Darcy focused on events from the previous century, the underlying pattern of decay and corruptive nature of the wild Irish sprang from an older tradition associated with Giraldus. Exploiting polemic rhetoric to optimal effect, Darcy's use historical argument was a distinctive renaissance phenomenon that was discernible in Finglas.[110] The earliest extant copy of Finglas' 'Breviate' dates to 1529 and although it became a highly influential treatise its initial impact is unclear.[111] Finglas was primarily concerned with south Leinster, Idrone and the Barrow valley, which generally became a major focus in terms of regional intervention in the 1520s. This strategically significant channel linked the Pale, Kilkenny and Waterford as Finglas heaps symbolic importance on the barony of Idrone as a focal point in the life of William Marshal's intermarriage and 'suffraunce' of the MacMurrough-Kavanagh.[112] Other examples of region-specific accounts of decay, sophisticated in nature, are known to have existed. Written in 'ballad royal' form (as with the earlier 1488 Waterford poem), an Oxford scholar Thomas Dormer was the author of 'The decay of Ross'.[113] Intense regional vested

---

[109] Unlike Inge, assuming his authorship of the 'State' (c. 1515), who came to entreat in favour of Gearóid Óg Fitzgerald, Darcy shifted his stance in the opposite direction: S. G. Ellis, 'An English gentleman and his community: Sir William Darcy of Platten' in Vincent Carey and Ute Lotz-Heumann (eds), *Taking sides? colonial and confessional mentalities in early modern Ireland* (Dublin, 2003), p. 33; David Edwards, *The Ormond lordship in County Kilkenny, 1515-1642: the rise and fall of Butler feudal power* (Dublin, 2003), pp 82-3; Bradshaw, *Const. rev.*, p. 37.

[110] Heffernan, *Tudor policy*, pp 29-34; Colm Lennon, *Sixteenth-century Ireland: the incomplete conquest* (Dublin, 1994), pp 82-3; Bradshaw, *Const. rev.*, pp 40-3, 50-7.

[111] Finglas will be discussed in more detail in the next chapter. See Maginn and Ellis for an overview of the different versions of the 'Breviate', and also Heffernan's article: Maginn and Ellis, *Tudor discov. Ire.*, pp 27-34; David Heffernan, 'Patrick Finglas' A Breviat of the conquest of Ireland and the decay of the same, c. 1535 and the Tudor Conquest of Ireland' in *Sixteenth Century Journal*, 49 (2017), pp 377-9; Bradshaw, *Const. rev.*, p. 53; White, 'Tudor plantations', p. 16.

[112] Maginn and Ellis, *Tudor discov. Ire.*, p. 69. For the symbolism of the region, see C. A. Empey, 'The liberties and counties of Carlow in the high middle ages' and Linda Doran, 'Medieval settlement hierarchy in Carlow and the "Carlow corridor" 1200-1550' in Thomas McGrath (ed.), *Carlow: history and society* (Dublin, 1995), pp 153-171, 173-212.

[113] The poem does not survive and next to nothing is known of the author except that he was in Oxford from 1525 to 1526, attained a BA and was a 'civilian, born at Ross': St John Seymour,

interests included most obviously Ormond under Piers as *de facto* eighth earl, but also the privileges of the port city of Waterford. In 1519, Thomas More relayed to Wolsey a 'supplication putt un to his grace by menne of Wattrford in the name of the citie', invoking the 'speciall favour' earned through loyalty during Yorkist rebellions against 'the kinge his father and other his progenitors for which he saith he bereth them as your grace well knowet'. Along with this historical consciousness, a sense of siege mentality was impressed upon Wolsey with 'mych beryng agaynste theym in Ireland and that the citie standeth so in the dayngir of the wild Irish'.[114]

Gearóid Óg Fitzgerald was restored with favour in September 1515 amidst the dissemination of conquest-orientated treatises at Court. It would be misleading to assume that articulate calls for reform and conquest were disregarded. The preservation of documents suggests the acquisition of intelligence and later 'bundles' filed by William Cecil Lord Burghley show Wolsey's active engagement with these records.[115] Kildare's recall in 1519 and the rather abrupt intervention with Surrey represented a turning point. His intense campaigning yielded initial promise which waned in the realisation that a prudent, cost-effective approach was necessary.[116]

Supported also by Piers Butler, Surrey enjoyed success against the midlands septs but more importantly secured the submission of O'Neill and O'Donnell. A marriage alliance was arranged between the latter and Darcy's daughter.[117] Surrey's failure to return Desmond to good relations with the crown was not helped by a Darcy-Butler agenda. Darcy's bifurcation of Geraldine malevolence and the loyal subjects had been promulgated six years earlier.[118] Surrey also contrasted the Geraldines with Piers Butler's 'true English hert', writing to Wolsey that he 'wold thErll of Desmond were of like wisedome and order'.[119] It is tempting

---

Anglo-Irish literature, 1200-1582 (Dublin, 1929), pp 29-30; *Register of the University of Oxford*, ed. C. W. Boase (2 vols, Oxford, 1885), i, 138.

[114] BL, Titus B.XI, ii, f. 341v.

[115] BL, Vitellius, C.XVII, f. 78v.

[116] S. G. Ellis, *Ireland in the age of the Tudors* (London, 1998), pp 119-25; Lennon, *Sixteenth-cen. Ire.*, pp 90-4; Maginn and Ellis, *Tudor discov. Ire.*, p. 129; Bradshaw, *Const. rev.*, pp 59-79; Brady, *Chief gov.*, p. 5. See also Edwards, *Ormond lordship*, p. 157.

[117] It transpired to be of little benefit: Ellis, 'Darcy of Platten', p. 37; Sparky Booker, *Cultural exchange and identity in late medieval Ireland: the English and Irish of the four obedient shires* (Cambridge, 2018), p. 164. Darcy advised against the O'Carroll and in favour of Ormond: LPL, MS 602, ff 52.

[118] A binary attitude regarding assimilation was aired in Darcy's 'Artycles': Booker, *Cult. exch. med. Ire.*, pp 136, 178-9.

[119] *S.P. Hen. VIII*, ii, 58. For the rise of Piers Butler, see C. A. Empey, 'From rags to riches: Piers Butler earl of Ormond, 1515-39' in *Butler Society Journal*, 2 (1984), pp 299-312; Edwards, *Ormond lordship*, pp 84-95, 155-6. There was apparently little contradiction in vouching for his 'true English heart' although he was immersed in native customs. To cite one roughly contemporaneous example, those of the Gaelic bardic *literati* served as witnesses to an indenture

to read the king's instructions to Surrey seeking 'amiable persuasions' rather than 'inforcement by strength or violence' in the light of that summer's grand diplomacy in France. While retaining subtle indications of conquest, ground at Court shifted in favour of diplomacy. Kildare (and Wiltshire) were among eleven earls 'to attende upon the kinges highness...with the Frenche king'.[120] After Kildare was released on sureties in late 1520, a draft submission for Gaelic lords (amended to also include English rebels) alluded to the history of the lordship.[121]

Meanwhile a 'device on how Ireland may be kept in obedience' (c. 1520) appealed to Wolsey's pre-eminence, 'being legate...comyssary with his ful powers and auctorite into Irland' to urgently act through the church. Advising the deputy to employ 'gentel means', a veneer of diplomacy covered an implied threat of force, with no intention to 'comyt warre agaynst man that with fayre means wyll doo their duety'.[122] It was argued that the poverty of Irish bishoprics exacerbated the cycle of decay, titles being of 'soo smale value that no Englyshman wyll accypt theym'. Native prelates were thus 'moost apt and redy to make warre and excite othres to moeve warr aganst the king and his deputy'.[123] This point was highlighted in the 'State' (c. 1515) by discussing the early church patricians.[124] The 'device' urged Wolsey to obtain a papal bull and exercise special powers to intervene accordingly. Potentially a catalyst for unity and security, the church could provide an avenue for coercion, 'clergy and freres to establish and enact that all men moeving warre against the kinges grace or his deputy bee accursid... sensure of cursing aftr most fereful and terrible manner'.[125]

The simple expediency of aristocratic delegation once again proved favourable as the allure of ambitions in Europe or further afield warranted fiscal prudence

---

between Piers Butler and Donal MacCarthy, lord of Carbery in 1512: *Ormond deeds*, iv, 12; Luke McInerney and Caroline Smiddy, 'The Clann Chraith bardic school of Burgess, south Tipperary' in Luke McInerney and Katharine Simms (eds), *Gaelic Ireland (c. 600-c. 1700), lordship, saints and learning: essays for the Irish chiefs' and clans' prize in history* (Dublin, 2021), p. 158.
[120] LPL, 602, f. 71; SP 1/19, f. 260r. For Wolsey's diplomatic ambitions and magnificence through peace see: Richardson, *Field of cloth of gold*, pp 2-15; Glenn Richardson, *Wolsey* (Oxford, 2020), pp 10-12, 16-41.
[121] The following 'armyes heretofore sent in the tymes' was struck in favour of 'armyes our progenitors and auncestors for the reducion of that land to vertuous lyving good ordre and politique govourn': BL, Titus, B.XI, f. 386r. Also, see *Expugnatio*, ed. Scott and Martin, p. 245 (II. 37).
[122] SP 60/1, f. 71v. A threat of force was always implicit in Tudor reform treatises: David Edwards, 'The escalation of violence in sixteenth-century Ireland' in David Edwards, PadraigLenihan and Clodagh Tait (eds), *Age of atrocity: violence and political conflict in early modern Ireland* (Dublin, 2007), pp 34-78.
[123] SP 60/1, f. 71r. Also, see Marian Lyons, 'The onset of religious reform: 1460-1550' in *CHI*, i, 498-504; Lennon, *Sixteenth-cen. Ire.*, p. 130.
[124] SP 60/1, f. 22v.
[125] SP 60/1, f. 71r. Also, see the curse against Thomas Fitzgerald: SP 60/2, f. 76r.

in Ireland.[126] Surrey was to secure the 'lymytes of defence' as the king had by then commanded, and so would emerge with 'acceptable pleasur and servyce as thowz ye conqueryd a grette part of that land' in the context of moving on to European diplomacy.[127] Appreciating that Ireland was regarded as a land of conquest, military aid was offered by Francis I.[128] Reinforcing the king's opinion, the sheer cost and scale to make the 'conquest be perffighted' was, as Surrey warned, prohibitive. Yet in advising the king, Surrey's reflections after a year in office in part measure the conquest of Ireland with campaigns elsewhere. Surrey spoke of the difficulties involved in relation to the thirteenth-century Edwardian conquest of Wales, citing geography and the constraints of distance.[129] After much scrutiny, the wild Irish were thoroughly robust and 'do lyve more hardly then any other people...in Christendome or Turky'.[130] Surrey understood the king's enthusiasm for conquest and desire for honour.[131] He was also alive to the immediate urgency of Scottish incursions in 'stopping of thErle of Argyles purpose in commyng to Irelande'. Furthermore, should war erupt between the Emperor and Francis I, 'by vertue of the treaties heretofore made, [he] shalbe required to geve ayde and assistance to the Prince invaded ayeinst the invasour...whiche...shall amounte to a right grete and marvelous charge'.[132] In 1521, the prevailing opinion was that Irish affairs yielded little honour, unlike pursuits elsewhere. The possibility of pressing obligations 'either to thEmperour or [the] Frense king...[upon which] gretely dependeth his honour' necessitated a more frugal approach in Ireland.[133]

Kildare's presence at the Field of the Cloth of Gold, was significant considering the 'weightie businesse' of continental diplomacy at hand. But it was also fitting given his political standing and myriad cultural pursuits.[134] While Surrey and the Irish council were reassured that Kildare's alleged 'conspiracies' would be 'tryed as...justice shall apperteigne', the earl himself was singularly privileged as an

---

[126] It has been argued as the inevitable outcome of seeking a 'politique' alternative: Bradshaw, *Cost. rev.*, p. 68.
[127] BL, Titus B.XII, f. 636v. See also SP 60/1, f. 62v.
[128] SP 60/1, f. 39v.
[129] *S.P. Hen. VIII*, ii, 73.
[130] *S.P. Hen. VIII*, ii, 74; Maginn and Ellis, *Tudor discov. Ire.*, pp 148-9.
[131] *LP*, iii, 189-91.
[132] SP 60/1, ff 57v, ff 58.
[133] SP 60/1, f. 61r. For the troubling condition of the Irish exchequer after Surrey, see Ellis, *Reform and revival*, pp 84, 104; Bradshaw, *Const. rev.*, p. 78; *S.P. Hen. VIII*, ii, 77-8. Treatises made in 1519-20 bound each prince by honour to the profit and 'weal ... to all Christendom': Edward Hall, *Vnion of the two noble and illustrate famelies of Lancastre and Yorke* (1548), p. 71. An optimistic mood can be seen in a c. 1521 memorial eagerly 'trustynge in the vertue and strengthe of treaties of pease': BL, Galba B.VII, f. 39v.
[134] SP 60/1, f. 37v. Also present at the summit were More and Andreas, works by whom printed in 1516 and 1517 respectively were added to Kildare's library: BL, Harleian MS 3756, f. 96v; Byrne, 'Earls of Kildare', pp 139, 145.

attending Irish-born lord at Balinghem. This appears to signal that he remained firmly in favour at Court throughout this period. Kildare was selected among the 'ffurst to attende upon the kinges grace' to 'the entervieu with the frenche king'. Present also was Thomas Boleyn who at the time was claimant to the earldom of Ormond and the Archbishop of Armagh John Kite, who was chosen among the prelates of the Church.[135]

The Cardinal's omnipotence offered hope for reformers in the colony, while a new archbishop occupied the Palace of St Sepulchre, his motto and arms freshly cut on its facade.[136] Kildare returned in 1523 where a council grateful for Wolsey's 'graciouse soliciting' suggested hopes for reform, although Ormond's limitations as deputy kept hopes to side-line Kildare in check.[137] The Geraldine position, in a sense legitimised through distinctive and broad cultural projections prompted the reformist response which was itself marked by characteristic humanist pursuits. The conquest-orientated rhetoric of the 1510s was thus preserved as key contributions in a conflict over differing visions of Ireland as a land of conquest. The particular circumstances of pre-Reformation renaissance diplomacy in Ireland ensured that critics of Kildare gained some traction at Court. The extent to which they were emboldened by the credence given to humanist 'conquest' literature up to this point is unclear, but it did little to allay the destabilisation of the lordship in the 1520s.

---

[135] SP 60/1, ff 37v-38r; SP 1/19, f. 260r.
[136] SP 60/1, f. 74r. For Palesmen's praise of Surrey, see Maginn and Ellis, *Tudor discov. Ire.*, p. 151; Heffernan, *Tudor policy*, pp 33-6, 45-6; Bradshaw, *Const. rev.*, p. 74.
[137] In 1521-2, Piers Butler was supported by the crown and Surrey: Edwards, *Ormond lordship*, pp 156-7.

5

Geraldine 'decay', 1522-34

Surrey's legacy as lord lieutenant in a sense splintered into separate facets. His learning curve in Irish matters and cognisance of the practical necessity of aristocratic delegation led to a *rapprochement* with Kildare (discussed in chapter six). But his time in Ireland stirred optimism among proponents of conquest. Kildare was reappointed in 1524 amid acrimonious relations with Ormond and growing contention in many quarters regarding the crown's Irish policy. Certain perspectives shifted over the course of the decade, most notably Surrey, and as it is here argued, those of his servant Thomas Bathe. Surrey (who succeeded his father as the third duke of Norfolk in May 1524) also maintained relations with both Piers Butler and a circle of moderate reformers. It is here proposed that Archbishop Inge, Patrick Bermingham and in particular Bathe came to take a less anti-Kildare view while Finglas, Rawson and Butler proponents hardened their stance. By the end of the decade, the 'Breviate' re-emerged c. 1529 as a notable addition to conquest-orientated literature of decay. In the preceding years, Robert Cowley was the most vocal and influential Butler advocate. Having initially served Kildare up to 1513 when he was dismissed by Gearóid Óg, Cowley became a secretary to Piers Butler and an implacable enemy of Kildare. Cowley, like Bathe, was a merchant with legal training. Both have been accredited authorship of the 'Discourse' (c. 1526), a long-overlooked document which can be compared with the 'State' (c. 1515) and the 'Breviate'.[1] Recent arguments have been made for Cowley's authorship, including a detailed case by Heffernan who has brought the entire document into print for the first time.[2] Heffernan points out that as Piers Butler was referred to as Ormond, it must predate 1528 and also traces

---

[1] SP 60/1, ff 130; *S.P. Hen. VIII*, ii, 142. White and Brady have put forward Bathe as the author: Dean White, 'The Tudor plantations in Ireland before 1571' (Ph.D., Trinity College Dublin, 1968), p. 49; Ciaran Brady, *Chief governors: the rise and fall of reform government in Tudor Ireland, 1536–1588* (Cambridge, 1994), p. 249. See also, Brendan Bradshaw, *Irish constitutional revolution of the sixteenth century* (Cambridge, 1979), pp 22, 41–3.

[2] David Heffernan, 'Robert Cowley's "A Discourse of the cause of the evil state of Ireland and of the remedies thereof", c. 1526' in *Analecta Hibernica*, 48 (2017), pp 1–30; David Heffernan, *Debating Tudor policy in sixteenth-century Ireland: 'reform' treatises and political discourse* (Manchester, 2018), pp 18–19, 33. Heffernan points to the tract's hostility toward Kildare and contextualises biographical evidence for Cowley. Mercantile interests are also cited. Both Bathe and Cowley matched this profile, the former having been 'customer of Carlyford': SP 60/1, ff 146; Heffernan, 'Cowley's "Discourse"', pp 5–6.

similarities between the 'Discourse' and Cowley's later policy proposals.[3] It appears that the 'Discourse' (c. 1526) was not the specific document of 'one Bath' refuted by Cowley in 1528. Chad Marshall questions Cowley's authorship, and given elements of doubt, he tentatively accredits Bathe as the author.[4] In what follows, it is proposed that the 'Discourse' was written by Bathe shortly after Kildare's restoration and when Surrey inherited his dukedom, before a revised 'boke' was offered in 1528 with a softened position regarding Kildare. Reflecting Norfolk's evolving perspectives, Bathe's favoured position may explain Cowley's bitter reaction. The final section of this chapter then explores the revival of the 'Breviate' and the rhetoric against Kildare up to the rebellion.

On the transition of power back to Kildare in May 1524, the 'Discourse' described O'Neill bearing the sword of state in Christ Church Cathedral as a 'monstrous sight to beholde'.[5] Composed between 1524 and 1528, the details here suggest an origin closer to 1524.[6] Written in the aftermath of the 'troble spoiles and enormyties doun' by the adherents of Kildare since 1520, it was O'Neill who at the earl's behest attacked the Pale upon Norfolk's arrival in Ireland.[7] The 'Discourse' covered most political issues of the 1520s and there are grounds for dating the treatise to the immediate aftermath of Kildare's reappointment as deputy. The most granular image and emotive passage related to these proceedings. At this stage, Cowley was presumably removed as clerk of the Privy Council and had returned to Whitehall. Although not likely to have been present at the ceremony, he would have agreed that the spectacle of O'Neill was an abomination.[8] The scene was described in Arthurian terms:

> the kynges sworde in Irlond may be resomblyd to kynge Arthures sege perelous which was ordeynyd but for one mane for Lancelotes sonnne. And if any other wolde attempte to sytte therein, he myght not escape without a grete daungere.

---

[3] See Heffernan, 'Cowley's "Discourse"', pp 8-11. Linguistic comparisons have been made between the 'Discourse' and other examples of Cowley's work: Fitzsimons, 'Cardinal Wolsey', p. 85.
[4] Marshall argues that Cowley was an established Irish figure, unlike the author of the 'Discourse'. Secondly, he states that the treatise is factionally neutral and therefore unlikely to be written by Cowley. A final reason is Cowley's policies, somewhat similar to some proposals in the 'Discourse', came later: Chad Marshall, 'The reform treatises and discourse of early Tudor Ireland, c. 1515-1541' (Ph.D., University of Tasmania, 2018), pp 202-5.
[5] BL, Lansdowne MS 159, f. 7v. Hall was less colourful in recording that 'the greate oneele bare the sworde': Edward Hall, *Vnion of the two noble and illustrate famelies of Lancastre and Yorke* (1548), p. 131.
[6] Heffernan, 'Robert Cowley's "Discourse"', p. 5.
[7] BL, Lansdowne MS 159, ff 7.
[8] Anthony McCormack and Terry Clavin, 'Cowley, Robert (d. 1546?)', *DIB*.

Soo it ys of the kinges sworde in Irlond, who so ever touchithe hit saveing one
man shall be putt to a grete extremitie and all his adherentes and partitakeres.[9]

As Surrey's servant and an associate of Inge and Bermingham, Bathe may have been in a position to have observed proceedings in person. The 'Discourse', as Heffernan stated, offers the most detailed account of Ireland at this time. Although more benign in terms of policy, it remains part of the anti-Kildare literature of decay. Given Bathe's relationship with Inge and Bermingham, they may have collaborated in appealing for Norfolk.[10] The 'Discourse' praised the duke while his landed interests in Idrone as Earl Marshal were presented in terms of the king's honour.[11] Securing peace with the lords of Ulster and Connaught was seen as a way to liberate the king's deputy to act freely in Leinster. This in turn was taken by seizing the barony of Idrone as the 'key of Ireland' through which the land was 'gotyn'.[12] Idrone was far more significant than its relatively modest size suggests. A range of geopolitical factors included its location in the Barrow valley, and its centrality on what Finglas referred to as the 'highe waye' between Dublin and Waterford.[13] It was also proximate to the core regions of the Kildare, Ormond and MacMurrough-Kavanagh lordships. Indeed, long after the Kildare rebellion the barony's importance remained undiminished. See, for example, the Butler revolt of 1569 which was precipitated by Lord Deputy Henry Sidney's granting of Idrone to Carew.[14] In the 'Discourse', accounts of the fertility of the country were tempered by fears that Cahir Art MacMurrough-Kavanagh would become as troublesome a Geraldine follower as the O'Connor Faly.[15]

Although addressed to Wolsey, the 'Discourse' was written in favour of Norfolk. Along with Inge, Bermingham and Bathe, Robert Cowley was thus inclined, having held the clerkship of the council up to 1523.[16] For a time, Piers Butler was considered by many including Norfolk as a counterweight to Kildare but

---

[9] The word 'not' was inserted above line: BL, Lansdowne MS 159, f. 7v.
[10] For instance, see SP 60/1, ff 130.
[11] BL, Lansdowne MS 159, ff 7v, 12, 13v.
[12] BL, Lansdowne MS 159, ff 14v, 12r, 16v (quote). This was similar to Finglas' 'Breviate'.
[13] Maginn and Ellis, *Tudor discov. Ire.*, p. 77.
[14] Brady, *Chief Gov.*, pp 132-40, 276-9; David Edwards, 'The Butler revolt of 1569' in *IHS*, 28 (1993), pp 228-55, esp. pp 245-6; David Edwards, *The Ormond lordship in County Kilkenny, 1515-1642: the rise and fall of Butler feudal power* (Dublin, 2003), pp 194-7; Nicholas Canny, *The Elizabethan conquest of Ireland: a pattern established, 1565-76* (Hassocks, 1976), pp 140-5; Heffernan, *Tudor policy*, pp 41, 126-37, 164.
[15] BL, Lansdowne MS 159, f. 13r. For example, in 1521 Stile warned Wolsey that defence against the O'Connor came at a great charge: SP 60/1, f. 67r. Also see Fiona Fitzsimons, 'The lordship of O'Connor Faly, 1520-70' in William Nolan and T. P. O'Neill (eds), *Offaly: history and society* (Dublin, 1998), pp 207-42.
[16] He was succeeded by John Alen: *S.P. Hen. VIII*, ii, 104; S. G. Ellis, *Reform and revival: English government in Ireland 1470-1534* (Woodbridge, 1986), p. 37.

there were limitations to his influence, especially regarding defence of the Pale. Indentures of 1524 show how Geraldine-Butler rivalry was delicately poised.[17] A lesser figure than Sir Piers may have been ineffective given the weakened Ormond position. It was, according to the 'Discourse', recognised that in times past that the Butlers 'doth good', noting elsewhere their stand against Geraldine Yorkists.[18] Their ascendancy under the White Earl and the Lancastrian crown was described as something of a benign intercession before having suffered the 'Garaldynes of the este...(and) of the weste' ever since.[19] Intrigue between Desmond and Francis I was a contributing factor to the author's emphasis that both Geraldine houses were 'foundid owte of one stocke'. Dark implications were then conjured with reference to the Yorkist revolts of the 1480s and 1490s.[20] In stressing his loyalty to the crown, Piers saw himself worthy of these 'auncesters by his [the king's] noble progenitors and specially in Waterford'.[21] Stoked by Kildare, the most recent violence and 'varyaunce' prompted ongoing doubts as to his viability as an alternative to the Geraldines.[22] Ambivalence was compounded by the dispute over the Ormond title, when Kildare was compelled to support the Boleyn claim in 1524. However, in regional terms, a loss of influence was offset by the translation of his brother Edmund as Archbishop of Cashel.

Other details, when discussed with wider events and certain strategic developments, may shed light on when the 'Discourse' was written. By means of the 'Discourse', Wolsey would have been notified of the supply of gunpowder and ordnance through Irish ports.[23] Piers captured Arklow from Maurice MacMurrough-Kavanagh in 1525 which the 'Discourse' did not mention in discussing regional policies and when outlining the 'sea on the iiiith side' of their sept.[24] Inscribed on the earliest surviving map of Ireland from the sixteenth century, precisely at the town of Arklow are the words 'erle of Ormond'. Dated to the 1520s, this seems to indicate that it was produced shortly after 1525 but this is by no means conclusive. It has been suggested that this very map was presented at Court along with the 'Discourse' which refers to an accompanying 'plat'.[25] In

---

[17] Christopher Maginn and S. G. Ellis, *Tudor discovery of Ireland* (Dublin, 2015), p. 152; Edwards, *Ormond lordship*, pp 155–6. The council had cautioned against the recall of Surrey: *S.P. Hen. VIII*, ii, 93.
[18] BL, Lansdowne MS 159, f. 7v.
[19] BL, Lansdowne MS 159, ff 6v, 7r.
[20] BL, Lansdowne MS 159, ff 6. By underlining both Fitzgerald houses as 'one stocke', Kildare was implicated in Desmond's actions. In a way, it was also an obscure and unintentional recognition of the broad identity then being projected by Kildare. See below, ch. 6.
[21] LPL, MS 602, ff 30.
[22] SP 60/1, f. 89r; BL, Lansdowne MS 159, ff 6r, 8r.
[23] BL, Lansdowne MS 159, f. 11v.
[24] BL, Lansdowne MS 159, f. 12r.
[25] BL, Augustus I.II, 21; BL, Lansdowne MS 159, f. 9r. Heffernan emphasises that this is almost

the 'Discourse', Arklow remained one of the 'crykes and pylles a mone Iryshemen' although in 1525 Kildare had recognised that 'Ormond kepeth...a pyle adjoynyng to the see, called Arclow'.[26] Nor did the 'Discourse' refer to Bishop Maurice Doran of Leighlin having been 'heynosly murdered', allegedly by 'Ormondes neigh kynnesman'.[27]

Since the Surrey experiment, Inge, Rawson and Bermingham impressed upon Wolsey the need to 'preserve' in his 'charitably bygonne enterprise'.[28] Repeatedly encouraged to enforce his legatine authority in Ireland since 1520 (by Rokeby, Alen and in an anonymous *c.* 1520 'device'), the 'Discourse' made a similar plea.[29] The tract was supportive of the Butlers but with reservations.[30] If written *c.* 1524-5, the 'Discourse' may have emerged amid fears that the accords of 1524 would be insufficient. Innovative proposals such as a plan to 'surrendre and yeld' lands would have appealed to Wolsey while the tract is presented in an articulate manner. Although a variety of approaches are outlined in the 'Discourse', as the case with the 'State' (*c.* 1515), the 'medicine' or solution, underlined by extended literary allusions was that of military conquest.[31]

Kildare and Piers were again summoned to Court by late 1526. Amid more 'envy and complaints' Kildare was examined before the king's council, to Wolsey's utter disdain for Geraldine intransigence.[32] There is little indication that the 'Discourse' had an immediate effect on policy but the appointment of Lord Delvin as governor in September 1527 was similar to proposals concerning the role of regional captains.[33] Richard Nugent, third baron of Delvin, was formerly

---

certainly the map that was referred to in the tract. See Heffernan, 'Cowley's "Discourse"', p. 7; J. H. Andrews, 'Colonial cartography in a European setting: the case of Tudor Ireland', in David Woodward (ed.), *The history of cartography: cartography in the European Renaissance* (6 vols, Chicago, 1987-2015), iii, 1673.

[26] BL, Lansdowne MS 159, f. 11v; S.P. Hen. VIII, ii, 122. Cowley later treated of 'that Arclo... a good haven': SP 60/3, f. 65v.

[27] *S.P. Hen. VIII*, ii, 122.

[28] SP 60/1, f. 74r.

[29] If written after Doran's murder, it may have alluded to the event. See BL, Lansdowne MS 159, f. 10v; *S.P. Hen. VIII*, ii, 103.

[30] They too were in part responsible for the decline of the Englishry: BL, Lansdowne MS 159, ff 9r-10r.

[31] BL, Lansdowne MS 159, f. 14v; BL, Add. MS 4792, f. 104v. For instance, see Wingfield to Wolsey: Vitellius B.XVIII, f. 117v. For the 'Discourse' and what was later termed 'surrender and regrant', Heffernan, 'Cowley's "Discourse"', p. 8. It was not until a 'Devices' (*c.* 1537), most likely written by Cusack, that such a policy would be proposed in detail: *'Reform' Treatises on Tudor Ireland*, ed. David Heffernan (Dublin, 2016), pp 1-6.

[32] ALC, 1527. Also, see BL, Lansdowne MS 159, f. 6r. Ellis compares complaints from the 1520s with those of the Talbot-Ormond feud: Ellis, *Reform and revival*, p. 52. Upon Kildare's departure Cahir MacMurorugh Kavanagh raided Kilkenny: Edwards, *Ormond lordship*, p. 159.

[33] BL, Lansdowne MS 159, f. 17v.

a Kildare ally but his capture by O'Connor Faly in May 1528 at the behest of the earl was enabled by Delvin having been 'not of power to defende' the Englishry.[34] The 'myssaventure' of Delvin was symptomatic of bitter factional divides and Kildare's ability to impose his will when removed from office.[35] As Ellis observes, in a battle of wills between Kildare and the king, the reliance on Delvin's localised *manraed* typified the crown's parsimonious, hopeful approach. Against advice to the contrary, it was essentially the king's decision to press on with the appointment of Delvin. Although Irish affairs remained a low priority, suggestions to appoint a Geraldine captain and ensure the defence of the Pale thus became a sensitive issue. The dramatic collapse of Delvin's vice-deputyship was unsurprising.[36] Piers Butler, recently ennobled earl of Ossory as Thomas Boleyn became Wiltshire and Ormond, was appointed as Delvin's replacement in August.[37] The 'Discourse' treated the continued Butler-Geraldine violence in Munster. After Dungarvan was besieged and granted to Ossory, Piers Butler received what had been described as the 'gretiste and principall...refuge and succore that there of dessmond hathe'.[38] Having been in league with France and the Emperor, Desmond was attainted in September 1528, placing Kildare in a complicated position at Court bearing in mind, as the 'Discourse' reminded, that they were of one stock.[39] In the tense circumstances of the mid-1520s, along with political proposals, much *gravitas* may have rested on the rhetorical pitch or symbolic import of a written treatise.

Norfolk, it seems, was of two minds. His initial heated reaction was to blame the malice between Kildare and Ossory for the land's problems, foreseeing no alternative but to launch a campaign as Henry II did with the first conquest. But within two months, he vouched for Bathe as 'bearer' of a dispatch to Wolsey, stressing the need to send Kildare 'thider'.[40] Bathe had hosted Norfolk (then Surrey) in his house in Drogheda and personal relations appear to have remained cordial.[41] Bathe worked closely with Norfolk throughout the decade and by 1528 had produced another treatise which Norfolk recommended to Wolsey. It seems

---

[34] SP 60/1, f. 108r. Family tradition in governing evidently mattered. His father governed in the late 1440s under Richard, duke of York.
[35] SP 60/1, f. 119r.
[36] S. G. Ellis, 'Defending the English Pale: The viceroyalty of Richard Nugent, third baron of Delvin, 1527-8' in *IHS*, 43 (2019), pp 1-11.
[37] At this time, he was reluctant to serve as deputy on the grounds of military shortcomings: Edwards, *Ormond lordship*, p. 159.
[38] The 'Discourse' adds that 'hit is the kinges playne enheritaunce and one of his chief honours of Irlond': BL, Lansdowne MS 159, f. 13v. In contrast, Ulster was stable at this time: Katharine Simms, *Gaelic Ulster in the middle ages: history, culture and society* (Dublin, 2020), p. 222.
[39] BL, Lansdowne MS 159, f. 6r.
[40] SP 60/1, f. 125v-126r; SP 60/1, ff 130; Ellis, 'Defending the English Pale', pp 1-11.
[41] SP 60/1, f. 127r.

that this 'boke', promptly denounced by Cowley, is lost.[42] However, if Bathe was the author of the 'Discourse' it is possible that the 'book' of 1528 was a revision of this work, while Finglas' 'Breviate' was also revived.[43] Instability in the lordship of the late 1520s sharpened Norfolk's learning curve, giving rise to his support of Kildare.[44] Norfolk recognised Kildare's extensive power networks in Ireland, which shaped his opinion by the end of the decade. Inge and Bermingham admitted that 'the strenght is by the Garrantynes'.[45] As with the 'State' (c. 1515) and Darcy's 'Artycles' (1515), the 'Discourse' sprang from a perceived crisis, which by 1528-9 had elicited its revision along with a revival of Finglas' 'Breviate'. Bathe appealed directly to the Cardinal (by then in a vulnerable position at Court) and amended his 'perceptions' to seek Kildare's return, while the 'Breviate' was revitalised in a push to seek the conquest of south Leinster. Both Finglas and Bathe were promoted by Norfolk, which indicated a willingness to consider divergent policies, as the duke himself was sought by a range of political figures.

Written by a 'most honest Englishman' (Bathe was described as a 'trew man'), the 'Breviate' was thus afforded credibility as a panicked response to a perceived severe crisis.[46] Appearing amid the uncertainty surrounding the Cardinal's fall and a second attempt to allay Geraldine-Butler feuding, the 'Breviate' also emerged as appeals for military intervention were overlooked. Finglas and in particular the Cowleys championed this more extreme approach. Finglas' work was disseminated as new strategies were proposed in the search for the optimal approach. In what was a challenge to Kildare, the revised 'Breviate' materialised at Court around the time of the Boleyn ascendancy and Ossory's replacement of Gearóid Óg.[47] A number of curiosities also arise from the various titles given to the treatise, some

---

[42] SP 60/1, f. 130r; LPL, MS 602, f. 56v; SP 60/1, ff 130; *S.P. Hen. VIII*, ii, 142.

[43] While the 'Breviate' was reissued, no distinctly humanist treatise by Finglas was produced.

[44] A closeness between Norfolk and Bathe was signified in his 'retournyng from Walsyngham, hath be here with me, and by hym I perceyve what myserable state' afflicted the lordship: SP 60/1, f. 130r.

[45] *S.P. Hen. VIII*, ii, 129.

[46] SP 60/1, f. 130r.

[47] 'An Abbreviate of the getting of Ireland and the decay of the same' (c. 1529) survives as an Elizabethan copy: LPL, MS 600, f. 209. In what follows, I have broadly followed the edition offered by Maginn and Ellis, *Tudor discov. Ire.*, pp 69-79. The earliest manuscript of these four versions are as follows (also in Maginn and Ellis). Version one (c. 1516) 'A brief note of the getting and decay of Ireland preferred to king Henry the eighth in about the viith yere of his reign': LPL, MS 635, f. 185, a late Elizabethan copy (available on microfilm, NLI, pos. 1707). Version two (c. 1529) 'An Abbreviate of the getting of Ireland and the decay of the same': LPL, MS 600, f. 209 (available on microfilm, NLI, pos. 1696). Version three (c. 1535) 'The decay of Ireland': LPL, MS 621, f. 92; BL, Add. MS 4763. Version four (c. 1535) 'An account of the conquest of Ireland, the decay of the same and a remedy for the oppression of Irish lords': SP 60/2, f. 17.

of which were copied much later in the century. The surviving copy of version one does not include the word 'Breviate', which has become synonymous with Finglas. It seems more accurate and appropriate to refer to the text as the 'Getting and decay'. The 'brief note' (c. 1516) which also survives as a later copy does not include the word breviate in the title.[48] Finglas became synonymous with the 'getting and decay' of Ireland, yet the pairing of these terms is slightly anomalous. It seems that Finglas distinguished between 'getting' and 'conquest'. While the latter is preferred throughout the text, the precise implications are unclear. The 'mooste parte' of the land was conquered by Henry II but the 'chief(est)' of the getting and conquering of Leynster' was 'Rycharde erle of Strangebowe who maryed MacMorrowghes daughter with whom aswell by the saide Mac Mottowghes gyfte as by conquest he had all Leynester and reduced it to good ordre and obedience of the kynges lawes'.[49] It could be that Finglas associated 'getting' with the blood of the MacMurrough which inevitably rendered 'all Leinster' prone to the organic process of decay.[50] By the use of both terms, there was a historical authenticity on account of the word 'conquest' along with the alarming decay of what had been imperfectly 'gotten'. The crown's obligation to secure Ireland is heightened by the decline of a conquest commanded by the king with papal 'lycence'. According to the 'Breviate', Leinster in particular was 'gotten' or perhaps given the organic nature of the term, begotten, and was bestowed as a 'gyft'.[51]

Little is known of the provenance of the c. 1529 'Abbreviate', aside from the likelihood of its production for a courtly reader. Influenced by the 'State' (c. 1515) and the 'Artycles' (1515), as a concise description and analysis of the colony, it proved a significant treatise in its own right.[52] The 'Breviate' opens with a geographical description which appears to inform a reader at Court seeking such information.[53] Like Darcy's 'Artycles', it offered a history of a decayed polity. Since the conquest, the 'chiefest' aspect of which was the 'gettyng and conqueryng

---

[48] The title may have been altered at a later date as Finglas became synonymous with 'getting and decay'. Although it can refer to the process of shortening, it was more commonly associated with the late sixteenth century and 'abbreviate' was a distinctly Elizabethan term.

[49] 'Chiefest': LPL, MS 635, f. 185r. See Maginn and Ellis, *Tudor discov. Ire.*, p. 69. Also, regarding the refortification of derelict posts see Brady, *Chief gov.*, pp 248-9.

[50] For Edmund Spenser's argument, see Ciaran Brady, 'Spenser, plantation and government policy' in R. A. McCabe (ed.), *Oxford handbook of Edmund Spenser* (Oxford, 2010), pp 86-105.

[51] Maginn and Ellis, *Tudor discov. Ire.*, p. 69.

[52] For overviews of the 'Breviate', see Maginn and Ellis, *Tudor discov. Ire.*; Ellis, *Ire. Tudors*, p. 29; Heffernan, 'Finglas' breviate', pp 371-3.

[53] Wolsey may have sought the 'brief note' c. 1516, while Gardiner or Cromwell perhaps did so in 1529. Finglas was appointed second justice of the common pleas in 1516: F. E. Ball, *The judges in Ireland, 1221-1921* (2 vols, London, 1926), i, 216; Maginn and Ellis, *Tudor discov. Ire.*, p. 24.

of Leynster', the MacMurrough presented an underlying incongruity.[54] William Marshal had preserved English order in the region but its decline thereafter occurred due to succession problems, absenteeism and crown neglect. In Finglas, this 'erle Marshall' was the last heroic figure of the conquest (after Henry II, Richard Fitzgilbert de Clare and Hugh de Lacy) as the Irish grew in strength after his death.[55] Finglas accounts for the decay of Ireland on a regional basis as the plight of extortions used by degenerate old colonial magnates had plagued the lordship for centuries. Finglas concludes that in order to reverse this affliction, the subjugation of MacMurrough, O'Byrne and O'Toole must precede the conquest and garrison of south Leinster. Foremost among his proposals were the fortification of key regional locations to make way for more expansive campaigns. Confiscated lands were to alleviate costs and absentee lords were to be severely penalised. Underlining the importance of the Barrow valley Finglas made a plea to 'put in the kynges mynde by this mean or a better to refourme this forsaide countree betuxte dublyne and Waterforde'.[56] Vested interests appear to be part of political interests and seem to have included the Butlers and the civic elite of Waterford while attention was also drawn to the Norfolk inheritance in south Leinster, specifically Idrone. With a didactic use of history, Finglas sought to revive interest in the colony.

Considering the wider circumstances across the Tudor realm, the c. 1516 version and the c. 1529 recension were part of a political intervention. The latter appears to have taken place around the time of the Boleyn ascendancy and the replacement of Kildare. With the absence of a coherent strategy, it may have been a challenge to Kildare at Court rather than in Ireland. The creation of Ossory also took place around the time the 'Breviate' was revived. By 1529, when the Cardinal was removed from office, secretary of state Stephen Gardiner or Norfolk may have turned to Finglas in seeking a fresh analysis of Irish affairs, considering a dire forecast that £20,000 'shall not repaire the hurtes that shalbe done or myd September'.[57] Precisely one month later, with the lordship in crisis Inge died of

---

[54] LPL, MS 635, f. 185r. The Hatfield manuscript differs slightly, accounting the 'chiefe of the gettyng': Maginn and Ellis, *Tudor discov. Ire.*, p. 69; Brady, *Chief gov.*, p. 249.

[55] See for example the aforementioned 'reede erll is dayes' as a historical frame of reference: SP 60/1, f. 7r.

[56] Maginn and Ellis, *Tudor discov. Ire.*, p. 79; David Heffernan, 'Patrick Finglas' A Breviat of the conquest of Ireland and the decay of the same, c. 1535 and the Tudor Conquest of Ireland' in *Sixteenth Century Journal*, 49 (2017), pp 372-3; Bradshaw, *Const. rev.*, pp 37-47. By 1515, Kildare had acquired a string of castles throughout Carlow which bolstered his position on the Ormond periphery: NLI, MS 25006, f. 1r; Edwards, *Ormond lordship*, p. 150.

[57] Inge was last mentioned as he sought unity between Kildare and Ossory, entrusted by Norfolk for the distribution of revenues to employ the military service of 'such Irishemen... next adjoynyng to the Inglishre and the mony to be distrybuted by the advyse of the Chaunsoler': SP 60/1, ff 130.

sweating sickness on 3 August 1528.[58] If Bathe filled something of a vacuum by becoming a voice in seeking amity between Ireland's feuding aristocracy, Finglas confirmed his position as an advocate for more extreme measures. His 'Breviate' (c. 1529) was timely, as Wolsey's fall reciprocated further changes in government. Moreover, with shifting ground at Court and in Ireland, the subsequent termination of the 'secret council' triumvirate of Alen, Bermingham and Rawson prompted a review of intelligence.[59]

Finglas reinforced his premise through the use of symbolism. In his use of history, the chronicles and the 'kinges recordis', Giraldus seems to have been the main inspiration. The barony of Idrone as the keystone of the colony were features of both the 'Breviate' and of the history of the conquest in general. It became a focal point where decay occurred after Willliam Marshal, a figure of importance in the *Expugnatio* and early Tudor conquest rhetoric.[60] Among the layers of historical argument and historical consciousness, as learned men, both Darcy and Finglas, associated the Earl Marshal with a virtuous colony before its lapse into Irishness. These themes were central to the *Expugnatio* while Finglas was aware of the Earl Marshal's symbolic appeal in Ireland and at Court. Darcy and Finglas studied at the Inns of Court, where a generation earlier 'no Irish person born' was to be admitted. In 1513, restrictions remained for 'gtm [gentlemen] of Ireland'. In 1503 Finglas was pardoned four vacations and elected steward in 1506.[61] William Marshal was entombed in Temple Church and centuries later graduates from the Inns ceremonially passed his effigy.[62] As the 'State' (c. 1515) was a redaction of the *Salus Populi*, the 'Breviate' likewise incorporated a range of sources alongside its main informant. In the 'Breviate', the history of the colony was carefully condensed ensuring that sufficient weight was given to Dermot MacMurrough's submission. The killing of Hugh de Lacy, 'traiterously slaine by a mason of his owne' while fortifying battlements, was a cautionary event. In something of an epitaph for a fallen conquest, Finglas then cited what is 'written in the Cronicles of Irland Quod ibi cessavit conquestus'.[63] Fearing the axes of the Irish with reference to de Lacy's death was also the concluding message of the

---

[58] *The book of obits and martyrology of the cathedral church of the Holy Trinity, commonly called Christ Church, Dublin*, ed. J. C. Crosthwaite (Dublin, 1844), p. 35.
[59] The venture was poorly financed. See copies of letters made by Archbishop Alen; SP 1/67, f. 35r.
[60] Their 'inclynacion to yrishe rule' was also a moral lapse: Maginn and Ellis, *Tudor discov. Ire.*, pp 69-71.
[61] *Records of the society of Lincoln's Inn*, ed. J. D. Walker (2 vols, London, 1897), i, 103, 192.
[62] I am grateful to John Shearer, verger at Temple Church for his assistance and insights.
[63] Maginn and Ellis here refer to *Chartularies of St Mary's Abbey, Dublin with the register of its house at Dunbrody and annals of Ireland*, ed. J. T. Gilbert (London, 1884, 2 vols), ii, 305. See Maginn and Ellis, *Tudor discov. Ire.*, p. 73.

Expugnatio.[64] This 'experience' was likely called upon in 1529 to 'reduce the lordes and gentlemen of this lande whiche ne of Englishe nation to due obedience of his graces laws which is veraye harde to doe onles the kynge with an armye represse Irishemen upon the bourdors to tribute in a good confourmyte'.[65] Consequently, it was through the conquest of the MacMurrough that allowed for the 'reformation of Leynster which was the keaye and high way for reformation'.[66]

The 'Breviate' effectively condensed past events with a *de casibus* rise and fall of the colony which may itself suggests a courtly readership. As with the 'State' (c. 1515) and the 'Artycles' (1515) there was a dynamic presentation of archaic literary sources. There is also evidence of shared readership with fellow council member (and long-time Kildare ally) William Preston, second Viscount Gormanston. Preston owned a copy of the 'Annales Hibernia' cited in the 'Breviate'. This manuscript came to be collated with the chartularies of St Mary's Abbey, whose abbot served with both Preston and Finglas on Surrey's council. Each had expressed their gratitude and impressed upon Wolsey the need for impartial government.[67] Inserted at the foot of the page recounting the death of Hugh de Lacy is an inscription made by a Tudor hand intended to prompt a reflection on the moral decline of the colony:

whate profit is of plente and grete treasure, And evyr i[n] wretdndnes to endure.[68]

---

[64] Gerald of Wales, *Expugnatio Hibernica, the conquest of Ireland*, ed. A. B. Scott and F. X. Martin (Dublin, 1978), pp 251-3 (II. 39). The late medieval Hiberno-English 'Butler Expugnatio' summarises 'Hugh de Lacy that to trusty was up-on hys Iresshmen and by trayson of ham was heded at dernagh...castels yn many places weren cast doun many men slawe to grete perrylle to all the land': TCD, MS 592, f. 28r. The corresponding section in the 'Bray Expugnatio' was highlighted with a decapitated head. As with the *Expugnatio*, a siege mentality and regional entrenchment co-exist with prophetic discourse in the 'Breviate'. The 'iiii saynctes (Patrick, Columba, Brechan and Molling) made prophecye that Englishmen should have conquered Irelande, saide that the saide Englishemen shoulde kepe the lande in prosperitie as long as they shoulde kepe ther owne laws and assone as they shoulde leave their own lawe and fall to Irishe order, then they should decay, thexperynce wherof is prowed true': Maginn and Ellis, *Tudor discov. Ire.*, p. 77.

[65] Maginn and Ellis, *Tudor discov. Ire.*, p. 77.

[66] The 'Butler Expugnatio' highlighted prophecies which foretold the bearing of 'fyr to Leynstre': TCD, MS 592, f. 7v.

[67] SP 60/1, f. 74r. Like Darcy, Preston may have drifted from the Geraldine orbit and become aligned with other Pale interests. He served on the council throughout the 1520s during which time, if there is truth in the tradition preserved in the Book of Howth, Preston's anti-Irish sentiment may have hardened. Gormanston reputedly said to the earl; 'we hath for the most number killed our enemies, and if we do the like with all the Irishmen that we have with us, it were a good deed': *Cal. Carew*, v. 185.

[68] The inscription appears at first to have been a rhyming couplet. The words 'plente and grete' were inserted above the line: Bodl., MS Laud Misc. 526, f. 2v.

There are tentative links with Finglas as it drew attention to past events narrated in the 'Breviate', in particular this citation of the 'Annales'. It is unclear who inscribed the endnote, nor is its precise implication discernible. However, it does show that historical argument was a contested sphere. It is arguably a perspective that highlighted the decay of Ireland and the vices of Kildare hegemony. The 'State' (c. 1515) similarly discussed: 'what is it to hym (Kildare) all the riches and honour of the worlde, yf he lose the honour and ryches eternall?'[69] This copy of the 'Annales' contained a reading aid that was later inserted to highlight the tenure of justiciar John Darcy in 1323.[70] In a contemporary hand, a folio page outlining the 'titil that the kynge of englande hath to Irland' followed the page indicating Preston's ownership and may have been added by the next owner of the text.[71] This also related to aspects of the 'Breviate' in the context of a decayed lordship. Taken as a whole, they are tropes from Giraldus but emphasised in this case as part of an attack against Geraldine power. The paths of Finglas and Preston crossed again as council members in 1528. Meanwhile, Ossory, Lord James Butler and Rawson advocated for Robert Cowley and appealed to Wolsey and Gardiner for support.[72]

Reports of seditious Geraldine 'confederacons' formed a climate where a revision of the 'Breviate' was possibly warranted by Gardiner as the new king's secretary.[73] Sir William Skeffington, master of the ordinance, was appointed deputy as Kildare was to assist this newcomer of low birth and for a time they seemed to effectively co-operate. The swift submission of O'Reilly to both figures preceded gains in Ulster, with Skeffington and O'Donnell in 'friendship and compact'.[74] Maginn and Ellis point to O'Donnell's submission at Drogheda in May 1531 and a clause to aid the king should he seek to reform Ireland.[75] The circumstances of this accord are noteworthy (see chapter six). It was perhaps wishful thinking to be a 'pollitickly ordered' strategy but it proved constructive for a time.[76] Hopes for the feuding old colonial magnates to 'joyne themselves in such conformytie as they

---

[69] SP 60/1, f. 22v.
[70] Bodl., MS Laud Misc. 526, f. 26v.
[71] Bodl., MS Laud Misc. 526, f. 42v.
[72] SP 60/1, ff 133r–136v. Ossory was instrumental in ensuring a flow of anti-Kildare rhetoric to court: Colm Lennon, *Sixteenth-century Ireland: the incomplete conquest* (Dublin, 1994), p. 86; Ellis, *Ire. Tudors*, p. 117. To many parties, Ossory was an acceptable alternative to Kildare. But among his difficulties was an inability to hold the Pale against the O'More and O'Connor Faly: Ellis, *Reform and revival*, pp 22–4; Maginn, '*Civ.*' *Gaelic Leinster*; p. 40.
[73] For relations between Butler and Gardiner, see SP 60/1, ff 132.
[74] ALC, 1532; S.P. Hen. VIII, ii, 156. Skeffington enjoyed the ready recognition of the Ulster lords: Simms, *Gaelic Ulster*, pp 202–3, 223–4.
[75] Maginn and Ellis, *Tudor discov. Ire.*, p. 151; S.P. Hen. VIII, ii, 152.
[76] Hall, *Vnion Lancastre and Yorke*, p. 193.

may accordyng to the kynges trust and expectacon', from a Geraldine perspective, was seen as a temporary arrangement as Kildare returned from England.[77] Intrigue between Desmond and the Emperor should have prompted Kildare to affirm his loyalty to the crown. Frustratingly, there is insufficient evidence for an in-depth study of Desmond-Hapsburg relations up to the 1520s.[78] Hapsburg communications with Desmond and his allies ('amiyes') were cut short with the death of the earl in July 1529.[79]

At Court, Kildare was also cleared of culpability by association as Wiltshire and Norfolk advocated Kildare's return. Meanwhile, Ossory's 'acqueyntaunce' with Cromwell and assurance that 'ye shall fynde me as reddy to accomplish your desires' reinforced factional divides.[80] The Butlers justifiably feared that Kildare was favoured by both Norfolk and Wiltshire. Furthermore, Ossory accused Kildare of inciting Wiltshire against him regarding claims over lands in Tullow and Arklow.[81] In reporting Kildare's usurpation of the king's patronage, Ossory declared the Barrow valley as the 'veray keyes of the cuntrey, wherby the said Erle of Kildare having possession therof hat opteyned of my lord of Wylshire a lees... [and intends] with strenght of his Irish alyes destrue me and wynne all the cuntrey from the king to him silf, which is his verey mynde.' Butler continued by stressing that 'garysons of thErldom of Ormond he wol at lenght make therof his owne enherytaunce'.[82] Not since the reign of Edward III had the manors of Tullow and Arklow been recovered, which 'were in the possession of Irishmen the space of thies 200 yeris'.[83] Mindful of the historical context, Wiltshire's lands were described as having been 'furst leesyd out in ferme to his auncestres and now [he] makith his awne enherytaunce therof by tytle of the sworde'.[84] Kildare believed

---

[77] SP 60/1, f. 142v.
[78] Micheál Ó Siochrú, 'Foreign involvement in the revolt of Silken Thomas, 1534-5' in *PRIA*, 96C (1996), pp 49-66, esp. pp 51-4; Thomas O'Connor, 'Ireland and Europe, 1580-1815: some historiographical remarks' in T. O'Connor (ed.), *The Irish in Europe, 1580-1815* (Dublin, 2001), pp 9-26, esp. pp 10-14; Anthony McCormack, *The earldom of Desmond, 1463-1583: the decline and crisis of a feudal lordship* (Dublin, 2005), pp 66-9.
[79] BL, Vespasian C.IV, f. 322r.
[80] Kildare had offered to 'procure hawks [and] falcons' for the Florentine Gherardini and Ossory likewise appealed to Cromwell by sending an 'Irish hawk' from Kilkenny to Austin Friars in 1532: *An account of the facsimiles of the National Manuscripts of Ireland*, ed. J. T. Gilbert (Dublin, 1889), p. 473; Diarmaid MacCulloch, *Thomas Cromwell: a life* (London, 2018), pp 66-7.
[81] Cromwell was reluctant to closely associate with any faction in Ireland according to: MacCulloch, *Thomas Cromwell*, p. 22-3. Bradshaw argued that this acquaintance has been overemphasised: Bradshaw, *Const. rev.*, p. 92.
[82] LPL, MS 616, f. 46r.
[83] LPL, MS 616, f. 46r.
[84] LPL, MS 616, ff 46. The militarisation of south Leinster occurred as Piers was allowed to gather forces to defend his *patria*. Edwards argues that in time this forced Kildare into rebellion. Edwards, *Ormond lordship*, pp 146-7, 160-2.

that alternative replacements in government had a short life span, an opinion reinforced since Surrey's lieutenancy. It was in Kildare's interest to co-operate with Skeffington, up to a point. After all, Geraldine prominence was recognised by means of a specific charge to defend the Pale. Skeffington's position became untenable when a parliamentary subsidy was refused in late 1531, by which stage Kildare and the deputy were at odds. In throwing his weight behind the Butlers, Skeffington had shown that a middle ground was diminishing. On the revoking of Kildare's rights to claim absentee lands in south Leinster, the Geraldines attacked members of Parliament passing through Idrone.[85] Cromwell had by then extended his horizons beyond the king's 'great matter' although Kildare's generous mandate on reappointment to office in 1532 indicated Ireland's low priority.[86]

But there was resolve at Court to curtail the power of the deputy as Kildare recommenced his governorship.[87] Cromwell followed Wolsey's efforts to establish networks of informants and this proved important. John Dethyke alerted Whitehall to Kildare's moving of the king's ordnance in September 1533 but the report also reflected a closeness between Cromwell and his Irish informants. As Cromwell's chaplain, Dethyke's sophisticated and scriptural correspondence cited proverbs in surmising the piety of Dublin citizens.[88] The episcopacy of Inge's successor, John Alen, proved a challenge to Kildare as much as an effort to reform. His tenure cast a different tone to his predecessors Rokeby and Inge. As Murray has shown, Alen's aggressive pursuit of his episcopal rights disturbed many vested interests, from the Pale community to those of the Kildare Geraldines.[89] Kildare

---

[85] See, LPL, MS 616, ff 46. Since Darcy's 'Artycles', proponents of conquest referred to the barony as the king's 'key highway'. Even in 1493, with de facto war between Kildare and Ormond, chief baron of the exchequer John Wyse reported the 'day to day... danger and peril of the road': *Statute rolls of the Irish parliament: Richard III - Henry VIII*, ed. Philomena Connolly (Dublin, 2002), p. 95.

[86] MacCulloch, *Thomas Cromwell*, p. 21. Kildare was quick to complain when restricted in making appointments to the office of chief remembrancer: Ellis, *Reform and revival*, p. 17.

[87] Lennon, *Sixteenth-cen. Ire.*, p. 105.

[88] Dethyke was on terms with his master's 'special good lady' and 'bedfellow': BL, Titus B.XI, ii, f. 346r. Cromwell's wife Elizabeth Wyckes died in 1529 but he fathered an illegitimate daughter who was born in the early 1530s: MacCulloch, *Thomas Cromwell*, pp 102-3. For Dethyke and Cromwell's propaganda campaign, see S. G. Ellis, 'The Kildare rebellion and the early Henrician reformation' in *HJ*, 19 (1976), p. 811; Brendan Bradshaw, 'Cromwellian Reform and the origins of the Kildare rebellion, 1533-4', in *Transactions of the Royal Historical Society*, 27 (1977), pp 76-7. For an indication of Kildare's treason, see D. B. Quinn, 'Henry VIII and Ireland, 1509-34' in *IHS*, p. 341.

[89] James Murray, 'Archbishop Alen, Tudor reform and the Kildare rebellion' in *PRIA*, 89C (1989), pp 1-10; James Murray, *Enforcing the English reformation in Ireland, clerical resistance and political conflict in the diocese of Dublin* (Cambridge, 2009), pp 21-8. During the 1520s, Kildare encountered bishops who acted independently, such as Dillon and Wellesley: Marian Lyons, *Church and society in County Kildare* (Dublin, 2000), p. 105; Marian Lyons, *Gearóid Óg Fitzgerald, ninth earl of Kildare* (Dundalk, 1998), pp 61-2.

ensured that the O'Byrnes and O'Tooles destroyed diocesan lands south of the Pale.[90] In striving for political as opposed to strictly ecclesiastical ends, Alen effectively operated through both canon and common law. A report to Cromwell in March 1532, proffered 'in haste', appropriately reflecting Alen's efficiency was predictably critical of Kildare, but it also showed a close relationship with the king's secretary. Having endured crippling praemunire charges for his association with Wolsey, seeking 'sum compassione' and a prebendary, Alen turned to Cromwell.[91] Having survived Wolsey's fall and the collapse of the 'secret council', Alen lamented the unruly marches of the Kildare governed lordship in terms of disorder and decay.[92] Both Alen and his cousin, namesake and clerk of the council (later lord chancellor) John Alen, were vehemently critical of Kildare. Yet after the killing of Ossory's son Thomas in 1532, the Cowleys and the earl entreated with additional vindictiveness and malice.

In late 1532 details of Kildare's campaigns in Ely were added to Cromwell's in-tray under 'intelligence out of Ireland by Waltr Cowley'. Carefully presented on paper with a watermark of a hand and five-pointed star, were accounts of Kildare having sustained a gunshot 'thorow the side...for the name and lordship of Okaroll'.[93] The council and Archbishop Alen shared a sense of historical consciousness, 'by the relation of aunciente men, in tymes past, within remembrance, all thInglish Lordes and gentils within the pale kepte retynewes of Irish yomen'.[94] A series of tropes, stemming from the conquest, included the centrality of English archery, where 'in tymes past' they were instrumental in 'feates of warre'.[95] In addition, Cowley's report of 1533 contrasted the 'honorable and wise' Butlers (including the archbishop of Cashel) with Geraldine indignity where the earl's brothers James, Richard and Walter Fitzgerald raided O'Toole's country 'escaping in the clothing of women'.[96]

---

[90] As Maginn points out, Geraldine-Butler feuding had obstructed attempts to reform the locality: Maginn, 'Civ.' Gaelic Leinster; pp 41, 62; Murray, 'Archbishop Alen', pp 1-10.
[91] This was highlighted by a manicle. A second, larger and distinctively sword shaped marginal highlight points to an apocryphal remark on performing duties in 'nether tyme of pece nore yet of warre': SP 60/1, f. 148r. Also, see Murray, 'Archbishop Alen', pp 1-16; Bradshaw, Const. rev., p. 91.
[92] SP 60/1, ff 149. Alen also wrote to Norfolk in 1529, to justify expenses of over £20 for repairs of the king's chancery 'within his Castell of Dublin which at my furst arriving I found here more like a swine stye then a stable': SP 1/67, f. 34r. For the administrative centralisation of the lordship in Dublin see Ellis, Reform and revival; Ellis, Ire. Tudors, pp 22-9, 43.
[93] SP 60/1, ff 152.
[94] See also the 'State' (c. 1515).
[95] S.P. Hen. VIII, ii, 163; Ellis, Reform and revival, p. 55. Traditionally, English archers were regarded as symbolically important: Expugnatio, ed. Scott and Martin, pp 183, 249 (II. 19, II. 38).
[96] SP 60/2, ff 5v, 7r; S.P. Hen. VIII, ii, 169. Gearóid Óg Fitzgerald had six sisters and seven half-brothers. I have followed the convention of most historians by simply referring to them as

John Alen, master of the rolls in July 1533, reinforced these themes. An earlier 'boke' was augmented by 'an addition' which (comparable to the 'Breviate') framed the geography, history and deep-rooted problems of Geraldine 'domynion'.[97] Alen justified an adequately financed English deputy to recover the king's 'grete inheritaunce' of the Cambro-Norman conquest which apparently was outlined at length in his original book ('as I elliswheare have said').[98] His narrative of the colony's decline under the Geraldines, highlighted by several manicles, included the well-known account of Sir Gerald Shanesson's remarks. Alen warned that the cycle of fifteenth-century Desmond-induced decay in Munster was recurring with the Leinster Fitzgeralds, a view shared by 'men of grete experience and wisdom'. His remark potentially encompassed a range of influences from Giraldus to Finglas.[99] With Shanesson as the 'chiefe organ pipe' of Kildare duplicity, 'from tyme to tyme' the earl had 'the kynges favours' but allegedly embraced Irish enemies as his 'brederne'.[100] The subsequent chapter of this study recounts the broad establishment of Kildare power that spanned generations, but here Alen conversely described a continual decay that bridged the eighth and ninth earls.[101] Furthermore, Alen argued for the morality of the conquest, 'as well to the greate and high daunger of Cristen soules innumerable'.[102] Writing at Court in late 1533 and mindful of appeals made over the previous decade, Walter Cowley optimistically reminded the king of his 'ardent deasire' to intervene in the lordship.[103]

In early 1534 with Kildare enroute to Whitehall, Cromwell was presented with a detailed set of articles seeking an English-born deputy to remedy a 'decayd' polity.[104] It seems that the royal chaplain Richard Rawson, brother of John (see chapter two), was sent to Ireland around the time Kildare travelled in the opposite direction as Cromwell bolstered lines of intelligence.[105] The misdemeanours of the old colonial magnates in general but Kildare in particular included the usurpation of a string of castles, manors and royal lands.[106] These articles also made didactic

---

his brothers: Marian Lyons, 'FitzGerald, Gerald (Gearóid Óg, Garrett McAlison) (1487–1534)', *DIB*.
[97] SP 60/2, f. 10r. Also, see Maginn and Ellis, *Tudor discov. Ire.*, p. 162.
[98] SP 60/2, f. 10r.
[99] SP 60/2, ff 10, 11r. The 1516 'brief note' as copied by an Elizabethan scribe, stated that Desmond, Kildare and Butler had 'henceforth' adopted Irish extortions in Munster, before crossing the word and replacing it with Ireland: LPL, MS 635, f. 185r.
[100] See also ch. 5, the 'Discourse' and Geraldine duplicity: BL, Lansdowne MS 159, ff 7.
[101] SP 60/2, f. 11r.
[102] SP 60/2, f. 12r.
[103] SP 60/2, f. 4v; Maginn and Ellis, *Tudor discov. Ire.*, p. 161; Bradshaw, *Const. rev.*, p. 96. Neither complaint proved particularly damaging: Brady, *Chief gov.*, p. 4.
[104] SP 60/2, ff 31r-32v; Maginn and Ellis, *Tudor discov. Ire.*, pp 49, 163; Ellis, *Reform and revival*, p. 19.
[105] *S.P. Hen. VIII*, ii, 201–2.
[106] Church possessions were also usurped: Murray, 'Archbishop Alen', pp 1–16; Maginn, 'Civ.'

use of the past in crafting an anti-Kildare history since the reign of Edward II. It was especially in the time of the eighth earl that Kildare 'dyd usurpe' the king's prerogatives and the common law to further decay through the 'wild Irish custome of extorcion'.[107] The '60 wynters' of Kildare tyranny described here was another of many such references. In this instance it referred to the deputyship of the seventh earl in 1474, as the Fraternity of Arms of St George was established, a wave of Scots entered Ulster and the earldom of Ormond was restored in Ireland.[108] Implicitly pejorative, the darkly suggestive long 'winter' of decay may offer a clue regarding patterns of readership and chronicling. Since Darcy's 'Artycles', certain landmark dates were underlined in the state paper and pseudo-state-paper narrative of Geraldine-induced decay.[109] The consultation of pre-existing textual records was of significance, while registers and chronicles were often peppered with contemporaneous marginal notes that emphasised certain observations.[110]

Aside from predictable polemic, Cromwell was well briefed in seeking a more systematic approach, pushing for greater uniformity with the norm of lowland England while reducing the role of the old colonial aristocracy. While still suffering from his wounds and with Thomas, Lord Offaly deputising, Kildare did not accept the 'articles' which Ossory had accepted. They were by no means draconian measures which perhaps indicates the earl's inflexibility.[111] Reflecting the support of Cromwell, Ossory's indenture came with the 'speciall affiaunce' of the king.[112] Its rhetoric placed Kildare in opposition to the morality of the conquest, 'thaugmentation of thonour of God in reducing the people to Cristen maners, upon manyfold enormities alleged and proved ayenst thErle of Kildare'.[113] In May, as Lord Dacre, warden of the west marches towards Scotland, was arrested on charges of treason, Thomas Cusack and Patrick Finglas (newly appointed chief justice of the king's bench) were dispatched to Ireland. It seemed that

---

Gaelic Leinster; p. 10.

[107] SP 60/2, f. 32r.

[108] *Statute rolls of the parliament of Ireland, twelfth and thirteenth to the twenty-first and twenty-second years of the reign of king Edward IV*, ed. James Morrisey (Dublin, 1939), pp 734-7; A. J. Otway-Ruthven, *A history of medieval Ireland* (London, 1968), p. 386.

[109] For collective memory and history in the writing of reform literature, see Heffernan, *Tudor policy*, pp 39, 90, 123

[110] Not to suggest a direct link here, but for example as James Murray has shown, Archbishop Alen scrutinised episcopal records in this way: Murray, 'Archbishop Alen', pp 1-16.

[111] Lyons, *Gearóid Óg Fitz.*, pp 53-7, 60; Bradshaw, *Const. rev.*, p. 102. Gearóid Óg was reported to have been gravely ill: *LP*, vii, 211-2; Laurence McCorristine, *The revolt of Silken Thomas: a challenge to Henry VIII* (Dublin, 1987), pp 62-3; Bradshaw, 'Cromwellian Reform', p. 84.

[112] It was filed with the following note; 'my lord of osserey is indent with the king for his sh[—] in Irland': SP 60/2, f. 41r. Also, see Bradshaw, *Const. rev.*, p. 97.

[113] SP 60/2, f. 41r. The Irish annals later recorded 'great complaints and accusations' against Kildare: AFM, 1534.

Skeffington was primed to replace Kildare as deputy.[114] Along with instructions for Lord Offaly, they carried a printed set of specifications, the *Ordinances for the Government of Ireland* (1534). There was little to distinguish the substance of the document from previous instructions although historians differ in their analysis.[115] Nonetheless, they presented a challenge to the Fitzgeralds as their 'pretended lybertie' of Kildare was to be abolished.[116] Influenced by reformers such as Alen, it was fitting that Finglas presented the *Ordinances* in person as they were largely shaped by the 'Breviate'.[117] Many of the *Ordinances* resembled the municipal, judicial and military content of earlier treatises, in particular the proposals of Finglas. The exchequer was empowered but geopolitical items were of more immediate significance with attention to the MacMurrough in south Leinster and O'Farrell of Annaly.[118]

Acquiescence with Cromwellian reform further aligned Ossory with Finglas and Alen. The *Ordinances* focused on south Leinster and restrictions were outlined on the raising of armed men in the counties of Kildare and Carlow, while 'thErle of Kyldare's londes to be cessed with men of warre, and other charges, as other lordes and gentilmens lands be in the same shires where his ben'.[119] Of note elsewhere was a telling indication of Hospitaller influence, whose role in matters of state steadily endured throughout the period. The importance of Rawson can be seen in the twenty 'able archers or gonners' for hosting to be supplied by

[114] As McCorristine argues, there was then little choice but to pursue the precarious yet well-established option of revolt: McCorristine, *Revolt of Silken Thomas*, p. 65. For crown policy against the border magnates at this moment, see S. G. Ellis, *Tudor frontiers and noble power: the making of the British state* (Oxford, 1995), pp 90-1, 247. Like Kildare, Dacre was a Norfolk ally who suffered a similar fate to Kildare: S. G. Ellis, 'A border baron and the Tudor state: the rise and fall of Lord Dacre of the North' in *Historical Journal*, 35 (1992), p. 275.

[115] McCorristine, *Revolt of Silken Thomas*, p. 55. The Ordinances have been misleadingly associated with the traditional concept of a Tudor conquest, yet they have been read in a nationalist light as an example of imperialist aggression: Edmund Curtis, *A history of medieval Ireland* (Dublin, 1938), p. 364. Bradshaw stated that it heralded the end of bastard feudalism: Bradshaw, 'Cromwellian reform', p. 85; Bradshaw, *Const. rev.*, pp 97, 101; Lyons, *Gearóid Óg Fitz.*, pp 54-5. The Ordinances have been seen as a continuation of Wolseian policy: S. G. Ellis, 'Thomas Cromwell and Ireland, 1532-1540' in *HJ*, 23 (1980), pp 500-2, 515; Ellis, *Reform and revival*, pp 35, 40-1, 134; Maginn and Ellis, *Tudor discov. Ire.*, pp 58-9; Brady, *Chief gov.*, pp 4-5.

[116] SP 60/2, 67r. It was, as Ellis observes, a move against all the nobility: Ellis, *Ire. Tudors*, pp 134-6. Brady states that the dismantling of this palatine jurisdiction was not a significant cause of the revolt: Brady, *Chief gov.*, p. 4.

[117] See Maginn and Ellis, *Tudor discov. Ire.*, pp 57-8; Bradshaw, *Const. rev.*, pp 99-100. Heffernan shows that the *Ordinances* were influenced by a range of documents as far back as the 'State' (c. 1515) and a 'Description of the power of Irishmen' (c. 1496): Heffernan, *Tudor policy*, pp 10-15.

[118] By September, Walter Cowley was made solicitor-general and Thomas Fitzgerald (Kildare's brother?) was replaced by Thomas Alen as exchequer clerk: *Patentee offices in Ireland, 1173-1826*, ed. J. L. J. Hughes (Dublin, 1960), p. 3.

[119] SP 60/2, ff 69v-70r.

Kilmainham (see chapter two). Among the lords spiritual, this was matched only by the archbishop of Dublin.[120]

Cromwell also made symbolic use of the king's printing press.[121] In 1533 Cromwell had begun to print a selection of statutes and ordinances, one of which, *Magna Carta and diuerse other statutes* (1534) related to Ireland.[122] By also circulating older legislation, the printing of the *Ordinances* was designed to create an atmosphere where the Irish extortions traditionally used by the old colonial magnates appeared unacceptable. As chancellor of the exchequer, he secured the printing of 'a true copy of the ordinaunces made in the tyme of Henry VI to be observed by the kynges eschequier', including three reprintings throughout 1533 and 1534. Aside from the practical implications of their content, these were public statements. Moreover, because they were published, universal support was implied. Opposition could be criticised as unpatriotic at best, and at worst as was commonplace at the Tudor Court, treasonous.[123]

If Stanihurst's scene of the council table on St Barnabas' Day was one of medieval drama, the murder in Artane just over a month later was a calamity with far-reaching and disastrous consequences.[124] It has long been written, and indeed accepted, that the 'dice were cast' when Offaly withdrew his allegiance in dramatic fashion on 11 June in St Mary's Abbey, but it is arguable that the Kildares truly crossed the Rubicon with the outrageous killing of Archbishop Alen.[125] The range of challenges faced by Kildare were in many ways exemplified by the bitter rancour with the archbishop. Factional divides and political reform appeared all the more threatening in conjunction with Alen's jurisdictional, ecclesiastical and landed pursuits.[126] The enmity between Kildare and Alen, with the latter's disregard for aristocratic privilege, destabilised the region and generated tension within the institutions of state.[127] He utilised both common and canon law to realign

---

[120] SP 60/2, f. 68r.

[121] The *Ordinances* for example, conclude by recognising Thomas Bartlet as 'Regius Impressor': SP 60/2, f. 71r.

[122] It contained a 'statute of Ireland', the thrust of which was to inform the king of a declining colony through absenteeism and intermarriage with the Gaelic Irish: *Magna Carta and diuerse other statutes* (1534), p. 149.

[123] *A true copy of the ordinaunce...of kynge Henry the vi to be observed in the...eschequier* (London, 1533).

[124] McCorristine critiques Stanihurst's aura of 'medieval drama': McCorristine, *Revolt of Silken Thomas*, p. 66.

[125] James Ware, *The antiquities and history of Ireland* (5 vols, Dublin, 1705), ii, 89.

[126] Murray, 'Archbishop Alen', pp 1–16. Bishop Wellesley acting independently by means of Norfolk's support at court: Lyons, *Church and soc.*; Lyons, *Gearóid Óg Fitz.*, pp 60-2. Put forward by both Wolsey and Cromwell, Alen had clashed with Kildare since 1529. By 1532 the earl had procured his removal as chancellor and the promotion of George Cromer, Archbishop of Armagh.

[127] Alen deprived Suffolk's chaplain of the prebendary of Mulhuddart: Murray, 'Archbishop

networks of patronage for the benefit of his diocesan and metropolitan jurisdictions. His actions proved contentious. For instance, Alen invoked an uncancelled instrument to establish a lordship in Dunboyke, Co. Wicklow to the detriment of Kildare's brother.[128] Alen stoked resentment by intervening in the affairs of the main religious houses of the Pale. He compelled the prior of St Wolstan's, Kildare to concede in a chancery inquisition to benefit his position as patron. This involved accusations against Gearóid Mór, referred to in the register as the 'old earl of Kildare' who allegedly presented an outside canon at the election of a former prior.[129] This indicated Alen's potential to testify against Kildare in the event of a trial after the 1534 rebellion. While not a reason for his murder, it was part of an overall picture where he became a threat. Beyond Dublin, Alen operated against Kildare through his archiepiscopal jurisdiction in Idrone and in Lecale by means of his stated prerogative as primate. Alen claimed 'five carucates [roughly 600 acres] in the comote of Odrone' near Baltinglass. In Lecale, Alen highlighted the incongruity of Niall O'Neill, son of the Geraldine in-law Con O'Neill, holding a valuable benefice in Downpatrick.[130] Given this context, the immediacy of events on 28 July 1534 as Alen fled for England showed the archbishop to be a liability who could not be allowed to present a case at Court that might destroy prospects of concessions from the king. Kildare did not have a theological agenda, but rather used such rhetoric to gather support through the Church in order to strengthen political power.

Although the Imperial ambassador Eustace Chapuys suspected that the king was willing to compromise even after this outrage, the murder of Alen was a turning point which would transform the complexion and *gravitas* of the revolt.[131] The concluding chapter returns to this point. In the face of short-term challenges and because of their perceived position of strength, the Kildares assumed a premeditated, temporary withdrawal of allegiance. What was thought to be transitory political reform prompted this attempt to maintain conservative noble governance which contrasted with Ossory's comparatively disadvantaged position. The extent of Geraldine *hubris*, however, was paralleled by the magnitude of their aristocratic project which continually broadened in scope in the decade prior to

---

Alen', pp 6-8.

[128] Alen cited a medieval escheat and a Butler genealogy to present Ormond as the rightful proprietor: Murray, 'Archbishop Alen', pp 3, 6-7; *Calendar of Archbishop Alen's register, c. 1172-1534*, ed. Charles MacNeill (Dublin, 1950), pp 291-2.

[129] Murray, 'Archbishop Alen', pp 6-7; *Alen Reg.*, pp 277, 291; Lyons, *Church and soc.*, pp 59, 60, 79.

[130] *Alen Reg.*, pp 17, 288.

[131] *Calendar of letters, despatches, and state papers relating to the negotiations between England and Spain preserved in the archives at Simancas and elsewhere*, ed. Pascual de Gayangos (13 vols, London, 1862-1919), v, 248-50.

1534.[132] Despite the advances in recent scholarship, it seems that fundamental understandings of the rebellion have not changed in a long time. A wider methodological approach is therefore required in revisiting this critical period, where new light can be shed on the context and circumstances of the rebellion.

---

[132] See Brady, *Chief gov.*, pp 4–5.

6

Aristocratic entente, Kildare c. 1524–34

With Kildare as the king's leading old colonial lord in Ireland, a major aristocratic *rapprochement* that spanned the Tudor realm materialised in the 1520s. With the support of Lord Grey of Dorset, Kildare returned to favour at Court and was allied with the Marques through marriage to Elizabeth Grey.[1] After supporting the Boleyn match (albeit with little choice) Kildare was of high standing in an aristocratic faction that also included Wiltshire and Norfolk. Since his governorship, Thomas Howard had been sought by various figures in Ireland but over the course of the decade he became aligned with Kildare. Although the flow of complaints against Kildare contributed to tensions and suspicion, this had long been a feature of Irish politics, and one which the ninth earl was generally confident he could transcend.[2] What follows is an account the Geraldine position from 1524, because as suggested above, a broad assessment from this perspective is required in order to more fully understand the true character of the rebellion. This is attempted, firstly by examining the shared interests of Kildare and Norfolk along with the wider strategies pursued by the earl. Finally, a specific courtly context is assessed in the hope of shedding fresh light on the cultural politics of the Kildare ascendancy.

Kildare campaigned widely across the island from 1524-6, firstly in support of Con Bacach O'Neill, whose appearance at Christ Church had so appalled the author of the 'Discourse'. The return of Kildare stabilised Ulster and as one of the earl's chief 'confederates', O'Neill also campaigned in the midlands.[3] While a crown commission regretted the 'divers oppressions' and 'varyaunce

---

[1] D. B. Quinn, 'Henry VIII and Ireland, 1509-34' in *IHS*, pp 229-30; S. G. Ellis, *Ireland in the age of the Tudors* (London, 1998), p. 124; Colm Lennon, *Sixteenth-century Ireland: the incomplete conquest* (Dublin, 1994), p. 94. Kildare's detention at court had its advantages. He did not have to rely on written correspondence or treatises: Christopher Maginn and S. G. Ellis, *Tudor discovery of Ireland* (Dublin, 2015), p. 142; Brendan Bradshaw, *Irish constitutional revolution of the sixteenth century* (Cambridge, 1979), p. 92.

[2] From a Court perspective, anything other than a stable, self-sustaining Lordship of Ireland was an unwanted burden. For example, see G. W. Bernard, *War, taxation and rebellion in early Tudor England: Henry VIII, Wolsey and the amicable grant of 1525* (Brighton, 1986).

[3] AFM, 1523; SP 60/1, f. 89r. Also, see Lennon, *Sixteenth-cen. Ire.*, p. 97; Marian Lyons, *Gearóid Óg Fitzgerald, ninth earl of Kildare* (Dundalk, 1998), p. 39. Geraldine influence in Ulster had a lasting effect since the 1460s: Katharine Simms, *Gaelic Ulster in the middle ages: history, culture and society* (Dublin, 2020), p. 220.

betwixt the said erles...of long season', concerns were overshadowed by articles of agreement between Desmond and Francis I, for the 'making of a warre' against Henry.[4] Kildare's power to arbitrate was demonstrated in the assembling of O'Neill and Hugh Dubh O'Donnell in prolonged attempts to compose terms which finally came to fruition in 1527 when Sir Thomas Fitzgerald (the earl's brother) deputised for Gearóid Óg.[5] Elsewhere in 1526 Kildare intervened in Breifne by imposing his candidate Fearghal O'Reilly before moving west to foray in Connaught. Certain regional interests in contested parts of south Leinster were important to the maintenance of this alliance. Norfolk's vast inheritance included estates and titles in Ireland, many of which were controlled by Kildare.[6] Straddling the main divide between the Kildare and Ormond heartlands, key estates included Idrone and the Barrow valley where the Geraldines had expanded since the turn of the century.[7] Because of a connection to the Earl Marshal (a point stressed by proponents of conquest, see chapter five) this specific region was of value both strategically and symbolically. Tullow and Carlow castles marked the southeast fringes of the main Kildare domain between the Wicklow mountains of the MacMurrough-Kavanagh and the Butler territories west of the Barrow. Further south, the seemingly innocuous but disputed locality of Fasagh Bentre was a chokepoint between the Blackstairs mountains and Brandon Hill leading towards Old Ross. It is unusual that this small area should have been brought to Cromwell's attention through Butler protests after 1530.[8] Norfolk possessions

---

[4] BL, Titus B.XI, ii, f. 302r. Up to the early 1530s, persuasion and co-operation between the leading nobility remained the priority of the crown: Ciaran Brady, *Chief governors: the rise and fall of reform government in Tudor Ireland, 1536-1588* (Cambridge, 1994), pp ix-xiv, 169. For a divergent view, see Brendan Bradshaw, 'Cromwellian Reform and the origins of the Kildare rebellion, 1533-4', in *Transactions of the Royal Historical Society*, 27 (1977), p. 80.

[5] *AFM*, 1524, 1525.

[6] For Norfolk's sudden rise in the mid-1520s, see D. M. Head, *The ebbs and flows of fortune: the life of Thomas Howard, third duke of Norfolk* (London, 1995); David Mathew, *The courtiers of Henry VIII* (London, 1970), p. 38.

[7] David Edwards, *The Ormond lordship in County Kilkenny, 1515-1642: the rise and fall of Butler feudal power* (Dublin, 2003), p. 153; NLI, 2506, f. 1r; *Calendar of the patent and close rolls of the chancery of Ireland in the reigns of Henry VIII, Edward VI, Mary and Elizabeth*, ed. J. Morrin (2 vols, Dublin, 1861), i, 150.

[8] 'Fasagh Bentre' or 'Fasagh of Beatre' was noted in 1528 by means of an indenture between Piers Rua and Kildare. This low lying heavily wooded parcel of land featured a reasonably sized castle despite clear topographical disadvantages. The castle in Fasagh Bentre was entirely surrounded by steep hills but a small tower on higher ground approximately 200m to the west was an extra defensive measure. For the strategic importance and historic symbolism of Idrone, see Emmett O'Byrne, '"A divided loyalty": the MacMurroughs, the Irish of Leinster and the crown of England, 1340-1420' in McGrath (ed.), *Carlow: history and society*, pp 273-306. For William Marshal generally see the following collection of essays, and for his regional associations in particular, see Adrian Empey, 'The evolution of the demesne in the lordship of

in the liberty of Wexford were extensive.[9] Since the reign of Edward IV an Act of Resumption ensured the protection of Norfolk estates in south Leinster which proved advantageous to the Geraldines at this time.[10] According to legislation from the 1540s, in 1524 Norfolk held 'as ancient inheritance...lordships of Caherlagh, Old Ross and divers other manors and lands in Ireland'.[11] In a sense, Norfolk was responsible for landed interests relating to the feuding earls and in the 1520s these estates were leased to Gearóid Óg. In 1526 Thomas Fitzmaurice Fitzgerald, cousin of Gearóid Óg, was conferred as captain of 'Old Ross' and the administration of Norfolk's Wexford estates, with custody of property in the region.[12]

Ecclesiastical politics in the region became heated from the mid-1520s. After Bishop Doran of Leighlin was 'heynously murdered', Kildare apprehended those culpable. The annals vividly proclaimed the perpetrators, Butlers and Maurice Mac-an-Abbadh MacMurrough, to have been justly 'flayed alive'. Kildare enjoyed the loyalty of the bishop of Ferns although he was subject to intense scrutiny from 1530-1. Bishop John Purcell (1519-31) was taken prisoner on 1 September 1531 for a debt of 200 marks claimed by the crown although he was released the following year.[13] As Ossory reminded Cromwell in 1531, the barony of Idrone and the shire of Carlow were the 'veray keyes' of the English lordship where Kildare, enabled by Wiltshire, 'with the strength of his Irishe

---

Leinster' in John Bradley, Cóilín Ó Drisceoil and Michael Potterton (eds), *William Marshal and Ireland* (Dublin, 2017), pp 41-77.

[9] Among the most important were New Ross, the rectory of 'Old Rosse', the castle and manor of Ross and the town of Rospont: *Irish fiants of the Tudor sovereigns*, ed. Edmund Burke (Dublin, 1994), p. 32; G. H. Orpen, *New Ross in the thirteenth century* (Dublin, 1911), p. 6.

[10] *Statute rolls of the parliament of Ireland, twelfth and thirteenth to the twenty-first and twenty-second years of the reign of king Edward IV*, ed. James Morrisey (Dublin, 1939), p. 54; *An account of the most important records of Great Britain*, ed. C. P. Cooper (London, 1832), p. 42.

[11] 'But making leases of divers of their holds and manors to the Earl of Kildare ... of the castells of Catherlagh Old Ross Arclow Tullagh in Offellay Killrush and other fortresses of the inheritance': *Reports on cases heard in the house of lords*, ed. Charles Clark and William Finnelly (12 vols, London, 1831-46), iv, 157; *Cal. pat. chan. Ire.*, i, 286. Also, see Marian Lyons, *Church and society in County Kildare* (Dublin, 2000), p. 148.

[12] Lyons, *Church and society*, p. 149. With the rise of the Geraldine ally Cahir MacMurrough-Kavanagh, their lordship was in turn incorporated into an aristocratic circle that spanned the Tudor realm. After 1511, for the splitting of the MacMurrough lineage into factions both for and against Kildare, see K. W. Nicholls, 'Late medieval Irish annals, two fragments' in *Peritia*, 2 (1983), p. 100.

[13] Also, see Marian Lyons, 'Onset of religious reform: 1460-1550' in *CHI*, i, 502-3. Purcell supported Gearóid Mór Fitzgerald and Lambert Simnel in 1486 as abbot of St Thomas's, Dublin. The dean of Ferns at this time was a Thomas Purcell, brother of the bishop. He seems to have been elected illegally by the chapter. As a result, he was forced to resign in 1531 and the bishop was removed from office in 1533: J. B. Leslie (ed.), *Ferns: clergy and parishes* (Dublin, 1936), p. 236.

alyes destrue me'.[14] Ossory was granted a lease of Norfolk estates in the region 'provided always' the exclusion of 'Carleagh'.[15] In 1533 a letter to the king from Kildare's cousin James Fitzgerald accused Ossory of forcing tenants from 'Norfolk's property' in Carlow.[16] This agreement was not renewed in that year which may have added to regional tensions.

Elizabeth Grey evidently took an immediate interest in Ireland and Lord Grey, having the ear of the king, presented a vitriolic series of articles against Ormond on behalf of Kildare.[17] Misdemeanours included the facilitation of piracy and enabling acts of atrocity. The articles were designed to appeal to the king's sense of piety and honour. The Ormond *patria* was allegedly devoid of Christianity as 'the myddes of Turkey'. By casting Butler as most 'evill disposed', the stability offered by Geraldine governance ensured good religion on behalf of the crown.[18] At the same time, the broad scope of Kildare's ecclesiastical influence in the name of the king 'in the west partes of this land emong the kynge's irish disobeygent subgets' was stressed. Through 'peyn and deligence', Geraldine 'vertue' was underlined as the preserve of 'right few persons in thEnglishry of this land' with a benefice 'in the Irishry not to be lightly had but by temporall power'. The Geraldines were by then reputed to show their indispensability in various ways. For example, when Kildare was examined at Court in 1527-8, his son-in-law audaciously captured Lord Delvin. Working O'Connor's wars to their advantage, an immediate aim was to reappoint Thomas Fitzgerald to office. Two months earlier, Con Bacach O'Neill requested freedom of movement through the Pale and in June 1528 Norfolk stated the need for amity between Kildare and Piers Butler.[19] The

---

[14] LPL, MS 616, f. 46r.

[15] Signed on 20 Mar. 1528, this lease specifically allocated to Piers Rua, Norfolk's 'manor and lordship of Old Rosses ... Fasagh of Beatre in Odrone ... from the bridge of Leghlin to new Rosse.' Also included was a large parcel of Wexford to new Ross, stretching 'to Ynyscorthy with the manor, castell and lordship of Femes, Tymouhy and Durburdiseyland': *Ormond deeds*, iv, 136. A rate of £20 annually for five years was stipulated. These areas had long been in the Ormond sphere of influence. See C. A. Empey, 'The Butler lordship in Ireland' (Ph.D., Trinity College Dublin, 1970); Edwards, *Ormond lordship*, pp 74, 150-1, 194-7.

[16] LP, xiv, 445.

[17] See for example, appeals to Wolsey and complaints against Piers Butler: SP 1/26, ff 185r-189r; BL, Titus B.XI, ii, f. 362r. Also, see Barbara Jean Harris, *English aristocratic women, 1450-1550: marriage and family, property and careers* (Oxford, 2002), pp 58-64; Damien Duffy, *Aristocratic women in Ireland, 1450-1660: the Ormond family, power and politics* (Woodbridge, 2021); S.P. Hen. VIII, ii, 120. LPL, MS 602, f. 34r. In terms of tone, there were similarities with earlier complaints by the countess of Kildare.

[18] S.P. Hen. VIII, ii, 122-3.

[19] As deputy, Ossory struggled to hold Desmond at bay to the detriment of the Pale and openly feared it 'no lesse dangerous to have werr on that other syde with o conour': SP 60/1, f. 132r. For the financial impact, including minister's fees lapsing into arrears, see S. G. Ellis, *Reform and revival: English government in Ireland 1470-1534* (Woodbridge, 1986), p. 85.

situation was complicated by the arrival of 'Sherake', Desmond's envoy at Toledo 'ffrom the partes off yrland' bearing gifts of hawks and greyhounds. There was a bill for Desmond's attainder c. 1528 although no parliament was held.[20]

At this juncture, Kildare's position of 'strength' was widely recognised even among his enemies. To illustrate, the potential of diplomacy and the ever present possibility of alternative courses of action, the emperor apparently conveyed to his ambassador Fernandez that the king's 'friends would be our friends...and foes our foes...should comprehend him in any treaty between us and the king of England... we have always endeavoured to continue in friendship.'[21] Norfolk's approval of Bathe's c. 1528 treatise, which apparently was more favourable to Kildare, reflected the duke's support for Geraldine-led governance. In this context, his assurance that 'pease shall ensew amonges Criston princes to the great laude off our master' was also an affirmation of unity and virtue through Geraldine influence.[22] It was also largely accepted that the old colonial ruling aristocracy under Kildare could restore stability.[23] Desmond-Hapsburg intrigue was abruptly ended with the death of the earl, sparing the crown a potentially threatening situation.[24]

Kildare's return under Skeffington as deputy was on the advice of the king's leading nobility at Court.[25] From Kildare's perspective, Skeffington posed little threat. The manner in which they effectively campaigned suggests a Geraldine confidence that the status quo would be restored especially as the cost of Skeffington's military was unsustainable.[26] The importance of Kildare was evident in Skeffington's instructions.[27] Other chronicles simplistically surmise

[20] BL, Vespasian C.IV, f. 264r; *LP*, iv, pp 24-5. I am grateful here for the advice of Professor Steven Ellis.
[21] *S.P. Hen. VIII*, ii, 129; *Cal. Carew*, i, 42-3.
[22] SP 60/1, f. 130r. See also above, ch.5. For the breakup of the Wolsey, Butler and Hugh Dubh O'Donnell axis, see Simms, *Gaelic Ulster*, pp 217-18.
[23] SP 60/1, f. 142v. Also, see Ellis, *Reform and revival*, p. 157. Apparently, this was a recurring pattern in the history of the colony. In the early fifteenth century, Archbishop Swayne made similar observations regarding the Talbot-Ormond feud: Simms, *Gaelic Ulster*, p. 222; Lennon, *Sixteenth-cen. Ire.*, p. 166.
[24] BL, Vespasian C.IV, f. 322r. Circumstances here remain unclear. The critical nature of the Hapsburg engagement during this period is a subject that merits further research. See Marian Lyons, *Franco-Irish relations, 1500-1610: politics, migration and trade* (Woodbridge, 2003), pp 27-8; Anthony McCormack, *The earldom of Desmond, 1463-1583: the decline and crisis of a feudal lordship* (Dublin, 2005), pp 43, 66-9; Micheál Ó Siochrú, 'Foreign involvement in the revolt of Silken Thomas, 1534-5' in *PRIA*, 96C (1996), pp 49-66.
[25] Norfolk had filled the vacuum after Wolsey's fall: Head, *Thomas Howard*, p. 103. It was not quite a return to traditional aristocratic delegation but there may have been a sense of anticipation in the annals as Kildare returned after a 'long time in the hands of the king' while as an afterthought, a 'Saxon Justiciary came with him': AFM, 1530; ALC, 1530.
[26] Brady, *Chief gov.*, p. 4; S. G. Ellis, 'Thomas Cromwell and Ireland, 1532-1540' in *HJ*, 23 (1980), pp 499-500.
[27] SP 60/1, f. 144r.

Ossory's 'litle resistance for lacke of power wherefore the kyng sent the erle of Kyldare into Ireland and with him Sir Wyllyam Skevyngton'. It was claimed that the lordship was consequently 'politckly ordered'.[28] O'Reilly, however, submitted voluntarily to Kildare and the deputy while Hugh Dubh O'Donnell followed suit by the following summer.[29] Skeffington's relationship with the northern lords was likely to have been boosted by Kildare's assistance. 'Friendship and compact' with O'Donnell was enabled through the co-operation of O'Neill.[30] Kildare was alive to Skeffington's inability to maintain armed forces indefinitely, but it seems that the deputy himself stoked Geraldine-Butler feuding for his ease of movement.[31] Good relations had evaporated by late summer 1531 and thereafter the deputy was essentially forced from office without the means to sustain his armed forces. At some stage early in his deputyship, Skeffington was offered gifts by John Wolfe, a Geraldine merchant involved in the production of metal items. This was another example of co-operation between Kildare and Skeffington before relations collapsed. Wolfe was a target of Kildare's enemies since Skeffington's first experience in Ireland with the secret council of 1528. Wolfe's debts were called into account and in November of that year, Kildare with the aid of Norfolk claimed 'no knowlage of the kinges pleasure' but hoped that his appearance before the council might be deferred according to his recognizances.[32] Five years later in 1533, his goods and the aforementioned gifts were in Skeffington's possession. In allegations that were similar to those against Prior James Keating with Gearóid Mór Fitzgerald, a Geraldine captain could embody Kildare's vices in a rhetorical attack on the earl. Wolfe was accused of exercising arbitrary and excessive power 'in the warrys, and that done many gay petye fetyes and at libertie to do right or wrong'. Thomas Lord Howth, who also was trusted by Wiltshire, was at hand to deny 'untriew' reports and argued the righteousness of Kildare's actions.[33]

When Ossory dismissed the 'pompe and rumoure' of Geraldine power, it proved to be a telling remark.[34] Kildare's entente with Wiltshire alarmed Ossory. Proponents of military conquest or regional entrenchment accentuated their claim to knowledge or experience of the land, but by doing so it exposed their comparative position of weakness. Conversely, among projections of Geraldine exceptionalism were broad, sophisticated cultural endeavours. Alen's well-known statement on Kildare's capacity to 'have the land in soche troble' was an

---

[28] Edward Hall, *Vnion of the two noble and illustrate famelies of Lancastre and Yorke* (1548), p. 153.
[29] *S.P. Hen. VIII*, ii, 151–3; Simms, *Gaelic Ulster*, p. 223.
[30] *S.P. Hen. VIII*, ii, 151–2; LPL, MS 603, ff 35; ALC, 1532; Simms, *Gaelic Ulster*, p. 223; Maginn and Ellis, *Tudor discov. Ire.*, p. 151.
[31] Lennon, *Sixteenth-cen. Ire.*, p. 104.
[32] BL, Vespasian F.XIII, f. 189r.
[33] SP 1/79, ff 81r, 83r.
[34] LPL, MS 616, f. 46v; Bradshaw, *Const. rev.*, p. 92.

admittance of the very 'power' Ossory had disparaged while pejorative allusions to Geraldine 'pompe' diverted from cultural aspects of deeper significance.[35]

At Court, Kildare was aligned with both Norfolk and Wiltshire by 1532. Norfolk was made a Knight of the Order of St Michael and also Earl Marshal of England having already held the title in Ireland even after little success in France up to 1533.[36] Chapuys appreciated how Norfolk valued Kildare's ability to control 'the affairs of Ireland'.[37] Meanwhile, Kildare campaigned widely and mobilised followers to intimidate members of parliament and intercept Butler intelligence.[38] To be sure, Gearóid Óg Fitzgerald faced greater opposition on both sides of the Irish Sea than his father, yet in 1532 his reappointment with favourable terms in the face of carefully formulated complaints reinforced a sense of assurance. At the time of the Boleyn coronation, Kildare could safeguard Wiltshire in the 'ordering of your said lands and teneiments but also in the prerog of your titles'. Kildare sought the office of chief justice of common pleas for his steward Richard Delahide and warned against Butler candidates stating that he 'would not think hit polytc in youe to suffer any of theim to optain that rowem [room]'.[39] It is possible that through Kildare gains in Ely, which came at a high price, lies a faint trace of the accord with Wiltshire. Clonony castle in MacCoghlan country, where Wiltshire's grand-daughters are buried, apparently came into Boleyn hands at some point in the early 1530s. Western Ely was a strange location for a Boleyn grave yet beside the keep 'under(neath) leys Elizabeth and mary bullyn daughters of Thomas Bullyn son of George bullyn viscount Rochford son of sir Thomas Bullyn earle of ormonde and wiltshire'.[40]

These developments were not played out simply on the level of political competition or overt factionalism. An additional level at which the struggle was ongoing was through the patterns of competition within court culture. The way in which the rarefied arena of court culture worked was also a means to display not just political aptitude but also a political perspective. In conjunction with a

---

[35] SP 60/2, f. 11r.
[36] L. & P. Hen. VIII, vii, 236–41; Head, Thomas Howard, pp 102–9. For Norfolk's statesmanship, see Calendar of State Papers Venice, ed. Rawdon Brown (11 vols, London, 1864), iv, 301.
[37] SP 1/78, ff 82; LPL, MS 616, f. 46r; Cal. S. P. Spain, v, 252–3.
[38] A revealing example can be found from 1526. For fear of being intercepted by the Geraldines, closing a report to Inge, an apprehensive James Butler 'dare not wrytt' more: SP 60/1, f. 119v.
[39] SP 1/78, f. 82r.
[40] In 1513 and 1533 the two earls were both wounded while campaigning in Ely (O'Carroll country). In 1519 a proxy battle between Kildare and Ormond was fought through a MacCoughlan dispute in west Ely which was notable for its use of firearms at Clonony castle: AFM, 1519, 1532, 1533.

wider aristocratic *rapprochement*, the ninth earl legitimised his position through a significant cultural offensive. In court society, political rivalries and competition were often mediated through cultural endeavour.[41] The Court provided a refined, regulated framework which extended beyond mere decorum. It was an all-encompassing arena of respectability wherein debate, discussion and even entertainment, to varying degrees, shaped political outcomes.[42] Indeed, this was the generation that produced Castiglione's *Il Cortegiano* (1528) or 'Book of the Courtier' which demonstrated how courtly norms had far-reaching implications. As court culture was bound by custom and decorum, the proper adherence to regulation and etiquette was in itself a form of competition. Rival aspirants and feuding magnates were compelled to conform to a rule-bound environment at Court under the king. Displaying an equitable temperament was a demonstration of intelligence, sophistication and trustworthiness.[43]

The precise nature of the transition between court culture and political action is obscure, due to the sophisticated nature of the process itself. However, this can be detected in how individuals displayed the merits and skills required for positions or favour. Participation in courtly rituals and their cultural endeavours was a means of disposing oneself for select duties. The entire court society, including the king, was bound in this complex, interdependent network. A bureaucratic, written verification of this process would have been incongruous and therefore concrete accounts of the process never existed. The granting of land, titles, positions and approval of policies were all the end result of a process that was generally not recorded but a socio-cultural footprint has survived to reflect this transmutation.[44] The granting of titles, positions, land and the approval of policy was the end result of a process that was not recorded but inferences can be made through the footprint of cultural patronage. Within the confines of this

---

[41] Court culture and politics is covered by a large bibliography. For instance, see Glenn Richardson, '"As presence did present them": personal gift-giving at the Field of cloth of gold' in Thomas Betteridge and Suzannah Lipscomb (eds), *Henry VIII and the court: art, politics and performance* (Abingdon, 2016), pp 47-64; Susan Brigden, 'Henry VIII and the crusade against England' in Lipscomb and Betteridge (eds), *Henry VIII and the court*, pp 215-34. David Starkey, *Henry: virtuous prince* (London, 2008); Mark Rankin, Christopher Highley and John King (eds), *Henry VIII and his afterlives: literature, politics and art* (Cambridge, 2009); Maria Hayward, *Rich apparel: clothing and the law in Henry VIII's England* (Abingdon, 2009).
[42] The court of Henry VIII had always embraced the transmutation between humanism and politics. Appropriate conduct at court had been put forward in John Skelton's *Speculum principis* (1501) which was taught to young Henry by the author himself: Starkey, *Henry: virtuous prince*, p. 37.
[43] Baldassarre Castilione, *The courtyer* (London, 1561).
[44] Norbert Elias, *The court society* (New York, 1983), pp 76, 142. A number of older studies remain useful: Alistair Fox, *Politics and literature in the reigns of Henry VII and Henry VIII* (Oxford, 1989); Sydney Anglo, *Spectacle, pageantry, and early Tudor policy* (Oxford, 1969).

cultural domain, the scope of Kildare patronage formed an impact from Gaelic lordships to the Tudor Court.

Firstly, in terms of literary patronage, the Geraldines projected broad interests. The catalogue of 'bokes remaynyng in the lyberary of Gerald FitzGerald erl of Kyldare the xv day of ffebruarii anno Henrici viii' (1531) can be compared with the earlier inventory of c. 1500.[45] As part of the *Kildare Rental*, the evolving library represented continuity under the ninth earl with military and political power as the basis for presentations through renaissance ideals. A general indication of what was added over this period sheds light on what was a long-term project. The library itself was a monumental statement, symbolic in terms of individual items and the sum of their parts. The expansive Kildare position under the ninth earl was exemplified by the themes represented in the texts acquired up to the early 1530s.[46]

Inspired by humanist learning and containing much historical material, it can be compared to the insular, alternate historical argument of the Butlers or a like-minded 'conquest' perspective.[47] Contemporary politics and the Tudor Court had directly influenced the library by 1531. It is uncertain precisely when More's *Utopia* and religious commentaries were acquired but it suggests intent to project a princely omnipotence in such matters.[48] Items in the collection can be seen to have broadly represented Geraldine visions of government. In 1529 a French translation of Erasmus' *Enchiridion* was added. Like More's *Utopia*, this could be read in a number of ways but the great possibilities of diplomacy and the potential to mediate are suggested.[49] Works by the Italian Lorenzo Valla, the royal tutor Bernard Andreas 'poete' and a French translation of Petrarch's *I Trionfi*, for example, testify to an engagement with humanist thought from across the continent. The wide variety of courtly lyrics acquired up to 1531 indicated how Gearóid Óg was alive to the rhythms of courtly presentation.[50] The fate of the

---

[45] Mac Niocaill's edition of BL Harleian 3756, f. 96v dates the catalogue as 'the 15 day of Februarii anno Henrici VIII 17' which is 1526. However, I concur with Aisling Byrne who notes that the roman numerals referring to the regnal year are 'xxii'. By comparing the letter form with the first 'x' and the 'v' in Henry's title, Byrne points out that Mac Niocaill was mistaken in this reading: Aisling Byrne, 'Earls of Kildare and their books at the end of the middle ages' in *The Library: Transactions of the Bibliographical Society*, 14 (2013), p. 135.

[46] The sheer rate of expansion denoted an upsurge in wealth and power: Byrne, 'Earls of Kildare', p. 138. See also above, ch. 3.

[47] See also Colm Lennon, 'The Fitzgeralds of Kildare and the building of a dynastic image, 1500-1630' in W. Nolan and T. McGrath (eds), *Kildare: history and society* (Dublin, 2006), p. 203. One of the latest additions was Alain Bouchart's 'Les croniques de la grand et petit bretaine' printed in 1531: Byrne, 'Earls of Kildare', p. 148.

[48] Lennon, *Sixteenth-cen. Ire.*, p. 83; Lyons, *Gearóid Óg Fitz.*, p. 23.

[49] Byrne, 'Earls of Kildare', p. 147.

[50] For instance, see 'Le comant de la roise', 'Le swong de virgier' and 'Le geardyn de plesence'.

earl's library can ultimately be linked to the catastrophe of 1534, although there was a reference to the library's 'great value' when it was pillaged in 1642.[51] Its subsequent though not immediate disappearance was one aspect of the cultural impact of the fall of Kildare.[52]

It was at the Tudor Court that the most recognisable piece of Geraldine-related literature was produced. Henry Howard's well-known sonnet the 'Fair Geraldine' or 'Description and praise of his loue Geraldine' has traditionally been read in the context of English sonnet literature.[53] But the wider Kildare aristocratic *rapprochement* is fundamental to understanding the politics of the 'Fair Geraldine'. It seems that the earliest printed version of the poem dates to 1557 with Richard Tottel's *Songes and sonettes written by...lord Henry Howard, late earle of Surrey, Thomas Wyatt the elder and others*. Entitled a 'Description and praise of his loue Geraldine' in this 1557 text (as with Stanihurst), it was not until the mid-seventeenth-century that the poem began to be referred to as the 'faire Geraldine'.[54] The sonnet has been dated *c*. 1537 due to the fact that this was around the time the 'fair Geraldine', young Elizabeth Fitzgerald returned to Court.[55] However, it is unlikely that the sonnet was composed in 1537, as has been suggested. The immediate aftermath of the execution of Thomas and his uncles would have been a most improbable time to 'praise' the Fitzgeralds, especially as disaffected Geraldines posed a growing threat. While a date of composition remains a matter of debate, the sonnet was plausibly written at an earlier stage.[56] Norfolk trumpeted his son's literary skills

---

[51] Byrne, 'Earls of Kildare', pp 133-4. Its precise contents cannot be determined in the 1640s. In August 1536 after Kildare was attainted, Cromwell was notified of the dismantling of the contents of the castle: SP 60/3, ff 139; C. W. Fitzgerald, *Earls of Kildare and their ancestors from 1057 to 1773* (Dublin, 1858), p. 258.

[52] A topical observation given the current archival project in reconstructing material lost in the Public Record Office of Ireland in 1922: Peter Crooks and Ciarán Wallace, 'The records of a country are its noblest inheritance (Beyond 2022: Ireland's Virtual Record Treasury Research Project)' in *HI*, 28, no. 3 (2020), pp 48-51. Recent excavations of the castle indicate that late medieval and sixteenth-centuries artefacts were essentially obliterated: Alan Hayden, 'Maynooth castle, co. Kildare: excavation of the donjon' (unpublished archaeological report lodged with the National Monuments Service, Ireland, 2013), p. 25.

[53] See also W. A. Sessions, *Henry Howard, the poet earl of Surrey: a life* (Oxford, 1999), pp 187-94.

[54] The extent to which the title is misleading adds to its underlying political import. The title does not 'praise' Elizabeth, but rather instead the Geraldine family name. The poem is neither a 'decription' of Elizabeth nor is she his love.

[55] Sessions, *Henry Howard*, pp 192-3. The corresponding line in the poem was conceivably an allusive reference to an earlier, perhaps even imagined encounter.

[56] Nor, as Robin Flower has inventively translated, was a different sonnet written in 1537 for another Geraldine, when Manus O'Donnell 'assiduously wooed' the widowed Eleanor McCarthy: *Love's bitter-sweet: translations from the Irish poets of the sixteenth and seventeenth centuries*, ed. Robin Flower (Dublin, 1925), pp 7-9; Brendan Bradshaw, 'Manus the magnificent: O'Donnell as a Renaissance prince' in Art Cosgrove and Donal McCartney (eds), *Studies in Irish history presented to R. Dudley Edwards* (Dublin, 1979), p. 36. It was not a sonnet at all, but it

in 1529 when he was aged twelve and young Henry Howard's relationship with Richmond was important.[57] They journeyed to Italy in 1532 where the boy poet took in the sights of 'Tuscan' and 'faire Florence', returning later that year which may have inspired the opening lines of the sonnet. A letter written from Chapuys to Charles V, well discussed in W. A. Sessions, entreats at length how Norfolk prized his son's valuable literary talents.[58] Norfolk's desire for his son to become 'preceptor and tutor' to Richmond was significant and from the outset, poetry and politics were to the fore with Surrey.

Until 1532 there had been speculation that Surrey would be betrothed to the king's eldest daughter and the following year marked a flurry of activity for the Howards.[59] Norfolk took an interest in courtly literature as Chapuys commented that the 'whole government [was] falling into [his] hands'.[60] The ambassador also spoke of Norfolk's praise for his son's literary talent. The early writings of young Henry were in part spurred by the prospect of political gain among his father's associates. With Kildare exonerated and serving as deputy in 1532, Norfolk pushed for marriage between his daughter Mary and Richmond. The following year, as the political climate in Ireland grew tempestuous, Chapuys noted how Norfolk began to move 'in tolerably good haste [especially since] it is also reported that the king is about to send his son Richmond to Ireland as governor of that country'.[61] Norfolk and Kildare had been working in a manner generally beneficial to each party, with a keen eye on imminent marriage arrangements. Having recently returned from 'faire Florence' and considering Norfolk's relations with Kildare, 1533 is a plausible date for the sonnet's inception. Clues in the verse aid this argument.[62] Elizabeth Fitzgerald was then five or six years of age. The 'childlike' image of the 'dedicatee' was underlined through reference to her birthplace and nursing in early infancy.[63] The tender youth of the poem's

---

may have been written in the later 1530s (see also below). Nevertheless, the politics of the 'faire Geraldine' merits further study: Sessions, *Henry Howard*, pp 187–94; *Verse in English from Tudor and Stuart Ireland*, ed. Andrew Carpenter (Cork, 2003), p. 44.

[57] Sessions, *Henry Howard*, p. 70; *Cal. S. P. Spain*, iii, 908.

[58] *Cal. S. P. Spain*, iii, 908.

[59] In 1533, the king's illegitimate son married Norfolk's daughter who thus became Mary Fitzroy, duchess of Richmond and Somerset. Along with a sketch of the young poet in 1533, Holbein also drew a black and coloured chalk portrait of Mary around this time.

[60] *Cal. S. P. Spain*, iv, 292.

[61] *Cal. S. P. Spain*, iv, 781; Sessions, *Henry Howard*, p. 81.

[62] This journey was 'with a kinges son' with whom his 'childishe yeres did passe': *Henry Howard, earl of Surrey: poems*, ed. Emrys Jones (Oxford, 1964), p. 27. For the 'self revelatory' nature of Surrey's poetry and his proximity to the throne, see Susan Brigden, 'Henry Howard, earl of Surrey, and the "Conjured League"' in *HJ*, 37 (1994), pp 508–10.

[63] Surrey's romantic image of Ireland as the 'western isle' with a 'pleasant shore' contrasted with earlier experiences. In 1520 Henry Howard was aged three when in the lordship with his family, where there was 'no place in this contre' with 'clene air' according to the then Lord

subject and the grandeur of the Kildares were outlined in the opening quatrain.[64] This regal image was a Geraldine projection in terms of aristocratic delegation and suitability for governance. Since the 'fostering' of Elizabeth in 1527, relations with Norfolk flourished and a carefully cultivated Kildare image evolved into the 1530s. In blunt political terms, the sonnet was less a 'description' and expression of 'loue' but an acknowledgement of Geraldine prowess and an affirmation of the Kildare-Norfolk *rapprochement*.[65]

New ground was struck with the patronage of pictorial art. The arrival and rise of Hans Holbein (the Younger) at Court, resulting in a 1530 portrait of Gearóid Óg, was part of a larger cultural movement in which Kildare was active. From an Irish perspective, he was its vanguard. Having been recommended by Erasmus, Holbein arrived in England in 1526 and from the outset served in close proximity to the crown. Holbein's work has been accredited as part of Renaissance political thought and a 'new diplomacy'.[66] His arrival at Court marked a shift from a particular emphasis on art as decorated tapestries and silver plate to portraiture, although visual art at the Tudor Court had always been highly politicised.[67] Holbein also painted Mary Howard, daughter of Norfolk, who was betrothed to the duke of Richmond in 1533. It appears that the 1530 portrait of Kildare was the first portrait painting of an Irish-born person which was made within their lifetime.[68]

Lieutenant Surrey: Tottel's *Songes and sonettes, written by the right honourable Lorde Henry Haward late Earle of Surrey, and others* [published by Richard Tottel] (London, 1574), pp. 6, 10; SP 60/1, f. 40r. Also, see Sessions, *Henry Howard*, p. 49.

[64] Also, see Seán Duffy, 'Gerald of Windsor and the origins of the Geraldines' in *Ger. Med. Ire.*, pp 21-2.

[65] For later Kildare patronage see John Scattergood, 'Humanism in Ireland in the sixteenth-century: the evidence of TCD MS 160' in Cormac Ó Cuilleanáin, Corinna Salvadori and John Scattergood (eds), *Italian culture: interactions, transpositions and translations* (Dublin, 2006), pp 72, 86-9.

[66] Osckar Batschman and Pascal Griener, *Hans Holbein* (London, 1997), p. 14. See also Kevin Sharpe, *Selling the Tudor monarchy: authority and image in sixteenth-century England* (New Haven, CT, 2009), pp 358-9. Portraits of the king fittingly presented him as a cultured patron. Noted early examples included a well-known piece by an unknown artist in 1511. For instance, see Neville Williams, *Henry VIII and his court* (London, 1971), pp 17-25.

[67] During the late 1520s the royal librarian Giles Duwey oversaw supported a remarkable quantity of manuscripts which had a concerted emphasis on the heraldic symbols of the Tudor dynasty in the decoration of borders: John Murdoch, Jim Murrell, Patrick Noon and Roy Strong (eds), *The English miniature* (Yale, 1981), p. 31.

[68] Portraiture was by then politicised in Ireland. For later examples see Jane Fenlon, 'Irish art and architecture, 1550-1730' in *CHI*, ii, 363-5. For Ormond's patronage see David Starkey, 'Holbein's Irish sitter?' in *Burlington Magazine*, 123 (1981), pp 300-3; Edwards, *Ormond lordship*, pp 92, 178. Of later interest is the example of Elizabethan opportunist Tom Lee, whose self-promotion included an audacious proposal for the marriage of his daughter to the son of the eleventh earl of Kildare: Hiram Morgan, 'Tom Lee: the posing peacemaker' in Brendan

As ruling magnates, it further demonstrated a capacity to wield power. As with the White Earl, courtly customs and cultural patronage could effectively transcend the gap between the old colonial nobility and the Gaelic lords. Geraldine patronage had long since retained a native complexion and it is likely that the collection of Irish texts in the Kildare library expanded as the second catalogue was compiled. Later sources can offer valuable glimpses on the Kildare's active use of books and the importance of Gaelic Irish both orally and textually. For example, the well-known 'Irish Primer' (c. 1560s) presented to queen Elizabeth referred to 'men yett lyving which knew Elizabeth Zouche...(who) learned to reade, write and prefectlye speake the tongue'. In this particular context, there is a source that merits further attention. It may possibly shed light on the various functions of the library but more importantly it indicates a Geraldine reputation for learning that spanned cultural.[69]

At some stage between 1531 and 1538 Manus O'Donnell composed a Gaelic lyric in praise of the ninth earl's daughter, Eleanor MacCarthy Fitzgerald.[70] While this marriage alliance took place after the rebellion as the 'Geraldine League' took shape, as it would later be named, it signified an earlier relationship between the families. It remains unclear precisely when the poem was written. Literary patronage, it must be emphasised, while courtly in nature, was produced for those of the native lords. Politics, both within and beyond Court were based on personal networks as much as institutional bodies. As Norbert Elias once observed, a sharing of cultural values was not necessary for an appreciation of the rhythms of courtly behaviour.[71] Even beyond the environs of Greenwich or Whitehall, courtly literature could form an aspect of the political process. Although O'Donnell's poem was written in Irish, Manus succeeded in demonstrating to Kildare, and a wider audience, a certain political aptitude regarding the etiquette of Tudor Court. In this context, other Tír Conaill pursuits may be considered.

Bradshaw, Andrew Hadfield, Willy Maley (eds), *Representing Ireland: literature and the origins of conflict, 1534–1660* (Cambridge, 1993), pp 141–2, 159.

[69] Benjamin Iveagh Library, Farmleigh, Dublin, Irish Primer, ff 3v–4r. Also, see Marie-Louise Coolohan, *Women, writing, and language in early modern Ireland* (Oxford, 2010), p. 125.

[70] She was widowed in 1531. Manus became the O'Donnell in 1537 and they married in 1538. See Darren McGettigan, 'O'Donnell, Manus (Ó Domhnaill, Maghnas) (d. 1563)', *DIB*; Brendan Bradshaw, 'Manus "the magnificent": O'Donnell as a Renaissance prince' in Art Cosgrove and Donal McCartney (eds), *Studies in Irish history presented to R. Dudley Edwards* (Dublin, 1979), pp 15–37; 'Manus O'Donnell and the earl's daughter' in *Transl. Irish poets*, ed. Robin Flower (Dublin, 1925), pp 7–9 (note the title of the poem is given by Flower); Katharine Simms, 'Bardic poetry as a historical source' in Tom Dunne (ed.), *The writer as witness: literature as historical evidence*. Historical Studies XVI (Cork, 1987), pp 58–75; Katharine Simms, 'Geraldines and Gaelic culture' in Peter Crooks and Sean Duffy (eds), *The Geraldines and medieval Ireland: the making of a myth* (Dublin, 2016), pp 264–77; Duffy, *Arist. women*, pp 90–1.

[71] Elias, *Court society*, p. 76; Natalie Mears, 'Courts, courtiers and culture in Tudor England' in *HJ*, 46 (2003), p. 704.

The ability to impose a lasting influence in Ulster and to balance O'Neill and O'Donnell was, as the Geraldines demonstrated, a mark of power. It is plausible that O'Donnell's submission to the crown in 1531 was secured by means of Skeffington relying on Kildare's co-operation.[72] The movement from shared cultural interests toward shared political interests accelerated in the 1530s and was likely to have been driven by renaissance influences. In a remarkable sign of cultural interchange, the Geraldine example was followed by Manus O'Donnell. In the following year, with the restoration of Gearóid Óg, a major hagiography was produced in the form of the *Beatha Colm Cille*. Commissioned by Manus, it was a politically charged work with a notable illustrated frontispiece of Columba, robed in Anglican style alongside two Tudor roses.[73] This 'Tudor Columba' was emblematic of a conciliatory approach and co-operation across cultural divides.[74] Precisely what the illustration represented is a matter of debate, but there is a hint of Geraldine instigation given the relationship between Manus and Kildare.[75]

---

[72] Skeffington's relationship with the northern lords has even been recognised in the annals: *ALC*, 1532.

[73] Bodl., MS Rawl. B 514, f. 2v; *Beatha Colaim Chille Life of Colum Cille: compiled by Manus O'Donnell in 1532*, eds Andrew O'Kelleher and Gertrude Schoepperle (Urbana, IL, 1918), p. xli; *The Life of Colum Cille by Manus O'Donnell*, ed. Brian Lacey (Dublin, 1998). The original hagiography was a lengthy manuscript by the seventh-century Donegal scribe, Adaman: *Life of Saint Columba, founder of Hy. written by Adamnan, ninth abbot of that monastery*, ed. William Reeves (Edinburgh, 1874). Other contemporaneous hagiographies were likewise used for political purposes. For the Book of Fenagh and Breifne propaganda, see Raymond Gillespie 'Saints and manuscripts in sixteenth-century Breifne' in *Breifne*, 11 (2008), pp 533-56; Raymond Gillespie, Salvador Ryan and Brendan Scott (eds), *Making the Book of Fenagh: context and text* (Cavan, 2016). It is arguable that such patronage represented the application of humanist ideas to politics, which in principle was similar to the symbolism associated with the Field of Cloth of Gold a decade earlier. For Manus O'Donnell and Tir Conaill patronage, see Bradshaw, 'Manus "the magnificent"', pp 30-2; Richard McCabe, 'Fighting words: writing the "Nine Years War"' in Thomas Herron and Michael Potterton (eds), *Ireland in the Renaissance c. 1540-1660* (Dublin, 2007), pp 109-110; Katharine Simms, 'Poems to the medieval Donegal chiefs' in William Nolan, Liam Ronayne and Mairead Dunlevy (eds), *Donegal: history and society* (Dublin, 1995), p. 194. For the material culture of Tir Conaill in the 1520s, an example of which was Manus' Lifford castle and its 'marble arches', see *The bardic poems of Tadgh Dall O'Huiginn*, ed. Eleanor Knott (2 vols, London, 1922), ii, 24. More generally, see Niamh Wycherley, 'The enduring power of the cult of relics: an Irish perspective' in Chris Jones, Conor Kostick and Klaus Oschema (eds), *Making the medieval relevant: how medieval studies contribute to improving our understanding of the present* (Boston, MA, 2020), pp 239-54.

[74] Indeed, the Ulster church had proven flexible in such matters. An exception was Archbishop of Armagh Octavian de Palatio who was less inclined to deal with the Irishry: Katharine Simms, 'The archbishops of Armagh and the O'Neills 1347-1471' in *IHS*, 19 (1974-5), pp 38-55; Simms, *Gaelic Ulster*; Sparky Booker, *Cultural exchange and identity in late medieval Ireland: the English and Irish of the four obedient shires* (Cambridge, 2018), pp 105-6. For supranationalism and the cult of Columba, see Booker, *Cult. exch. med. Ire.*, pp 137-40.

[75] In the late 1520s, Manus distanced himself from his father's policies. He was a cousin of

This may have been an early indication of a *rapprochement* between the O'Donnells, traditional enemies of the O'Neill and the house of Kildare, which would later issue in the guardianship of young Gerald Fitzgerald, the eleventh earl.[76]

Co-operation with the leading Gaelic nobility in Ulster but also in Leinster, as with the MacMurrough-Kavanagh, dovetailed with the Geraldine conception of aristocratic rule.[77] Their obvious strategic relevance in relation to the Barrow valley could be underlined in other respects. The significance of Dermot MacMurrough in chronicles was manifested in the historical argument of 'conquest' lobbyists such as Finglas and Darcy. The symbolism of the ancient kingship of Leinster becomes especially relevant on an aristocratic level and through material culture. In accounts of the twelfth-century conquest, MacMurrough's submission confirmed their place among the nobility from the outset. The MacMurrough-Kavanagh continually claimed the ancient kingship of Leinster over the centuries and although they were a Gaelic lordship in decline, they saw themselves in elevated terms. An impressive seal matrix survives from the late fifteenth century and a rare extant secular metal artefact from the period is the MacMurrough-Kavanagh 'charter horn'. The horn itself dates to the fourteenth century but an ornamental metal stand was forged in the early 1500s.[78]

The events of 1534 have tended to overshadow the preceding period of intense cultural activity and it is remarkable that the 1533 Kildare Rent Table remains one of the most underappreciated monuments from Renaissance Ireland. Conveying

---

Con Bacach and aided Kildare in wielding peace between the Ulster lords in 1527: AU, 1527; Simms, *Gaelic Ulster*, pp 221–2. It had always been necessary for a ruling magnate to engage through ecclesiastical patronage in order to bridge cultural differences where the Latin church provided a common ground: Booker, *Cult. exch. med. Ire.*, pp 98–100; Katherine Walsh, 'The clerical estate in later medieval Ireland: alien settlement and society in medieval Ireland' in John Bradley (ed.), *Settlement and society in medieval Ireland* (Kilkenny, 1988), pp 361–78. Also, see Brendan Bradshaw, 'Sword and strategy in the reformation in Ireland' in *HJ*, 21 (1978), pp 745–502. The fluidity of the Irish world requires an appreciation of its textual, visual and oral tribrid nature. The Kildare library was a testament to the ninth earl's broad appreciation of Christian humanism. See also Raymond Gillespie, *Reading Ireland: print, reading and social change in early modern Ireland* (Manchester, 2005), p. 28.

[76] Vincent Carey, *Surviving the Tudors: the 'wizard' earl of Kildare and English rule in Ireland, 1537–1586* (Dublin, 2002), pp 47–9.

[77] See esp., S. G. Ellis, *Tudor frontiers and noble power: the making of the British state* (Oxford, 1995), p. 11.

[78] Edmund Curtis, 'Some further medieval seals out of the Ormond archives, including that of Donal Reagh MacMurrough-Kavanagh, king of Leinster' in *JRSA*, 7 (1937), p. 76; P. F. Wallace and Raghnall O'Floinn (eds), *Treasures of the National Museum of Ireland* (Dublin, 2002), p. 260. See ch. 1 for the wider symbolism of this artefact, and for the broad projections of the white earl of Ormond when the MacMurrough-Kavanagh were under their influence. Art MacMurrough-Kavanagh refurbished of the book of Mulling as 'Arturus Rex, Dominus Lagenie': Katharine Simms, 'The barefoot kings: literary image and reality in later medieval Ireland' in *PHCC*, 30 (2010), p. 7.

the sophistication and continuity of Geraldine authority, the table was in ways a refined material manifestation of the *Kildare Rental*.[79] As a tangible, functional construct, it ritualised the tributes and income received by the earl.[80] It was in August of that year as the table was formally unveiled, that Kildare impressed upon Wiltshire his stance on the 'good payment' of revenues and the 'ordering of your said landes'.[81] A Council House was incorporated into Maynooth castle as by 1533 the annual income of Kildare exceeded £2,000. It is believed that the Rent Table stood in this building.[82] Inscribed on the octagonal border in decorative style and raised lettering is the following:

GERALDUS COMES KILDARIE FILIUS GERALDI [coat of arms] A.D. M CCCCCXXXIII [coat of arms] SI DIEU PLET CROMABO [coat of arms][83]

It gestured toward a Geraldine European lineage and their 'auncient seate' as Ireland's foremost magnate. In well-preserved masonry, the legs and edges of the table are ornately decorated. Two of these feature a Kildare coat of arms and in distinctively humanist fashion, there are two nude figures. Even a fragmentary glimpse of Kildare culture patronage in the early 1530s uncovers an image of opulence and majesty, which in turn reinforced a sense of exceptionalism and legitimacy.[84] On consideration, it may not be an overstatement to characterise Geraldine pursuits as those of a renaissance prince in the glory that was Maynooth. Historians have long acknowledged the *hubris* of Kildare at the point of rebellion, but the Geraldine sense of exceptionalism was even more pronounced than hitherto appreciated.[85] Presuming the tacit partiality of their aristocratic

---

[79] *Ger. Med. Ire.*, preface, p. 19; Thomas Herron, 'Introduction: a fragmented Renaissance' in Thomas Herron and Michael Potterton (eds), *Ireland in the Renaissance c. 1540–1660* (Dublin, 2007), pp 19-39; E. S. Eames and Thomas Fanning, *Irish medieval tiles: decorated medieval paving tiles in Ireland with an inventory of sites and designs and a visual index* (Dublin, 1988), p. 48; Fitzgerald, *Earls Kildare*, p. 120.

[80] Fixed cash payments and leases were likely to have been regulated here: Brady, *Chief gov.*, p. 173. As Gillespie observes, Kildare exercised control over such arrangements. A 1532 monetary defence arrangement between Kildare and MacRanald of the Glens was sealed with the Maynooth chantry college signet on the part of the latter: Gillespie, *Reading Ire.*, p. 29.

[81] SP 1/78, ff 82.

[82] Marian Lyons, 'Kildare ascendancy' in Patrick Cosgrove, Terence Dooley and Karol Mullaney-Dignam (eds), *Aspects of aristocratic life: essays on the Fitzgeralds and Carton House* (Dublin, 2014), p. 54; Raymond Gillespie, 'The Fitzgeralds and the making of the manor of Maynooth' in Patrick Cosgrove, Terence Dooley and Karol Mullaney-Dignam (eds), *Aspects of aristocratic life: essays on the Fitzgeralds and Carton House* (Dublin, 2014), pp 34-46.

[83] I am grateful to Brenda Malone, National Museum of Ireland (Collins Barracks), for granting access to view this artefact.

[84] *Crown surveys of lands, 1540–1, with the Kildare Rental begun in 1518*, ed. Gearóid MacNiocaill (Dublin, 1992); Lyons, 'Kildare ascendancy', pp 53-4; Lennon, *Sixteenth-cen. Ire.*, pp 72-3.

[85] Lennon, *Sixteenth-cen. Ire.*; Lennon, 'Fitzgeralds of Kildare', pp 195-211; Lyons, 'Kildare

allies at Court, they sought to capitalise on the weaknesses of the crown from the vantage point of the long-term governance of the lordship. The recent tenure of Skeffington with the expediency of Cromwell's policies confirmed the crown's limited position.[86] Drawing largely, but not exclusively from the State Papers, scholars generally concur that the rumbling crises of the decades preceding 1534 were stoked by a series of disjointed, reactionary crown responses. Furthermore, it is generally agreed that the rebellion itself was a more immediate miscalculation which speedily expanded with catastrophic consequences. Nonetheless, despite the challenges faced by the Kildares in general and the predicament of the ninth earl in particular, they faced the summer of 1534 from what they saw as a position of strength.[87]

---

ascendancy', pp 47–59. Ironically, the Florentine Gherardini were reputed for arrogance and a 'distain of the people' according to a late medieval chronicle ('in odio al popolo'): Florence, Biblioteca Nazionale Centrale di Firenze, MS Banco Rari 23, f. 52v.

[86] Brady, *Chief gov.*, pp 1–3, 17–8.

[87] For many years, the traditional narrative was that of Stanihurst's romanticised 'lord Thomas being youthfull, rash and head-long...assuring himselfe that the knot of all the force of Ireland was twisted under his girdle': Raphael Holinshed, *Chronicles of England, Scotlande and Irelande* (6 vols., London, 1807–8), i, 89. Quinn argued against this being an impulsive act and was among the first to caution historians as to the lack of reliable evidence, urging a critical approach to a wider context: Quinn, 'Hen. VIII and Ire.', pp 328–32; Bradshaw, *Const. rev.*, pp 60–80. For the international context of the rebellion, see Ó Siochrú, 'Foreign involvement', pp 49–66. For conflict between Archbishop Alen and Kildare, see James Murray, 'Archbishop Alen, Tudor reform and the Kildare rebellion' in *PRIA*, 89C (1989), pp 1–16. For the course of the rebellion, see McCorristine, *Revolt of Silken Thomas*, pp 59–84.

7

Rebellion, State Paper Dark Age, 1534–40

Exploding within an already toxic political atmosphere, the outbreak of rebellion was a source of profound bewilderment for both sympathisers and enemies alike. A shocked Thomas Finglas did not even remotely anticipate Offaly's actions 'as fere as [he] had knowlege at that tyme' and Robert Cowley was quick to deem the 'seducyous proditorious rebelling' as heresy. Framing the westward conquest as a crusade, Ossory's indenture of 1534 had portrayed the king as a 'vertuous and most cristen prince' in reducing Ireland to 'Cristen manners'.[1] Having failed to take Dublin, Thomas moved to secure Maynooth and the south Leinster buffer between Kildare and Ormond.[2] The arrival of Skeffington with a force of 2,300 men eventually allowed for the rebellion to be quelled with a great deal of ferocity as the shires of Kildare, Meath and environs were laid waste. Aylmer, Alen and Brabazon later commented on the destruction, as the former liberty of Kildare was 'all brent'.[3] The Pale was rocked by violent exchanges and the infamous incidence of slaughter was the 'pardon' of Maynooth.[4] After the fall

---

[1] SP 60/2, ff 42v–43r, 48r, f. 50r; Ciaran Brady, *The chief governors: the rise and fall of reform government in Tudor Ireland, 1536–1588* (Cambridge, 1994), pp xii–xiv, 1–4. Kildare had also underestimated Cromwell's intelligence in Ireland: Micheál Ó Siochrú, 'Foreign involvement in the revolt of Silken Thomas, 1534-5' in *PRIA*, 96C (1996), p. 65.

[2] As Ellis states, at this point the defence of Maynooth was seen as a greater priority: S. G. Ellis, 'Siegecraft on the Tudor frontier: the siege of Dublin, 1534 and the crisis of the Kildare rebellion' in *Historical Research*, 92 (2019), pp 705–19; Laurence McCorristine, *Revolt of Silken Thomas: a challenge to Henry VIII* (Dublin, 1987), p. 91. Rawson conveyed a sense of alarm and violence; 'tiranny withowte marse... allso aluryd Oconnor unto hym and all other Irichemen that he can gett be in hys ayde burnyng and distroying your gracys Inglyche subjectes': *S.P. Hen. VIII*, ii, 201–2. While citizens were sympathetic to the Kildare cause, the city stood largely independent: Colm Lennon, *The lords of Dublin in the age of reformation* (Dublin, 1989), p. 36.

[3] SP 60/2, f. 145r; Brendan Bradshaw, *Irish constitutional revolution of the sixteenth century* (Cambridge, 1979), p. 104.

[4] Also see McCorristine, *Revolt of Silken Thomas*, pp 79–119; Ellis, *Ire. Tudors*, pp 134–41; S. G. Ellis, 'Henry VIII, rebellion and the rule of law' in *Historical Journal*, 24 (1981), pp 513–31; S. G. Ellis, *Tudor frontiers and noble power: the making of the British state* (Oxford, 1995), pp 209–23; Colm Lennon, *Sixteenth-century Ireland: the incomplete conquest* (Dublin, 1994), pp 109–13; Ó Siochrú, 'Foreign involvement', pp 65–9; Marian Lyons, *Gearóid Óg Fitzgerald, ninth earl of Kildare* (Dundalk, 1998), pp 51–69. The cost of suppressing the rebellion was alarming: S. G. Ellis, *Ireland's English Pale* (Woodbridge, 2021), pp 136–43; Brady, *Chief gov.*, pp 20–9; MacCulloch, *Thomas Cromwell*, p. 260. For the need to verify Stanihurst's account of the rebellion, see Ellis, 'Siegecraft on the Tudor frontier, pp 705–19; Ciarán Brady, 'The myth of

of Maynooth, with Kildare in retreat, there was a significant loss of momentum for the rebels.[5] Fitzgerald's appeal to Rome in May 1535 was less a theological move and more an act of desperation born of necessity. An absolution from Rome was required to preserve support for the rebellion but it also obstructed paths to a possible resolution with the crown.[6] It was Lord Leonard Grey as marshal of the army who relayed the surrender of Kildare in August 1535. Thomas was then bound for Court with the promise of a pardon.

Cowley's reproof of Offaly's stance as the 'popes secte and bande' obscured a more complex picture.[7] Yet there was always an ecclesiastical, if not religious, aspect to the rebellion even as recent scholarship has moved away from religion as its main cause.[8] While the Reformation exposed a weakness in the crown's position, the break with Rome also ran against Kildare's pan-cultural patronage and influence. As a result, a blind spot for Kildare was a failure to appreciate the significance of the Henrician religious Reformation. Perhaps having perceived the king to have been vulnerable because the Reformation individualised England, the extent to which a theological context drove the rebellion was a further miscalculation. Although the rebellion was mainly a secular event, ecclesiastical interests had long been a means for any ruling magnate to maintain and project authority. Kildare's political strength and ecclesiastical patronage were intertwined.[9] It is also difficult to reconcile how Fitzgerald would forsake the support of his aristocratic allies at Court, who themselves were compelled to support the king's supremacy.[10] Seduced by the European humanist ideal of Christendom and their own exceptionalism, they were confident that a compromise would emerge given

---

"Silken Thomas"' in Peter Crooks and Sean Duffy (eds), *The Geraldines and medieval Ireland: the making of a myth* (Dublin, 2016), pp 379-98. For recent excavations of the castle and the obliteration of late medieval and sixteenth-centuries artefacts: Alan Hayden, 'Maynooth castle, co. Kildare: excavation of the donjon' (unpublished archaeological report lodged with the National Monuments Service, Ireland, 2013), p. 25.

[5] S. G. Ellis, 'The Tudors and the origins of the modern Irish states: a standing army' in Thomas Bartlett and Keith Jeffery (eds), *Military history of Ireland* (Cambridge, 1996), p. 130; McCorristine, *Revolt of Silken Thomas*, p. 138.

[6] Chapuys indicated that the king may have been open to compromise even after the killing of Alen: *Cal. S. P. Spain*, v, 248-50.

[7] SP 60/2, f. 48r; James Murray, *Enforcing the English reformation in Ireland, clerical resistance and political conflict in the diocese of Dublin* (Cambridge, 2009), p. 82. Also, see MacCulloch, *Thomas Cromwell*, p. 117.

[8] For a traditional view, see Robert Dudley Edwards, *Church and state in Tudor Ireland* (Dublin, 1935). This perspective is somewhat echoed in Henry Jefferies, *The Irish church and the Tudor reformations* (Dublin, 2010).

[9] For polemic with ecclesiastical allusions, see the allegations presented to Grey a decade earlier, where the Butlers were equated to the heathen Turks: *S.P. Hen. VIII*, ii, 123.

[10] D. M. Head, *The ebbs and flows of fortune: the life of Thomas Howard, third duke of Norfolk* (London, 1995), pp 87-8, 103.

the wider historic unity under the papacy. However, in keeping with his father's policy, Offaly had initially kept a wide berth from Desmond-Hapsburg intrigue.[11]

They were on dangerous ground and enormous vested interests were at stake.[12] Projections of Kildare-led conservative aristocratic governance found purchase with ecclesiastical patronage and strengthened by the unifying force of Catholicism. Long-standing contention concerning the highly politicised Knights Hospitallers, for example, epitomised this overlap. Prior John Rawson also played a role in the arrest of Kildare's brethren who were delivered from Kilmainham.[13] Rawson remained faithful to the king even though the Hospitallers were in a sense more closely bound to the wider battle for Christendom under the Papal banner. In fact, he was one of few leading Irish clergymen to steadfastly support the crown throughout the rebellion. Fitzgerald seems to have avoided inflicting damage on Kilmainham property even during the siege of Dublin as he controlled 'free passage...too and fro in the Pale'. Some Palesmen later testified that a priory granary was burned by the rebels at some stage in 1535.[14]

The 'great curse' against Thomas Fitzgerald for the murder of Alen was declared publicly once Skeffington secured a foothold in Drogheda and Dublin in October or November of 1534. It invoked the anti-Geraldine rhetoric of decay, inverting the image of Kildare-led governance to the despotic 'wycked Pharoo'.[15] It was a move to emphasise the rebellion as a religious crusade although historians

---

[11] Detailed sources for Kildare's appeals to Rome and the emperor were possibly lost: Micheál Ó Siochrú, 'Foreign involvement', pp 49, 50-5.

[12] S. G. Ellis, *Ireland in the age of the Tudors* (London, 1998), pp 192-9, 211-14; Murray, *Enf. Eng. ref. Ire.*, pp 23-34, 46; Brendan Bradshaw, *Dissolution of the religious orders in Ireland under Henry VIII* (Dublin, 1974) pp 4, 8-37.

[13] The Geraldines were more concerned with Archbishop Alen. Kildare's retribution against Rawson was futile: SP 60/3, ff 153; Gregory O'Malley, *The Knights Hospitaller of the English langue, 1460-1565* (Oxford, 2005), p. 251; Brendan Scott, 'The Knights Hospitaller in Tudor Ireland: their dissolution and attempted revival' in Martin Browne and Colman Ó Clabaigh (eds), *Soldiers of Christ: the Knights Hospitaller and the Knights Templar in medieval Ireland* (Dublin, 2016), p. 49. For difficulties in dissolving the Hospitallers, see Bradshaw, *Dissolution*, pp 28-9, 78-80. Murray, *Enf. Eng. ref. Ire.*, pp 79, 122; Lennon, *Lords of Dublin*, pp 130-1.

[14] *Cal. S. P. Spain*, v, 164; *Extents of Irish monastic possessions 1540-1541*, ed. N. B. White (Dublin, 1943), p. 182; Holinshed, *Chronicles*, i, 91; Murray, *Enf. Eng. ref. Ire.*, pp 83-91. For the traditional character of the Dublin church, see Peadar Slattery, *Social life in pre-reformation Dublin 1450-1540* (Dublin, 2019), pp 145-74. Also, for earlier interventions and Hospitaller influence see Agnes Conway, *Henry VII's relations with Scotland and Ireland 1485-1498* (Cambridge, 1932) pp 143, 210, 218-19.

[15] SP 60/2, f. 76v-77r. Aggrieved enemies of the white earl saw him in similar terms 'more cruel than Pharaoh': Peter Crooks, 'Factionalism and noble power in English Ireland, c. 1361-1423' (Ph.D., Trinity College Dublin, 2007), p. 375; *CPR*, x, 497. It was a strong political statement. Murray has shown that there was little personal sympathy for the murdered archbishop: James Murray, 'Archbishop Alen, Tudor reform and the Kildare rebellion' in *PRIA*, 89C (1989), pp 1-16. As with the *Ordinances*, the 'curse' was enumerated among the state papers as a key source

have downplayed its practical implications.[16] In order to minimise the fallout over the killing of Alen, Kildare sent his chaplain Charles Reynolds to appeal for papal assistance in December 1534.[17] Neither Papal nor Spanish aid materialised.[18] It was in late autumn of 1536 with the Pilgrimage of Grace that Thomas' crusading overtures appeared in the most damning light.

In September 1535, Norfolk pressed for lenient treatment of Kildare, pointing to a worrying lack of 'credight' offered by alternative governors such as the Butlers. He warned Cromwell of a disastrous scenario where 'his grace shalbe inforced incontinent to procede to the general conquest of the londe' without the stability provided by Kildare. A financially crippling campaign was unavoidable according to the duke, 'onles they do parle'. This involved Kildare being in 'pryson for a tyme' and eventually restored.[19] The politics of Catholicism was part of this context. The process of excommunicating the king had begun under Clement VII in July 1533 and although this came into effect in September of that year it was not formally promulgated until Paul III in 1538. The king's re-fellowship under the papacy and a compromise with the Kildares was technically possible, even for quite some time after Thomas was first brought to the Tower. At the time Offaly renounced his allegiance, Norfolk had been on diplomatic duties at the French Court. By the end of the month he was appointed lord high steward at the trial of Lord Dacre.[20] When the rebellion escalated, he soured at the prospect of being sent to Ireland, and according to Chapuys, Norfolk saw 'nothing but harm from one side or another'. This report by Chapuys would be something of a harbinger for Grey's deputyship as Norfolk astutely weighed the scenario. His tentative

---

pertaining to the 'correspondence' between the governments of England and Ireland. They provide examples of an inherent state paper bias: SP 60/2, ff 76v-77r.

[16] Murray, *Enf. Eng. ref. Ire.*, pp 82-3; Ellis, *Ire. Tudors*, pp 135-9; Murray, 'Archbishop Alen', pp 1-16.

[17] Reynolds, or 'Magranyll' in chancery records, was a clergyman from Breifne. Hailing from an ecclesiastical dynasty in west Ulster, and not the church *inter Anglicos*. He studied in Oxford and according to the Imperial ambassador in Rome he convincingly put forward the Kildare case. For education of the clergy, see Marian Lyons, 'The onset of religious reform: 1460-1550' in *CHI*, i, 503. His documentation included a 'printed paper in English' recounting the heresies of the king, a 'copy of a manuscript paper, showing how, in the times of Pope Innocent III King John had acknowledged in the presence of Pandolfo his legate, that he had been justly deprived of his kingdom, and had received it again as a fief of the Apostolic See': *Calendar of the patent and close rolls of the chancery of Ireland in the reigns of Henry VIII, Edward VI, Mary and Elizabeth*, ed. J. Morrin (2 vols, Dublin, 1861), i, 2; *Alumni Oxonienses, 1500-1714*, ed. James Parker (2 vols, Oxford, 1891), i, 261; *Cal. S. P. Spain*, v, 164; Murray, *Enf. Eng. ref. Ire.*, pp 86-8.

[18] Ó Siochrú, 'Foreign involvement', p. 49; Ellis, *Ire. Tudors*, p. 137.

[19] SP 60/2, ff 154r-156r.

[20] *LP*, vii, 782; viii, 240.

inclination for Kildare was thus a signal that his doom was not sealed.[21] Moreover, the 'forsayd pardon' of Thomas was on the honour of Grey who was appointed as governor as Fitzgerald's destiny hung in the balance.[22]

The fate of the tenth earl in the Tower may also be considered in relation to the portrait that appears to have been made at some stage between late 1535 and February 1537. It is probable that Holbein drew Fisher in the Tower before his execution in 1535 and in doing so preserved his likeness while being resigned to a dignified *quietus*. Kildare's circumstances differed. The portrait of Thomas may have been commissioned for precisely the same reasons his father had done so in 1530.[23] Thomas wrote of his mean conditions in his cell in appealing to O'Brien of Thomond but the portrait suggests a different narrative and it is likely that Thomas anticipated his restoration at some stage.[24] The fall of Wiltshire and the Boleyns did not aid Kildare's chances of rehabilitation but while Thomas was detained, Grey's deputyship began to incur costs. By June 1536 the failure to pay arrears stoked dissent among the crown's standing army in Ireland. Grey's dilemma, as Brady outlines, was his charge to impose order and raise revenue while being curtailed with finite resources. The suppression of Kildare had drained crown treasure which left Grey to rely on using extortions that in turn left him vulnerable to accusations.[25] With the Pilgrimage of Grace the question of Kildare was postponed as steps were taken by Norfolk to quell the rebellion. It was as late as May of that year that the attainder against the Kildare Geraldines was passed. After sixteen months of imprisonment, on 3 February 1537, Thomas Fitzgerald, along with his five uncles, was executed at Tyburn, leaving the crown committed to some form of new departure in governing Ireland.[26]

No regional interest had been more vocal than the lobby for south Leinster; however there was a sense of déjà vu regarding related pleas on behalf of Waterford. Cromwell had been warned by Wyse of Waterford that the emperor's 'practise is

---

[21] *LP*, vii, 486.

[22] *LP*, xxi, 599; SP 60/2, f. 151r.

[23] The original is lost but a copy was made around the late eighteenth or early nineteenth century. Thomas is described therein as the 'earle of Kildare' which must postdate the death of Gearóid Óg. This copy is housed in the Stapleton Historical Collection, London: 'History of Ireland', online at carmichealdigitalprojects.org. Two artists, Lucas Horenbout and Holbein are known to have resided at court during this period: Derek Wilson, *Hans Holbein: portrait of an unknown man* (London, 2006), p. 225; Roy Strong, *Artists of the Tudor court: the portrait miniature rediscovered 1520–1620* (London, 1983), p. 6.

[24] SP 60/3, f. 196r; *S.P. Hen. VIII*, ii, 402-3; McCorristine, *Revolt of Silken Thomas*, pp 126-8, 153.

[25] Brady, *Chief gov.*, pp 17-33.

[26] McCorristine, *Revolt of Silken Thomas*, pp 130-2; Lennon, *Sixteenth-cen. Ire.*, p. 112; Ellis, *Ire. Tudors*, pp 141-2.

to wyn the Garaltynes' as the rebellion validated long-standing complaints that the Fitzgerald sect had decayed the colony.[27] When Gearóid Óg departed for England in February 1534 Richard Rawson ('your gracys chapelyn') travelled in the opposite direction. Shortly thereafter John Rawson had presented to the king the 'fears' of the 'mayr of your graces siutie of Waterford'. By the autumn the prior was a trustworthy voice to advise the king that Richard 'repeirythe now unto your Hyghtnes with dylygens who can informe your Grasse as he hathe sene and harde in Ireland'. The influential prior of Kilmainham was a credible figure to alert the king to dangers faced by the city in the face of invasion.[28]

Similar to the Butlers and like-minded proponents of 'conquest', Wyse made polemic use of historical argument and literature. There appeared in correspondence with Court, a 'copie of a letter' which was the ballad royal verse against the Geraldines in the 'tyme of their rebellion' (1487). With Grey appointed lord deputy, it was Thomas Cromwell who shared this ballad and urged the king in 'remembraunce' of the city's 'publique weale', sending a 'capp of llideguaunce [allegiance]' as an 'evident token of our favours'.[29] The poem was circulated at Court in the years after 1534, in time crystalising into something of an established account of Geraldine degeneration. Elizabethan commentators later appraised 'for wise it is remembred [and] circumstances may not be forgotten, be well preparid', which could also be a conceit in allusion to the author. Taking instruction from this evidently familiar 'Englysh ryme as followeth', the opening couplet was then cited. This apparently sufficed to prompt the reader.[30] The king's secretary was reminded of Waterford's tradition of loyalty in the face of Geraldine hostility. Early in Grey's deputyship in the summer of 1536, when anticipating a campaign to reform south Leinster, Wyse made it clear to Cromwell that 'Fernes in McMorow is the countre...necessay to be had for the king'. While doing so he alluded to Cromwell's Italianate learning. Anticipating Grey's campaigns in Thomond, he cited Petrarch's *Rerum Memorandum Libri* when he foresaw that 'we are like to have som sport procul ab urbana luxuria [far from urban luxury] with the desmondes and breenys'.[31] Other fragments of Wyse's literary historical argument may also

---

[27] BL, Titus B.XI, ii, f. 359r; Diarmaid MacCulloch, *Thomas Cromwell: a life* (London, 2018), pp 256-7; Ó Siochrú, 'Foreign involvement', p. 54.

[28] S.P. Hen. VIII, ii, 201-2, 244.

[29] SP 60/2, 52v. For Cromwell and Waterford, see BL, Titus B.XI, ii, f. 359r. See also above, ch. 2, and accounts of the late 1480s: BL, Add. MS 4792, ff 56.

[30] SP 63/214, f. 20r. Bradshaw remarked that reformers failed regarding immediate policy but succeeded in establishing more long-term developments: Bradshaw, *Const. rev.*, p. 33.

[31] SP 60/3, f. 106r. See *Rerum Memorandum Libri*, III. 69, found in Petrarca, Francesco, *Opera quae extant omnia etc.* (Basil, 1581), p. 448. The text was in print and circulated in England by the 1530s: Roberto Weiss, *Humanism in England during the fifteenth century* (Oxford, 1941), p. 64; Roberto Weiss, 'New Light on Humanism in England during the fifteenth century' in *Journal of the Warburg and Courtauld Institutes* 14 (1951), p. 21. Also of interest is Edmund Bonner, bishop

be gleaned from contemporaneous readership of the *Song of Piers de Bermingham* (1308). It was a fourteenth-century manuscript which belonged to the Wyse family, but evidence exists for its oral performance in the sixteenth century.[32]

In the wake of 'manyfold enormyties alleged and proved ayenst thErle of Kildare', the Butlers could justifiably foresee a favourable rearrangement of south Leinster given Cromwell's 'speciall affiaunce in their polesye'.[33] During the rebellion Brabazon declared that the banishment of MacMurrough and conquest of O'Toole and O'Byrne was 'easie to be done'. For the remainder of the decade, this call was echoed.[34] The pace of change quickened with Lord Deputy Grey, Archbishop George Browne (consecrated March 1536) and the Reformation parliament of May 1536 which speedily enacted supremacy legislation.[35] Aptly enough, in June, Cowley sought with 'great hast' the confiscation of the 'Kewanaghes and brines'. He then added that 'such oportunytie' to recover the 'hole domynion' was not possible since before the rise of the Geraldines 'theise hundrith yeres past'.[36] A string of similar petitions had been made by late autumn, many of which reinforced earlier themes.[37]

Attention was directed toward former Norfolk possessions in Fasagh, Carlow, Tullow and Old Ross.[38] Norfolk's castles and manors in Idrone and Wexford were subject to fierce fighting in order to repel the Geraldine Cahir

---

of London in 1529 (Wolsey's former chaplain) to Cromwell 'willing to make me a good ytalian pmsed unto me long agoe the triumphs of Petrarche in the ytalian tongue': SP 1/57, f. 75r. Also see MacCulloch, *Thomas Cromwell*, pp 27-8, 238. For the *Rerum* as a reworking of Cicero, see Barbara C. Bowen, 'Ciceronian wit and Renaissance rhetoric' in *Rhetorica* 16 (1998), p. 411.

[32] Written in trochaic trimeter, a stressed foot in Tudor hand (the word 'he') was inserted at the following to sustain the flow of the metre; 'Sire Pers sei ham com | He receivid al and some': BL, Harleian MS 913, f. 51v. This line referred to Bermingham on campaign against O'Connor Faly. See also *Anglo-Irish poems of the middle ages*, ed. Angela Lucas (Dublin, 1995), pp 27-42, 46-172; Robin Frame, 'Contexts, divisions and unities: perspectives from the later middle ages' in *CHI*, i, pp 535-6.

[33] SP 60/2, f. 41r.

[34] SP 60/2, f. 156r; David Heffernan, *Debating Tudor policy in sixteenth-century Ireland: 'reform' treatises and political discourse* (Manchester, 2018), pp 36-44; Christopher Maginn, *'Civilizing' Gaelic Leinster: the extension of Tudor rule in the O'Byrne and O'Toole Lordships* (Dublin, 2005), pp 46-53.

[35] SP/60/3, f. 159v-160r; Murray, *Enf. Eng. ref. Ire.*, pp 78, 88-90, 99-108.

[36] *S.P. Hen. VIII*, ii, pp 332-3; SP/60/3, f. 93r. Historians have pointed to Grey's success against the O'Tooles and pleas to move elsewhere in south Leinster: Heffernan, *Tudor policy*, pp 36-7; Maginn, 'Civ.' *Gaelic Leinster*, p. 62; Christopher Maginn and S. G. Ellis, *Tudor discovery of Ireland* (Dublin, 2015), p. 167.

[37] See for example Ossory's instructions to Cowley, Sept. 1535 in making a case for intervention in Idrone and south Leinster: SP 60/2, ff 129r, 130.

[38] They were administered in the 'king's service' according to Kildare in 1525 despite attacks by 'Ormondes servauntes': *S.P. Hen. VIII*, ii, 123.

MacMurrough-Kavanagh in 1535.[39] Robert Cowley meanwhile pressed for the walling of Leighlin and Fassagh to defend the 'contree of Odron', attaching the correspondence with his 'boke whiche (he) last delivered to your wisdom'.[40] Cowley maintained that by attending to Idrone 'then shall all Leynester be clier Englissh without any of the Irisshery amongest them'.[41] Here Cowley notoriously proposed to 'brenne and distroye [their lands] so as the Irisshery shall not lyve thereupon'.[42] Cowley the elder followed by evoking the heroics of the Cambro-Norman conquest in south Leinster. An additional memorandum declared that the 'hole countie of Wexford and divers other possessions be resumed' to the crown. Cowley emphasised that under Geraldine control, the 'Inglish blodde of the Ynglish conqueste ys in maner worne out of this lande'.[43]

Finglas's 'Breviate' was again revived in the aftermath of 1534.[44] After the fall of Kildare, Finglas was made baron of the exchequer for life and his son Thomas, who wrote and delivered a copy (version four) of the 'Breviate', was appointed protonotary and chirographer of common pleas. Prior to this, Thomas seems to have followed in his father's footsteps at the Inns of Court, where a 'Fynglasse' was elected escheator in 1533.[45] The post-rebellion revisions of the 'Breviate' included an extended historical narrative which still centred on south Leinster, while confiscated lands were also discussed. Alen placed the reduction of Leinster in its historical context as an opportunity not seen 'these 250 yeres'. Concerted attempts were made to persuade the king that it would be 'honorable, nedefull and in theynde profectable' to focus on south Leinster 'betwexte dublin and Waterforde'. An artificial proximity to mainland Britain was given as 'those partes of Leynster [namely] McMurgho...next to your Realm of Englande'.[46] Frequent references to the king's 'progenitors' for centuries rooted such rhetoric in the mythology and history of the conquest. However, in conceptual terms, a troubling incongruity had by then appeared. The continued emphasis of Giraldus and

---

[39] SP 60/2, f. 130v.
[40] SP 60/3, ff 68v–69r.
[41] SP 60/3, f. 66r.
[42] SP 60/3, ff 69; Heffernan, *Tudor policy*, p. 68.
[43] SP 60/3, f. 93v. See also articles written by Robert Cowley in Oct. 1536 which drew attention to south Leinster and the king's titular prestige of the Earl Marshal. SP 60/3, ff 141v–142v.
[44] Heffernan dates versions three and four to 1535. See Heffernan, 'Finglas' breviate', p. 371–9, esp. p. 377; Maginn and Ellis, *Tudor discov. Ire.*, pp 27–34.
[45] If so, he was also placed to make the symbolic link between the rights of a neglected colony and Marshal's remains at Lincoln's Inn, both in the written 'kings recordes' and the material evidence in Temple church: *Records of the society of Lincoln's Inn*, ed. J. D. Walker (2 vols, London, 1897), i, 236.
[46] SP 60/3, ff 155, 165v, 175r; Bradshaw, *Const. rev.*, pp 109, 114. It is useful here to consider the broader analysis offered by Ellis in *Tudor frontiers*, pp 64, 126–32.

the twelfth-century papal conquest of Christendom directly contradicted the Reformation legislation, itself barely a few months old.

※

Over the following year, enemies descended upon Grey from many quarters. Grey's opponents denounced him as a papist and in this context, enmity between Grey and Browne ran deep. Grey viewed Browne as an obstacle to his aim of gathering support among former Geraldine sympathisers. Conversely, the archbishop saw the deputy as an impediment to crown ecclesiastical policy and English order with his adherence to a treasonous papal ideology.[47] Not only did Grey stand independent of the Butlers and like-minded Pale interests, he sought a broad following among supporters of the Kildare Geraldines. Browne's ecclesiastical responsibility as a Reformation archbishop thus generated enormous tension with the embattled deputy.

The famous Butler allegation that Grey was the 'Erle of Kildare newly borne again' was justified.[48] He was circumspect about the restoration of Kildare, for example when he suggested to Cromwell it was best to withhold a decision and allow 'tyme [as] we trust to have knowlege from your lordship how all things shall procede'.[49] But the day before he wrote, the earl and his uncles were executed. The reported shock of the commons at the prospect of Kildare's return, as mentioned by Grey, contrasted with the 'lamentations' of the annals after the event.[50] But Grey may be credited with striving to impose stability by governing with a broad geopolitical scope and in taking steps toward the establishment of a central administration. It was a tall order amid the turmoil of post-rebellion dissent and Grey's priority had been to stabilise the Munster Geraldines while he came to terms with O'More and he found O'Neill to be, albeit ominously, 'very tractable in words'. His interests clashed with those of the Butlers. Mistrust would have been stirred by an accord between the deputy and the Fitzpatrick of Upper Ossory.[51] Along with Cromwell, Grey had been praised for steering the Reformation parliament of 1536-7, speedily enacting legislation and the confiscation of some monastic and Geraldine lands.[52] Cromwell's attention on Ireland, however, was very much sporadic as he entrusted Grey with affairs.[53]

---

[47] S.P. Hen. VIII, ii, 569; Murray, Enf. Eng. ref. Ire., pp 109-12, 182; Brady, Chief gov., p. 23-30.
[48] BL, Titus B.XI, f. 356r.
[49] SP 60/4, f. 10r; Bradshaw, Const. rev., p. 177.
[50] SP 60/4, f. 10r; AFM, 1537.
[51] See esp., Brady, Chief gov., pp 13-17; Bradshaw, Const. rev., pp 177-95; S.P. Hen. VIII, ii, 334, 384.
[52] S. G. Ellis, 'Thomas Cromwell and Ireland, 1532-1540' in HJ, 23 (1980), pp 508-10; Heffernan, Tudor policy, p. 55.
[53] They were close allies. In 1539, Cromwell employed Grey's nephew in his household: Brady, Chief gov., p. 42.

Proponents for regional entrenchment or 'conquest' had appeared triumphant when Grey was first appointed governor, as he appeared amenable to their bidding. The advent of such strategies was seen as a final vindication after the rebellion; however it merely served to compound their eventual disillusion with Grey. The Butlers adamantly declared to Grey the pressing matter of honour should 'he and his blood [be] put from their inheritaunce, which they have possessed from the conquest'.[54] Furthermore, Grey's reluctance to enforce the religious Reformation exacerbated hostility with Browne and the deputy's problems mounted as unreconciled Geraldines grew increasingly militant.[55] By the summer of 1537 the commission under St Leger and Paulet was formed to investigate the ill-governed lordship. Grey had accused Brabazon, Agard, Poole, Cusack and Walter Cowley as the 'most grownde of the devision here'.[56] Well before the commission arrived (in September) 'conquest' lobbyists had denounced Grey by means of uncompromising rhetoric projected through historical argument and symbolism. Although the findings of the investigation were pleasing to those such as the Butlers, Cromwell remained inactive. It would become merely the first in a series of bitter disappointments as costly approaches were averted. For instance, the king's command to 'all consider what importable charges We have been at lately...aswel how presently to gratifie Us with some recompence'.[57] The council responded to Cromwell, with a passage highlighted by a line at the margin and that honour was to be gained by 'annexed rewle and riches...for the reformacion of this lande is not yet come'.[58]

Still, 'conquest' orientated memoranda were produced at astounding rates.[59] The Cowley petitions presented the Butler programme for 'conquest' while Alen, Brabazon, Cusack and Finglas argued along similar lines and with similar rhetoric.[60] The post-rebellion state memoranda retold the history of a colony decayed by the Geraldines with increased zeal. The preceding themes of 'conquest' discourse, in terms of rhetoric and symbol, continued to draw from Giraldus and the English mythology of the conquest. With Alen and Cowley, there was also a curious accentuation of the eastern lordship as essentially an extension

---

[54] SP 60/4, f. 10r. Also see Brendan Kane, *Politics and culture of honour in Britain and Ireland, c. 1541–1641* (Cambridge, 2010), pp 1–19, 23, 33–5.
[55] Brady, *Chief gov.*, pp 16–7.
[56] SP 60/3, f. 169v.
[57] *S.P. Hen. VIII*, ii, 403. The sentiment recurs through 1537, 'vayne consumption' of revenues yielding 'little honour or profit': SP 60/4, f. 33v.
[58] SP 60/4, f. 60v.
[59] Heffernan, *Tudor policy*; David Heffernan, 'The reduction of Leinster and the origins of the Tudor conquest of Ireland, c. 1534–46' in *IHS*, 40 (2016), pp 1–21. Since the late twentieth century, a number of studies examined the push for policy in this period: Dean White, 'The Tudor plantations in Ireland before 1571' (Ph.D., Trinity College Dublin, 1968); Bradshaw, *Const. rev.*; Brady, *Chief gov.*; Maginn and Ellis, *Tudor discov. Ire.*
[60] Heffernan emphasises the aggressive nature of Alen's proposals.

of west Wales. The proximity of Ireland's south-eastern seaboard to mainland Britain appears to have been exaggerated to present policies in a favourable light. Framed by the binary of Geraldine decay, the honour and morality of a westward 'conquest' for true religion was all the more pronounced.[61]

Within a week of Geraldine 'heddes set up about the cittie' of London, a centrepiece reform treatise, the 'Memoriall, or note for the wynnyng of Leynster' was sent to the king and council.[62] The author is uncredited but if not written by Finglas, it was strongly influenced by the 'Breviate'. The council advised that the 'Memoriall' was to be sent with the lord treasurer, James Butler. The Cowleys were therefore also likely candidates.[63] The substance and rhetoric of the 'Memoriall' encapsulated the Butler 'conquest' approach. It ambitiously proposed a radical 'conquest' of south Leinster through the occupation of many former Kildare strongholds and the disposal of lands to 'certein gentilmen of Ingland.' Ormond lands in south Leinster and east Munster would benefit in terms of strategic value and the defence of the Englishry should these proposals be implemented. An earldom of Carlow was to be created as the house of Kildare was dismantled. Polemic content of the 'Memoriall' portrayed the strategic and symbolic value of south Leinster in general and Idrone in particular as it was the Geraldines as 'actors or abbettors' who were the 'cheef soar bile' of the colony. The MacMurrough-Kavanaghs were the first Irish enemy to be removed and should the Geraldines be entirely subdued there would be none 'to haunte' the king's highway between Dublin and Waterford.[64] Evoking the *res gestae* of the original conquest:

> the nobilitie of those Inglishemen, wich came in at the conqwest, is much to be extolled and noted, wich being to souch an interprise but a few in number, how valiauntly and circumspectlye ded thei procede and agayne, after what soarte thei made fortresses, and inhabited as thei went what travayle, what paynes,

---

[61] For examples of treatises based on such historical argument, see Alen to St Leger: SP 60/5, f. 27r and Luttrell to St Leger, SP 60/5, ff 41. For an example of historical argument and a concerted appeal to the king's sense of honour, both highlighted with a marginal reading aid: SP 60/4, f. 60v. Also see Kane's conceptual study; Ireland was land of conquest which brought power, but in the post-1540 environment, justice brought legitimacy: Kane, *Pol. culture of honour*, p. 84.

[62] *The chronicle of the Grey Friars of London*, ed. C. G. Nichols (London, 1852), p. 39; McCorristine, *Revolt of Silken Thomas*, p. 131; SP 60/4, ff 19r-25r.

[63] Heffernan underlines its importance. Drawing analogies between its ambitious aims and the Breviate, he also cites the later influence of the 'Memoriall' through John Alen: Heffernan *Tudor Policy*, pp 14, 41-7. Also see Maginn, 'Civ.' *Gaelic Leinster*, pp 36-7, 52-3; Maginn and Ellis, *Tudor discov. Ire.*, p. 33; Brady, *Chief gov.*, p. 249.

[64] SP 60/4, ff 19r, 20r. Also, see the 'perils' described by John Wyse in 1493: *Statute rolls of the Irish parliament: Richard III - Henry VIII*, ed. Philomena Connolly (Dublin, 2002), p. 28; Heffernan, *Tudor policy*, p. 95.

what diligence usid thei therin? Thei sought neither for delicate fare, neither desired thei to lye in walled townes, uppon soft beddes, but pursued their enemies, untill thei had banyshed theym: for, if thei had don the contrarie, as souldiers do now a dayes, thei had neiver achived ther purpas.[65]

Apparently influenced by Giraldus, failure to intervene accordingly would be to the crown's shame since the 'naked Scotts out of the Isles' could secure a foothold in Ulster. The 'Memoriall' contributed this English mythology of the conquest, stressing the region to be 'directly agaynst Northwales and Southwales'.[66] Pushing this concept further, Leinster was 'next to the socor and domynon of Inglande'.[67] Of relevance here was Cromwell's expansion of the Tudor bureaucracy and the marcher lordships of Wales.[68] Part of a geopolitical agenda in presenting a Leinster extension of mainland Britain was to downplay the dangers of the Irish Sea. This was an understandable concern, as can be seen in a diverse range of sources. See for example details of the 'gret labour and payn' endured by Edgecombe before arriving on Irish shores in the summer of 1488. These perils were attested to in Caxton's printing of the *Polychronicon* (1502): 'the see that is bytwene brytaye and Irlonde is al the yere ful of grete waves'. Of more immediate relevance, Norfolk cryptically remarked in autumn 1534 that only a 'bridge' would induce him to return to the lordship.[69]

Along with the Butlers, Alen, Brabazon and Browne evidently supplied information for the crown commission of 1537-8 which superseded the lord deputy.[70] Shortly after the commissioners departed, Archbishop Brown himself was troublingly impeded when the Dublin clergy refused the 'Form of Beads'. He reported to Cromwell with dismay that there was 'scarse one that favoureth Goddes worde', famously citing the obstinacy of one Humphrey of St Audoen's.[71] Articles against Grey revealed deep resentment of the deputy who governed autocratically and allegedly abandoned the process of reform.

In what was arguably Cromwell's most important intervention in Ireland, the commission had aimed to regularise the garrison system.[72] Grey apparently

---

[65] SP 60/4, ff 23.
[66] SP 60/4, f. 19r.
[67] SP 60/4, ff 19.
[68] Ellis, *Tudor frontiers*, pp 4, 21-31, 43-4, 257; S. G. Ellis and Christopher Maginn, *The making of the British Isles: The state of Britain and Ireland, 1450-1660* (London, 2007), pp 2-10, 97-105.
[69] BL, Titus B.XI, ff 282r; *Cal. S.P. Spain*, v, 255. Also, see Slattery, *Social life in pre-reformation Dublin*, p. 18.
[70] Brady, *Chief gov.*, pp 20-4, 42.
[71] *S.P. Hen. VIII*, iii, 7; Murray, *Enf. Eng. ref. Ire.*, pp 109-11. Having been a loyal bastion, the city witnessed divisions at this juncture: Murray, *Enf. Eng. ref. Ire.*, pp 82-3; Slattery, *Social life in pre-reformation Dublin*, pp 20-1, 35-9.
[72] MacCulloch, *Thomas Cromwell*, p. 260; Brady, *Chief gov.*, pp 20-4; Ellis, 'Cromwell and

destabilised the lordship, hindering 'therle of Ossorys son' in their duties 'to serve the king' apprehending rebels in south Leinster.[73] Regional problems were compounded by the 'mortal' enmity stirred by Grey with the MacMurrough-Kavanagh. Led by the former Geraldine Cahir McArt, the coveted eastern Ormond interests were reduced to disorder.[74] The commission itself was regarded as a success. According to Barnewall in April 1538, it had uncovered 'moche of the mysdemenurs here'.[75] But despite the damning revelations, no action was taken until 1540 as Cromwell gambled to allow an old ally to strengthen the crown's regional position in mid-Leinster.[76] The findings were concealed until later as St Leger had initially sided with the Butlers.[77] It was at some point between April 1538 and early 1540 that in spite of a worsening situation, St Leger became convinced that a costly military strategy would not be approved. He prudently observed in January 1538 that the land was 'moche easiyar wonne than kept'.[78] Mounting frustration on the part of 'conquest' proponents manifested in hostile depositions where Cromwell was subject to a range of attacks. Loaded allusions, while seemingly obscure, can be revealing in the context of rhetorical influences. George Paulet, a Geraldine sympathiser, was alleged to have spoken negatively of

> my lorde pryve seal for some practise hath sent (a) Walshe man (to) Saint Patrickes to ensershe and have intelligence pryvely of a certain prophesye that a pellycane shulde come out of Irlande into Englande whiche shulde doo many mervaillous thinges.

The intention here was to discredit Cromwell and ensure the garrison of Carlow and Kildare along with elsewhere in south Leinster.[79] These were slanderous allegations that appear to have been coined to suggest Cromwell's knowledge and consideration of the Butler 'conquest' strategy and its projections through Giraldus.

Ireland'; Heffernan, *Tudor policy*, p. 61.
[73] *S.P. Hen. VIII*, iii, 37.
[74] *S.P. Hen. VIII*, iii, 42.
[75] SP 60/6, f. 89r.
[76] SP 60/6, f. 5v; *S.P. Hen. VIII*, ii, 535.
[77] Bradshaw, *Const. rev.*, pp 164-85; Brady, *Chief gov.*, p. 42.
[78] SP 60/6, f. 5r.
[79] SP 60/6, f. 48v. For the prophecies of Merlin (of Celidon) and the Leinster region, see Gerald of Wales, *Expugnatio Hibernica, the conquest of Ireland*, ed. A. B. Scott and F. X. Martin (Dublin, 1978), pp 31, 65, 97. One prophecy is followed by an account of Irish lords eating the 'loathed' flesh of the crane, in obedience to the king: *Expugnatio*, ed. Scott and Martin, p. 97. The above reference may be a seditious inversion of what may have been a well-known account. Merlin's prophecy highlighted in the 'Butler Expugnatio' manuscript regarding 'fyre' from the east: TCD, MS 592, f. 12v. Also, see contemporary printed versions of Geoffrey of Monmouth and Merlin's 'lion out of Irland ... (that) shall tremble the land that...shall be called England as an aspen leef': *Chronicles of England*, ed. William Caxton (1480), pp 75-6.

But after the tremendous cost of defeating Kildare, Cromwell had no intention of allowing the Butlers to regain their former position of ascendancy as in the time of the White Earl. Indeed, given optimal circumstances, Sir Piers was capable of becoming an overmighty magnate. Restored to the earldom of Ormond, he died in 1539 as he continued to seek an antiquated policy of regional entrenchment. He was interred alongside his forefathers in St Canice's in an expensive yet stylistically archaic tomb.[80] Financial reasons aside, Cromwell saw strategic shortcomings in the region-specific 'conquest' agenda as he viewed the Tudor state as a broad entity.[81] The vast quantity of 'conquest' polemic varied in sophistication and certain points of emphasis but the above core themes remained constant.[82] It is arguable that Cromwell decided against this approach from an early stage. A further complicating factor was the symbolic implications associated with the traditional 'conquest' and the Henrician religious Reformation.

A 'conquest' strategy enjoyed an advantage as it opposed, in principle, the unified European concept of Christendom, which had been projected by the lately treasonous Geraldines. Yet while 'conquest' in this sense was anti-Catholic, it was an imperfect fit for the king's reformed church outside the see of Rome. Projected through tropes linked to the *Expugnatio*, this 'conquest' approach ran contrary to the king's supremacy. The concept of an Irish church that predated the twelfth-century conquest was a preferable basis for the Henrician Reformation.[83] Whereas the Cambro-Norman conquest was a papal intervention to rectify the degenerate Celtic church, its original licence was a worry for Anglicanism or its Irish equivalent. But the king's supremacy rendered the Latin church itself degenerate and by anterior emphasis, justified the pre-conquest Irish church. Problematic for the Butlers was that such reform essentially required a broad, pan-cultural approach. Although there was a desire for both 'conquest' and reformation, it was impossible to achieve both. Giraldus as a projection of strategy

---

[80] Paul Cockerham, '"To mak a tombe for the earl of Ormon and to set it up in Iarland": Renaissance ideas in Irish funeral monuments' in Thomas Herron and Michael Potterton (eds), *Ireland in the Renaissance* (Dublin, 2007), pp 195–230, esp. 197–200; Susan Flavin, *Consumption and culture in sixteenth-century Ireland: saffron, stockings and silk* (Woodbridge, 2014), pp 85, 94–5, 140; E. W. Heckett, 'Tomb effigies and archaic dress in sixteenth-century Ireland' in Catherine Richardson (ed.), *Clothing culture, 1350–1650* (Aldershot, 2004), pp 63–75. For later Ormondist reform proposals up to 1539, see *S.P. Hen. VIII*, iii, 448; SP 60/6, f. 62r. Also, see David Edwards, *The Ormond lordship in County Kilkenny, 1515–1642: the rise and fall of Butler feudal power* (Dublin, 2003), p. 145.

[81] Ellis and Maginn, *Making of the British Isles*, pp 363–9; Ellis, *Tudor frontiers*, p. 173; MacCulloch, *Thomas Cromwell*, pp 23, 132; S. G. Ellis, *Reform and revival: English government in Ireland 1470–1534* (Woodbridge, 1986), p. 179.

[82] See Heffernan, *Tudor policy*, ch. 1, pp 218–21.

[83] Murray, *Enf. Eng. ref. Ire.*, pp 34–57; Ellis, *Ire. Tudors*, pp 191–209; Alan Ford, '"That noble dream", objectivity and the writing of Irish Church history' in Mark Empey, Alan Ford and Miriam Moffitt (eds), *The Church of Ireland and its past* (Dublin, 2017), pp 3–4.

was therefore at odds with ecclesiastical changes in what proved to be the sheer internal conflict of Tudor policy in Ireland.[84] Strained relations between officials caused further instability. Aside from Browne's bitter conflict with Grey, he clashed with the more conservative bishop of Meath, Edward Staples who in turn quarrelled with Grey and lost favour with Cromwell.[85] Staples's preference for education and persuasion contrasted with Browne's bullish approach. As an enemy of Grey, Browne was a natural ally for Alen and the Butlers (aside from the above contradictions) but his headstrong desire to impose ecclesiastical reform on a reluctant clergy generated conflict. Browne's official 'Form of Beads' denounced breviaries and 'other bokes' where the pope was recognised, which technically included the *Expugnatio*. At the very least it was problematic for the use of Giraldus as a projection of policy.[86]

Although he campaigned widely and for the most part effectively, Grey's most notable victory at Bellahoe against O'Neill and O'Donnell in 1539 was overshadowed by recurring violence and raids on the Pale. The alliance of Ulster lords sometimes referred to as the Geraldine league, along with O'Connor (Sligo) and O'Brien presented a dangerous situation.[87] Plagued by accusations that he supported the exiled Geraldine heir, young Gerald Fitzgerald's presence in Europe also prompted anxiety and suspicion. Fitzgerald's arrival at Cardinal Reginald Pole's Court in Florence, as Vincent Carey suggests, was more than a familial occasion.[88] Meanwhile, Cowley's reports of attacks and the 'fyre of destruction' marked another push for 'conquest'. But it was ultimately to no avail as momentum shifted to alternative solutions.[89] Two years had passed since the commission but Grey's recall in May 1540 and sudden imprisonment

---

[84] Also see Murray, *Enf. Eng. ref. Ire.*, pp 48–9.

[85] Brendan Scott, *Religion and reformation in the Tudor diocese of Meath* (Dublin, 2007), pp 35–46, 97; Bradshaw, *Const. rev.*, pp 155–7, 165, 193–5; Brendan Bradshaw, 'George Browne, first reformation archbishop of Dublin, 1536–1554' in *Journal of Ecclesiastical History*, 21 (1970), pp 301–26; Murray, *Enf. Eng. ref. Ire.*, pp 82–124, 157–8, 199–202; James Murray, 'Ecclesiastical justice and the enforcement of the reformation: the case of Archbishop Browne and the clergy of Dublin, 1536–1554' in Alan Ford, James McGuire and Kenneth Milne (eds), *As by law established: The Church of Ireland since the reformation* (Dublin, 1995), pp 33–51; Heffernan, *Tudor policy*, pp 56–9.

[86] SP 60/6, f. 79r.

[87] Maginn, '*Civ.*' *Gaelic Leinster*, p. 62. By early 1541 the rehabilitation of Desmond under the pretender James FitzJohn had changed the complexion of the alliance as Manus O'Donnell colluded with James V of Scotland: Anthony McCormack, *The earldom of Desmond, 1463–1583: the decline and crisis of a feudal lordship* (Dublin, 2005), pp 70–6; Ellis, *Ire. Tudors*, pp 148–9; Brady, *Chief gov.*, pp 22–4; Bradshaw, *Const. rev.*, pp 174–85.

[88] Vincent Carey, *Surviving the Tudors: the 'wizard' earl of Kildare and English rule in Ireland, 1537–1586* (Dublin, 2002), p. 44–9.

[89] SP 60/8, f. 59r; AFM, 1539. For example, see Thomas Cusack's 'Devise': *S.P. Hen. VIII*, iii, 179; Heffernan, *Tudor policy*, p. 47.

on 12 June occurred alongside the swift downfall of Cromwell, months after being granted the earldom of Essex.[90] After Bellahoe, and certain of Cromwell's backing, Grey was apparently confident of securing support for garrisons and a strong military policy.[91] With his destruction, there were dramatic consequences for all those associated with Cromwell, including Grey and Arthur Plantagenet Viscount Lisle, in what was essentially a palace coup d'état. St Leger contributed to the undoing of Grey by affirming the long-standing allegations put forward by 'conquest' proponents.[92]

Few would have anticipated the new departure heralded by St Leger, and fewer still would have foreseen its positive impact in the mid-1540s.[93] Cromwell's execution paved the way for the governorship of St Leger, whose conciliatory methods of co-option, known to posterity as 'surrender and regrant', signalled the rejection of a traditional 'conquest' strategy. As the post-Grey recourse to diplomacy sealed the perdition of this Butler, or anti-Geraldine agenda, Cowley influence evaporated. Early in 1542 the king was convinced that Robert Cowley was a 'man seditious and full of contention and disobedyence which is to be abhorred in any man but chiefly in a counsailor'.[94] While finding glory, honour and 'conquest' appealing, the king was unwilling to deplete the treasury for an Irish war, even if (and perhaps more so because) the Lordship was elevated in status from a lordship to a kingdom in its own right. After Grey's ruin it became obvious that Butler pleas were overlooked. Their underlying priority to destroy the MacMurrough and to establish suzerainty over lords in mid-Leinster, along with the very principle of the original conquest, ran against the imperative of reformation and by 1540, also the process of reform.[95] Since 1537, St Leger had gradually come to appreciate the

---

[90] MacCulloch, *Thomas Cromwell*, pp 371–8.
[91] Brady, *Chief gov.*, pp 23–5; Heffernan, *Tudor policy*, pp 41–50.
[92] Brady, *Chief gov.*, pp 23–5; Ellis, *Ire. Tudors*, pp 147–9.
[93] Cusack's 'Device' (c. 1537) proposed a very similar approach for south Leinster: *'Reform' Treatises*, pp 1–6; Brady, *Chief gov.*, pp 29–42, 270; Bradshaw, *Const. rev.*, pp 197–235; Maginn, 'Civ.' Gaelic Leinster, p. 63–85; Heffernan, *Tudor policy*, pp 11–12, 27, 33–47. It was a shift from Kildare's affinity-based authority to more legalistic crown authority: Emmett O'Byrne, 'The Tudor state and the Irish of east Leinster, 1535–54' in Michael Potterton and Thomas Herron (eds), *Dublin and the Pale in the Renaissance, c. 1540–1660* (Dublin, 2007), pp 68–92. For the early stages of this experiment, see Brady, *Chief gov.*, Brendan Bradshaw, 'The English Reformation and identity formation in Ireland and Wales' in Brendan Bradshaw and Peter Roberts (eds), *British consciousness and identity: the making of Britain, 1533–1707* (Cambridge, 1998), pp 43–111.
[94] S.P. Hen. VIII, iii, 369; Edwards, *Ormond lordship*, p. 170. This would prove to be a recurring problem. See Valerie McGowan-Doyle, 'Elizabeth I, the Old English, and the rhetoric of counsel' in Brendan Kane and Valerie McGowan-Doyle (eds), *Elizabeth I and Ireland* (Cambridge, 2014), pp 163–83; Heffernan, *Tudor policy*, pp 182–95.
[95] For example, see Ossory to Walter Cowley in 1535, who urged to intervene in Leix. A coded reading aid ('p[–]x') in the margin of the correspondence highlighted its importance: SP 60/2, 130v.

impracticality of 'conquest' which was all the more unfeasible on the grounds of its basis in a twelfth-century Christian ideology.[96]

Further validation was given with his appointment and mandate to implement radical constitutional change as governor. The elegant way in which the kingly title resolved this contradiction was by asserting through anteriority that Ireland had always been a unified polity.[97] For instance, following the landmark accord with Con Bacach O'Neill and his ennoblement at Court, when he was made an earl in 1542, in principle, Tyrone always had been a subject of the crown.[98] In strategic terms, the subsequent agreements with Gaelic lords also bore similarities to the former Geraldine means of co-option. By solving the problem of reformation and circumventing the pitfall of ruinous military expenditure, the crown veered from a 'conquest' strategy at the very moment its proponents were most optimistic. What subsequently transpired proved a far cry from regional entrenchment. It was with some ambivalence that James Butler (though admittedly well compensated) presided over the pronouncement of the 'act for the kingly title' in the Gaelic tongue.[99] The house of Ormond had failed to sway policy but the ninth earl nevertheless found himself presiding over a constitutional venture where, in other circumstances, the Geraldines or even the Butlers themselves could have led as the king's foremost old colonial lord. From a crown standpoint, 'conquest' was relievedly set aside as diplomatic manoeuvres proved effective. However, in each case and especially with the latter, this would only be for a time.[100]

---

[96] When writing to St Leger in 1538, Staples sought to remedy the problem of the colony's papal licence within the emerging ecclesiastical framework: *S.P. Hen. VIII*, iii, 305.

[97] *S.P. Hen. VIII*, iii, 370. For its limitations, see Peter Crooks, 'The structure of politics in theory and practice, 1210- 1541' in *CHI*, i, 467-8.

[98] LPL, MS 603, f. 76r; *Cal. Carew*, i, 198-9.

[99] According to Bradshaw this was a 'liberal revolution': Bradshaw, *Const. rev.*, p. 189; Heffernan, *Tudor policy*, pp 42-54, 218; Brady, *Chief gov.*, p. 25; Ciaran Brady, 'Comparable histories?: Tudor reform in Wales and Ireland' in S. G. Ellis and Sarah Barber (eds), *Conquest and union: fashioning a British state, 1485-1725* (London, 1995), pp 75-7; S. G. Ellis, 'Tudor state formation and the shaping of the British Isles' in S. G. Ellis and Sarah Barber (eds), *Conquest and union: fashioning a British state, 1485-1725* (London, 1995), p. 56; Ellis, *Ire. Tudors*, pp 156-7; Edwards, *Ormond lordship*, p. 169; Nicholas Canny, *From reformation to restoration: Ireland, 1534-1660* (Dublin, 1987), pp 41-2. See also Christopher Maginn, '"Surrender and regrant" in the historiography of sixteenth-century Ireland' in *Sixteenth Century Journal*, 38 (2007), pp 955-74.

[100] Brady, *Chief gov.*, pp xv, 291-300; Heffernan, *Tudor policy*, pp 217-19; Nicholas Canny, *The Elizabethan conquest of Ireland: a pattern established, 1565-76* (Hassocks, 1976), p. 33; Nicholas Canny, *Making Ireland British, 1580-1650* (Oxford, 2001), pp 45-8, 178; David Edwards, Pádraig Lenihan, and Clodaigh Tait (eds) *Age of atrocity: violence and political conflict in early modern Ireland* (Dublin, 2007), editorial introduction and David Edwards, 'Escalation of violence in sixteenth-century Ireland', pp 34-78; Edwards, *Ormond lordship*, p. 92; Christopher Maginn, *William Cecil, Ireland, and the Tudor State* (Oxford, 2012), pp 33-6, 39-51; Lennon, *Sixteenth-cen. Ire.*, pp 166-77; Ellis, *Ire. Tudors*, pp 149-60, 352-6.

Conclusion

When John Harington translated the *Orlando Furioso* in 1591, he airbrushed the earls of Desmond from the relevant line in canto ten and replaced them with the Butlers of Ormond, who were then moved by the poet ahead of Kildare as the land's foremost peer: 'and of these bands the Lords and leaders are, the noble Earls of Ormond and Kildare'.[1] Even if one were familiar with Ariosto's original Italian, this may appear as a seemingly innocuous piece of poetic licence. Given the recent Munster wars it was perhaps politic to omit the Desmond Fitzgeralds. Did Harington anticipate a courtly reception and seek to avoid offence by elevating the queen's old colonial cousins? To speculate here is intriguing but ultimately futile. What can be determined is that at a stroke, in this snippet of verse the original context was entirely distorted. Unintentionally, Harington's Elizabethan audience along with subsequent generations were denied a fragmentary glimpse of what originally were late medieval Geraldine Italianate overtures. Kildare-Ormond rivalry in the politics of the 1510s and their respective projections in terms of their relation to political power were also obscured, rooted as they were in conditions specific to Ireland's early Tudor renaissance. In time, with the descent of layers of historiographical complexity, a veil was drawn over these particular circumstances in the historical record. There may be additional meaning in Davies' remark that the 'people of this land', both Irish and English, desired to be governed by 'great persons'. Therefore, considering what has been discussed, especially in chapters three and six, the above extract from Harington's verse is profoundly revealing. In this context, the cultural crisis of the fall of the Geraldines and the emergence of a 'reformed' humanism that overshadowed inveterate traditions merits further study.[2]

---

[1] *Orlando furioso in English heroical verse*, by Iohn Haringto[n] (1591), p. 78. For Harington and Ireland, see Paul E. J. Hammer, '"Base rogues" and "gentlemen of quality": the earl of Essex's Irish knights and royal displeasure in 1599' in Brendan Kane and Valerie McGowan-Doyle (eds), *Elizabeth I and Ireland* (Cambridge, 2014), pp 185, 194. See also, Patricia Palmer, *Severed head and the grafted tongue: literature, translation and violence in early modern Ireland* (Cambridge, 2019), pp 36–65; John Harington, *A short view of the state of Ireland written in 1605* (Oxford, 1879); Jason Scott-Warren, *Sir John Harington and the gook as gift* (Oxford, 2001), pp 20–2.

[2] John Davies, *A discoverie of the true causes why Ireland was never entirely subdued* (1612), p. 217; James Murray, *Enforcing the English reformation in Ireland, clerical resistance and political conflict in the diocese of Dublin* (Cambridge, 2009), pp 5–12, 93. See also Colm Lennon, 'Protestant reformations, 1550–1641' in *CHI*, ii, 197–200, 212–13. Historians differ regarding a scholastic or humanist breach. For a sense of continuity, see Ian Campbell, 'Irish political thought and

CONCLUSION

The paradigm of the State Papers has provided a convincing illusion in recounting the anti-Geraldine narrative of 'conquest' up to and after the 1534 rebellion. The perspective of those seeking to challenge the status quo as they pushed for an entrenched regional intervention reverberates in the flood of state correspondence from 1534. Yet there was continuity with the rhetoric of dissenting voices that preceded even the rise of Kildare. With this in mind, the opening chapters here have considered the cultural politics of the Ormond ascendancy under the White Earl, moving toward a shifting of strategy and rhetoric emphasis with the rise of the Geraldines. The *Expugnatio* as a representation of regional entrenchment and as a core tenet of a punitive policy became a weapon for those outside power. But as a vision for the colony, it was part of a wider struggle. Alongside the consideration of neglected sources, the approach taken in this study has been to give balance to each opposing perspective within an account of the specified period. Also present throughout this book, either directly or indirectly, is that problematic yet enriching archival observation: that embedded in the original state paper volumes and later selectively arranged in the nineteenth-century publications is the 'conquest' perspective. From critical readings of this polemical material and by gathering alternative, albeit fragmentary sources, a different story may be reconstructed. While closure for many issues remains elusive, a main objective here has been to offer a fresh dimension to the mysteries surrounding the fall of the Geraldines. Arising from the Kildare rebellion, the contradictions discussed above, both political and ecclesiastical, culminate in a final complicating twist. As the Geraldine project was destroyed, the Butler or 'conquest' campaign itself, which in principle challenged the Henrician religious Reformation, stumbled and ran aground within a few years of the first deputyship of Sir Anthony St Leger. Butler expectations that St Leger would be a willing supporter of a renewed conquest were quickly shattered. To their dismay, far from pursuing a strategy of military conquest, St Leger embarked upon the most ambitious and innovative conciliatory approach to extend English government in Ireland since the reign of Richard II.

Although the promise of St Leger's initiatives proved a false dawn, it would be a mistake to presume that policy was simply overturned as 'conquest' once reform began to collapse as it did when the mid-Tudor crisis ensured a critical loss of momentum.[3] This was, as historians have perceptively understood,

---

intellectual history, 1550-1730' in *CHI*, ii, 506-28; Ian Campbell, *Renaissance humanism and ethnicity before race: the Irish and the English in the seventeenth century* (Manchester, 2013). For the evolution of a reformed humanism, see Scattergood, 'Humanism in Ireland in the sixteenth century: the evidence of TCD MS 160', pp 69-89, 86-9. For an alternative view, see Bradshaw, Const. rev.; Brendan Bradshaw, 'Transalpine humanism' in J. H. Burns and Mark Goldie (eds), *The Cambridge history of political thought* (Cambridge, 1991), pp 95-131.

[3] Ciaran Brady, *Chief governors: the rise and fall of reform government in Tudor Ireland, 1536-1588*

the era of reform.[4] That it failed should not conceal the subsequent tension between strategies of broad governance – which became reform – and aggressive, punitive strategies of conquest. A range of these approaches recurred time and again in different guises, thus characterising the strained politics of the later sixteenth century. Such tensions, as they materialised, found expression through sharply contrasting policies whose mutual opposition was accentuated by the intensely competitive and divisive atmosphere of the late Tudor Court. But it is important to emphasise that the chronically unsettled conditions within which such later competing policies emerged had its roots far deeper than the vagaries of Elizabethan court politics. Throughout the later Middle Ages, bitter and enduring antagonisms were at times violently overt but always latent among the old colonial elites. Flaring and subsiding with the ebb and flow of a particular lord's power, they were frequently exploited and exacerbated by those in a position of strength but also by those seeking to govern on behalf of the crown. Moreover, regardless of the underlying motives of those in office or of those proximate to power in Ireland, the matter did not receive sustained attention at Court. While these tensions were not necessarily a harbinger of the upheaval to come, their long-standing existence nonetheless presaged that the crown's problems in Ireland were likely to remain neglected and unresolved until the brutal finality of military conquest.

(Cambridge, 1994), pp 45-71; Brendan Bradshaw, *Irish constitutional revolution of the sixteenth century* (Cambridge, 1979), pp 258-67.

[4] Bradshaw, *Const. rev.*, pp 32-57, 164-85, 189-92; S. G. Ellis, *Reform and revival: English government in Ireland 1470-1534* (Woodbridge, 1986), pp 206-13; Brady, *Chief gov.*, pp 11-44. For the policies of the 1540s, see Christopher Maginn, '"Surrender and regrant" in the historiography of sixteenth-century Ireland' in *Sixteenth Century Journal*, 38 (2007), pp 955-74. For conquest, see Nicholas Canny, *Elizabethan conquest of Ireland: a pattern established, 1565-76* (Hassocks, 1976). Broadly, for contention over policy from the Yorkist period to the late sixteenth century, see Christopher Maginn and S. G. Ellis, *Tudor discovery of Ireland* (Dublin, 2015), pp 17-30, 113-56; Ciaran Brady, 'Politics, policy and power, 1550-1603' in *CHI*, ii, pp 23-47; David Heffernan, *Debating Tudor policy in sixteenth-century Ireland: 'reform' treatises and political discourse* (Manchester, 2018).

Bibliography

Manuscripts

Biblioteca Nazionale Centrale di Firenze, Florence

Palatini Machiavelli I.52, (https://teca.bncf.firenze.sbn.it/ImageViewer/servlet/ImageViewer?idr=BNCF0003854502)
MS Banco Rari 23, (https://teca.bncf.firenze.sbn.it/ImageViewer/servlet/ImageViewer?idr=BNCF00004585788)

Bodleian Library, Oxford

MSS Laud Misc. 526, 610
MSS Rawlinson B 484, B 490, B 501, B 514

British Library, London

Additional MSS 4763, 4787, 4791, 4792, 40674
Augustus I.II
Caligula D.VI, E.I
Cotton MSS
Galba B.III, B.VI, B.VII
Harleian MSS 433, 913, 3756
Lansdowne MS 159
Otho C.IX, C.XI
Royal MSS E.IV, 15 E.VI
Royal MS 10, B.IX (from microfilm, NLI, pos. 1451)
Titus B.VIII, B.IX, B.XI (i, ii), B.XII
Vespasian C.IV, D.X, F.XIII
Vitellius B.II, B.XVIII, C.XVII

Benjamin Iveagh Library, Farmleigh, Dublin

Irish Primer (Irish Alphabet Presented by Lord Delvin to Queen Elizabeth)

BIBLIOGRAPHY

John Rylands Library, Manchester

Crawford MS 54 (from microfilm, NLI, pos. 4797)

Lambeth Palace Library, London

MSS 598, 602, 603, 616, 621, 632, 635
MS 600 (from microfilm, NLI, pos. 1696)

National Library of Ireland, Dublin

MSS 2507, 5769, 25006, D 1855, D 1790

The National Archives, Kew

SP 1, State Papers, Foreign and Domestic, Henry VIII
SP 46, State Papers, Domestic, Supplementary
SP 60, State Papers, Ireland, Henry VIII

Trinity College Dublin

MSS 592, 842

Printed Sources

An account of the facsimiles of the national manuscripts of Ireland, ed. J. T. Gilbert (Dublin, 1889)
An account of the most important records of Great Britain, ed. C. P. Cooper (London, 1832)
The act book of the diocese of Armagh 1518–1522, ed. John MacCafferty (Dublin, 2020)
Alumni Oxonienses, 1500–1714, ed. James Parker (2 vols, Oxford, 1891)
Andrea Ammonii carmina omnia, ed. Clemente Pizzi (Florence, 1958)
Anglo-Irish poems of the middle ages, ed. Angela Lucas (Dublin, 1995)
The Annals of John Clyn, ed. Bernadette Williams (Dublin, 2007)
The Annals of Loch Cé: a chronicle of Irish affairs, 1014–1690, ed. W. M. Hennessy (2 vols, London, 1871)
Annála Ríoghachta Éireann: Annals of the kingdom of Ireland by the Four Masters from the earliest period to the year 1616, ed. J. O'Donovan (7 vols, Dublin, 1851)

BIBLIOGRAPHY

Annála Uladh: the Annals of Ulster, ed. B. MacCarthy (1895)

'Appendix to the unpublished Geraldine Documents: the Gherardini of Tuscany', Abraham Fitzgibbon, in *Journal of the Royal Historical and Archaeological Association of Ireland*, iv (1877)

Ariosto, L., *Orlando Furioso: an English prose translation*, ed. Guido Waldman (Oxford, 1974)

Athenae Cantabrigienses 1500–1585, eds H. C. Cooper and Thompson Cooper (London, 1858)

The bardic poems of Tadgh Dall O'Huiginn, ed. Eleanor Knott (London, 1922)

Beatha Colaim Chille Life of Colum Cille: compiled by Manus O'Donnell in 1532, eds Andrew O'Kelleher and Gertrude Schoepperle (Urbana, IL, 1918)

The book of obits and martyrology of the cathedral church of the Holy Trinity, commonly called Christ Church, Dublin, ed. John C. Crosthwaite (Dublin, 1844)

Calendar of Archbishop Alen's register, c. 1172–1534, ed. Charles McNeill (Dublin, 1950)

Calendar of the Carew manuscripts preserved in the archiepiscopal library at Lambeth, 1515–1574, eds W. Bullen and J. S. Brewer (6 vols, London, 1867–73)

Calendar of Close Rolls Henry VI: 1451–1461, ed. C. T. Flower (London, 1947)

Calendar of entries in the Papal registers relating to Great Britain and Ireland, eds J. A. Twemlow, iii–xvii, Michael J. Haren, xviii (23 vols, London, 1897–2008)

Calendar of letters, despatches, and State Papers ... England and Spain, eds G. A. Bergenroth, i–ii, P. de Gayangos, iii–vii, M. A. S. Hume, viii, M. A. S. Hume and R. Tyler, ix and R. Tyler, x–xiii (13 vols, London, 1862–1919)

Calendar of the patent and close rolls of the chancery of Ireland in the reigns of Henry VIII, Edward VI, Mary and Elizabeth, ed. James Morrin (2 vols, Dublin, 1861)

Calendar of Ormond deeds, ed. Edmund Curtis (6 vols, Dublin, 1932–43)

Calendar of State Papers Ireland, Tudor period, 1509–1547, eds Steven G. Ellis and James Murray (Dublin, 2017)

Calendar of State Papers and manuscripts in the archives and collections of Milan, 1385–1618, ed. A. B. Hinds (16 vols, London, 1912)

Calendar of State Papers relating to Ireland of the reigns of Henry VIII, Edward VI, Mary and Elizabeth, ed. Hans Hamilton (11 vols, London, 1860)

Calendar of State Papers Venice, ed. Rawdon Brown (11 vols, London, 1864)

Campion, Edmund, *A historie of Ireland* (Dublin, 1809)

Caoursin, Guillaume, *The siege of Rhodes* (London, 1482)

Castilione, Baldassarre, *The courtyer* (London, 1561)

Chartularies of St Mary's Abbey, Dublin with the register of its house at Dunbrody and annals of Ireland, ed. J. T. Gilbert (2 vols, London, 1884)

Chaucer, Geoffrey, *Troylus and Cresyde* (1483)

The chronicle of the Grey Friars of London, ed. C. G. Nichols (London, 1852)

Chronicles of England, ed. William Caxton (1480)

BIBLIOGRAPHY

Collectanea de rebus Hibernicis, ed. Walter Harris (20 vols, Dublin, 1786)
Collection des voyages des souverains des Pays-Bas, ed. Charles Piot Gachard (4 vols, Brussels, 1881)
The complete English poems of John Skelton, ed. John Scattergood (Liverpool, 2015)
Crown surveys of lands, 1540-1, with the Kildare rental begun in 1518, ed. Gearoid Mac Niocaill (Dublin, 1992)
Davies, John, *A discoverie of the true causes why Ireland was never entirely subdued* (1612)
Dignitas Decani St Patrick's Cathedral Dublin, ed. Newport White (Dublin, 1957)
Dizionaris biografico delgi Italiani, ed. Gilbert Tournoy (Rome, 1989)
Extents of Irish monastic possessions, 1540-1541, ed. Newport White (Dublin, 1943).
Gerald of Wales, *Expugnatio Hibernica, the conquest of Ireland*, eds A. B. Scott and F. X. Martin (Dublin, 1978)
The great parchment book of Waterford: liber antiquissimus civitatis Waterfordiae, ed. Niall J. Byrne (Dublin, 2007)
Harington, John, *Orlando furioso in English heroical verse, by Iohn Haringto[n]* (1591)
Harington, John, *A short view of the state of Ireland written in 1605* (Oxford, 1879)
Henry Howard, earl of Surrey: poems, ed. Emrys Jones (Oxford, 1964)
Hibernica or some antient pieces relating to Ireland, ed. Walter Harris (Dublin, 1750)
Historical collections of a citizen of London in the fifteenth century, ed. James Gairdner (London, 1876)
Historia Regis Henrici Septimi a Bernardo Andrea, ed. James Gairdner (London, 1858)
History of the Church of Ireland, ed. Richard Mant (London, 1839)
Holinshed, Raphael, *Chronicles of England, Scotlande and Irelande* (6 vols, London, 1807-8)
Ireland under Elizabeth and James the First described by Edmund Spenser, by Sir John Davies and by Fynes Moryson, ed. Henry Morley (London, 1890)
Irish fiants of the Tudor sovereigns, ed. Edmund Burke (Dublin, 1994)
Issues of the exchequer from Henry III to Henry VI, ed. Frederick Devon (London, 1837)
Landino, Cristoforo, *Opere del divino poeta Danthe consuoi cometi* (Milan, 1520)
Lazzari, Alfonso, *Ugolino e Michele Verino: studii biografici e critici, contributo alla storia dell'umanesimo in Firenze* (Florence, 1897)
Le Fèvre, Raoul, *Recuyell of the Historyes of Troye* (Bruges, 1473)
Letters and papers, foreign and domestic, Henry VIII, eds J. S. Brewer, R. H. Brodie and James Gairdner (21 vols, London, 1862-1932)
Letters and papers illustrative of the reigns of Richard III and Henry VII, ed. James Gairdner (3 vols, London, 1863)
The libelle of Englyshe polycye, ed. George Warner (Oxford, 1926)
The Life of Colum Cille by Manus O'Donnell, ed. Brian Lacey (Dublin, 1998)

BIBLIOGRAPHY

Life of Saint Columba, founder of Hy. written by Adamnan, ninth abbot of that monastery, ed. William Reeves (Edinburgh, 1874)

Love's bitter-sweet: translations from the Irish poets of the sixteenth and seventeenth centuries, ed. Robin Flower (Dublin, 1925)

Mahaffy, J. P., 'Two early tours in Ireland', in *Hermathena*, 40 (1914), pp 10-11

Materials illustrative of the reign of Henry VII, ed. William Campbell (2 vols, London, 1877)

Memorials of Henry VII, ed. James Gairdner (London, 1858)

Original letters illustrative of English history, ed. Henry Ellis (11 vols, London, 1824-6)

Orlando Furioso: a new verse translation, ed. David R. Slavitt (London, 2009)

Patentee offices in Ireland 1173-1826, ed. J. L. J. Hughes (Dublin, 1960)

Petrarca, Francesco, *Opera quae extant omnia etc.* (Basil, 1581)

Poems on the Butlers of Ormond, Cahir and Dunboyne AD 1400-1650, ed. James Carney (Dublin, 1945)

Poems on marcher lords: from a sixteenth-century Tipperary manuscript, eds Anne O'Sullivan and Pádraig Ó Riain (London, 1987)

Political poems and songs relating to English history, ed. Thomas Wright (2 vols, London, 1861)

Popular songs of Ireland, ed. Crofton Croker (Dublin, 1866)

Proceedings and ordinances of the Privy Council of England, ed. Nicolas Harris (7 vols, London, 1834-7)

Records of the society of Lincoln's Inn, ed. J. D. Walker (2 vols, London, 1897)

The Red Book of the Earls of Kildare, ed. Gearoid Mac Niocaill (Dublin, 1964)

The Red Book of Ormond, ed. N. B. White (Dublin, 1932)

'Reform' treatises on Tudor Ireland, ed. David Heffernan (Dublin, 2016)

The register of John Swayne, archbishop of Armagh and primate of Ireland, 1418-1439, with some entries of earlier and later archbishops, ed. D. A. Chart (Belfast, 1935)

The register of St Saviour's Chantry of Waterford, eds Niall Byrne, Michael Byrne, K. W. Nicholls (Dublin, 2013)

Register of the University of Oxford, ed. C. W. Boase (2 vols, London, 1885)

Registrum de Kilmainham: register of chapter acts of the Hospital of Saint John of Jerusalem in Ireland, 1326-1339, ed. Charles McNeill (Dublin, 1932)

Registrum Iohannis Mey. The Register of John Mey, Archbishop of Armagh, 1443-1456, ed. W. G. H. Quigley (Belfast, 1972)

Registrum Octaviani alias Liber Niger, ed. Mario A. Sughi (2 vols, Dublin, 1999)

Reports on cases heard in the house of lords, eds Charles Clark and William Finnelly (12 vols, London, 1831-46)

'Robert Cowley's "A discourse of the cause of the evil state of Ireland and of the remedies thereof", c. 1526', David Heffernan, in *Analecta Hibernica*, 48 (2017), pp 1-30

BIBLIOGRAPHY

A roll of the proceedings of the king's council in Ireland, ed. James Graves (London, 1877)

Select cases in the council of Henry VII, ed. Bernard Quaritch (London, 1958)

Skelton, John, *Pithy pleasaunt and profitable works of maister Skelton* (London, 1568)

Smith, Aquilla, 'On the Irish coins of Edward IV' in *Transactions of the Royal Irish Academy*, 19 (1841), pp 31-49

The social state of the southern and eastern counties of Ireland in the sixteenth-century, eds H. J. Hore and J. Graves (Dublin, 1870)

Songes and sonettes, written by the right honourable Lorde Henry Haward late Earle of Surrey, and others [published by Richard Tottel] (London, 1574)

State Papers, Henry VIII (11 vols, London, 1830-52)

Statute rolls of the Irish parliament Richard III – Henry VIII, ed. Philomena Connolly (Dublin, 2002)

Statute rolls of the parliament of Ireland, first to the twelfth years of the reign of king Edward IV, ed. H. F. Berry (Dublin, 1914)

Statute rolls of the parliament of Ireland, twelfth and thirteenth to the twenty-first and twenty-second years of the reign of king Edward IV, ed. James Morrisey (Dublin, 1939)

Three prose versions of the Secreta Secretorum, ed. Robert Steele (London, 1898)

A true copy of the ordinaunce...of kynge Henry the vi to be observed in the...eschequier (London, 1533)

Vergil, Polydore, *The Anglica historia of Polydore Vergil, A.D. 1485-1537* (London, 1950)

Verino, Ugolino di, *De illustration urbis Florentiae* (Paris, 1790)

Verse in English from Tudor and Stuart Ireland, ed. Andrew Carpenter (Cork, 2003)

Ware, James, *The antiquities and history of Ireland* (5 vols, Dublin, 1705)

The whole works of Sir James Ware concerning Ireland, ed. Walter Harris (2 vols, Dublin, 1764)

Secondary Works

Andrews, J. H., 'Colonial cartography in a European setting: the case of Tudor Ireland' in David Woodward (ed.), *The history of cartography: cartography in the European Renaissance* (6 vols, Chicago, 1987-2015), iii, pp 1670-83

Anglo, Sydney, *Spectacle, pageantry, and early Tudor policy* (Oxford, 1969)

Bagwell, Richard, *Ireland under the Tudors* (3 vols, London, 1885)

Ball, F. E., *The judges in Ireland, 1221-1921* (2 vols, London, 1926)

Batschman, Osckar and Pascal Griener, *Hans Holbein* (London, 1997)

Berdan, John, *Early Tudor poetry* (New York, 1920)

Bennett, Michael, 'The Libelle of English policy: the matter of Ireland' in Linda

Clark (ed.), *The fifteenth century XV: writing, records and rhetoric* (Woodbridge, 2017), pp 1-20

Bennett, Michael, 'Late medieval Ireland in a wider world' in Brendan Smith (ed.), *The Cambridge history of Ireland* (3 vols, Cambridge, 2018), i, pp 329-52

Bernard, G. W., *War, taxation and rebellion in early Tudor England: Henry VIII, Wolsey and the amicable grant of 1525* (Brighton, 1986)

Bieler, Ludwig, *Ireland, harbinger of the middle ages* (Oxford, 1963)

Blamires, Alcuin, *Chaucer, ethics and gender* (Oxford, 2006)

Boas, George, *Primitivism and related ideas in the middle ages* (Baltimore, MD, 1948)

Booker, Sparky, *Cultural exchange and identity in late medieval Ireland: the English and Irish of the four obedient shires* (Cambridge, 2018)

Booker, Sparky, 'The Geraldines and the Irish: intermarriage, ecclesiastical patronage and status' in Peter Crooks and Seán Duffy (eds), *The Geraldines and medieval Ireland: the making of a myth* (Dublin, 2016), pp 292-324

Booker, Sparky, 'The Knight's Tale' in Sparky Booker and Cherie N. Peters (eds), *Tales of medieval Dublin* (Dublin, 2014), pp 135-48

Bowen, Barbara C., 'Ciceronian wit and Renaissance rhetoric' in *Rhetorica* 16 (1998), pp 409-29

Bowers, Roger, 'The cultivation and orbit of Thomas Wolsey' in S. J. Gunn and P. G. Lindley (eds), *Cardinal Wolsey, church, state and art* (New York, 1991), pp 178-218

Bradley, John, Cóilín Ó Drisceoil and Michael Potterton (eds), *William Marshal and Ireland* (Dublin, 2017)

Bradshaw, Brendan, *'And so began the Irish nation': Nationality, national consciousness and nationalism in pre-modern Ireland* (London, 2015)

Bradshaw, Brendan, 'Cromwellian Reform and the origins of the Kildare rebellion, 1533-4' in *Transactions of the Royal Historical Society*, 27 (1977), pp 69-93

Bradshaw, Brendan, *Dissolution of the religious orders in Ireland under Henry VIII* (Dublin, 1974)

Bradshaw, Brendan, 'George Browne, first reformation archbishop of Dublin, 1536-1554' in *Journal of Ecclesiastical History*, 21 (1970), pp 301-26

Bradshaw, Brendan, *The Irish constitutional revolution of the sixteenth century* (Cambridge, 1979)

Bradshaw, Brendan, 'Manus "the magnificent": O'Donnell as renaissance prince' in Art Cosgrove and Donal McCartney (eds), *Studies in Irish History presented to R. Dudley Edwards* (Dublin, 1979), pp 15-37

Bradshaw, Brendan, 'The English Reformation and identity formation in Ireland and Wales' in Brendan Bradshaw and Peter Roberts (eds), *British consciousness and identity: the making of Britain, 1533-1707* (Cambridge, 1998), pp 43-111

Bradshaw, Brendan, 'Sword and strategy in the reformation in Ireland' in *Historical Journal*, 21 (1978), pp 475-502

BIBLIOGRAPHY

Bradshaw, Brendan, 'Transalpine humanism' in J. H. Burns and Mark Goldie (eds), *The Cambridge history of political thought* (Cambridge, 1991), pp 95-131

Bradshaw, Brendan, Andrew Hadfield and Willy Maley (eds), *Representing Ireland: literature and the origins of conflict, 1534-1660* (Cambridge, 1993)

Brady, Ciaran, *The chief governors: the rise and fall of reform government in Tudor Ireland, 1536-1588* (Cambridge, 1994)

Brady, Ciaran, 'Comparable histories?: Tudor reform in Wales and Ireland' in Steven G. Ellis and Sarah Barber (eds), *Conquest and union: fashioning a British state, 1485-1725* (London, 1995), pp 64-86

Brady, Ciaran, '"Constructive and instrumental": The dilemma of Ireland's first "new historians"' in Ciaran Brady (ed.), *Interpreting Irish history: the debate on historical revisionism* (Dublin, 1994), pp 3-31

Brady, Ciaran, 'From policy to power: the evolution of Tudor reform strategies in sixteenth-century Ireland' in Brian MacCuarta (ed.), *Reshaping Ireland, 1550-1700: colonisation and its consequences, essays presented to Nicholas Canny* (Dublin, 2011), pp 21-42

Brady, Ciaran, 'Making good: new perspectives on the English in early modern Ireland' in Ciaran Brady and Jane Ohlmeyer (eds), *British interventions in early modern Ireland* (Cambridge, 2005), pp 1-27

Brady, Ciaran, 'The myth of "Silken Thomas"' in Peter Crooks and Seán Duffy (eds), *The Geraldines and medieval Ireland: the making of a myth* (Dublin, 2016), pp 379-98

Brady, Ciaran, 'Politics, policy and power, 1550-1603' in Jane Ohlmeyer (ed.), *The Cambridge history of Ireland* (3 vols, Cambridge, 2018), ii, pp 23-47

Brady, Ciaran, *Shane O'Neill* (Dundalk, 1996)

Brady, Ciaran, 'Spenser, plantation and government policy' in R. A. McCabe (ed.), *The Oxford handbook of Edmund Spenser* (Oxford, 2010), pp 86-105

Brady, Ciaran, *A viceroy's vindication?: Sir Henry Sidney's memoir of service in Ireland 1556-1578* (Cork, 2002)

Brady, Ciaran and Raymond Gillespie (eds), *Natives and newcomers: essays on the making of Irish colonial society, 1534-1641* (Dublin, 1986)

Brand, C. P., *Ludovico Ariosto: a preface to the Orlando Furioso* (Edinburgh, 1974)

Brigden, Susan, *London and the reformation* (Oxford, 1989)

Brigden, Susan, 'Henry Howard, earl of Surrey, and the "Conjured League"' in *Historical Journal*, 37 (1994), pp 507-37

Brigden, Susan, *New worlds, lost worlds: the rule of the Tudors, 1485-1603* (London, 2001)

Brigden, Susan, *Thomas Wyatt: the heart's forest* (London, 2014)

Brigden, Susan, 'Henry VIII and the crusade against England' in Thomas Betteridge and Suzannah Lipscomb (eds), *Henry VIII and the court: art, politics and patronage* (Abingdon, 2016)

BIBLIOGRAPHY

Bryan, Donough, *The great earl of Kildare* (Dublin, 1933)

Budra, Paul, *A mirror for magistrates and the de Casibus tradition* (London, 2000)

Byrne, Aisling, 'The earls of Kildare and their books at the end of the middle ages' in *The Library: Transactions of the Bibliographical Society*, 14 (2013), pp 129-53

Byrne, Aisling, 'Family, locality and nationality: vernacular adaptations of the Expugnatio Hibernica in late medieval Ireland' in *Medium Ævum*, 82 (2013), pp 101-18

Byrne, Aisling, 'The Geraldines and the culture of the wider world' in Peter Crooks and Seán Duffy (eds), *The Geraldines and medieval Ireland: the making of a myth* (Dublin, 2016), pp 278-91

Campbell, Gordon L., *Strange creatures: anthropology in antiquity* (London, 2006)

Campbell, Ian, 'Irish political thought and intellectual history, 1550-1730' in Jane Ohlmeyer (ed.), *The Cambridge history of Ireland* (3 vols, Cambridge, 2018), ii, 506-28

Campbell, Ian, *Renaissance humanism and ethnicity before race: the Irish and the English in the seventeenth century* (Manchester, 2013)

Canny, Nicholas, *The Elizabethan conquest of Ireland: a pattern established, 1565-76* (Hassocks, 1976)

Canny, Nicholas, *From reformation to restoration: Ireland, 1534-1660* (Dublin, 1987)

Canny, Nicholas, *Making Ireland British, 1580-1650* (Oxford, 2001)

Carey, Vincent, 'Neither good English nor good Irish: Bi-lingualism and identity formation in sixteenth-century Ireland' in Hiram Morgan (ed.) *Political ideology in Ireland 1541-1641* (Dublin, 1999), pp 45-61

Carey, Vincent, 'John Derricke's image of Ireland, Sir Henry Sidney, and the massacre at Mullaghmast, 1578' in *IHS*, 31 (1998-9), pp 305-27

Carey, Vincent, *Surviving the Tudors: the 'wizard' earl of Kildare and English rule in Ireland, 1537-1586* (Dublin, 2002)

Carlson, David R., 'Three Tudor epigrams' in *Humanistica Lovaniensia: Journal of Neo-Latin Studies*, 45 (1996), pp 189-200

Cartwright, Kent, *A companion to Tudor literature* (Oxford, 2010)

Cary, George, *The medieval Alexander* (Cambridge, 1956)

Clarke, H. B., 'Angliores ipsis Anglis: the place of medieval Dubliners in English history' in H. B. Clarke, Jacinta Prunty and Mark Hennessy (eds), *Surveying Ireland's past: multidisciplinary essays in honour of Anngret Simms* (Dublin, 2004), pp 41-72

Cockerham, Paul, '"To mak a tombe for the earl of Ormon and to set it up in Iarland": renaissance ideas in Irish funeral monuments' in Thomas Herron and Michael Potterton (eds), *Ireland in the Renaissance* (Dublin, 2007), pp 195-230

Connolly, S. J., *Contested island: Ireland 1460-1630* (Oxford, 2007)

Conway, Agnes, *Henry VII's relations with Scotland and Ireland* (Cambridge, 1932)

BIBLIOGRAPHY

Coolohan, Marie-Louise, *Women, writing, and language in early modern Ireland* (Oxford, 2010)

Covington, Sarah, Valerie McGowan-Doyle and Vincent Carey (eds), *Early modern Ireland: new sources, methods and perspectives* (London, 2018)

Cosgrove, Art, 'The Gaelic resurgence and the Geraldine supremacy: c. 1400-1534' in T. W. Moody and F. X. Martin (eds), *The course of Irish history* (Cork, 1967), pp 158-73

Cosgrove, Art, 'The execution of the earl of Desmond, 1468' in *Journal of the Kerry Archaeological and Historical Society*, 8 (1975), pp 11-27

Cosgrove, Art, 'Ireland beyond the Pale 1399-1460' in Art Cosgrove (ed.), *A New History of Ireland*, ii (Oxford, 1987), pp 569-90

Crawford, H. S., 'Mural painting in Holycross abbey' in *JRSA*, 5 (1915), pp 149-50

Crawford, John and Raymond Gillespie (eds), *St Patrick's Cathedral, Dublin: a history* (Dublin, 2009)

Crooks, Peter, 'The ascent and descent of Desmond under Lancaster and York' in Peter Crooks and Seán Duffy (eds), *The Geraldines and medieval Ireland: the making of a myth* (Dublin, 2016) pp 223-63

Crooks, Peter, 'Factions, feuds and noble power in the lordship of Ireland, c. 1356-1496' in *IHS*, 35 (2006-7), pp 425-54

Crooks, Peter, 'The structure of politics in theory and practice: colonial Ireland, 1210-1541', in Brendan Smith (ed.), *The Cambridge history of Ireland*, i (Cambridge, 2018), pp 441-68

Crooks, Peter and Ciarán Wallace, 'The records of a country are its noblest inheritance (the Beyond 2022: Ireland's Virtual Record Treasury Research Project)' in *HI*, 28, no. 3 (2020), pp 48-51

Cunningham, Sean, *Henry VII* (London, 2007)

Curtis, Edmund, *A history of Ireland* (New York, 1939)

Curtis, Edmund, *A history of medieval Ireland* (Dublin, 1938)

Curtis, Edmund, 'Richard, duke of York, as viceroy of Ireland, 1447-1460; with unpublished materials for his relations with native chiefs' in *Journal of the Royal Society of Antiquaries of Ireland*, 2 (1932), pp 158-86

Curtis, Edmund, 'Some further medieval seals out of the Ormond archives, including that of Donal Reagh MacMurrough-Kavanagh, king of Leinster' in *Journal of the Royal Society of Antiquaries of Ireland*, 7 (1937), pp 72-6

Darcy, Eamon, *The Irish rebellion of 1641 and the wars of the three kingdoms* (Woodbridge, 2013)

Dillon, Miles, 'Laud Misc. 610 (cont.)' in *Celtica*, 6 (1963), pp 135-55

Doran, Linda, 'Medieval settlement hierarchy in Carlow and the "Carlow corridor" 1200-1550' in Thomas McGrath (ed.), *Carlow: history and society, interdisciplinary essays on the history of an Irish county* (Dublin, 1995), pp 173-212

Due, Bodil, 'Alexander's inspiration and ideas' in Jesper Carlsen, Bodil Due, Otto Steen Due and Birte Poulsen (eds), *Alexander the Great: reality and myth* (Rome, 1993), pp 53–60

Duffy, Damien, *Aristocratic women in Ireland, 1450–1660: the Ormond family, power and politics* (Woodbridge, 2021)

Duffy, Seán, *Ireland in the middle ages* (Dublin, 1997)

Duffy, Seán, 'Gerald of Windsor and the origins of the Geraldines' in Peter Crooks and Seán Duffy (eds), *The Geraldines and medieval Ireland: the making of a myth* (Dublin, 2016), pp 21–52

Dyck, Andrew, *A commentary on Cicero, de Legibus* (Ann Arbor, MI, 2004)

Eames, Elizabeth S. and Thomas Fanning, *Irish medieval tiles: decorated medieval paving tiles in Ireland with an inventory of sites and designs and a visual index* (Dublin, 1988)

Edwards, David, 'The Butler revolt of 1569' in *IHS*, 28:111 (1993), pp 228–55

Edwards, David, 'The escalation of violence in sixteenth-century Ireland' in David Edwards, Pádraig Lenihan and Clodagh Tait (eds), *Age of atrocity: violence and political conflict in early modern Ireland* (Dublin, 2007), pp 34–78

Edwards, David, *The Ormond lordship in County Kilkenny, 1515–1642: the rise and fall of Butler feudal power* (Dublin, 2003)

Edwards, David, 'Spenser's *View* and martial law in Ireland' in Hiram Morgan (ed.), *Political ideology in Ireland, 1541–1641* (Dublin, 1999), pp 127–57

Edwards, David, Pádraig Lenihan, and Clodaigh Tait (eds), *Age of atrocity: violence and political conflict in early modern Ireland* (Dublin, 2007)

Edwards, R. D., *Church and state in Tudor Ireland* (Dublin, 1935)

Edwards, R. D. and T. W. Moody, 'The history of Poynings' Law: Part I, 1494–1615' in *IHS*, 2 (1940–1), pp 415–24

Egan, Simon, 'A playground of the Scots? Gaelic Ireland and the Stewart monarchy in the late fourteenth and fifteenth centuries' in Linda Clark (ed.), *The fifteenth century XVI* (Woodbridge, 2018), pp 105–21

Egan, Simon, 'An Irish context to a Scottish disaster: James IV, the O'Donnells of Tyrconnell and the road to Flodden' in Katharine Simms and Joseph Mannion (eds), *Politics, kinship and culture in Gaelic Ireland, c. 1100-c. 1690: essays for the Irish chiefs' and clans' prize in history* (2 vols, Dublin, 2018), ii, 10–16

Egan, Simon, 'Lordship and dynasty in the late medieval Irish sea world: the Hiberno-Scottish Nexus' in *Cambrian Medieval Celtic Studies*, 78 (2019), pp 1–44

Elias, Norbert, *The court society* (New York, 1983)

Ellis, Steven G., 'A border baron and the Tudor state: the rise and fall of Lord Dacre of the North' in *Historical Journal*, 35 (1992), pp 253–77

Ellis, S. G., 'A crisis of lordship: Robert Ogle, fifth Lord Ogle, and the rule of early Tudor Northumberland' in *Northern History*, 55 (2018), pp 61–75

BIBLIOGRAPHY

Ellis, S. G., 'Civilizing the natives: state formation and the Tudor monarchy, c. 1400-1603' in S. G. Ellis and Lud'a Klusáková (eds), *Imagining frontiers: contesting identities* (Pisa, 2007), pp 77-92

Ellis, S. G., 'Defending the English Pale: The viceroyalty of Richard Nugent, third baron of Delvin, 1527-8' in *IHS*, 43 (2019), pp 1-11

Ellis, S. G., 'An English gentleman and his community: Sir William Darcy of Platten' in Vincent Carey and Ute Lotz-Heumann (eds), *Taking sides? Colonial and confessional mentalities in early modern Ireland: essays in honour of Karl Bottigheimer* (Dublin, 2003), pp 19-41

Ellis, S. G., 'The English Pale: a 'failed entity'?' in *HI*, 19, no. 2 (2011), pp 14-17

Ellis, S. G., 'The great earl of Kildare (1456-1513) and the creation of the English Pale' in Peter Crooks and Seán Duffy (eds), *The Geraldines and medieval Ireland: the making of a myth* (Dublin, 2016), pp 325-41

Ellis, S. G., 'Henry VII and Ireland, 1491-1496' in James Lydon (ed.), *England and Ireland in the later middle ages: essays in honour of Jocelyn Otway-Ruthven* (Dublin, 1981), pp 237-54

Ellis, S. G., 'Henry VIII, rebellion and the rule of law' in *Historical Journal*, 24 (1981), pp 513-31

Ellis, S. G., *Ireland in the age of the Tudors 1477-1603* (London, 1998)

Ellis, S. G., *Ireland's English Pale, 1470-1550: The making of a Tudor region* (Woodbridge, 2021)

Ellis, S. G., 'The Kildare rebellion and the early Henrician reformation' in *Historical Journal*, 19 (1976), pp 807-30

Ellis, S. G., 'Nationalist historiography and the English and Gaelic worlds in the late middle ages' in *IHS*, 25 (1986-7), pp 1-18

Ellis, S. G., *Reform and revival: English government in Ireland 1470-1534* (Woodbridge, 1986)

Ellis, S. G., 'Siegecraft on the Tudor frontier: the siege of Dublin, 1534 and the crisis of the Kildare rebellion' in *Historical Research*, 92 (2019), pp 705-19

Ellis, S. G., 'Taxation and defence in late medieval Ireland: the survival of scutage' in *Journal of the Royal Society of Antiquaries of Ireland*, 107 (1977), pp 5-28

Ellis, S. G., 'The Tudors and the origins of the modern Irish state: a standing army' in Thomas Bartlett and Keith Jeffery (eds), *A military history of Ireland* (Cambridge, 1996), pp 116-35

Ellis, S. G., 'Thomas Cromwell and Ireland, 1532-1540' in *Historical Journal*, 23 (1980), pp 497-519

Ellis, S. G., *Tudor frontiers and noble power: the making of the British state* (Oxford, 1995)

Ellis, S. G., *Tudor Ireland: crown, community and the conflict of cultures, 1470-1603* (London, 1985)

BIBLIOGRAPHY

Ellis, S. G., 'Tudor state formation and the shaping of the British Isles' in S. G. Ellis and Sarah Barber (eds), *Conquest and union: fashioning a British state, 1485–1725* (London, 1995), pp 40–63

Ellis, S. G. and Christopher Maginn, *The making of the British Isles: The state of Britain and Ireland, 1450–1660* (London, 2007)

Elton, G. R., *The Tudor revolution in government* (London, 1953)

Empey, Adrian, 'The evolution of the demesne in the lordship of Leinster' in John Bradley, Cóilín Ó Drisceoil and Michael Potterton (eds), *William Marshal and Ireland* (Dublin, 2017), pp 41–77

Empey, C. A., 'The Butler Lordship' in *Journal of the Butler Society*, 13 (1970–71), pp 174–85

Empey, C. A., 'From rags to riches: Piers Butler earl of Ormond, 1515-39' in *Butler Society Journal*, 2 (1984), pp 299–312

Empey, C. A., 'The liberties and counties of Carlow in the high middle ages' in Thomas McGrath (ed.), *Carlow: history and society, interdisciplinary essays on the history of an Irish county* (Dublin, 1995), pp 153–71

Empey, C. A. and Katharine Simms, 'The ordinances of the White Earl and the problem of coign in the later Middle Ages', in *Proceedings of the Royal Irish Academy*, 75C (1975), pp 161–87

Esposito, Mario, 'The English conquest of Ireland' in *Notes and Queries*, 75 (1917), pp 495–6

Falkiner, C. L., 'The Hospital of St John of Jerusalem in Ireland' in *PRIA*, 26 (1906–7), pp 275–17

Fenlon, Jane, 'Irish art and architecture, 1550–1730' in Jane Ohlmeyer (ed.), *The Cambridge history of Ireland*, ii (Cambridge, 2018), pp 346–84

Ferster, Judith, *Fictions of advice: the literature and politics of counsel in late medieval England* (Philadelphia, 1996)

Ferguson, Arthur B., *Clio unbound: perception of the social and cultural past in renaissance England* (Durham, NC, 1979)

Ferguson, Arthur B., *The articulate citizen and the English Renaissance* (Durham, NC, 1965)

Fitzgerald, Brian, *The Geraldines: an experiment in Irish government, 1165–1601* (London, 1951)

Fitzgerald, Charles W., *The earls of Kildare and their ancestors from 1057 to 1773* (Dublin, 1858)

Fitzgibbon, Abraham, 'Appendix to the unpublished Geraldine documents: the Gherardini of Tuscany' in *JRHA*, 4 (1877), pp 247–9

Fitzsimons, Fiona, 'Cardinal Wolsey, the native affinities and the failure of reform in Henrician Ireland' in David Edwards (ed.), *Regions and rulers in Ireland 1100–1650* (Dublin, 2004), pp 78–121

Fitzsimons, Fiona, 'The lordship of O'Connor Faly, 1520-70' in William Nolan and Timothy P. O'Neill (eds), *Offaly: history and society, interdisciplinary essays on the history of an Irish county* (Dublin, 1998), pp 207-42

Flavin, Susan, *Consumption and culture in sixteenth-century Ireland: saffron, stockings and silk* (Woodbridge, 2014)

Fletcher, A. J., *Drama and the performing arts in pre-Cromwellian Ireland: a repertory of sources and documents from the earliest times until c. 1642* (Cambridge, 2001)

Flower, Robin, *The Irish tradition* (Oxford, 1947)

Ford, Alan, 'The Irish historical renaissance and the shaping of Protestant history' in Alan Ford and John McCafferty (eds), *The origins of sectarianism in early modern Ireland* (Cambridge, 2005), pp 127-57

Ford, Alan, '"That noble dream", objectivity and the writing of Irish Church history' in Mark Empey, Alan Ford and Miriam Moffitt (eds), *The Church of Ireland and its past* (Dublin, 2017), pp 1-18

Fox, Adam, *Oral and literate culture in England, 1500-1700* (Oxford, 2000)

Fox, Alistair, *Politics and literature in the reigns of Henry VII and Henry VIII* (Oxford, 1989)

Fox, Alistair and John Guy (eds), *Reassessing the Henrician age: humanism, politics and reform, 1500-1550* (Oxford, 1986)

Frame, Robin, *Colonial Ireland, 1169-1369* (Dublin, 1981)

Frame, Robin, 'Contexts, divisions and unities: perspectives from the later middle ages' in Brendan Smith (ed.), *The Cambridge history of Ireland*, i (Cambridge, 2018), pp 523-550

Froude, J. A., *The English in Ireland* (3 vols, London, 1884)

Gillespie, Raymond, 'The Fitzgeralds and the making of the manor of Maynooth' in Patrick Cosgrove, Terence Dooley and Karol Mullaney-Dignam (eds), *Aspects of aristocratic life: essays on the Fitzgeralds and Carton House* (Dublin, 2014), pp 34-46

Gillespie, Raymond, *Reading Ireland: print, reading and social change in early modern Ireland* (Manchester, 2005)

Gillespie, Raymond, 'Books, politics and society in renaissance Dublin', in Kathleen Miller and Crawford Gribben (eds), *Dublin: Renaissance city of literature* (Manchester, 2017), pp 38-54

Gillespie, Raymond, 'Saints and manuscripts in sixteenth-century Breifne' in *Breifne*, 11 (2008), pp 533-56

Gillespie, Raymond, Salvador Ryan and Brendan Scott (eds), *Making the Book of Fenagh: context and text* (Cavan, 2016)

Gillingham, John, *The English in the twelfth century: imperialism, national identity and political values* (Woodbridge, 2000)

Good, Jonathan, *The cult of St George in medieval England* (Woodbridge, 2009)

BIBLIOGRAPHY

Griffin, Carrie and Emer Purcell (eds), *Text, transmission and transformation in the European middle ages, 1000–1500* (Turnhout, 2018)

Griffiths, R. A., *The Reign of Henry VI* (London, 1981)

Griffith, M. C., 'The Talbot-Ormond struggle for control of the Anglo-Irish government, 1414-47' in *IHS*, 2 (1940-1), pp 376-97

Gunn, S. J. and P. G. Lindley (eds), *Cardinal Wolsey, church, state and art* (New York, 1991)

Guy, John, *Henry VIII: The quest for fame* (London, 2018)

Guy, John, *The reign of Elizabeth I: court and culture in the last decade* (Cambridge, 1995)

Guy, John, 'The rhetoric of counsel in early modern England' in Dale Hook (ed.), *Tudor political culture* (Cambridge, 1995) pp 242-310

Guy, John, *The Tudor monarchy* (London, 1997)

Gwyn, Peter, *The king's cardinal: the rise and fall of Thomas Wolsey* (London, 1990)

Hammer, Paul E. J., '"Base rogues" and "gentlemen of quality": the earl of Essex's Irish knights and royal displeasure in 1599' in Brendan Kane and Valerie McGowan-Doyle (eds), *Elizabeth I and Ireland* (Cambridge, 2014), pp 184-208

Haren, Michael, 'Social structures of the Irish church: a new source in papal penitentiary dispensations for illegitimacy' in Ludwig Schmugge (ed.), *Illegitimität im Spätmittelalter* (Munich, 1994), pp 207-26

Harris, Barbara Jean, *English aristocratic women, 1450–1550: marriage and family, property and careers* (Oxford, 2002)

Hayden, Alan, 'Maynooth castle, Co. Kildare: excavation of the donjon' (unpublished archaeological report lodged with the National Monuments Service, Ireland, 2013)

Hayes-McCoy, G. A., *Irish battles: a military history of Ireland* (Belfast, 1989)

Hayward, Maria, *Rich apparel: clothing and the law Henry VIII's England* (Abingdon, 2009)

Hayward, Maria, 'Rich pickings: Henry VIII's use of confiscation and its significance for the development of the royal collection' in Suzannah Lipscomb and Thomas Betteridge (eds), *Henry VIII and the court: art, politics and performance* (Abingdon, 2013), pp 29-46

Haywood, Eric, 'Humanism's priorities and empire's prerogatives: Polydore Vergil's *Description of Ireland*' in *Proceedings of the Royal Irish Academy*, 109C (2009), pp 195-236

Head, D. M., *The ebbs and flows of fortune: the life of Thomas Howard, third duke of Norfolk* (London, 1995)

Healy, William, *The history and antiquities of County Kilkenny* (Kilkenny, 1893)

Healy, John, *Maynooth College 1795–1895: its centenary history* (Dublin, 1895)

Heckett, E. W., 'Tomb effigies and archaic dress in sixteenth-century Ireland' in Catherine Richardson (ed.), *Clothing culture, 1350–1650* (Aldershot, 2004), pp 63–75

Heffernan, David, 'Complaint and reform in late Elizabethan Dublin, 1579-94', in Kathleen Miller and Crawford Gribben (eds), *Dublin: Renaissance city of literature* (Manchester, 2017), pp 73–98

Heffernan, David, *Debating Tudor policy in sixteenth-century Ireland: 'reform' treatises and political discourse* (Manchester, 2018)

Heffernan, David, 'Patrick Finglas' A Breviat of the conquest of Ireland and the decay of the same, c. 1535 and the Tudor Conquest of Ireland' in *Sixteenth Century Journal*, 49 (2017), pp 369–88

Heffernan, David, 'The reduction of Leinster and the origins of the Tudor conquest of Ireland, c. 1534-46' in *IHS*, 40 (2016), pp 1–21

Heffernan, David, 'Robert Cowley's "A Discourse of the cause of the evil state of Ireland and of the remedies thereof", c. 1526' in *Analecta Hibernica*, 48 (2017), pp 1–30

Henry, Françoise and Geneviève Marsh-Micheli, 'Manuscripts and illuminations, 1169–1603' in A. Cosgrove (ed.), ii, *A New History of Ireland* (Oxford, 1987), pp 781–815

Herron, Thomas, 'Introduction: a fragmented Renaissance', in Thomas Herron and Michael Potterton (eds), *Ireland in the Renaissance c. 1540–1660* (Dublin, 2007), pp 19–39

Herron, Thomas and Brendan Kane, *Nobility and newcomers in Renaissance Ireland* (Washington, DC, 2013)

Herron, Thomas and Michael Potterton (eds), *Ireland in the Renaissance, c. 1540–1660* (Dublin, 2007)

Hickey, Elizabeth, 'Royal heraldry and some Irish arms at Trim' in *Ríocht na Midhe*, 8 (1998-9), pp 129–40

Hodgen, Margaret, *Early anthropology in the sixteenth and seventeenth centuries* (London, 1964)

Hoffman, Eva, *Late medieval art of the Mediterranean world* (Oxford, 2007)

Hurlock, Kathryn, 'Crusading rhetoric and Anglo-Irish relations, c. 1300–1600' in Edward Coleman, Paul Duffy and Tadhg O'Keeffe (eds), *Ireland and the Crusades* (Dublin, 2022), pp 164–77

Jefferies, Henry A., *Priests and prelates of Armagh in the age of reformations, 1518–1558* (Dublin, 1997)

Jefferies, Henry A., *The Irish church and the Tudor reformations* (Dublin, 2010)

Jones, Randolph, 'Janico Markys, Dublin and the coronation of 'Edward VI' in 1487' in Seán Duffy (ed.), *Medieval Dublin XIV: Proceedings of the friends of medieval Dublin symposium 2012* (Dublin, 2014), pp 185–209

Kane, Brendan, 'Did the Tudors read Giraldus? Gerald of Wales and early modern polemical historiography' in Georgia Henley and A. J. McMullen (eds), *New perspectives on Gerald of Wales* (Cardiff, 2018), pp 259–84

Kane, Brendan, *The politics and culture of honour in Britain and Ireland, c. 1541–1641* (Cambridge, 2010)

Kane, Brendan, 'A world of honour: aristocratic *mentalité*' in Jane Ohlmeyer (ed.), *The Cambridge history of Ireland*, ii (Cambridge, 2018), pp 482–505

Kane, Brendan and Valerie McGowan-Doyle (eds), *Elizabeth I and Ireland* (Cambridge, 2014)

Kelly, James, *Poynings' law and the making of law in Ireland, 1660–1800* (Dublin, 2007)

Kenny, Colum, *King's Inns and the kingdom of Ireland* (Dublin, 1992)

Koenigsberger, Dorothy, *Renaissance man and creative thinking: a history of concepts of harmony, 1400–1700* (Hassocks, 1979)

Leask, Harold G., *Irish churches and monastic buildings* (3 vols, Dundalk, 1960)

Lennon, Colm, 'The confraternities and cultural duality in Ireland, 1450–1550' in Christopher F. Black and Pamela Gravestock (eds), *Early modern confraternities in Europe and the Americas: international and interdisciplinary perspectives* (Aldershot, 2007), pp 35–52

Lennon, Colm, 'The Fitzgeralds of Kildare and the building of a dynastic image, 1500–1630' in William Nolan and Thomas McGrath (eds), *Kildare: history and society, interdisciplinary essays on the history of an Irish county* (Dublin, 2006), pp 195–211

Lennon, Colm, *The lords of Dublin in the age of reformation* (Dublin, 1989)

Lennon, Colm, 'The making of the Geraldines: the Kildare Fitzgeralds and their historians' in Patrick Cosgrove, Terence Dooley and Karol Mullaney-Dignam (eds), *Aspects of aristocratic life: essays on the Fitzgeralds and Carton House* (Dublin, 2014), pp 71–8

Lennon, Colm, 'Pedagogy and reform: the influence of Peter White on Irish scholarship in the Renaissance' in Thomas Herron and Michael Potterton (eds), *Ireland in the Renaissance c. 1540–1660* (Dublin, 2007), pp 43–51

Lennon, Colm, 'Protestant reformations, 1550–1641' in Jane Ohlmeyer (ed.), *The Cambridge history of Ireland*, ii (Cambridge, 2018), pp 196–219

Lennon, Colm, *Sixteenth-century Ireland: the incomplete conquest* (Dublin, 1994)

Leslie, J. B., *Ferns: clergy and parishes* (Dublin, 1936)

Lovejoy, Arthur and George Boas, *Primitivism and related ideas in antiquity* (Baltimore, MD, 1935)

Lydon, James, *Ireland in the later middle ages* (Dublin, 1973)

Lydon, James, *The lordship of Ireland in the middle ages* (Toronto, 1972)

Lyons, Marian, *Church and society in County Kildare* (Dublin, 2000)

Lyons, Marian, 'The foundation of the Geraldine College of the Blessed Virgin Mary, Maynooth, 1518' in *Journal of the County Kildare Archaeological Society*, 18 (1994-5), pp 134-50

Lyons, Marian, *Franco-Irish relations, 1500-1610: Politics, migration and trade* (Woodbridge, 2003)

Lyons, Marian, *Gearóid Óg Fitzgerald, ninth earl of Kildare* (Dundalk, 1998)

Lyons, Marian, 'The onset of religious reform: 1460-1550' in Brendan Smith (ed.), *The Cambridge history of Ireland*, i (Cambridge, 2018), pp 498-522

Lyons, Marian, 'The Kildare ascendancy' in Patrick Cosgrove, Terence Dooley and Karol Mullaney-Dignam (eds), *Aspects of aristocratic life: essays on the Fitzgeralds and Carton House* (Dublin, 2014), pp 48-59

Lyons, Marian, 'Sidelights on the Kildare ascendancy: A survey of Geraldine involvement in the Church, c. 1470-c. 1520' in *Archivium Hibernicum*, 48 (1994), pp 73-87

Mac Cárthaigh, Eoin, 'Dia libh, a uaisle Éireann (1641)' in *Ériu*, 52 (2002), pp 89-121

Mac Cárthaigh, Eoin, 'The O'Donnells at war in the 1640s and early 1650s' (Pamphlet), Paul Walsh Memorial Lecture 7 (Maynooth, 2022)

MacCulloch, Diarmaid, *Thomas Cromwell: A life* (London, 2018)

MacLeod, Catriona, 'Fifteenth-century vestments in Waterford' in *Journal of the Royal Society of Antiquaries of Ireland*, 52 (1952), pp 85-98

MacNeill, Eoin, *Phases of Irish history* (Dublin, 1919)

MacNiocaill, Gearoid, 'Registrum cantariae S. Salvatoris, Waterfordensis' in *Analecta Hibernica*, 23 (1964), pp 136-222

Maginn, Christopher, *'Civilizing' Gaelic Leinster: the extension of Tudor rule in the O'Byrne and O'Toole lordships* (Dublin, 2005)

Maginn, Christopher, 'Continuity and change: 1470-1550' in Brendan Smith (ed.), *The Cambridge history of Ireland*, i (Cambridge, 2018), pp 300-28

Maginn, Christopher, 'Gaelic Ireland's English frontiers in the late middle ages' in *Proceedings of the Royal Irish Academy*, 110C (2010), pp 173-90

Maginn, Christopher, '"Surrender and regrant" in the historiography of sixteenth-century Ireland' in *Sixteenth Century Journal*, 38 (2007), pp 955-74

Maginn, Christopher, *William Cecil, Ireland, and the Tudor State* (Oxford, 2012)

Maginn, Christopher and S. G. Ellis, *The Tudor discovery of Ireland* (Dublin, 2015)

Mahaffy, J. P., 'Two early tours in Ireland' in *Hermathena*, 40 (1914), pp 1-16

Maley, Willy, *Salvaging Spenser: colonialism, culture and identity* (Manchester, 1997)

Martin, F. X., 'The crowning of a king at Dublin, 24 May 1487' in *Hermathena*, 144 (1988), pp 7-34

Matthew, Elizabeth, 'Henry V and the proposal for an Irish crusade' in Brendan Smith (ed.), *Ireland and the English world in the late Middle Ages* (Basingstoke, 2009), pp 161-75

Mathew, David, *The courtiers of Henry VIII* (London, 1970)

Maxwell, Constantia, *Irish history from contemporary sources 1509–1610* (London, 1923)

McCabe, Richard, 'Fighting words: writing the "Nine Years War"' in Thomas Herron and Michael Potterton (eds), *Ireland in the Renaissance c. 1540–1660* (Dublin, 2007), pp 105–21

McCauley, Barbara L., 'Giraldus "Silvester" of Wales and his *Prophetic history of Ireland*: Merlin's role in the *Expugnatio Hibernica*' in *Quondam et Futurus*, 3 (1993), pp 41–62

McCormack, Anthony, *The earldom of Desmond, 1463–1583: the decline and crisis of a feudal lordship* (Dublin, 2005)

McCorristine, Laurence, *The revolt of Silken Thomas: a challenge to Henry VIII* (Dublin, 1987)

McGowan-Doyle, Valerie, *The Book of Howth: Elizabethan conquest and the Old English* (Cork, 2011)

McGowan-Doyle, Valerie, 'Elizabeth I, the Old English, and the rhetoric of counsel' in Brendan Kane and Valerie McGowan-Doyle (eds), *Elizabeth I and Ireland* (Cambridge, 2014), pp 163–83

McGroarty, Kieran, 'Did Alexander the Great read Xenophon?' in Mark Humphries and Brian McGing (eds), *Hermthena: a Trinity College Dublin Review, in honour of George Huxley* (Dublin, 2006), pp 105–24

McInerney, Luke and Caroline Smiddy, 'The Clann Chraith bardic school of Burgess, south Tipperary' in Luke McInerney and Katharine Simms (eds), *Gaelic Ireland (c. 600–c. 1700), Lordship, saints and learning: essays for the Irish chiefs' and clans' prize in history* (Dublin, 2021), pp 153–73

Mears, Natalie, 'Courts, courtiers and culture in Tudor England' in *Historical Journal*, 46 (2003), pp 703–22

Mears, Natalie, *Queenship and political discourse in the Elizabethan realms* (Cambridge, 2005)

Miles, Brent, *Heroic saga and classical epic in medieval Ireland* (Woodbridge, 2011)

Mitchell, R. J., *John Tiptoft (1427–1470)* (London, 1938)

Montaño, John Patrick, *The roots of English colonialism in Ireland* (Cambridge, 2011)

Moody, T. W. and Martin, F. X. (eds), *The course of Irish history* (Cork, 1967)

More, Thomas, *History of Ireland* (4 vols, Paris, 1840)

Morgan, Hiram, 'Giraldus Cambrensis and the Tudor conquest of Ireland' in Hiram Morgan (ed.), *Political ideology in Ireland 1541–1641* (Dublin, 1999)

Morgan, Hiram, 'Tom Lee: the posing peacemaker' in Brendan Bradshaw, Andrew Hadfield and Willy Maley (eds), *Representing Ireland: literature and the origins of conflict, 1534–1660* (Cambridge, 1993), pp 132–65

Morgan, Hiram, with Dorothy Convery, *Ireland 1518: Archduke Ferdinand's visit to Kinsale and the Dürer connection* (Cork, 2015)

Morgan, Hiram, 'Archduke Ferdinand's visit to Kinsale in Ireland, an extract from Le Premier voyage de Charles-Quint en Espagne, de 1517 à 1518', online at celt.ucc.ie

Moss, Rachel, *Art and devotion in late medieval Ireland* (Dublin, 2006)

Murdoch, John, Jim Murrell, Patrick Noon and Roy Strong (eds), *The English miniature* (Yale, 1981)

Murray, James, 'Archbishop Alen, Tudor reform and the Kildare rebellion' in *Proceedings of the Royal Irish Academy*, 89C (1989), pp 1-16

Murray, James, 'Ecclesiastical justice and the enforcement of the reformation: the case of Archbishop Browne and the clergy of Dublin, 1536-1554' in Alan Ford, James McGuire and Kenneth Milne (eds), *As by law established: The Church of Ireland since the reformation* (Dublin, 1995), pp 33-51

Murray, James, *Enforcing the English reformation in Ireland, clerical resistance and political conflict in the diocese of Dublin* (Cambridge, 2009)

Nelson, William, *John Skelton: laureate* (New York, 1939)

Newns, Brian, 'The hospice of St Thomas and the English crown 1474-1538' in John F. Allen (ed.), *The English hospice in Rome* (Gloucester, 2005), pp 145-92

Nicholls, Kenneth W., 'Anglo-French Ireland and after' in *Peritia*, 1 (1982), pp 370-403

Nicholls, K. W., 'The development of lordship in County Cork' in Patrick O'Flanagan and C. G. Buttimer (eds), *Cork: history and society, interdisciplinary essays on the history of an Irish county* (Dublin, 1993), pp 156-211

Nicholls, K. W., *Gaelic and gaelicised Ireland in the middle ages* (Dublin, 1972)

Nicholls, K. W., 'Late medieval Irish annals, two fragments', in *Peritia*, 2 (1983), pp 87-102

Nicholson, Helen, 'The Hospitallers and Templars' involvement in warfare on the frontiers of the British Isles in the late thirteenth and early fourteenth centuries' in Jürgen Sarnowsky (ed.), *Ordines militaris colloquia Torunesia historica* (Toru, 2012), pp 105-19

Ó Cathain, Diarmaid, 'Some reflexes of Latin learning and of the renaissance in Ireland, c. 1450-c. 1600' in Jason Harris and K. C. Sidwell (eds), *Making Ireland Roman: Irish neo-Latin writers and the republic of letters* (Cork, 2009), pp 14-37

O'Byrne, Emmett, 'A divided loyalty': the MacMurroughs, the Irish of Leinster and the crown of England, 1340-1420' in Thomas McGrath (ed.), *Carlow: history and society, interdisciplinary essays on the history of an Irish county* (Dublin, 1995), pp 273-306

O'Byrne, Emmett, 'The Tudor state and the Irish of east Leinster, 1535-54' in Thomas Herron and Michael Potterton (eds), *Dublin and the Pale in the Renaissance c. 1540-1660* (Dublin, 2007), pp 68-92

O'Byrne, Theresa, 'Centre or periphery? The role of Dublin in James Yonge's *Memoriale* (1412)' in Kathleen Miller and Crawford Gribben (eds), *Dublin: Renaissance city of literature* (Manchester, 2017), pp 16-37

Ó Cléirigh, Cormac, 'The O'Connor Faly lordship of Offaly, 1395-1513' in *Proceedings of the Royal Irish Academy*, 96C (1996), pp 87-102

Ó Conbhuidhe, Colmcille, *The Cistercian abbeys of Tipperary* (Dublin, 1999)

O'Connor, Thomas, 'Ireland and Europe, 1580-1815: some historiographical remarks' in T. O'Connor (ed.), *The Irish in Europe, 1580-1815* (Dublin, 2001), pp 9-26

O'Keeffe, Tadgh, *Medieval Irish buildings* (Dublin, 2015)

O'Malley, Gregory, *The Knights Hospitaller of the English langue, 1460-1565* (Oxford, 2005)

Ó Siochrú, Micheál, 'Foreign involvement in the revolt of Silken Thomas, 1534-5' *Proceedings of the Royal Irish Academy*, 96C (1996), pp 49-66

O'Sullivan, Anne and William Ó'Sullivan, 'Three notes on Laud Misc. 610 (or the Book of Pottlerath)' in *Celtica* 9 (1971), pp 135-51

O'Sullivan, Harold, 'Dynamics of regional development' in Ciaran Brady and Jane Ohlmeyer (eds), *British interventions in early modern Ireland* (Cambridge, 2005), pp 49-72

Orpen, G. H., *Ireland under the Normans, 1216-1333* (4 vols, Oxford, 1920)

Orpen, G. H., *New Ross in the thirteenth century* (Dublin, 1911)

Otway-Ruthven, A. J., *A history of medieval Ireland* (London, 1968)

Ovenden, Richard, *Burning the books: a history of the deliberate destruction of knowledge* (London, 2020)

Palmer, Patricia, *Language and conquest in early modern Ireland: English renaissance literature and Elizabethan imperial expansion* (Cambridge, 2001)

Palmer, Patricia, *The severed head and the grafted tongue: literature, translation and violence in early modern Ireland* (Cambridge, 2019)

Pender, Seamus, 'O Clery Genealogies' in *Analecta Hibernica*, 18 (1951), pp 169-72

Penn, Thomas, *Winter king: Henry VII and the dawn of Tudor England* (London, 2011)

Petrina, Alexandra, *Cultural politics in fifteenth-century England: The case of Humphrey, duke of Gloucester* (Boston, MA, 2004)

Plummer, Charles, 'Colophons and marginalia of Irish scribes' in *Proceedings of the British Academy*, 11 (1926), pp 11-44

Pollnitz, Aysha, *Princely education in early modern Britain* (Cambridge, 2015)

Potterton, Michael, 'The Fitzgeralds, Florence, St Fiachra and a few fragments' in Thomas Herron and Michael Potterton (eds), *Dublin and the Pale in the Renaissance c. 1540-1660* (Dublin, 2007), pp 19-47

Potterton, Michael, *Medieval Trim: history and archaeology* (Dublin, 2005)

Potterton, Michael and Thomas Herron (eds), *Dublin and the Pale in the Renaissance c. 1540-1600* (Dublin, 2011)

Power, Gerald, *A European frontier elite: the nobility of the English Pale in Tudor Ireland, 1496-1566* (Hannover, 2012)

Quinn, David B., 'Anglo-Irish local government 1485-1534' in *IHS*, 1 (1938-9), pp 366-81

Quinn, D. B., 'Aristocratic autonomy, 1460-1494' in Art Cosgrove (ed.), *A New History of Ireland*, ii (Oxford, 1987), pp 591-618

Quinn, D. B., 'The early interpretation of Poynings' Law, 1494-1534' in *IHS*, 2 (1940-1), pp 241-54

Quinn, D. B., *The Elizabethans and the Irish* (Washington, DC, 1966)

Quinn, D. B., 'Guide to English financial records for Irish history, 1461-1558, with illustrative extracts, 1461-1509' in *AH*, 10 (1941), pp 17-27

Quinn, D. B., 'Henry VIII and Ireland, 1509-1534' in *IHS*, 12 (1960-1), pp 318-44

Quinn, D. B., 'The hegemony of the earls of Kildare, 1494-1520' in Art Cosgrove (ed.), *A New History of Ireland*, ii (Oxford, 1987), pp 638-61

Quinn, D. B., 'The re-emergence of English policy as a major factor in Irish affairs, 1520-34' in Art Cosgrove (ed.), *A New History of Ireland*, ii (Oxford, 1987), pp 662-87

Ralph, Karen, 'Medieval antiquarianism: the Butlers and artistic patronage in fifteenth-century Ireland' in *Eolas*, 7 (2014), pp 2-27

Rankin, Mark, Christopher Highley and John King (eds), *Henry VIII and his afterlives: literature, politics and art* (Cambridge, 2009)

Richardson, Glenn, *The Field of Cloth of Gold* (London, 2013)

Richardson, Glenn, '"As presence did present them": personal gift-giving at the Field of Cloth of Gold' in Suzannah Lipscomb and Thomas Betteridge (eds), *Henry VIII and the court: art, politics and performance* (Abingdon, 2013), pp 47-64

Richardson, Glenn, *Wolsey* (Oxford, 2020)

Richter, Michael, *Giraldus Cambrensis: the growth of the Welsh nation* (Aberystwyth, 1972)

Roe, Helen, *Medieval fonts of Meath* (Navan, 1968)

Ruddick, Andrea, *English identity and political culture in the fourteenth century* (Cambridge, 2013)

Sayles, G. O., 'The vindication of the earl of Kildare from treason, 1496' in *IHS*, 7 (1950-1), pp 37-47

Scattergood, John, 'Humanism in Ireland in the sixteenth-century: the evidence of TCD MS 160' in Cormac Ó Cuilleanáin, Corinna Salvadori and John Scattergood (eds), *Italian culture: interactions, transpositions and translations* (Dublin, 2006), pp 69-89

BIBLIOGRAPHY

Scattergood, V. J., 'The libelle of Englyshe polycye: the nation and its place' in Helen Cooney (ed.), Nation, Court and culture: new essays on fifteenth-century English poetry (Dublin, 2001), pp 28–49

Scott, Brendan, 'The Knights Hospitaller in Tudor Ireland: their dissolution and attempted revival' in Martin Browne and Colman Ó Clabaigh (eds), Soldiers of Christ: the Knights Hospitaller and the Knights Templar in medieval Ireland (Dublin, 2016), pp 47–60

Scott, Brendan, Religion and reformation in the Tudor diocese of Meath (Dublin, 2007)

Scott-Warren, Jason, Sir John Harington and the gook as gift (Oxford, 2001)

Sessions, W. A., Henry Howard, the poet earl of Surrey (London, 2003)

Seymour, Edward, Christ Church Cathedral, Dublin (Dublin, 1869)

Seymour, St John, Anglo-Irish literature, 1200–1582 (Dublin, 1929)

Sharpe, Kevin, Selling the Tudor monarchy: authority and image in sixteenth-century England (New Haven, CT, 2009)

Simms, Katharine, 'The archbishops of Armagh and the O'Neills 1347–1471' in IHS, 19 (1974–5), pp 38–55

Simms, Katharine, 'Bardic poetry as a historical source' in Tom Dunne (ed.), The writer as witness, Historical Studies XVI (Cork, 1987), pp 58–75

Simms, Katharine, 'Bards and barons: the Anglo-Irish aristocracy and the native culture' in Robert Bartlett and Angus MacKay (eds), Medieval frontier societies (Oxford, 1992), pp 177–97

Simms, Katharine, 'The barefoot kings: literary image and reality in later medieval Ireland' in Proceedings of the Harvard Celtic Colloquium, 30 (2010), pp 1–21

Simms, Katharine, 'Gaelic culture and society' in Brendan Smith (ed.), The Cambridge history of Ireland, i (Cambridge, 2018), pp 415–440

Simms, Katharine, Gaelic Ulster in the middle ages: history, culture and society (Dublin, 2020)

Simms, Katharine, 'Geraldines and Gaelic culture' in Peter Crooks and Seán Duffy (eds), The Geraldines and medieval Ireland: the making of a myth (Dublin, 2016), pp 264–77

Simms, Katharine, '"The King's friend": O'Neill, the crown and the earldom of Ulster' in James Lydon (ed.), England and Ireland in the later middle ages: essays in honour of Jocelyn Otway-Ruthven (Dublin, 1981), pp 214–36

Simms, Katharine, From Kings to warlords: the changing political structure of Gaelic Ireland in the later middle ages (Woodbridge, 1987)

Simms, Katharine, 'Poems to the medieval Donegal chiefs' in William Nolan, Liam Ronayne and Mairead Dunlevy (eds), Donegal, history and society: interdisciplinary essays on the history of an Irish county (Dublin, 1995), pp 183–97

Simpson, James, Reform and cultural revolution: the Oxford English literary history, 1350–1547 (Oxford, 2002)

BIBLIOGRAPHY

Simpson, Linzi, 'The early Geraldine castles of Ireland: some case studies' in Peter Crooks and Seán Duffy (eds), *The Geraldines and medieval Ireland: the making of a myth* (Dublin, 2016), pp 93–156

Slattery, Peadar, *Social life in pre-reformation Dublin 1450–1540* (Dublin, 2019)

Smith, Brendan, *Crisis and survival in late medieval Ireland: the English of Louth and their neighbours, 1330–1450* (Oxford, 2013)

Stalley, Roger, 'The architecture of the cathedral and priory buildings, 1250–1530' in Kenneth Milne (ed.), *Christ Church Cathedral, Dublin: a history* (Dublin, 2000), pp 95–128

Stalley, Roger, *The Cistercian monasteries of Ireland* (New Haven, CT, 1987)

Starkey, David (ed.), *The English court from the wars of the Roses to the civil war* (London, 1987)

Starkey, David, *Henry: virtuous prince* (London, 2008)

Starkey, David, 'Holbein's Irish sitter?' in *Burlington Magazine*, 123 (1981), pp 300–3

Stoneman, Richard, *Alexander the Great: a life in legend* (New Haven, 2008)

Strong, Roy, *Artists of the Tudor Court: the portrait miniature rediscovered 1520–1620* (London, 1983)

Sutton, Anne, 'The Hospital of St Thomas of Acre of London: the search for patronage, liturgical improvement, and a school, under Master John Neel, 1420–63' in Clive Burgess and Martin Heale (eds), *The late medieval English college and its context* (York, 2008), pp 199–229

Tournoy, Gilbert, 'The unrecorded poetical production of Andreas Ammonius' in *Humanistica Lovaniensia: Journal of Neo-Latin Studies*, 37 (1988), pp 255–64

Vale, Malcolm, *The princely court: medieval courts and culture in north-west Europe, 1270–1380* (Oxford, 2001)

Vale, Malcolm, *War and chivalry: warfare and aristocratic culture in England, France and Burgundy at the end of the middle ages* (London, 1981)

Valkenburg, A., 'A study in diplomacy, Gerald, eleventh earl of Kildare 1525–85' in *JKA*, 14 (1965), pp 293–315

Van der Velden, Hugo, 'A prayer roll of Henry Beauchamp, earl of Warwick' in J. F. Hamburger and A. S. Korteweg (eds), *Tributes in honor of James H. Marrow: studies in painting and manuscript illumination of the late middle ages and northern renaissance* (London, 2006), pp 521–50

Virtuani, Paolo, '*Tuitio fidei*? The Irish Hospitallers at war' in Edward Coleman, Paul Duffy and Tadhg O'Keeffe (eds), *Ireland and the Crusades* (Dublin, 2022), pp 121–8

Wachowich, Cameron, 'In search of worlds to conquer: echoes of Alexander the Great in medieval Ireland' in *Proceedings of the Harvard Celtic Colloquium*, 36 (2016), pp 215–30

Walker, Greg, *John Skelton and the politics of the 1520s* (Cambridge, 1988)

Wallace, David, *Chaucerian Polity* (Stanford, 1997)

Wallace, P. F. and Raghnall O'Floinn (eds), *Treasures of the National Museum of Ireland* (Dublin, 2002)

Walsh, Katherine, 'The clerical estate in later medieval Ireland: alien settlement and society in medieval Ireland' in John Bradley (ed.), *Settlement and society in medieval Ireland* (Kilkenny, 1988), pp 361-78

Weiss, Roberto, *Humanism in England during the fifteenth century* (Oxford, 1941)

Weiss, Roberto, 'New Light on Humanism in England during the fifteenth century' in *Journal of the Warburg and Courtauld Institutes* 14 (1951), pp 21-33

Whiting, B. J. and H. W. Whiting, *Proverbs, sentences, and proverbial phrases from English writings mainly before 1500* (Cambridge, MA, 1968)

Whelan, Caoimhe, 'The notary's tale' in Sparky Booker and Cherie N. Peters (eds), *Tales of medieval Dublin* (Dublin, 2014), pp 113-34

Whelan, Caoimhe, 'James Yonge and the writing of history in late medieval Dublin' in Seán Duffy (ed.), *Medieval Dublin XIII* (Dublin, 2011), pp 183-95

Whelan, Caoimhe, 'The *Expugnatio Hibernica* in medieval Ireland' in Georgia Henley and A. J. McMullen (eds), *New perspectives on Gerald of Wales* (Cardiff, 2018), pp 243-58

Whelan, Caoimhe, 'Translating the *Expugnatio Hibernica*: A vernacular English history in late medieval Ireland' in Carrie Griffin and Emer Purcell (eds), *Text, transmission and transformation in the European middle ages, 1000-1500* (Turnhout, 2018), pp 165-92

Williams, Neville, *Henry VIII and his court* (London, 1971)

Willoughby, James, 'The library of the English hospital in Rome before 1527' in *La Bibliofilia*, 113 (2011), pp 155-74

Wilson, Derek, *Hans Holbein: portrait of an unknown man* (London, 2006)

Woods, Herbert, *A guide to the records deposited in the Public Record Office of Ireland* (Dublin, 1919)

Woolf, D. R., *Reading history in early modern England* (Cambridge, 2000)

Wycherley, Niamh, 'The enduring power of the cult of relics: an Irish perspective' in Chris Jones, Conor Kostick and Klaus Oschema (eds), *Making the medieval relevant: how medieval studies contribute to improving our understanding of the present* (Boston, MA, 2020), pp 239-54

Theses

Beresford, David, 'The Butlers in England and Ireland, 1405-1515' (Ph.D., Trinity College Dublin, 1999)

Crooks, Peter, 'Factionalism and Noble Power in English Ireland, c. 1361-1423' (Ph.D., Trinity College Dublin, 2007)

Empey, C. A., 'The Butler lordship in Ireland' (Ph.D., Trinity College Dublin, 1970)

Kelly, Alan, 'Classical thought and primitivism in English depictions of Ireland: a case study of John Derricke's *Image of Ireland*, 1581' (M.A., Maynooth University, 2005)

Marshall, Chad, 'The reform treatises and discourse of early Tudor Ireland, c. 1515-1541' (Ph.D., University of Tasmania, 2018)

Matthew, E. A. E., 'The governing of the Lancastrian lordship of Ireland in the time of James Butler, fourth earl of Ormond c. 1420-1452 (Ph.D., Durham University, 1994)'

McCauley, Barbara L., 'A critical edition of the English conquest of Ireland, a medieval Hiberno-English manuscript from the Latin of Giraldus Cambrensis' Expugnatio Hibernica' (Ph.D., Florida State University, 1993)

Moore, Catharine, 'The library lists of the eighth and ninth earls of Kildare' (M.A., Trinity College Dublin, 1997)

Whelan, Caoimhe, 'Translating Cambrensis: The history of the late medieval English conquest of Ireland' (Ph.D., Trinity College Dublin, 2015)

White, Dean, 'The Tudor plantations in Ireland before 1571' (Ph.D., Trinity College Dublin, 1968)

Index

Alen, John, chancellor 113-14, 146-8
Alen, John, archbishop of Dublin 6, 57 n.71, 85, 108, 112-17, 140
Alexander ('The Great'), of Macedon, cult of 22, 23 n.42, 39, 51, 65 n.36, 66, 70
Annaly, Irish lordship 116
Ariosto, Ludovico 68-9, 154
Ammonius, Andreas 53-4, 58, 91
Andreas, Bernard 54, 86 n.55, 91, 128
Arklow 102, 111
Armagh, archdiocese of 18, 78
Arthurian (romance) 26, 91, 100
Athlone 84-5
Athy 35

Bray, Reginald 42
Browne, George, archbishop of Dublin 143-8, 151
Baltinglass 118
Bann, fishery 50
Barrow, valley 2, 5, 19, 32, 35-7, 49, 52, 81, 94, 101, 107, 111, 121
Bathe, Thomas 28, 71, 87, 99-101, 104-5, 124
Becket, Thomas (d. 1170), archbishop of Canterbury 25, 47-8
Bermingham, Patrick, lord chief justice 87, 99, 101-8
 Piers de (d. 1308) 143
Bellahoe (1539), battle of 151-2
Bere, Richard 86
Blackstairs, mountains 121
Blount, William, lord Mountjoy 53-4
Boleyn, Anne, queen of England, marquess of Pembroke 16, 126
 Thomas, 1st earl of Wiltshire, 1st earl of Ormond 25, 72, 98, 102, 104-5, 107, 120, 126, 141
Brabazon, Sir William, undertreasurer 137, 143, 146, 148
Brigid, St 45 n.6, 78 n.16, 89
Bruni, Leonardo 30

Burgundy, duchy of 39, 69
Butler (of Cahir) 18-20, 26-7, 49
Butler, Edmund macRichard (d. 1464) 19-20, 27, 30-1
 Edmund (d. 1551), archbishop of Cashel 102, 113
 James, 4th earl (the White Earl) of Ormond 1, 16-27, 36, 43-51, 55, 66, 72, 102, 132, 134, 139, 150, 155
 James, 5th earl of Ormond 49, 51
 James, 9th earl of Ormond 153
 John, 6th earl of Ormond 2, 28-9, 50
 John, mayor of Waterford 52
 James, Lord Butler 110
 Piers, 8th earl of Ormond, 1st earl of Ossory 37, 41, 55-6, 61, 78, 93, 95-103, 123-4, 150
 Thomas, 7th earl of Ormond 3, 38, 51, 53, 61

Cantwell, John, archbishop of Cashel 39
Carrick 17, 27
Carbery, Irish lordship 63, 69
Carlow, castle 35, 61
 county 35, 94, 107, 116, 121-3, 141, 149
Carrickfergus 63
Cashel, synod of (1172) 46
Castiglione, Baldassare 64, 127
Castledermot 49, 61
Catherine of Aragon, queen of England 71
Caxton, William 88, 147
Cecil, William (d. 1598), lord Burghley 95
Charles V (king of Spain, Holy Roman Emperor) 71, 79, 97, 104, 111, 124, 130, 141
Chaucer, Geoffrey 86-9
 Troilus and Cresidye 86 n.60, 87-8, 89 n.77

INDEX

Clanrickard Burke 36, 61
Clement VII, pope 140
Clonony, castle 126
Cogan, Miles de (d. 1182) 47
Colman, Thomas 85, 88
Columba, St 109 n.64, 133
Connaught 24, 30, 36-7, 61, 77 n.10, 101, 121
Connesburgh, Edmund, archbishop of Armagh 39, 50
conquest (of Ireland), Cambro-Norman ix, 3, 5, 22, 38, 41, 44, 46, 66-7, 74, 104, 107, 164, 114, 144, 146-7, 150
  Tudor 9, 43, 49, 116, 156
Constantinople 56, 82
Cooley, barony 35, 80
Courcy, John de (d. 1219), lord of Ulster 50 n.30, 59 n.89
Cowley, Robert 5-6, 71, 113, 137-8, 143-4, 152
Cowley, Walter 5-6, 99-101, 103, 105, 110, 113-14, 116, 145, 152
coyne and livery 3 n.5, 20, 28-9, 53, 59, 77, 80, 93
Cromer, George, archbishop of Armagh 117
Cromwell, Thomas, earl of Essex, king's principal secretary 6, 63, 68, 106, 111-17, 122, 129, 136-7, 140-3, 145-6, 147-52
Cusacke, Thomas 103, 115, 146, 151-2

Dacre, William, 3rd Baron Dacre 115-16, 140
Dante Alighieri (d. 1321) 66
Darcy, John (d. 1483) 59, 110
  Sir William 4, 28-9, 45, 50, 59, 76, 80-1, 92-5, 105-6, 108-9, 112, 115, 134
Davies, Sir John (d. 1626), attorney-general of Ireland 9, 28-9, 154
Delahide, Richard 126
Delvin, baron of see Nugent
Desmond, earl of see Fitzgerald
Dethyke, John 112
Doran, Maurice, bishop of Leighlin 103, 112
Dormer, Thomas 94
Drogheda 28, 31, 104, 110, 139

Dublin, city 11, 29, 32, 34-5, 37, 47, 62, 80, 101, 118, 137, 139, 144, 147
  Christ Church cathedral 3, 47, 73-4, 100, 108, 120
  St Patrick's cathedral 18, 73, 87
Dungarvan 104
Dunsany 31
Dungannon 61

Earl Marshal, the 52, 56, 80, 94, 101, 106-8, 121, 126, 144. See also Marshal, William
Edgecombe, Sir Richard 36, 40, 51-3, 71, 148
Edward VI, Yorkist pretender 35-6, 52, 54, 122. See also Simnel, Lambert
Edward IV, king of England 2, 33-4, 38-9, 50, 57, 122
Ely, Irish lordship 113, 126. See also O'Carroll
England 1, 11, 13, 19, 21, 28, 33, 38, 41, 53, 67-70, 74, 85, 92, 111, 115, 118, 126, 138, 142, 149
English, culture 4, 14, 26, 34-5, 41, 43-9, 53-6, 60-2, 66, 77, 80, 88, 90-2, 95, 113-14, 123, 145-8
  language 4, 39, 43-9, 52, 69, 83, 89-90, 129, 140
  common law 10-11, 32, 34 n.113, 44, 60-3, 106-7, 109, 113, 115, 117, 155
English Pale in Ireland see Pale, the (and Palesmen)
Erasmus, Desiderius (of Rotterdam) 86, 128, 131
Este, (d'Este family, Ferrara) 69
Estrete, John 40
Expugnatio Hibernica see Giraldus Cambrensis

Fasagh Bentre (Fassaghbantry) 121, 123, 143-4
Ferns, diocese of 122
Finglas, Patrick, chief baron of the exchequer 5, 7, 29, 92-4, 99, 101, 105-10, 114-16, 134, 144, 146-7
  Thomas 137

INDEX

Field of Cloth of Gold 92, 96-7, 127 n.41, 133
FitzEustace, Alison, first wife of 8th earl of Kildare 41
  Sir Roland, Lord Portlester 40-1, 56
Fitzgerald (of Leinster), Elizabeth (d. 1590), daughter of the 9th earl of Kildare 129-30
  Gerald, 5th earl of Kildare 18
  Gearóid Mór, 8th earl (Gerald, the Great Earl) of Kildare 1-5, 11, 33-4, 36-7, 40-1, 51, 53, 57-64, 68, 74, 78, 118, 125
  Gearóid Óg, 9th earl (Gerald) of Kildare 5, 58, 62-3, 65, 69, 72, 74, 76, 80, 94-5, 99, 105, 113-17, 121-2, 126, 128, 131, 133, 141-2
  Gerald, 11th earl of Kildare 57, 131, 134
  Margaret, daughter of 8th earl, wife of Piers Butler 37, 51
  Thomas, 10th earl of Kildare 1, 6, 8, 41, 139, 141
  Thomas, 7th earl of Kildare 1-2, 31-4, 38-40, 48, 50, 65, 70, 72, 74, 115
  Sir Thomas, brother of the 9th earl 121, 123
Fitzgerald family (of Munster), James, 6th earl of Desmond 30, 93
  James, 11th earl of Desmond 139
  Maurice, 10th earl of Desmond 111, 124
  Thomas, 8th earl of Desmond 2, 28-32
Fitzgerald, Thomas, prior of Kilmainham 17-18, 54-6
FitzGilbert, Richard de Clare, 'Strongbow' (d. 1176) 43, 107
FitzRoy, Henry, duke of Richmond and Somerset 130
FitzSimons, Walter, archbishop of Dublin 85
Flattisbury, Philip 22, 62, 66
Florence 151. See also Gherardini (of Florence)
Fox, Richard, bishop of Winchester, lord privy seal 54, 76, 86
France 1, 16, 21, 24, 66-7, 74, 90, 92, 96, 104, 126

Francis I, king of France 79, 97, 102, 121
Fraternity of Arms of St George 32, 38-40, 64, 70, 115

Galway 62
Gardiner, Stephen, bishop of Winchester 106 n.53, 107, 110
Geoffrey of Monmouth (d. 1155), chronicler 90, 149
Gerald of Wales see *Giraldus Cambrensis*
Geraldines, Geraldine family see Fitzgerald
Geraldini, Alessandro, bishop of Santa Domingo 71-2
Gherardini (of Florence) 3, 30, 48, 66-70, 130, 136, 151
Gigli, Sylvester 54, 85
Giraldus Cambrensis (d. 1223), *Expugnatio Hibernica* 3-4, 20-3, 43-51, 54-5, 58, 67, 74, 88-93, 108-9, 113, 149-51
  later influence of 4, 20, 42-50, 88-94, 108, 110, 114, 144, 146, 148-51
  Topographia Hibernica 46-8, 89-90
Gormanston, Lord see Preston
Gouernaunce of Prynces ('Secreta Secretorum') 23, 65
Greencastle 81
Greenwich 71, 92
Gregory I, pope 89
Grey, Elizabeth, second wife of 9th earl of Kildare 120, 123
  Henry, Lord Grey of Ruthin 2, 33
  Leonard, Lord Grey 138, 140-52

Harington, John (d. 1612) 154
Henry II, king of England 43, 104, 106-7
Henry VI, king of England 2, 30, 117
Henry VII (Henry Tudor), king of England 35-42, 47, 52-4, 57-8, 60, 62-4, 77
Henry VIII, king of England and Ireland 12, 17, 28, 48, 51, 54, 57, 59, 71, 69, 71, 77-9, 92-3, 96-7, 106, 110-11, 114-15, 117-18, 123-4, 130-1, 137-42, 144, 147, 152

185

INDEX

Higden, Ranulph (d. 1364)   90
Holbein, Hans (the Younger)   130-1, 141
Holy Land, the   55
Homeric (literary tradition)   54, 84
Howard, Thomas, earl of Surrey, 3rd duke of Norfolk   5, 79, 87, 94-105, 107, 109-13, 116-17, 120-6, 129-31, 138, 140-1, 143, 148
   Henry, earl of Surrey, 4th duke of Norfolk   14, 91, 129-30

Inge, Hugh, archbishop of Dublin   76, 78-82, 84-7, 94, 99, 101, 103, 105, 107, 112, 126
Idrone   94, 101, 107-8, 112, 118, 121-2, 143-4, 147
Ireland, English lordship of   1-2, 9, 11, 16, 27-8, 31-2, 36, 41, 44, 46, 51-3, 55, 58, 63, 76-80, 85-8, 90, 94, 98, 105-7, 112-14, 125, 130 n.63, 136, 146-9, 152-3
   chancery   113 n.92
   exchequer   41, 116-17, 144
   revenues   17, 28, 32, 38, 41, 55, 58, 77, 107 n.57, 141
Irish, lords   1-2, 3 n.5, 18, 21-3, 25, 46, 61, 76-9, 96, 107, 111, 123, 132, 134, 153
   customs and culture   10, 13-14, 17 n.6, 22, 25-7, 43 n.1, 44, 46, 48-58, 60 n.3, 65 n.36, 72 n.17, 83, 86, 89, 91, 94, 95 n.119, 97, 108, 109 n.64, 114 n.99, 115, 117, 131-3, 134 n.75, 149 n.79, 150, 154
   law   36, 77 n.10, 83

James III, king of Scotland   52 n.39
James IV, king of Scotland   11 n.33, 36, 57 n.78
James V, king of Scotland   151 n.87
John of Fordun (d. 1384), chronicler   90
Juvenal (d. second century), poet   65
Julius II, pope   54 n.53, 85

Kavanaghs see MacMurrough-Kavanagh
Kay, John   57
   Kilsaran, manor   57-8

Keating, James, prior of Kilmainham   28, 40-1, 56-8, 125
Kent, Thomas   61
Kilcullen, manor   35
Kildare, bishop of   72 n.75
   county   2, 18-19, 34, 36 n.130, 116, 137
   house of see Fitzgerald
   liberty of   116, 137
   rebellion   viii-ix, 1-2, 6-9, 12, 69, 111 n.84, 118-19, 120, 132, 135-46, 155
Kilkenny, castle   16
   county   19, 24, 37-8
   town   29, 39 n.152, 94, 103 n.32
Kilmainham see Order of Knights of the Hospital of Saint John of Jerusalem
Kinsale   79
Kite, John, archbishop of Armagh   76, 78-9, 80 n.28, 81, 84, 98
Knevet, Anthony   71
Knight, William   79
Knockdoe (1504), battle of   3, 62
Knights Hospitaller see Order of Knights of the Hospital of Saint John of Jerusalem

Landino, Cristoforo   66-7
Lacy, Hugh de (d. 1186), lord of Meath   107-9
Lea, manor   35
Lecale   32, 41, 61, 118
Leighlin castle   35, 123 n.15
Leighlinbridge   103, 122
Leinster, kingship of   25 n.52, 43 n.1, 72, 134
   strategic importance of   3-4, 12, 32, 37, 49, 106-7, 121, 137, 141-2
Leo X, pope   79
Limerick, city   33, 39 n.152
   county   2, 20
   diocese of   73
Lomley, Marmaduke   56-7, 58 n.81
Louth (Uriel), county   12 n.35, 17, 58, 80 n.27
Lydgate, John   84 n.45, 87 n.67

MacCarthy (of Carbery)   63, 96 n.119

INDEX

MacCoghlan, Irish lord   126
MacMurrough-Kavanagh, Irish lord   25 n.52, 47, 61, 72, 94, 101-2, 106-7, 116, 121, 134, 143, 147, 149, 152
  Cahir McArt   101, 103 n.32, 122 n.12, 143
  Dermot   43, 108-9, 134
MacWilliam Burke   28
Marshal, William (d. 1219), earl of Pembroke   94, 106-8, 121
Maynooth, castle   48, 69-72, 135, 137-8
  College of the Blessed Virgin Mary   72-3
  library   49
  manor   2, 32 n.98, 63
Machiavelli, Niccoló   68-9
Maguire, Irish lord   61
Medici, Julius de, cardinal   54 n.53, 55
Meath, bishop of   50, 78 n.17, 82, 84-6, 151
  county   34, 36 n.128, 85-6, 93, 137
More, Sir Thomas   89 n.73, 95
Morrett, manor   35
Munster   16, 18, 20, 26-7, 28 n.71, 32, 93, 104, 114, 147, 154

Netherlands (Low Countries)   57, 69
Nugent, Richard, 1st baron of Delvin   17,
  Richard, 3rd baron of Delvin   103-4, 123

O'Brien (of Thomond), Irish lord   62, 77, 141, 151
O'Byrne, Irish lord   107, 112-13, 143
O'Carrolls (of Ely), Irish lord   95 n.117, 126 n.40
O'Connor (of Sligo), Irish lord   151
O'Connor Faly, Irish lord   31-2, 36 n.128, 53, 101, 103-4, 110 n.72, 123, 143 n.32
O'Daly, Dominicus (d. 1662)   67
O'Dempsey, Irish lord   23
O'Donnell (of Tirconnell), Irish lord   17, 29-30, 34, 36, 61, 78, 95, 110, 121
  Hugh Dubh   63, 121, 124 n.22, 125
  Manus   129 n.56, 132-4, 151 n.87
O'More, Irish lord   110 n.72, 145

O'Neill (of Clandeboye), Hugh Boy   81
O'Neill (of Tyrone), Irish lord   17, 36, 63, 80, 95, 151
  Con Bacach, 1st earl of Tyrone   120-1, 123, 125, 133, 145, 153
  Con Mór (d. 1493)   34, 100
  Henry (d. 1489)   61
  Niall, son of Con Mór   118
  Shane, son of Con Bacach (d. 1567)   23 n.44
Octavian, Caesar Augustus (d. 14 CE)   53-4
Orlando Furioso see Ariosto, Ludovico
Order of the Garter   3, 24 n.48, 28 n.72, 62-3, 70
Ordinances for the government of Ireland (1534)   116-17
Order of Knights of the Hospital of Saint John of Jerusalem   12, 17-18, 28, 39, 40-1, 54-5, 57, 73-4, 77, 116-17, 139, 142
O'Reilly, Irish lord   17, 110, 121, 125
Ormond, Sir James   37-8, 41, 52, 61. *See also* Butler
Ossory *see* Butler, Piers
O'Toole, Irish lord   35, 107, 113, 143
Oxford, New College   79, 84

Page, John   56
Palatio de, Octavian, archbishop of Armagh   52, 57, 133 n.74
Pale, the (and Palesmen)   2, 4, 11 n.32, 15, 29, 34, 49-50, 52, 60-2, 77 n.8, 94, 98 n.136, 100, 102, 104, 109 n.67, 110 n.72, 112-13, 118, 123, 137, 139, 145, 151
Paul III, pope   140
Paulet, George   146, 149
parliament of Ireland   3, 19, 20 n.31, 28-9, 32-5, 36 n.128, 38, 41, 52, 56, 61, 124, 126, 143, 145
Petrarch, Francesco (d. 1374)   128, 142-3
Philostratus, Lucius Flavius (d. 250 CE)   71
Piltown (1462), battle of   2, 28-31, 49
Plantagenet, Richard, duke of York   17, 20-1, 24-5, 28
Pole, Reginald, cardinal   151
Portlester *see* FitzEustace

187

INDEX

Powerscourt 35
Poynings, Sir Edward 3, 38, 41-2, 52
Preston, Christopher, Lord
    Gormanston 20-1
  William, 2nd Viscount
    Gormanston 109-10
Purcell, John, bishop of Ferns 122

Rathangan, manor 32, 35
Rawson, John, prior of Kilmainham 54, 55 n.58, 57-8, 74, 77, 78 n.11, 99, 103, 108, 110, 116, 137 n.2, 139, 142
  Richard 114, 142
Reynolds, Charles 140
Rhodes, siege of (1480) 57
  siege of (1522) 58
Richard II, king of England 2, 21
Richard III, king of England 33, 35, 73 n.84
Rokeby, William, archbishop of Dublin 72, 76, 78-9, 81, 84-7, 103

St John, Elizabeth, second wife of 8th earl of Kildare 3, 35, 41, 62, 90, 81 n.30, 92
St Leger, Sir Anthony 7 n.16, 146-7, 149, 152, 153 n.96, 155
Scotland 34, 50, 85, 88, 115
Seix, Edmund 58
Shanesson, Sir Gerald 37, 114
Shakespeare, William 16, 76
Sherwood, William, bishop of Meath 50, 56
Simnel, Lambert 35-6, 52, 54, 122
Skeffington, Sir William 80 n.27, 110, 112, 115-16, 124-5, 133-4, 136-7, 139
Skelton, John 86 n.55, 91, 127 n.42,
Spain 71, 79
Spenser, Edmund (d. 1599) 2, 9, 28 n.70, 106 n.50
Spinelly, Thomas 79, 88
Stanihurst, Richard (d. 1618) 65, 81, 117, 129, 136 n.87, 137 n.4
Staples, Edward, bishop of Meath 151, 153 n.96
'surrender and regrant' 103, 152, 156 n.4
Surrey, earl of *see* Howard, Thomas

Swayne, John, archbishop of Armagh 20-1, 124 n.23

Talbot, Sir John, earl of Shrewsbury and Waterford 16, 20-2, 23-4, 26, 64
  Richard, archbishop of Dublin 17-18
  Thomas 28
Temple Church, London 108, 144 n.45
Tiptoft, Sir John, earl of Worcester 2, 31
Topographia Hibernica see Giraldus Cambrensis
Tottel, Richard (d. 1594) 129,
Towton (1461), battle of 28, 49
Turks, the 52, 55, 56 n.65, 91, 97, 123, 138 n.9
Tullow 111, 121, 143
Trim 25, 39
Troilus and Cresidye see Chaucer, Geoffrey

Ulster 2, 12, 17, 19-20, 30, 32, 34, 37-8, 62, 77, 80-1, 101, 110, 120, 133-4, 151
  earldom of 17, 61
  Scottish threat to 34, 50, 61, 63, 77 n.9, 115, 148

Verino, Ugolino di 66
Verney, Ralph 42, 61
Virgil (poet, d. 19 BCE) 65
Vergil, Polydore 53 n.51, 64, 86 n.61

Wakefield (1460), battle of 28
Wales 97, 146-8
Waterford 5, 19, 21, 29, 37-8, 39 n.152, 47, 51-2, 61, 74, 77, 94-5, 101-2, 107, 141-2, 144, 147
Wise [Wyse], John, chief baron of the exchequer 37, 52, 77, 112 n.85, 141-3, 147 n.64
Wolfe, John 125
Wolsey, Thomas, cardinal 52, 53 n.49, 71-3, 76-82, 85-92, 98, 101-4, 106 n.53, 108-10, 112-13, 117 n.126, 124 n.22, 124 n.25
Wyatt, Thomas 91

Yong, James 22-4, 46 n.9

Zouche, Elizabeth, wife of 9th earl of Kildare 62, 132

Irish Historical Monographs previous volumes

I. Ruling Ireland 1685–1742: Politics, Politicians and Parties, *D. W. Hayton*, 2004
II. Lord Broghill and the Cromwellian Union with Ireland and Scotland, *Patrick Little*, 2004
III. Irish Migrants in New Zealand, 1840–1937: 'The Desired Haven', *Angela McCarthy*, 2005
IV. The Fenian Ideal and Irish Nationalism, 1882–1916, *M. J. Kelly*, 2006
V. Loyalism in Ireland, 1789–1829, *Allan Blackstock*, 2007
VI. Constructing the Past: Writing Irish History, 1600–1800, edited by *Mark Williams and Stephen Forrest*, 2010
VII. The Making of the Irish Protestant Ascendancy: The Life of William Conolly, 1662–1729, *Patrick Walsh*, 2010
VIII. The Militia in Eighteenth-Century Ireland: In Defence of the Protestant Interest, *Neal Garnham*, 2012
IX. The Anglo-Irish Experience, 1680–1730: Religion, Identity and Patriotism, *D. W. Hayton*, 2012
X. The Presbyterians of Ulster, 1680–1730, *Robert Whan*, 2013
XI. The Welsh and the Shaping of Early Modern Ireland, 1558–1641, *Rhys Morgan*, 2014
XII. The Irish in the Spanish Armies in the Seventeenth Century, *Eduardo de Mesa*, 2014
XIII. Consumption and Culture in Sixteenth-Century Ireland: Saffron, Stockings and Silk, *Susan Flavin*, 2014
XIV. Elite Women in Ascendancy Ireland, 1690–1745: Imitation and Innovation, *Rachel Wilson*, 2015
XV. The Stuart Restoration and the English in Ireland, *Danielle McCormack*, 2016
XVI. Charity Movements in Eighteenth-Century Ireland: Philanthropy and Improvement, *Karen Sonnelitter*, 2016
XVII. Hugh de Lacy, First Earl of Ulster: Rising and Falling in Angevin Ireland, *Daniel Brown*, 2016
XVIII. Catholic Survival in Protestant Ireland, 1660–1711: Colonel John Browne, Landownership and the Articles of Limerick, *Eoin Kinsella*, 2018
XIX. Popular Protest and Policing in Ascendancy Ireland, 1691–1761, *Timothy D. Watt*, 2018
XX. The Old English in Early Modern Ireland: The Palesmen and the Nine Years' War, 1594–1603, *Ruth A. Canning*, 2019
XXI. Political Conflict in East Ulster, 1920–22: Revolution and Reprisal, *Christopher Magill*, 2020

XXII. Aristocratic Women in Ireland, 1450-1660: The Ormond Family, Power and Politics, *Damien Duffy*, 2021
XXIII. The Jacobite Duchess: Frances Jennings, Duchess of Tyrconnell, c.1649-1731, *Frances Nolan*, 2021
XXIV. Ireland's English Pale, 1470-1550: The Making of a Tudor Region, *Steven G. Ellis*, 2021
XXV. Irish Women in Religious Orders, 1530-1700: Suppression, Migration and Reintegration, *Bronagh Ann McShane*, 2022
XXVI. Ireland and Empire in the Late Nineteenth Century, *Fergal O'Leary*, 2023
XXVII. Ireland's Sea Fisheries, 1400-1600: Economics, Environment and Ecology, *Patrick W. Hayes*

Printed in the United States
by Baker & Taylor Publisher Services